THE CULTURAL TURN IN SPORT PSYCHOLOGY

THE CULTURAL TURN IN SPORT PSYCHOLOGY

Tatiana V. Ryba, Ph.D.
University of Jyväskylä

Robert J. Schinke, Ph.D.
Laurentian University

Gershon Tenenbaum, Ph.D.
Florida State University

Editors

FiT

Fitness Information Technology
a Division of the International Center
for Performance Excellence
West Virginia University
262 Coliseum, WVU-PASS
PO Box 6116
Morgantown, WV 26506-6116

Copyright © 2010, West Virginia University

Library of Congress Card Catalog Number: 2009939898

ISBN: 978-1-935412-03-8

Cover Composition: Bellerophon Productions
Cover Photo: Paul Cooklin (www.paulcooklin.com)
Production Editor: Val Gittings
Copyeditor: Maria denBoer
Typesetter: Bellerophon Productions
Printed by Sheridan Books, Inc.

10 9 8 7 6 5 4 3 2 1

Fitness Information Technology
A Division of the International Center for Performance Excellence
West Virginia University
262 Coliseum, WVU-PASS
PO Box 6116
Morgantown, WV 26506-6116
800.477.4348 (toll free)
304.293.6888 (phone)
304.293.6658 (fax)
Email: fitcustomerservice@mail.wvu.edu
Website: www.fitinfotech.com

CONTENTS

PART III • APPLIED ARENAS

FOREWORD

Many academics are using the metaphor of waves these days to describe the evolution of their fields. It's nice to see curves coming to the fore, moving past the geometric gridlock of past disciplines to gain a deeper understanding of disciplinary and subdisciplinary transformation. Maureen Weiss (2008) talks about riding the waves — smooth, choppy, or turbulent — of the changes in sport psychology over the past three decades in the search for a transformed sport and exercise psychology that is interdisciplinary and more keenly focused upon scientific impact and the translation of research into practice. Tatiana Ryba and Handel Wright aim to stir up more turbulent waves with their suggestions in Chapter 1 of this book that the knowledge base in sport psychology is in need of radical revision and expansion — notably the inference that the "science" of sport psychology is deeply and unforgivingly embedded in a traditional male-oriented Western epistemology that has disenfranchised members of the sporting community and its audience who do not — or cannot — climb the white picket fence that surrounds it.

This book provides multiple new and interesting perspectives of sport psychology as a way of opening up the field to critical inquiry, including a variety of emerging theories and provocative questions; an expanded range of methodologies, such as ethnography, narrative inquiry, and biography; and a particular focus upon ethical ways of "doing" and consuming sport psychology. Through a broad range of contributions from seasoned and new scholars it brings to bear a series of rich insights from cultural studies that demand ways of opening the study of sport psychology to issues of transnational, gendered, and sexual identities; new methodologies; the nature of expertise and professional practice; and the basis of the science of sport psychology itself.

In a global world with increasingly complex issues around topics of embodiment and the rapidly changing and expanding nature of the sporting enterprise, these broadened perspectives on sport psychology are both enlightening and valuable. They portend closer attention to situated ethical issues through a critical examination of the moral aspects of sport psychology practice and the theories that support it. They renew attention to the need to intensify an interrogation of whiteness in relation to white athletic privilege and the politicization of black athletes in the United States and elsewhere. They demand a heightened feminist consciousness in relation to sporting opportunity and the wider world of physical activity and require an end to heterosexual privilege by queering the study and practice of sport psychology. They ask the reader to think beyond Western ways of knowing and doing by respecting indigenous knowledges and conceiving of alternative ways of viewing the practices of sport and physical activity.

In light of this new and creative perspective the section on the application of sport psychology practices is especially valuable. Given the technological advances of the 21st century, issues of disability in sport are in urgent need of revision and a cultural studies approach is extremely promising at all levels of analysis. The discussion around disability in sport and exercise psychology speaks to and for the growing power of the disability lobby in sport as well as the opening up of elite and everyday sport to persons yearning to participate, despite physical obstacles to their mobility and multiple objections to their participation. Career development and transition similarly beg to be opened to a cultural studies approach that can amplify issues of power and embodiment in relation to aging and injury as well as gender, class, and race. This project therefore is an incredibly promising opening to new vistas in the study of sport psychology and its practices, engendering new waves of exploration in a revitalized sport psychology for the future.

—Patricia Vertinsky
University of British Columbia

Reference

Weiss, M. (2008). "Riding the wave": Transforming sport and exercise psychology within an interdisciplinary vision." *Quest*, *60*(1), 63-83.

SITUATING THE CULTURAL TURN IN SPORT AND EXERCISE PSYCHOLOGY

This book is positioned in relation to contemporary epistemological debates about the challenges and possibilities of the cultural turn. The contributing authors examine the impact of the turn to culture on sport and exercise psychology and offer new directions in the theory and practice of psychological research in the field.

The cultural turn as a permutation of the postmodernist critique of the production of knowledge swept through social sciences in the 1960s (Bonnell & Hunt, 1999). The parent field of psychology became a stage of heated intellectual debates about the future of the discipline in the 1980s. Psychologists influenced by post-structuralist theorizing brought attention to the role of language in the constitution of social and psychological life and critiqued psychology's reliance on cognition as an all-purpose explanatory strategy (see Ewards & Potter, 1992; Henriques et al., 1984). In the 1990s, cultural and indigenous psychologists intervened in the ongoing debates, highlighting cultural construction of the subject. Drawing on the work of feminist, queer, and postcolonial scholars, cultural and indigenous psychologists critiqued the hegemonic Western psychology for taking up the person as an independent and autonomous individual, neglecting the ways in which cultural context and social practices permeate and constitute the individual psyche (Hwang, 2003; Shi-xu, 2002). While some scholars of sport and exercise psychology began to situate themselves and their methodologies in a cultural studies paradigm, cultural modes of analysis of psyche and behavior are yet to enter mainstream research practices of sport and exercise psychologists. To modify Bonnell and Hunt's disciplinary assessment of sociology: "[sport psychologists] have insisted on the scientific foundations of their research, and they have been somewhat slow . . . to embrace discursive understandings of culture and to undertake research on the various forms of cultural representation" (1999, p. 5).

The issues brought about by the cultural turn relate to epistemological, analytical, and moral/ethical concerns that challenge conventional theories of representation of older paradigms. Language
and culture are fundamental to our embodied experience of and in
the world. Cultural psychological theories highlight the fact that our
psyche is cultural and political, and not simply a matter of neurological processes and cognition of the individual subject. This includes
recognizing the enactive power of culture in lives of both the research
participants and the researchers. A serious engagement with postmodernist, post-structuralist, and postcolonial critiques of grand
narratives of science, therefore, is not an idle academic exercise but is
integral to intellectual vitality and credibility of our field.

Most contributors to this anthology situate their essays in the interdisciplinary practice of cultural studies, grappling with the issues
raised by cultural theories in the past decades. Each author has a
somewhat different understanding of what is at stake. We believe
that ambiguity and the presence of tensions among the interpretive
repertoires used by researchers is a constitutive part of the intellectual work marked by the cultural turn. Nevertheless, there are certain unifying characteristics that signal a cultural studies project.
The following abbreviated list offered by Wright (cited in Ryba,
2005) pinpoints integral characteristics that would delineate a cultural studies work:

> *Interdisciplinary, anti-disciplinary, and post-disciplinary* — refuses to
> adhere to traditional disciplinary boundaries; draws upon a se-
> lection of traditional disciplines; transgresses and transcends
> disciplinary boundaries.
>
> *Heavily informed by theory (especially cutting-edge theorizing)* — instead
> of dogmatically adhering to a certain theoretical position, bor-
> rows from and intersects with a number of theories and theo-
> rists; theoretical framework is determined by one's own politics
> and its relevance to one's work.
>
> *Political* — concerned with issues of power, social difference, and
> justice; critically examines sociocultural, transnational identity/
> identification; draws on and forwards identity politics dis-
> courses; generally works toward progressive social change.
>
> *Praxis-driven* — intends to bring theory and practice together; not
> a purely academic endeavor but one that attempts to address
> real contemporary sociopolitical and cultural issues.

Contextual—positioned within a particular context; the method, theory, and politics of critical inquiry are connected to specificity of the geographical location and historical conjuncture.

Self-reflective—realizes the potential incongruity and transient nature of the knowledge it produces; resists creating and endorsing canons.

The organization of this volume tracks the contours of a cultural discourse of sport and exercise psychology, from the general trends to the specific arenas. Part I contests traditional mapping of the field, including its paradigmatic alliances, historicity, and professional practices. The contributing authors trouble the discipline's representation by critically engaging the politics of difference in their analyses. Part II isolates the major discursive fields in sport and exercise psychology, such as whiteness studies, queer and gender studies, and indigenous studies. The authors track the inroads of these intellectual strands to sport and exercise psychology, highlighting the role of critical discourses in making the cultural praxis trajectory. Part III examines the utility of cultural modes of analysis in specific arenas of sport and exercise psychology. The contributors draw on their vast experience of articulating psychological theories with local specificity to offer new directions for the research and practice in the field. We conclude the book with intent to provoke further epistemological debates in the field while proposing the possibilities for varying levels of engagement with the cultural turn. Two contributors situate their arguments in positivism and post-structuralism, respectively, to examine what difference the cultural turn makes in sport and exercise psychology.

The authors of the essays in this volume demonstrate the systematic engagement with a variety of sociocultural theories and culturally oriented research methodologies. We believe they make a significant contribution to reshaping the future of sport and exercise psychology. It is our hope that this project will provide conceptual grounds for new researchers in the field to anchor their studies in the cultural praxis discourse of sport and exercise psychology.

—Tatiana V. Ryba
Robert J. Schinke
Gershon Tenenbaum

References

Bonnell, V. E., & Hunt, L. (Eds.). (1999). *Beyond the cultural turn*. Berkeley, CA: University of California Press.

Edwards, D., & Potter, J. (1992). *Discursive psychology*. London: Sage.

Henriques, J., Hollway, W., Urwin, C., Venn, C., & Walkerdine, V. (Eds.). (1984). *Changing the subject: Psychology, social regulation and subjectivity*. London: Methuen.

Hwang, K. K. (2003). In search of a new paradigm for cultural psychology. *Asian Journal of Social Psychology, 6,* 287–291.

Ryba, T. V. (2005). Cultural studies theory. In D. Levinson & K. Christensen (Eds.), *Berkshire encyclopedia of world sport* (pp. 409–414). Great Barrington, MA: Berkshire.

Shi-xu. (2002). The discourse of cultural psychology. *Culture & Psychology, 8,* 65–78.

PART I

(RE)PRESENTING SPORT PSYCHOLOGY

1

SPORT PSYCHOLOGY AND THE CULTURAL TURN: NOTES TOWARD CULTURAL PRAXIS

Tatiana V. Ryba and Handel Kashope Wright

CHAPTER SUMMARY

Sport[1] psychology as cultural praxis is a critical discourse that emerged as an attempt to broaden the epistemological spectrum of theory and practice in the field (Ryba & Wright, 2005). Much of the knowledge base in sport and exercise psychology was developed by inference from positivistic research and practice with white male athletes. The Western ethnocentric bias inherent in mainstream sport psychology disconnects disenfranchised members of the sporting community, such as women, people of color, and queer individuals, from "their social relations and their own ways of thinking, feeling and interacting with the world" (Smith, 1999, p. 28). Building on interdisciplinary cultural studies as well as the pioneering work of feminist, critical race, and queer scholars of sport, cultural praxis articulates cultural studies scholarship with sport psychological problematics as a way of opening up sport psychological studies to issues of transnational identities, competing notions and sites of belonging, and contested cultures, which are enmeshed with power and ethics and which constitute the pressing actuality of our increasingly complex world. In this essay, we offer an overview of cultural studies and its potential (and necessarily difficult) articulation with sport psychology, which becomes more apparent in subsequent chapters of the book as the authors unearth and interrogate implicit ideological assumptions of our professional practices (inclusive of research, pedagogy, and consulting) in their areas of expertise. We then engage the cultural praxis heuristic model to propose a trajectory of sport psychology that is ethically and politically concerned about marginalized groups.

Sport Psychology and the Cultural Turn

In this essay we trouble the way traditional sport psychology maps its research and practice. We use the cultural studies as praxis model to propose a cultural discourse of sport psychology that deals with issues of marginalization, representation, and social justice through theory, research, and practice in sport and exercise psychology. Within the proposed framework, practice is conceptualized as merging with cutting-edge theorizing and the politics of difference into cultural praxis. We engage the concept of identity as a thread to show how sport psychology can be a discourse that deals with a more overt and nuanced representation of athletes/exercisers and issues of justice.

Race as a form of identity points to issues of representation in sport psychology and offers an example of how difference has (not) been taken up by traditional researchers. In 1990, Joan Duda and Maria Allison challenged scholars of sport and exercise psychology to give serious consideration to the role of race and ethnicity in producing human behavior. They reasoned that the failure to address cultural identity/identification in sport and exercise not only has moral consequences of diminishing ethnic minorities' experiences but also "leaves the theoretical understanding of the human condition in these contexts biased and distorted at best" (p. 115). Much to the authors' credit, they recognized and pointed to methodological limitations of traditional research designs in the psychological study of culture. While arguing from within the cross-cultural discourse, Duda and Allison asserted that simply adding culture (i.e., the mere adoption of race/ethnicity as a categorical variable) will do very little to advance our understanding of motivation and meaning of sport and exercise among diverse ethnic groups. Rearticulating the human psyche as constituted by historically specific, social, and cultural discourses that produce culturally situated knowledge is central to the cultural turn rhetoric. Hence, we recognize Duda and Allison's call for the interpretive methodological framework, which included addressing cultural identifications at a conceptual level in research, as an early precursor of the turn to cultural theory and methodology in sport psychology.

Since the time of Duda and Allison's article, there has been an increase in cross-cultural research activity in the field. Much of the work was devoted to cultural validation of psychological instruments and identification of cultural similarities/variations in psychological constructs across cultures. Duda and Allison's challenge to begin to incorporate culture at a conceptual level (i.e., contextualizing the results within the cultural specificity of a sociocultural group) was not answered, for the most part, by cross-cultural researchers. Ram, Starek, and Johnson (2004) conducted a content analysis of articles published in three leading U.S.-based journals—*Journal of Sport and Exercise Psychology* (1988–2000), *Journal of Applied Sport Psychology* (1989–2000), and *The Sport Psychologist* (1987–2000)—and concluded that, of all the articles published, only 15 and 4 papers looked at race/ethnicity and sexuality, respectively, in a conceptual way to inform the results obtained.

The failure of cross-cultural sport psychologists to work with conceptual difficulties of culture observed by Ram et al. is hardly surprising if we consider the philosophical assumptions underpinning cross-cultural research. Cross-cultural psychology was conceived within mainstream psychology and shares its parent discipline's desire for universal truth and procedure-driven inquiry (Moghaddam & Studer, 1997). The following quote from Jaan Valsiner (2004) points to the implications of resting knowledge claims on method: "The result of using methods that superimpose their implicit assumptions upon the data construction is the construction of epistemological 'blind spots'—the method begins to determine the general ways in which researchers think" (p. 11). Indeed, methodological issues are inseparable from ontological and epistemological assumptions that underpin our inquiry. Quantitative methods presuppose realist ontology, making it problematic for cross-cultural researchers to incorporate a social constructionist understanding of culture since such arrangement would lead to the study's epistemological antinomy. If, for example, we subscribe to the objective, independent, and single version of reality, conceptualizing culture as a coherent entity that exists outside of us, then our inevitable methodological choice is to study the effect of culture (often based on geographical location and ethnic or linguistic group) on psychological processes and behaviors of sport and exercise participants. Incorporating culture at a conceptual level most likely results in taking up culture as relational process rather than causal entity, as fragmented rather than holistic, and as negotiated and constructed rather than as "given," transmitted through processes of socialization and acculturation (Friedman, 1996). If these lines of reasoning make sense, then the ethical and political ramifications of research practices become apparent. Paraphrasing Weedon (1997), we pose the following questions for reflection. Are queer (or black, female) athletes essentially different from straight (or white, male) athletes (i.e., due to their sexuality, race, or gender)? Or are they socially constituted as different and because of their sociocultural location exhibit behavioral and/or emotional responses different from those of their normative counterparts?

The turn to cultural theory in social sciences, often associated with the "booming" of cultural studies internationally and especially in the United States since the 1990s (Storey, 1996), has been relatively invisible in sport and exercise psychology. We believe it was due to to the pioneering efforts of feminist sport psychologists, notably Dorothy Harris, Carole Oglesby, Diane Gill, and Vikki Krane, that issues of difference, identity, power, meaning, reflexivity, and praxis—all of which are central to cultural studies scholarship—were brought into debates over knowledge production and legitimation as part of the ongoing crisis of representation in sport psychology. Metaphorically, the feminist scholars have paved the way for developing scholars in the field to enter the cultural studies paradigm.[2] It is testimony to the growing theoretical and political influence of feminist work that many authors in this book demonstrate a pronounced and prolonged engagement with feminist theorizing as a means of centering culture in research and practice of sport psychology.

Continuing the feminist legacy in the field, sport psychology as cultural praxis is a psychological imaginary that is ethically and politically concerned with equity, sociocultural justice, and the representation of the marginalized. The heuristic draws on cultural studies in general and the "cultural studies as praxis" model proposed by Handel Wright in particular (see Ryba & Wright, 2005; Wright, 2001/2002, for in-depth discussion) to broaden the focus on difference to include transnational identities, competing notions and sites of belonging, and contested cultures. Diversifying the field does not merely mean an inclusion of nonwhite subjects in our studies since such an "add on" approach often reasserts the centrality of the hegemonic white (and often male, heterosexual) way of knowing by virtue of "othering."[3] Diversifying the field against the backdrop of the cultural turn means a serious engagement with and reexamination of ontological, epistemological, analytical, and political underpinnings of sport psychological research. We proceed by introducing cultural studies and pointing to its intersection with sport studies, outlining the articulation of sport psychology with cultural studies as praxis and explicating how sport psychology as cultural praxis can and, in fact, is leading to the evolution of a radically expanded and altered psychology of sport.

What Is Cultural Studies Anyway?[4]

Cultural studies is a generic term that can refer variously to the general study of culture, the study of intercultural relations, the study of cultural production and consumption, and a form of cultural critique. The cultural studies discourse that has been taken up by the scholars of sport, particularly in the English-speaking world, is derived from a discourse that had its institutional origins at the Centre for Contemporary Cultural Studies (CCCS) at the University of Birmingham, England, in the 1960s. British cultural studies emerged as an attempt to understand the changing sociopolitical and cultural environment of post-World War II Britain. This attempt to make meaning of the then contemporary culture meant undertaking such projects as studying movements and subcultures as "hippies" and "skin heads" (Clarke, 1973); examining the role of popular culture and the cultural industries in the production of meaning (Hall, 1977; Peters, 1976); retelling history from the perspectives of previously marginalized groups in society (e.g., "herstory," or history from women's perspective, and also undertaking "history from below," or history from the perspective of the working class) (Women's Studies Group, 1978; CCCS, 1982b); examination and critique of police brutality directed at black and working-class populations (CCCS, 1982a); and critical analysis and theorizing of the phenomenon of Thatcherite Britain (Hall, 1988).

Most accounts of the origin of cultural studies point to a period marked by crises of identity in the social sciences and humanities as the environment of ferment and foment in which the new, interdisciplinary, and indeed anti-disciplinary field of cultural studies could emerge and thrive (Gray & McGuigan, 1993). The narrative is of a distinctly British and singular history, conceived with the seminal work of three founding fathers, Raymond Williams, Richard Hoggart, and E. P. Thompson, and born in 1964 with the establishment of the Centre for Contemporary Cultural Studies at the University of Birmingham (the center that named the new field "cultural studies"). Though it quickly became quite interdisciplinary, English studies and sociology were the first discourses that cultural studies spoke as a toddler. This neat, singular, British academic narrative of origin has been muddied considerably by some figures who have asserted that arguments could be made, for example, for an African (theater), Russian (culturology), African American (black studies), or Appala-

chian (progressive education) origin of cultural studies rather than a
white British (English and sociology) origin (Wright, 1995, 1998).
Similarly, others have argued for an activist and performative acts
origin rather than an academic origin of cultural studies (Davies,
1995). Ioan Davies, for example, has put forward the following alternative narrative of the origin of cultural studies:

> Those of us who marched to Aldermaston and back in the 1950s
> and early 1960s, who helped establish the New Left Club . . .
> who discovered Jazz with Eric Hobsbawm, who taught evening
> classes for the Workers' Educational Association, who fought
> with Fife Socialist League who defended (equally) Tom
> M'boya, Lenny Bruce, Wole Soyinka, CLR James, Vic Allen
> are surprised to discover that what we were doing was invent-
> ing Cultural Studies. (p. 31)

What we have in Davies's account is an identification of leftist political activism and performative acts rather than academic work and
struggle over the crises in the disciplines as the origin of cultural
studies. These alternative narratives serve in part to confound cultural studies' purported and ironically "singular geographical and
specific racial and cultural (read white, male, working class, British)
origin" (Wright, 1995, p. 159). The point of the resulting multiplicity of narratives of the origin and history of cultural studies is not to
have readers discern which version is "accurate" but to acknowledge
that the history of cultural studies should be conceptualized as being
as open-ended and fluid as its discourse and praxis. As some cultural
studies theorists have pointed out, we ought not to look to a particular school nor to the emergence of institutionalized cultural studies
as a singular, definitive origin, but rather to a messy situation of difficult to pinpoint conjunctures of political activism, performative
acts, and intellectual and academic work at various moments and
sites (Gilroy, 1991; Wright, 1998).

The CCCS projects displayed a variety of theoretical and methodological approaches since the investigated issues were considered
to be more important than the disciplinary constraints placed on
what questions one could ask and examine within an individual discipline. Thus, a radical ground-breaking discourse was developed at
the CCCS that allowed British intellectuals to undertake progressive activism in an academic setting and to address pressing issues of
social justice in and through culture in an interdisciplinary and also

anti-disciplinary manner. Drawing from various disciplines, reading the latest theory, and undertaking theorizing of their own, and generally working for progressive social change, they undertook mainly ethnographic studies to examine how power and privilege operated in culture and society and to give a voice to oppressed and marginalized groups. Hence cultural studies at the CCCS was a project of double articulation of culture in an intellectual and a political sense, where "'culture' is simultaneously the ground on which analysis proceeds, the object of study, and the site of political critique and intervention" (Nelson, Treichler, & Grossberg, 1992, p. 5).

Once cultural studies was established as a discourse that dealt primarily with class issues, feminist and race theory and politics were used to strongly introduce women and gender issues, and black identity and race issues, and thus intervene in cultural studies itself and change the discourse from within (CCCS, 1982a, b; Women's Studies Group, 1978). While different cultural studies theorists and activists would emphasize different characteristics or aspects, or even reject certain aspects, it is important to note that "openness" (in terms of theoretical and methodological approaches and in terms of content) is a pivotal characteristic of cultural studies (Gray & McGuigan, 1993). As Stuart Hall (1990) once observed, "cultural studies is not one thing. It has never been one thing" (p. 11). The fact that the "definition, scope, and concerns of cultural studies are . . . constantly differed and differing" (Wright, 1995, p. 158) within various contexts has resulted in the mushrooming development of diverse versions of cultural studies. The various discourses of cultural studies are distinguishable by such factors as geographical location (e.g., British, Canadian, American, African, Nordic, Australian, Asian, etc.), close disciplinary affiliation (e.g., closely related to communications and media studies, English and literary studies, sociology and anthropology, history, etc.) and variations on theory/ practice balance (while cultural studies is supposed to involve the blending of theory and practice in praxis, some versions are almost purely theoretical while others maintain strong connections with grassroots activism). In the mid 1980s to early 1990s, the cultural studies' axis shifted from England to the United States, where "many academic institutions—presses, journals, hiring committees, conferences, university curricula—have created significant investment opportunities in cultural studies" (Nelson et al., 1992, p. 1). The rise of cultural studies in the United States was also associated with the cultural turn in social sciences, which was in part the incarnation of the growth of such intellectual trends as postmodernism, post-structuralism, and semiotics. Politically, the cultural turn signaled profound social changes taking place outside the academy as well as within and produced in conjunction with global cultural flows.

Given the complexity and diversity of cultural studies, which has moved from England to become a global discourse, it is useful to highlight the characteristics of a cultural studies project that holds the potential to transform the psychology of sport and exercise into a discourse that deals with issues of representation in a more nuanced and politicized way. First, cultural studies is a discourse interested in issues of identity/identification, representation, and the politics of sociocultural diversity. It provides a conceptual framework to engage with a dazzling plurality of difference — racial, sexual, transcultural, and intercultural — necessary for understanding contemporary unstable ethnoscapes. Second, cultural studies is a form of praxis. The project is informed by cutting-edge theorizing but also by blending theory with practice and empirical research to engender progressive social change. Third, cultural studies is disputed and contested in terms of its disciplinary origins and its relationship with the disciplines. Of major relevance to our work is that cultural studies has engaged not only principal humanities and social sciences disciplines like English, history, and sociology, but also the more practice-based, applied fields such as education and sport studies. Finally, cultural studies rejects taking up knowledge as neutral and an end in itself and has been a foment home for developing analytical tools to examine ideological, moral, and ethical implications of the Western power-knowledge. With its characteristics as outlined above, therefore, cultural studies emerges as an important discursive framework for instituting and understanding the cultural turn in sport and exercise psychology.

Cultural Studies Intersection with Sport Studies

Originally, sport was not established as a substantial part of academic scholarship. Sport activities were studied primarily within the context of cultural practices by anthropologists and/or historians. Generally subscribing to the arbitrary division between high and low culture, most scholars considered sport to be an unworthy subject for academic pursuit. Ironically, this marginalization was endorsed by both progressive and conservative politics (Blake, 1996).

For the Left, examining sport meant diverting attention from "real" political issues that were at stake. The Right, on the other hand, wanted to perpetuate the assumed unproblematic nature of sport — "a blissful unawareness about the social relations that control sport and other forms of physical activity, a frightening naiveté about the social context and material conditions underlying physical culture" (Sage, 1998, p. 13).

Pioneering sociohistorical texts by C. L. R. James (1963), Tony Mason (1989), and Wray Vamplew (1988), who produced important insights into sport as everyday practices, professional sport in Britain, and the relationship between sport and colonialism; E. P. Thompson (1966), who highlighted the relationship between sport and working-class culture; and Jennifer Hargreaves (1982) and Pierre Bourdieu (1978), who undertook the theorizing of how sport fits in the social structure of modern societies, helped the study of sport to be accepted by traditional disciplines. However, it was a slow process and sport as an object of study remained on the margins of what became its sociocultural foundations (history, sociology, philosophy). Andrew Blake (1996) has observed that

> sociologists and historians tended firstly to ignore sport; then, when from mid-1960s they began to consider it, they saw it within these frameworks as either unimportant leisure practices or as harmful economic and ideological aspects of the class system. (p. 14)

Though some figures (e.g., Blake, 1996; John Hargreaves, 1982) have asserted that cultural studies followed the established academic pattern of marginalizing sport, others have argued that this was not the case, that cultural studies did take up sport as a significant sociocultural phenomenon. As Andrews and Loy (1993) have rightly pointed out, since the days of the CCCS cultural studies has engaged "the study of sport as a cultural practice" (p. 255) in its larger project of taking popular culture seriously. From Birmingham onwards, cultural studies projects have questioned sport practices deconstructively, revealing the constructedness of what had been assumed "natural" and reading actively against the grain of the common sense and taken-for-grantedness of sport as a neutral, apolitical activity.

The cultural studies' conceptual framework has blended well with critical approaches to sport studies (e.g., feminist, neo-Marxist, queer) because these theoretical approaches share with cultural stud-

ies a number of characteristics—for example, a distrust of the ideological assumptions underpinning the cultural and academic canon
and a critique of the regulatory power of the canon to naturalize
certain "truths"; a focus on the object of study without close adherence to the constraints of a single and singular discipline; and the
centrality of issues of power and production of meaning. Critical
scholars of sport, including Jennifer Hargreaves (1994), John Hoberman (1992), Helen Lenskyi (1986), William Morgan (1994),
George Sage (1998), and Patricia Vertinsky (1994), for example, in-
jected critical approaches into their fields by undertaking analyses
of sport and exercise practices in conjunction with political econo-
my, body politics, ideology, and power relations. These scholars have
argued that the study of sport and exercise must be based on an understanding of their relationships with other everyday sociocultural
and political issues of contemporary societies. C. L. Cole (1993) put
forward a cogent summary of this position when she stressed:

> . . . sport is always already embedded in a theoretical/political
> position since any conceptualization of sport presupposes a re-
> lationship between power/knowledge and meaning/politics and
> is embedded in a theory of power, its operations and mecha-
> nisms (typically liberal and/or repressive), and corresponding
> strategies of resistance and change. (p. 78)

Cole (1993, 1998) went further by pointing to the importance of a
social analysis informed by cultural theories, which involves unearthing a cultural practice contingent on a specific historical conjuncture to produce a contextual map of the social formation. She
urged the rethinking of the very foundations of sport sociology, as-
serting centrality of the body in the contextual matrix of social, political, economic, and technological articulations of sport. Thus, cultural studies emphasis on the body and the body practices as sites of
popular pleasure, cultural production, and circulation of meanings
has arguably been the catalyst in sport studies' (re)turn to embodied
physical culture and the emergence of physical cultural studies.

There is a wide variety of theories of the body and not all of them,
of course, are associated with the cultural turn. Nonetheless, the
(re)discovery of the body by sport sociologists was triggered by the
cultural turn and holds significant implications for the psychological
study of sport and exercise. Physical culture scholarship (see Harg-

reaves & Vertinsky, 2007, as a prime example) highlighted the body in motion as cultural interface of personal experiences, meanings, and subjectivities through which broader social, economic, political, and technological contingencies are articulated (Andrews, 2008). The important point here is that an understanding of embodiment as a sociocultural constitution of the body imbued with power, begs for reconceptualization of the psyche as socioculturally constituted and constituting in its articulation with "genetically endowed corporeality." Allan Ingham (1997; Ingham, Blissmer, & Davidson, 1999) was among the first scholars of sport who attempted to reconcile the Cartesian split of scientific discourses in relation to personality, still hegemonic in sport psychology. Ingham (quoted in Andrews, 2008, p. 53) asserted:

> We need to know how social structures and cultures impact our social presentation of our 'embodied' selves and how our embodied selves reproduce and transform structures and cultures; how our attitudes towards our bodies relate to our self- and social identities.

Hence, sport sociologists influenced by cultural studies contributed tremendously to our understanding of contemporary sporting cultures as sites of (re)construction of the embodied self. What seems to be missing, however, is the concern with needs and wants of a specific person. "There is no record of suffering, alienation, and distortion as revealed *through* the subjectival first person. . . . The focus on subjectivities and difference . . . thus tends to be apolitical in the sense of *praxis*" (Ingham et al., 1999, p. 239). As a corrective, sport psychologists are in a prime position to reassert emotional and (un)conscious psychic events of the person as they articulate with social structures and cultures. In this sense, sport and exercise psychology as a discourse is not only embedded in power relations but is powerful itself in its ability to frame its object and subject of study. We propose the sport psychology as cultural praxis heuristic as a direction for the field that situates its work in the contextual *glocal*[5] matrix of contemporary sporting culture to understand its discursive enabling-constraining effects on the *lived* experience of oppression and empowerment. The praxis component of the heuristic works in tandem with analytical components of theory and research to engender social change in the field in general and in everyday lives of specific people in particular.

Articulating Sport Psychology as Cultural Praxis

Early work in the field that was explicitly positioned within the cultural studies paradigm became visible in early 2000s. Vikki Krane (2001) incorporated feminist cultural studies to address issues of gender and sexuality by putting forward a "lesbian feminist epistemology" in sport psychology. Ted Butryn (2002) utilized a cultural studies discourse to problematize race in general and whiteness as a racial identity in particular. Leslee Fisher, Ted Butryn, and Emily Roper (2003) pointed to utility of cultural studies in examining issues of power, privilege, and justice in research and applied work. The aforementioned essays invoked various aspects of cultural studies to challenge sport psychology scholars and practitioners to move out of the entrenched disciplinary "box" (see also Vealey, 2006).

Sport psychology as cultural praxis (Ryba, 2003; Ryba & Wright, 2005) was conceived as an articulation of cultural studies with sport psychology as a disciplinary discourse. In other words, instead of utilizing cultural studies to address certain issues in sport psychology, cultural praxis reconceptualizes the field to provoke sport and exercise psychology into a new trajectory "where [it] hardly recognizes in becoming otherwise, the unforeseeable that [it is] already becoming" (Patti Lather, cited in Ryba, 2005, p. iv). The heuristic is a vision of the field that is evolving from being a tightly specialized, white (in terms of the conceptual models), performance discourse to one that is an aspect of the interdisciplinary project of critical sport studies. The proposed heuristic is interdisciplinary, multidisciplinary, and focused on issues of sociocultural difference and social justice (with a particular emphasis on a reconceptualization of the athlete's identity); blends theoretical and practice work together in praxis; and favors progressive forms of qualitative research, especially what Lather (1991) has called "research as praxis."

The starting point of the heuristic is to work with the broad elements of theory, practice, and research in a reflexive process of articulating theoretical insights with local cultures and specific subjectivities. As underscored by Wright (2001/2002), these elements are not held apart and taken up separately but rather are considered as inextricably linked, blended together with progressive politics that focuses on social difference, equity, and justice, in praxis. The provided summary is something of an oversimplification since cultural studies comes with a built-in activist component and a preferred range of research approaches, and cultural theories draw on diverse ideological and analytical repertoires to tease out subjectivity, identity, and experience. Similarly, sport psychology literature is underpinned by disciplinary-based theories and professional ethics. Finally, there is both a diverse set of theories and forms of action involved in qualitative research. Due to inherent complexity of its components, it is difficult to develop a coherent description of the heuristic. The globalizing social sphere saturated with ambiguity of cultural meanings also means that sport psychology as cultural praxis is constantly redefined by local specificity. For sport psychology researchers, we suggest the cultural praxis heuristic as an analytical space where the dazzling plurality of difference is taken as constitutive of psychic realities that have real, material effects on actual lived experiences.

For the purpose of this essay, it is necessary to tease out the interwoven strands of cultural praxis (i.e., theory, practice, and research). As we have pointed out, simultaneous inter-/anti-/post-/disciplinarity are integral developments that now characterize cultural studies. When cultural studies is articulated with sport psychology, these characteristics promote the latter as a comprehensive and plaint discourse and praxis. In other words, cultural studies provokes sport psychology out of its historically inherited disciplinary adherence into becoming an aspect of inter-/anti-/post-/disciplinarity. "Doing" sport psychology as an interdisciplinary multicultural project allows the field to transcend tradition, to see itself as part of the more comprehensive sport studies scholarship, and to open up to understanding psychological issues in relation to historically contingent, *glocal* cultural narratives.

In a cultural praxis framework, the (re)examination of identity in general and the identity of the athlete in particular becomes a central concern. Hermans and Dimaggio (2007) contended that practicing psychologists witness an increasing impact of globalization on self and identity, highlighting the experience of uncertainty as integral in a dialogical analysis of self and identity. The economic, technological, and moral effects of globalization have been under scrutiny of the historians and sociologists of sport (Bale & Maguire, 1994). Yet, psychological challenges brought about by global migration and recent transformations of the international sports system remain relatively unexamined. The pressing research themes, such as cultural adaptation of displaced athletes and exercisers, require rethinking of identity in relation to current epistemological issues.[6] In what follows, we give a very brief indication of how each of the three elements of the cultural praxis heuristic — theory, practice, and research — would affect and change sport psychology.

In terms of theory, we could use post-structuralist theory as one of several possible examples. Post-structuralist perspectives (e.g., Butler, 1990; Foucault, 1982, 1995; Weedon, 1997) offer a theorization of the subject that is radically different from the liberal humanist perspective that is central to Western academic and civic discourses and is still taken for granted by the dominant sport psychological discourse. Instead of essentializing aspects of the "self," scholars influenced by various post-structuralist theories explicate the role of competing discourses in temporarily "fixing" subjectivity on behalf of particular power relation and social interests. We advocate the notion of identity as a number of "identifications come to light" (Fuss, 1995) and as a concept that though "under erasure" can be usefully deployed strategically (Hall, 1996), with the caveat that any declaration of identity be recognized as positional, selective, and provisional (Wright, 2003). The complexity of identity means that one cannot merely replace one form of identity with another. For example, the African athlete who comes to the United States on a sport scholarship does not automatically cease to be a continental African athlete and become a "black" athlete upon entering an American college. Rather, this athlete's identity is a series of complementary and contradictory identifications operating simultaneously, with some coming to the foreground or receding depending on context (e.g., the athlete lives and studies in the United States but she is not an American citizen, she is "black" but not African American, she is simultaneously a continental and a diasporic African). The athlete's experiences are shaped by her identity and vice versa. Ann Gray (2003) pointed to the inextricable interrelationship between experience and identity when she asserted that "experience can be understood as a discursive 'site of articulation' upon and through which subjectivities and identities are shaped and constructed" (p. 25).

Contrary to working with the athlete as disembodied, decontextualized, and autonomous, sport psychology as cultural praxis draws on post-structuralist conceptions and, therefore, considers the athlete to be an *embodied* subject of multiple discourses (e.g., race, gender, sexuality, etc.), a member of numerous social and cultural groups, and a part of sport as an institution immersed in a particular sociocultural and historical context. Such multiplicity of subject positions, often engaged in tensions, negotiations, and conflicts, comes together in one athlete who is both subjected to and an active agent of various discourses. By suggesting that subjectivity is fluid, poststructuralist theorizing opens subjectivity/identity to change and transformation and has much to offer sport psychology in terms of enhancing our understanding of athletes' sporting experiences as well as developing new forms of therapeutic interventions (see Leahy & Harrigan, 2006, and Thorpe, 2008, as examples of this work).

The practice component of the heuristic is informed by critical pedagogy (Freire, 1970; Giroux, 1988; McLaren, 2003) and aims at transgressing the "performance discourse" in which "the emotions are to be managed and the motivations are to be honed in ways that enhance performance" (Ingham et al., 1999, p. 240). In line with earlier calls for social justice in physical education and kinesiology (cf. Gill, 2007; Sage, 1993), we advocate addressing politics of difference through the co-participatory and transformative practice of sport psychology that emphasizes inclusion, enjoyment, equity, and pedagogy of possibility. Drawing on Paulo Freire (1970, 1985), athletes are approached as experts of their individual experiences, who co-participate in the applied consultancy work always already knowing about their performing bodies and who have agency and the potential to negotiate power in their dealings with institutions and with corporate sporting culture. Cultural praxis fosters progressive social change in the field by means of demystifying power relations and challenging taken-for-granted normative systems of the lived culture. As Freire observed, human reality is not static and a given destiny, but rather fluid and transformable. At the center of his understanding of praxis is education that serves as a catalyst for reflecting on the conditions of our lives and becoming agents of social transformation for ourselves and society as a whole. From this perspective, the role of the sport psychologist shifts from merely attempting to improve athletes' performance in a narrowly focused, functionalist sense to assisting athletes in the process of "conscienticization"[7] and creating possibilities for performance enhancement, athlete self-assurance, and empowerment, and indeed social transformations to occur.

In order to accomplish this task, the training and work of the sport psychologist takes the educational model seriously and infuses it with critical pedagogy. Taking seriously the Freirean and critical pedagogy notion that education and pedagogy are always already political, the sport psychology educational model in this conception

goes beyond teaching athletes to develop psychological skills and beyond the notions of performance enhancement as neutral and an end
in itself. We will not rehash convincing arguments published elsewhere that sport psychology has been carving a narrow disciplinary
track that objectifies the athlete insofar as the athlete's body is viewed
as an instrument that needs to be worked and fine-tuned to achieve
a desired outcome; that the performance discourse is structurally
and ideologically induced to reproduce systems of domination in
(post)capitalist societies; and that sport psychologists are unwit-
tingly complacent in colonizing the athlete's subjectivity by adjusting
the athlete's responses to hegemonic normative systems of oppression and exploitation (see, e.g., Coakley, 1992; Hoberman, 1992; Ingham et al., 1999; Ryba & Schinke, 2009). The reader is encouraged
to wrestle with the aforementioned texts to gain insights into the inner workings of the knowledge production in the field. We, moreover, reiterate our previous assertion (Ryba & Wright, 2005) that
the incorporation of critical pedagogy makes for a sport psychology
educational model that rejects both the myth of neutrality and the
insidious endorsement of oppression and exploitation that it masks.
The overt politicization of applied work in the field and infusion of
its educational model with critical pedagogy facilitate the production of a cultural praxis trajectory in sport psychology.

Praxis as a form of theory-driven practice points to the importance of understanding epistemological and political assumptions of
everyday professional practices. Much of the critical scholarship
that deconstructs a taken-for-granted sport psychological imaginary
draws on social and cultural theories and is often published in sociological and cultural studies journals. Hence, it is not enough to advocate blending of theory and practice in praxis; the theory component ought to draw on cultural and critical sport studies in addition
to theoretical models in sport and exercise psychology. The incorporation of critical theories in applied context will likely result in the
articulation of foundational psychological theories with a critical
reading of the context through the prism of specific subjectivity, thus
enhancing sport psychological theory with lived culture of practice.

The research component of the heuristic plays an integral role in
engendering praxis. Despite the proclaimed methodological openness of cultural studies (Nelson et al., 1992), certain approaches
have been more prevalent in cultural studies work than others. Cultural studies has tended to favor qualitative over quantitative meth-

odologies, a critical paradigm over post-positivism, and critical forms of ethnography more than any other research tradition. Emphasizing this point, Gray (2003) has identified ethnographic research as an approach to "doing" cultural studies, thereby endorsing empirical research as a factor that engenders cultural studies as praxis.

Sport psychology, on the other hand, has traditionally been quantitative and positivistic (Vealey, 2006). Gradually, under the influence of feminist and existential/humanist epistemologies, the field of sport psychology is becoming more qualitative friendly. Cultural studies methodological intervention has the potential to open up sport psychological research to greater acceptance of qualitative studies and a wider variety of qualitative approaches and traditions (e.g., narratives, discourse analysis, semiotics and visual ethnography, institutional ethnography, and participatory action research). The transformative power of research as praxis is evident in both research and applied settings.

As a research example, we highlight the project developed by Robert Schinke and colleagues in collaboration with a Canadian Aboriginal community, the Wikwemikong, to demonstrate how pressing contextual issues intervened within the academic project to alter the direction, and indeed the moral significance, of the conducted research. The project began as a traditional sport psychological investigation into adaptation strategies of elite Canadian Aboriginal athletes who train and compete within the mainstream sport system (Schinke et al., 2006). The research questions arose from the academic context and, by the authors' admissions, reflected interests of Schinke et al. Although the research team quickly became aware of the epistemological challenges of adapting psychological constructs to the parameters of local culture, it took three years of collaborative work with the community to gain a better understanding of what kind of questions needed to be addressed in Wikwemikong. Of major concern to the community elders were issues related to health and well-being of the Wikwemikong youth. They were applied issues that would instigate social change on the reserve. By encouraging community members to take an active role in and the ownership of research, the team of academic and community-appointed co-researchers succeeded in mobilizing resources and expertise to develop sport and physical activity programming that would address pressing health and well-being issues of Wikwemikong youth. Hence, the research project that began as a post-positivistic apolitical endeavor has been transformed into a timely cultural praxis work (see Blodgett et al., in press, and Schinke et al., 2009, for reflexive reports about the progressive integration of Wikwemikong's cultural practices in successive multicultural projects).

In applied settings, practitioners need theoretical knowledge and analytical skills to make sense of competing information when assessing a situation. Practitioners rely on their knowing-in-action, which is mostly tacit and revealed through spontaneous behavior of skillful practice. According to Donald Schön (1983), "When someone reflects-in-action, he becomes a researcher in the practice context. He is not dependent on the categories of established theory and technique, but constructs a new theory of the unique case" (p. 68). When the practice situation cannot be mapped onto a "classic" case or concrete category of applied theory, we do not have a problem to solve. Schön has argued that the emphasis on problem solving, which is an approach to professional practice grounded in assumptions of logical positivism, needs to be redirected to problem *setting*. Problem setting is the process by which

> we select what we will treat as the "things" of the situation . . . set the boundaries of our attention to it, and . . . impose upon it a coherence which allows us to say what is wrong and in what directions the situation needs to be changed. (p. 40)

In other words, practitioners need to do some work or *construct* problems from the fragmented and fuzzy situations that make no sense by naming the things that are perceived as relevant and important and setting them into the frame of a specific problem. When we consider how to motivate athletes, for example, we usually deal with many things at once (e.g., team culture, personal values, coaching style). Because achievement motivation is a multidimensional construct that spills over psychological, social, cultural, and ideological issues, we need to untangle and map particular features of the practice situation onto the categories of a certain theoretical model of motivation. Hence by naming the features we find relevant, we *"frame the context in which we will attend to them"* (p. 40).

If we take Schön's assertion seriously, it becomes evident that our own psychosocial location in the world, cultural history, and disciplinary norms influence what pieces of information we consider important, what data we simply ignore or avoid noticing, and what kind of inferences we make in our assessment of the problem. Without a critical reflection on our actions of problem setting, we might be reducing professional assessment to mental shortcuts, tapped into the collective historical and commonsense Eurocentric knowledge. In the framework of cultural praxis, therefore, practitioners work with the elements of theory, research, and reflection-in-action articulated with lived culture. The overarching goal of practice shifts from problem solving (when problem is located within the sport or exercise participant) to "unfixing" the subject position (aiming at instigating personal transformation) while working toward the social change in the field.

Conclusion

Building on the progressive work of scholars like George Sage (1993), who challenged physical educators to look at their work in connection to the larger sociopolitical context and become agents of social change; Brenda Bredemeier (2001), who proposed to ground sport psychology research in feminist praxis; and Handel Wright (2001/2002), who developed the cultural studies as social justice praxis model, we have pointed in this chapter to the implications of the intersection of sport psychology with cultural studies as a discursive site of cultural praxis. Such an articulation provides an important framework for instituting and understanding the cultural turn in sport psychology (i.e., what difference the cultural turn makes in terms of addressing identity and the politics of difference, in terms of disciplinarity and its limits and in terms of the theory/practice binary in the field of sport psychology). Articulating sport psychology as cultural praxis contributes to bridging the dichotomies between academic and applied work, theory and practice, text and lived culture. While we acknowledge the constraints we all operate under in the academy and the perennial threat posed by theoreticism to academic work as praxis work,[8] we nevertheless believe that it is possible and valuable to undertake work in the academy that goes beyond various binaries (e.g., academic/practitioner, university/sporting field, theorizing/coaching). Cultural studies as a form of praxis, therefore, facilitates the integration of academic and applied work in sport and exercise psychology as a way of undertaking interdisciplinary, praxis work in the field.

In the age of economic and political uncertainty that has resulted in the global flows of migrants transcending material and imaginary borders, it is integral to locate our research questions in the contextual *glocal* matrix of contemporary sporting/physical cultures that enact and are enacted by the subject. Within the hegemonic performance discourse, pressures to conform to a fairly narrow range of acceptable disciplinary practices have produced sport psychological theory and practice that prescribes a regime of constant adjustment of subjectivity, despite the neoliberal rhetoric of diversity. In a globalized society "without borders" the pressures to conform are intensified due to a floating image of "opportunity" and "fair competition" that projects desires as increasingly realizable. To modify Vertinsky (2002), new technologies are less a script for freedom than subjection of difference to the demand to fit in and perform. The potential of psychological violence is ubiquitous as subjection "consists precisely in this fundamental dependency on a discourse we never chose but that, paradoxically, initiates and sustains our agency" (Butler, 1997, p. 2). As a profession, we should not be glossing over the profound implications of practicing the performance discourse for identity, subjectivity, and well-being of sport and exercise participants.

The cultural turn in sport and exercise psychology has created the condition of possibility to reexamine the key theoretical and political assumptions that underlie our disciplinary practices and to analyze effects of these working assumptions on how marginalized populations are studied and represented in and through sport psychological research. The cultural praxis heuristic advances sport psychological studies into new spaces where the politics of difference is taken up as constitutive of psychic realities. What we offer in the notion of sport psychology as cultural praxis is a discursive framework to address the urgency of sociocultural difference in theory, practice, and research in the field. By opening up the ways of thinking about subjectivity, identity, and representation; academic and applied work; knowledge production; and reasserting the lived materiality of psychic events as they articulate with social structures and cultures, sport psychology as cultural praxis makes for a radically expanded and altered trajectory of sport and exercise psychology.

References

Ahmed, S. (2000). *Strange encounters: Embodied others and post-coloniality*. London & New York: Routledge.

Andrews, D. L. (2008). Kinesiology's inconvenient truth and the physical cultural studies imperative. *Quest, 60,* 45–62.

Andrews, D. L., & Loy, J. (1993). British cultural studies and sport: Past encounters and future possibilities. *Quest, 45,* 255–276.

Bale, J., & Maguire, J. (Eds.). (1994). *The global sports arena: Athletic talent mi-*

gration in an interdependent world. London: Frank Cass & Co. Ltd.

Blake, A. (1996). *The body language: The meaning of modern sport*. London: Lawrence & Wishart.

Blodgett, A. T., Schinke, R. J., Fisher, L. A., Yungblut, H. E., Recollet-Saikkonene, D., Peltier, D., et al. (in press). Praxis and community-level sport programming strategies in a Canadian aboriginal reserve. *International Journal of Sport and Exercise Psychology*.

Bourdieu, P. (1978). Sport and social class. *Social Science Information, 17*, 819–840.

Bredemeier, B. (2001). Feminist praxis in sport psychology research. *The Sport Psychologist, 15*, 412–418.

Butler, J. (1990). *Gender trouble*. London: Routledge.

Butler, J. (1997). *The psychic life of power*. Stanford, CA: Stanford University Press.

Butryn, T. M. (2002). Critically examining white racial identity and privilege in sport psychology consulting. *The Sport Psychologist, 16*, 316–336.

Centre for Contemporary Cultural Studies. (1982a). *The empire strikes back: Race and racism in 70s Britain*. London: Hutchinson.

Centre for Contemporary Cultural Studies. (1982b). *Making histories: Studies in history-writing and politics*. London: Hutchinson.

Clarke, J. (1973). Football hooliganism and the skinheads. *Centre for Contemporary Cultural Studies Stencilled Occasional Paper Series, 42*.

Coakley, J. (1992). Burnout among adolescent athletes: A personal failure or social problem? *Sociology of Sport Journal, 9*, 271–285.

Cole, C. L. (1993). Resisting the canon: Feminist cultural studies, sport, and technologies of the body. *Journal of Sport & Social Issues, 17*(2), 77–97.

Cole, C. L. (1998). Addiction, exercise, and cyborgs: Technologies of deviant bodies. In G. Rail (Ed.), *Sport and post-*

modern culture (pp. 261–276). Albany: State University of New York Press.

Davies, I. (1995). *Cultural studies and beyond: Fragments of empire*. New York: Routledge.

Duda, J. L., & Allison, M. T. (1990). Cross-cultural analysis in exercise and sport psychology: A void in the field. *Journal of Sport and Exercise Psychology, 12*, 114–131.

Fisher, L. A., Butryn, T. M., & Roper, E. (2003). Diversifying sport psychology through cultural studies: A promising perspective. *The Sport Psychologist, 17*, 391–405.

Foucault, M. (1982). The subject and power. In H. Dreyfus, & P. Rabinow (Eds.), *Michel Foucault: Beyond structuralism and hermeneutics* (pp. 208–226). Brighton, England: Harvester.

Foucault, M. (1995). *Discipline and punish: The birth of the prison* (Trans. A. Sheridan). (2nd ed.). New York: Vintage.

Freire, P. (1970). *Pedagogy of the oppressed*. New York: Continuum.

Freire, P. (1985). *The politics of education: Culture, power, and liberation*. South Hadley, MA: Bergin & Garvey.

Friedman, J. (1996). *Cultural identity and global process*. London: Sage.

Fuss, D.(1995). *Identification papers*. New York: Routledge.

Gill, D. L. (2007). Integration: The key to sustaining kinesiology in higher education. *Quest, 59*, 269–286.

Gilroy, P. (1991). *There ain't no black in the union jack: The cultural politics of race and nation*. Chicago: University of Chicago Press.

Giroux, H. (1988). *Schooling and the struggle for public life: Critical pedagogy in the modern age*. Minneapolis: University of Minnesota Press.

Gray, A. (2003). *Research practice for cultural studies*. London: Sage.

Gray, A., & McGuigan, J. (Eds.). (1993). *Studying culture: An introductory reader*. London: Arnold.

Gunew, S. (2004). *Haunted nations: The*

colonial dimensions of multiculturalism. London & New York: Routledge.

Hall, S. (1977). Culture, the media and the "ideological effect." In J. Curran, M. Gurevitch, & J. Woollacott (Eds.), *Mass communications and society* (pp. 56–90). London: Arnold.

Hall, S. (1988). The toad in the garden: Thatcherism among the theorists. In C. Nelson & L. Grossberg (Eds.), *Marxism and the interpretation of culture.* London: Macmillan.

Hall, S. (1990). The emergence of cultural studies and the crisis of the humanities. *October, 53,* 11–90.

Hall, S. (1992). Cultural studies and its theoretical legacies. In L. Grossberg, C. Nelson, & P. A. Treichler (Eds.), *Cultural studies* (pp. 277–294). London & New York: Routledge.

Hall, S. (1996). Introduction: Who needs identity? In S. Hall & P. du Gay (Eds.), *Questions of cultural identity.* London: Sage.

Hargreaves, J. (Ed.). (1982). *Sport, culture, and ideology.* London: Routledge & Kegan Paul.

Hargreaves, J. (1982). Sport, culture, and ideology. In J. Hargreaves (Ed.), *Sport, culture, and ideology* (pp. 30–61). London: Routledge & Kegan Paul.

Hargreaves, J. (1994). *Sporting females: Critical issues in the history and sociology of women's sports.* London: Routledge.

Hargreaves, J., & Vertinsky, P. A. (Eds.). (2007). *Physical culture, power, and the body.* London: Routledge.

Hermans, H. J. M., & Dimaggio, G. (2007). Self, identity, and globalization in times of uncertainty: A dialogical analysis. *Review of General Psychology, 11*(1), 31–61.

Hoberman, J. (1992). *Mortal engines: The science of performance and the dehumanization of sport.* New York: The Free Press.

Ingham, A. G. (1997). Toward a department of physical cultural studies and an end to tribal warfare. In J. Fernandez-Balboa (Ed.), *Critical postmodernism in*

human movement, physical education, and sport (pp. 157–182). Albany: State University of New York Press.

Ingham, A. G., Blissmer, B. J., & Davidson, K. W. (1999). The expandable prolympic self: Going beyond the boundaries of the sociology and psychology of sport. *Sociology of Sport Journal, 16,* 236–268.

James, C. L. R. (1963). *Beyond a boundary.* London: Stanley Paul.

Johnson, R. (1996). What is cultural studies anyway? In J. Storey (Ed.), *What is cultural studies: A reader* (pp. 75–114). London: Arnold.

Krane, V. (2001). One lesbian feminist epistemology: Integrating feminist standpoint, queer theory, and feminist cultural studies. *The Sport Psychologist, 15,* 401–411.

Lather, P. (1991). *Getting smart: Feminist research and pedagogy with/in the postmodern.* London: Routledge.

Leahy, T., & Harrigan, R. (2006). Using narrative therapy in sport psychology practice: Application to a psychoeducational body image program. *The Sport Psychologist, 20,* 480–494.

Lenskyj, H. (1986). *Out of bounds: Women, sport, and sexuality.* Toronto: Women's Press.

Mason, T. (Ed.). (1989). *Sport in Britain: A social history.* Cambridge, England: Cambridge University Press.

McLaren, P. (2003). *Life in schools: An introduction to critical pedagogy in the foundations of education* (4th ed.). Boston: Allyn & Bacon.

Moghaddam, F. M., & Studer, C. (1997). Cross-cultural psychology: The frustrated gadfly's promises, potentialities, and futures. In D. Fox & I. Prilleltensky (Eds.), *Critical psychology: An introduction* (pp. 185–201). Thousand Oaks, CA: Sage.

Morgan, W. (1994). *Leftist theories of sport: A critique and reconstruction.* Urbana, IL: University of Illinois Press.

Nelson, C., Treichler, P. A., & Grossberg,

L. (1992). Cultural studies: An introduction. In L. Grossberg, C. Nelson, & P. A. Treichler (Eds.), *Cultural studies* (pp. 1–18). London & New York: Routledge.

Peters, R. (1976). Television coverage of sport. *Centre for Contemporary Cultural Studies Stencilled Occasional Paper Series, 48.*

Ram, N., Starek, J., & Johnson, J. (2004). Race, ethnicity, and sexual orientation: Still a void in sport and exercise psychology. *Journal of Sport & Exercise Psychology, 26,* 250–268.

Ryba, T. V. (2003). From mental game to cultural praxis: Implications of a cultural studies model for transforming sport psychology. *Cultural Studies Association (U.S.) Founding Conference*, Pittsburgh, PA.

Ryba, T. V. (2005). *Applied sport psychology: Unearthing and contextualizing a dual genealogy.* Doctoral dissertation, University of Tennessee.

Ryba, T. V., & Schinke, R. J. (Eds.). (2009). Decolonizing methodologies: Approaches to sport and exercise psychology from the margins (Special Issue). *International Journal of Sport and Exercise Psychology, 7*(3).

Ryba, T. V., & Wright, H. K. (2005). From mental game to cultural praxis: A cultural studies model's implications for the future of sport psychology. *Quest, 57,* 192–212.

Sage, G. H. (1993). Sport and physical education in the new world order: Dare we be agents of social change? *Quest, 45,* 151–164.

Sage, G. H. (1998). *Power and ideology in American sport: A critical perspective.* Champaign, IL: Human Kinetics.

Schinke, R. J., Peltier, D., Hanrahan, S., Eys, M. A., Recollet-Saikkonene, D., Yungblut, H. E., et al. (2009). The progressive integration of Canadian indigenous culture within a sport psychology bicultural research team. *International Journal of Sport and Exercise Psychology, 7*(3), 309–322.

Schinke, R. J., Gauthier, A., Dubuc, N., & Crowder, T. (2007). Understanding athlete adaptation in the national hockey league through an archival data source. *The Sport Psychologist, 21,* 277–287.

Schinke, R., Michel, G., Gauthier, A., Pickard, P., Danielson, R., Peltier, D., et al. (2006). The adaptation to the mainstream in elite sport: A Canadian aboriginal perspective. *The Sport Psychologist, 20*(4), 435–448.

Schön, D. (1983). *The reflective practitioner: How professionals think in action.* London: Temple Smith.

Smith, L. T. (1999). *Decolonizing methodologies: Research and indigenous peoples.* Dunedin, New Zealand: University of Otago Press.

Storey, J. (Ed.). (1996). *What is cultural studies: A reader.* London: Arnold.

Thompson, E. P. (1966). *The making of the English working class.* New York: Random House.

Thorpe, H. (2008). Foucault, technologies of self, and the media: Discourses of femininity in snowboarding culture. *Journal of Sport & Social Issues, 32,* 199–229.

Valsiner, J. (2004). Three years later: Culture in psychology—between social positioning and producing new knowledge. *Culture & Psychology, 10*(5), 5–27.

Vamplew, W. (1988). *Pay up and play the game: Professional sport in Britain, 1875–1914.* Cambridge, England: Cambridge University Press.

Vealey, R. S. (2006). Smocks and jocks outside the box: The paradigmatic evolution of sport and exercise psychology. *Quest, 58,* 128–159.

Vertinsky, P. A. (1994). *The eternally wounded woman: Women, doctors and exercise in the late nineteenth century.* Champaign: University of Illinois Press.

Vertinsky, P. A. (2002). Embodying normalcy: Anthropometry and the long arm of William H. Sheldon's somatotyping project. *Journal of Sport History, 29,* 95–133.

Weedon, C. (1997). *Feminist practice & post-*

structuralist theory (2nd ed.). Cambridge, England: Blackwell.

Weedon, C. (2004). *Identity and culture: Narratives of difference and belonging.* Maiden head, England. Open University Press.

Women's Studies Group, CCCS. (1978). *Women take issue.* London: Hutchinson.

Wright, H. K. (1995). Would we know African cultural studies if we saw it? *The Review of Education/Pedagogy/Cultural Studies, 17,* 157–165.

Wright, H. K. (1998). Dare we de-centre Birmingham? Troubling the origins and trajectories of cultural studies. *European Journal of Cultural Studies, 1,* 33–56.

Wright, H. K. (2001/2002). Cultural studies and service learning for social justice. *Tennessee Education, 31/32,* 11–16.

Wright, H. K. (2003). Cultural studies as praxis: (making) an autobiographical case. *Cultural Studies, 17,* 805–822.

Notes

1. David Andrews (2008) has recently mused that *sport* is one of the most ambiguous and least useful words with which to frame an area of study. Indeed, sport as a cultural practice can be engaged in a multiplicity of ways. The meaning of sport varies across times, spaces, and cultures. For some, sport signals a system of rigorous talent selection through a web of state-sponsored sport schools for children and youth. For others, sport signifies a loosely organized network of physical activity sites, such as playgrounds, recreation and leisure facilities, community centers, and the like. While sport and exercise psychology has been arbitrarily divided into two discourses that emphasize either performance or well-being as their respective concerns, we feel that the boundary is highly contested and porous at best. Therefore, sport psychology as cultural praxis decolonizes the word *sport* from its traditional usage in sport psychology to open it to a rearticulation based on various expressions of human movement. Most contributing authors in this book, while attempting to delimit theoretical insights and consequent recommendations to either sport or exercise, felt that it is more productive to locate psychological, cultural, social, and ideological analyses of subjectivities and active bodies in "spatial and historical specificity" (Andrews, 2008, p. 50).

2. In sketching the contours of a cultural studies scholarship in sport psychology, it is imperative to acknowledge the sport psychology program at the University of Tennessee, housed within the Cultural Studies Unit during 1994–2003, as a rich ferment for innovative cultural discourse of sport psychology. Central to that rich ferment is the intellectual influence of Handel Kashope Wright, who was brought to the University of Tennessee as a cultural studies specialist to develop a program that would promote and link critical work in foundations of education (history, anthropology, sociology, and philosophy), cultural studies in education, and sport studies (sociocultural foundations of sport and sport psychology). The intellectual tradition rooted in Tennessee is well represented on the short list of scholars who work explicitly within a cultural studies framework in the field: Leslee Fisher teaches sport and exercise psychology at the university and Ted Butryn, Emily Roper, Kerrie Kauer, and Tatiana Ryba are graduates of Tennessee's "old" doctoral program in sport psychology (i.e., when it was juxtaposed with cultural studies).

3. As defined by Weedon (2004), "othering" refers to the process of "constructing another people or group as radically different to oneself or one's own group, usually on the basis of racist and/or ethnocentric discourses" (p. 166). Postcolonial scholars explicate the process of "othering" found in Western scientific discourses and offer nuanced analyses of how supposedly progressive discourses,

such as multiculturalism and cross-cultural psychology, recenter the white subject (see Ahmed, 2000; Gunew, 2004; Moghaddam & Studer, 1997).

4. We title this subheading after a seminal paper by Richard Johnson (1996) "What Is Cultural Studies Anyway?" First published in 1986, Johnson's paper is significant because it is a relatively early detailed explication of cultural studies, written by one of the acknowledged founders of institutionalized cultural studies (Johnson was the founder and first director of the first cultural studies center and program, the Centre for Contemporary Cultural Studies, University of Birmingham, England). Perhaps more important, it is significant because it was an early indication of what has become a perennial preoccupation in the field, namely, constant self-examination and explication. Because cultural studies is constantly expanding and mutating, and because it has always been a fairly complex anti-/inter-/post-/diciplinary field, there is a tendency to focus repeatedly on (re)defining it and examining its scope and its changing relationships with traditional disciplines. In fact, the book in which the paper is reprinted, John Storey's (1996) *What Is Cultural Studies*, is a collection of essays, each of which could be said to provide an answer to this pivotal question.

5. The local-global nexus, such as approaching local issues from a global perspective.

6. We acknowledge early work of Robert Schinke and colleagues into adaptation strategies of Canadian Aboriginal and immigrant athletes as a shift to culture in sport psychological research (see Schinke et al., 2006; Schinke et al., 2007). Within a cultural praxis framework, we advocate for further investigation of this problematic that troubles and attempts to rethink traditional notions of adaptation, acculturation, and such.

7. "Conscienticization" is a principal concept in Paulo Freire's liberation pedagogy. The assumption is that dehumanization, although a concrete historical fact, is *not* a given destiny but the result of an unjust order. The oppressed can remove barriers to total liberation when they become critically aware of the injustice in the world and perform acts that destroy it. In a way, the process of conscienticization is a deconstruction of the naturalized social order, creation of new understanding of reality and how one is positioned in society, and a starting point for doing something to change oneself and society for the better.

8. Stuart Hall (1992), for example, had been aware of the danger of armchair theorizing as long ago as the 1970s and warned of it in the early 1990s.

2

HISTORICIZING SPORT PSYCHOLOGY

Anthony P. Kontos

CHAPTER SUMMARY

This chapter provides a critical historical review of the development of research in sport psychology. In so doing, I attempt to deconstruct the "white picket fence," ordered depiction of the history of sport psychology research to reflect a more representative view that includes the sociocultural issues that helped shape its development. In the introduction, I argue for a reexamination of the history of sport psychology that focuses on global and sociocultural influences instead of the traditional Western, ethnocentric viewpoint. Issues related to adopting a "presentist" historical perspective are emphasized in this section. I then critically examine the development of key research questions and topics in the field of sport psychology from the late 1800s to the present. Emphasis is placed on the influence of key sociocultural institutions that shaped the direction, some might argue, misdirection, of the development of sport psychology research. Although I examine several key sport psychology research questions from my admittedly primarily North American perspective, I attempt to provide multiple discourses of the history of sport psychology. Next, I examine the ongoing and future history issues in the field as they relate to the cultural praxis emphasis of this book. I have included these sections to offer the reader perspective on the rapidly evolving development of sport psychology research during the past decade. Next, I provide a brief review of cultural praxis content evidence in research from current sport psychology professional journals. Finally, in the conclusion, I highlight the need for a cultural praxis approach to sport psychology research as the field continues its development.

Historicizing Sport Psychology: White Picket Fences and the Caveat of Presentist Monocultural History

Typically, the history of sport psychology research is depicted in a consistent, ordered, and linear manner, analogous to a "white picket fence," wherein the dominant paradigm of each period of the field's development is highlighted along with its key figures and milestone accomplishments in research and practice (e.g., Weinberg & Gould, 2007; Williams & Straub, 2007). As such, readers are introduced to Norman Triplett's pioneering research on cycling performance in the presence of others (i.e., social facilitation) in the late 1890s while at Indiana University (Triplett, 1898); Coleman Griffith's "first sport psychology laboratory" and research-practitioner methodology researching athletes at the University of Illinois from the 1920s to 1940s; the considerable influence of Franklin Henry on connecting the academic (i.e., courses) and research side of sport psychology at the University of California at Berkley; the influence of Bruce Olgilvie and Thomas Tutko's seminal work on applied sport psychology during the early 1970s at San José State University; and so on to the "multidisciplinary science and practice" (Weinberg & Gould, 2007, p. 10) of present-day sport psychology researchers. Feltz and I (2002) adopted a similar approach to historicizing sport psychology research in Horn's (2002) *Advances in Sport Psychology*. It is important to be aware of sport psychology's historical development, key figures, and milestone achievements, as they offer an historical roadmap for how research in the field has evolved from its beginnings to its current state. However, as with any roadmap we use to navigate to our destination, there are numerous routes we can take to arrive at the same place and different stops we can take along the way. Unfortunately, most of the road maps of sport psychology research provided by authors of sport psychology books rarely waiver from the largely North American/Western European myopic view of the field's development. However, recent examinations of the development of Russian sport psychology in the *Journal of Applied Sport Psychology* by Ryba and colleagues (2005, 2006) have provided a hopeful start to an expanded global view of the development of the field.

The linear and sometimes nostalgic (i.e., focusing on sport psychology's successes and "good old days") approach to the development of sport psychology research, particularly the field's formative years, is reflective of the hegemonic forces that created and fostered its development; namely, white male perspectives and positivistic psychology. This approach to historicizing sport psychology also parallels that which has dominated the broader field of psychology (see Hothersall, 2004). Although this hegemonic approach to the history of sport psychology research lends itself nicely to the "white picket fence" image, it provides little context for the current development of our field. Moreover, there is little mention in the historical reviews of sport psychology research of the influences of the social, political, cultural, and institutional forces that shaped its development. As a result, the history of sport psychology research as it is taught in the survey-style courses in which it is typically and briefly covered is presented as a largely North American and white male endeavor. Nonetheless, some researchers such as Vealey (2006) have advocated for a paradigmatic shift away from this historical "box" or context in which the development of sport psychology has traditionally been framed. Similarly, Gill (1995) provided a much-needed new perspective on the traditional history of sport psychology by decentering traditional father figures of sport psychology and "replacing" women such as Dorothy Harris and Carole Ogelsby from the margins of the field's development to its center.

The purpose of this chapter is to challenge the "white picket fence," hegemonic image of the development of sport psychology research by exploring the sociocultural and other forces that influenced its development. Ryba (Ryba, 2005; Ryba & Wright, 2005) argued that the field of sport psychology is entering a multidisciplinary phase, or "cultural praxis." The term *cultural praxis* refers to the coalescence of a discipline into an interdisciplinary/multidisciplinary approach that encompasses sociocultural and social justice themes, and combines practice and theory (Ryba, 2005). Practically, such an approach integrates the traditional sport psychology forces (e.g., performance enhancement, quantitative research, theory, and concepts adapted from the broader field of psychology) with both global (e.g., cross-cultural, international) and interdisciplinary (e.g., exercise physiology, counseling) influences. Consequently, in the critical historical review of sport psychology research that follows, I have purposely attempted to reexamine the development of sport psychology research through a cultural praxis lens.

A Note about "Presentist" History

When examining the historical development of research in a discipline such as sport psychology, it is easy to adopt a "presentist" viewpoint, which entails viewing the past through a "lens of the present." This "presentist," or "whig history," as Fancher (1987) called it, reflects the natural tendency of people to frame and evaluate the past in juxtaposition with present-day knowledge. For example, one might reflect on the dominant personality paradigm in sport psychology research and practice during the 1960s and early 1970s as unidimensional, "shot-gun" (Ryan, 1968), and short-sighted (given the lack of change one can effect on personality motives or traits). However, this and other historical trends in sport psychology, regardless of the current perception of them, are important to explore as they have helped shape present-day research in sport psychology. More important, an examination of the history of sport psychology research must include the failures and shortcomings of researchers in addition to their successes and revolutionary ideas. For example, the current (i.e., Wonderlic) and past (Athletic Motivation Inventory) use of culturally biased sport intelligence testing as means for sport selection has served to reinforce racial/ethnic stereotypes and maintain social class and power for affluent white males. The evolution of sport psychology research did not follow a linear trajectory to its present state, but was littered with ups and downs, some positive, some negative. In summary, it is important to maintain a more open perspective on the history and development of sport psychology, as many of today's applied practices and research topics will no doubt be viewed 50 years from now by future sport psychology professionals with a skeptical, "presentist" eye.

Cultural History: Toward a Cultural Praxis

Another key to examining the history of research in a discipline is to include multiple cultural perspectives of its development. Such an approach allows for a deconstruction of history into cultural history, which as Poster (1997) maintained, must consider the distinct influences of gender, ethnicity, and class. Ryba and Wright (2005) argued for a more inclusive and collaborative approach to research in sport psychology that brings culture (i.e., ethnicity, class, and gender) into the core of sport psychology research rather than relegating it to the fringes as a contextual variable to consider in one's statistical analyses. By shifting sport psychology research toward such a cultural praxis, be it multicultural, theory-practice, or academic-applied, the isolated monolithic pillars that have dominated sport psychology can be connected under a unified cultural roof. As Butryn (2002) noted, such a unification and collaboration of cultures will increase sport psychology researchers' ability to effect positive social change. Although the information in this chapter may not result directly in positive social change, I hope to provide an historical context from which researchers in sport psychology can begin to do so. Hence, in the sociocultural review of the history of sport psychology research that follows, I have adopted a purposely open and, when possible, multicultural perspective in examining the events, people, and cultural and institutional influences that led the development of research in the sport psychology to its current state. Hopefully, in so doing, the information will help to, as Poster (1997) said, "enliven" the field of sport psychology.

A Sociocultural Review of Sport Psychology's Development

This section examines the development of several key sport psychology research topics or problems from its beginnings in the late 1890s to its current state. Particular emphasis is placed on the influence of sociocultural forces on the field's development. I also attempt to integrate into the ethnocentric, North American/Western European view of sport psychology a more globally infused perspective. Finally, I structure my discussion around problems, issues, and conditions that drove research, rather than on the research per se. Such an approach has been advocated for some time in sport psychology (e.g., Martens, 1987; Vealey, 2006). For each of the topics in the linear presentation of the history of psychology in this section, I have hopefully provided at least one alternative historical narrative as suggested by Wright (1998), or at the very least juxtaposed sociocultural context for the development of research in our field.

First, I provide a brief historical example of a problem from performance enhancement in wartime in Ancient Greece to highlight the long-running connection between sport psychology problems and the sociocultural, institutional, and hegemonic forces of society. Following this example, I contrast the development of the sport psychology technique with the issues of privilege and power of the time. I then make an analogy from the parallels of the example to the traditional approach of sport psychology in relation to the proposed move to cultural praxis advocated in this book.

Ancient Roots of Sport Psychology:
Performance Enhancement for the Privileged

Although sport psychology's modern roots extend only to the late 1800s, historians have indicated that sport psychology can extend its roots even further back to Ancient Greece and Asia (Mahoney, 1989). Both Ancient Greek and Eastern cultures emphasized the importance of the mind-body connection. This connection emanated from both religious/philosophical (e.g., Aristotle, Confucius) and more pragmatic military sources, and provides an historical parallel for the focus on certain sport psychology problems, such as the performance enhancement emphasis that persists in our field to this day. Moreover, the dominant hegemonic forces (e.g., upper class, young, male) of the time period combined with institutional (e.g., religion, military) forces to influence the emphasis of learning and advancement. For example, a significant performance issue in war was (and continues to be) that soldiers were fearful or anxious, which affected their ability to fight effectively during battle. The Spartans of Ancient Greece were undoubtedly aware of this performance issue. Consequently, they adopted a practical mind-body approach to training their soldiers that focused on learning to embrace and manage fear (i.e., arousal regulation) during combat such that concentration and physical performance would be enhanced (cf. Pressfield, 1998).

This performance enhancement example demonstrates the influence of privilege and power and the monocultural perspective that continues to persist in contemporary sport psychology (Ryba, 2005). In the preceding example, the effects of an underlying caste (i.e., class) system dictated who would benefit from such practical knowledge. Specifically, the privilege and power of the Spartiate (ruling male warrior class) ensured that they controlled access to knowledge and benefited from that knowledge. Moreover, the application of the knowledge gained in combat and training was rarely passed along to the perioikoi (second-class male merchants occasionally used in battle) or helots (enslaved population with no rights) to better their situations. In fact, it was more likely that knowledge was purposely withheld from these lower classes to reinforce the dominant hegemony of the Spartiates. Moreover, females were not engaged directly in battle, and although they were given more freedom than many of their contemporaries, they were not provided with intimate knowledge of Spartiate training or techniques (Plutarch, 1921). Ironically, the current example focuses on a limited application of a technique to battle, rather than generalizing it to other areas of life such as sport. One can draw parallels from this example to modern sport psychology's focus on elite male athletes from high-profile sports that benefits a small minority of sport participants, the proprietary for-profit approach to performance enhancement (such as the personality profiling for athlete success of Tutko, Lyon, and Ogilvie in 1969 that was subsequently challenged by Martens in

1975) that limits access to those with money (i.e., privilege), and general lack of focus on social change within sport psychology.

Roots of Sport Psychology Research: Triplett as a Portent for the Psychology-Kinesiology Schism

The contribution of Norman Triplett at Indiana and Clark universities and later at the Kansas Normal School to the development of sport psychology cannot be understated. His work in social psychology extended what until the late 1890s was mostly reaction time and motor learning-based research to the first incarnation of sport psychology research. His pioneering thesis work at Indiana University on performance in competitive cycling in the presence of others is regarded as the first sport psychology research publication (Mahoney & Suinn, 1986) and a seminal work in social psychology (Allport, 1954). Given the challenges to the recognition and acceptance of modern sport psychology within the context of the broader field of psychology, it is ironic that one of psychology's pioneering researchers focused his research on sport. The recognition of Triplett's early contributions to psychology provided an historical leg on which subsequent research in sport psychology could stand. However, as Brawley and Martin (1995) indicated, sport psychology researchers' reliance on the broad field of psychology for theory and topics may not have always been in the best interest of the field's development.

Unlike his successor, Coleman Griffith, Triplett focused considerable effort on training and teaching future professionals and promoting sport psychology to the public (Davis, Huss, & Becker, 1995). The training that he provided his students was largely psychologically based, as Triplett himself was trained as a psychologist. Triplett's, and later Griffith's, background in psychology set the stage for the formative development of sport psychology from largely psychological, rather than physical education (i.e., kinesiology), roots. This is not to say that the field of physical education did not influence early sport psychology, as it clearly did (see Vealey, 2006); however, early research in sport psychology that started under the broad umbrella of psychology helped to substantiate it initially as part of psychology. Not surprisingly, the lineage of sport psychology continues to be viewed along two divergent histories with either a psychological or kinesiological origin. This division continues today in the schism between psychology-based applied training and work, and kinesiology-based educational training and research (Kontos & Feltz,

2008). This split is also evident in the continuum of professional sport psychology organizations from applied/psychological in nature (e.g., American Psychological Association [APA]- Division 47) to mixed (e.g., Association for Applied Sport Psychology [AASP]), to theoretical/kinesiology focused (e.g., North American Society for the Psychology of Sport and Physical Activity [NASPSPA]).

The Research to Practice Paradigm in Sport Psychology: Beyond Griffith

Coleman Griffith, who was trained as a psychologist, conducted much of the early published research in sport psychology in North America. However, as I discuss in the following paragraphs, simultaneous and similar research efforts were being undertaken by researchers in Russia. At the same time, however, dominant hegemonic forces limited the involvement of women in early sport psychology research. Griffith's research was largely problem-focused and reflected the trend in psychology research that involved taking experimental research into the field to solve problems (Gould & Pick, 1995). The focus on the promotion of professional development within physical education paralleled the problem-solving focus of research in sport psychology (Gill, 1995). Griffith's focus on coaching and athlete performance enhancement is not surprising given the explosion of organized sports that occurred at the beginning of the 1920s (Mrozek, 1983). It is important to note that like Griffith, most of the key figures in sport psychology were tied to universities, which during the first half of the 20th century were places of wealth and social standing. Moreover, organized sports in the 1920s through 1940s were the domain of upper-class white males (Coakley, 2004). A great example of this upper-class focus of sport during the 1924 Olympic Games is provided in the film *Chariots of Fire*. Hence, much of the research and applied focus of the early period of sport psychology's development focused on elite, upper-class, white, collegiate performers and individuals with privilege and power. It is equally important to note that women and minorities were largely excluded from research and applied work, as they were not provided access to universities and organized sport in significant numbers until later in the century.

At the same time Griffith was honing his research to practice paradigm in North America, researchers elsewhere were developing similar approaches to research in sport psychology. One example of the concurrent development of sport psychology research that was occurring during the mid-1900s was in Leningrad, Russia, where Avksenty Puni was developing the first Russian sport psychology program at Lesgaft Institute of Physical Culture and conducting applied research. His most recognized research centered on the psychological preparation of athletes and included aspects such as goal setting, motivation, and the role of coaches in psychological preparation (Ryba et al., 2005). Dominant hegemonic forces at this time in Russia, such as politics (e.g., communism and sport as a representation of communist ideals), gender (e.g., males and females both viewed as competitive athletes for the Communist Party), and the professionalization (i.e., movement away from participation and toward competition) of sport shaped the focus of Puni's research. Surprisingly, Puni was not a Communist Party member. Moreover, according to Ryba et al. (2005), Puni's writing and research pertained to both male and female athletes. Puni was first introduced to a broad sport psychology audience in 2005 by Ryba and colleagues, who acknowledged that, unlike Griffith, Puni was joined by contemporary and rival, Piotr Roudik, at the Russian State Academy of Physical Culture in Moscow. This rivalry may have spurred the development of many sport psychology professionals in Russia who can trace their lineage back to Puni and Roudik. In contrast, Griffith produced few trained professionals in sport psychology, and the influence of his research outside of academe to the general population was limited. Although Griffith and Puni shared a research-practitioner focus, they differed in their approach to involving others in their work, hence affecting the subsequent development of sport psychology in Russia and in North America during the 1940s-1960s.

As yet, I have barely acknowledged the role of women in sport psychology in this overview of the development of the field. This exclusion is due in large part to the broader exclusion of women from academic and research positions (where much of sport psychology development was occurring), and emphasis on their participation versus competition in sport and exercise at this time (Gill, 1995). Moreover, when women attempted to enter into academic and research roles they were not provided with the same training, support, and opportunities as men (Safrit, 1984). As the broader field of physical education began to disaggregate into subdisciplines such as motor learning and sport psychology, which focused more on research and less on professional practice, the presence of women in these emerging subdisciplines waned (Gill, 1995). Consequently, there is only one female contemporary in sport psychology for Griffith and Puni: Dorothy Yates, who was a psychologist and instructor at San Jose State College and Stanford University (Kornspan & Mac-Cracken, 2001). She was able to gain recognition for her work and publications in mental training, although, like Griffith, she too did not directly promote the development of a legacy for women in the field. Nonetheless, she and other women (e.g., Ruth Glassow and Mabel Lee) who were prominent in the physical education profession would serve as the foundation and inspiration for later contributions of women in sport psychology such as Dorothy Harris and Carole Ogelsby.

The Search for the Athletic Personality: Ethnocentric Assumptions of an Ideal for Sport

Much of the research conducted in sport psychology in the late 1930s through 1960s centered on personality, much as it did in the field of psychology (e.g., Allport, 1937). Again, here we have evidence for sport psychology's parallel development with the overarching field of psychology. Unfortunately, the early research into personality in sport was plagued by methodological shortcomings, including convenience sampling and a-theoretical, shotgun methods (Kontos & Feltz, 2008). In addition, the research into personality in sport assumed that there was an ideal personality built around masculine, male hegemonic values. This masculinization of personality and behavior promoted a male hegemonic model for success in sport. Ironically, the categorization of traits such as leadership, competitiveness, and assertiveness as masculine was subsequently used to portray any successful female athletes as overly masculine (Gill, 2000). Multiple, individualized perspectives on personality in sport (Ryba, 2005) were not considered. Factors such as race/ethnicity, gender, and age were rarely included in research on personality in sport, and were negated through the use of monocultural and biased personality measures. Due to researchers' limited view of personality in sport, the research in this area provided little evidence of a single personality being predictive of performance (Silva & Weinberg, 1984). Hence, sport psychology researchers (e.g., Martens, 1975) began to question the utility of this line of research. These researchers

(Martens, 1970, 1975) believed that sport psychology research would benefit from a more social-psychological model that focused on theory-driven research.

Social Psychology: Feminism and the Beginnings of Movement toward Praxis

Researchers in sport psychology during the 1970s began to shift their focus toward the interactions of social factors in sport and physical activity. This shift represented a frustration with the lack of validity of personality as a predictor of success in sport, as much as it reflected the prevailing shift in psychology and society in general. Much of the research at this time is viewed as "classic" or seminal to the field of sport psychology research. However, here again, the notion of seminal research is influenced by the power and privilege of who is conducting the research. As Vealey (2006) noted, this era of sport psychology research was influenced by the first generation of dedicated sport psychology researchers and academicians, such as Dan Landers, William Morgan, Glyn Roberts, Bert Carron, and Rainer Martens. Although the contribution of these mostly North American researchers to sport psychology is substantial to say the least, their contributions were still representative of a prevailing white male hegemony that dominated sport psychology. However, a shift toward greater inclusion of women sport psychology researchers was beginning to take hold.

Here for the second time in the history of our field, the influence of women in sport psychology, specifically Dorothy Harris and Carole Ogelsby, provides a different and long overdue alternative perspective to the development of our field. Their prominence in the field coincided with adoption of Title IX in 1972 and with a larger feminist movement for women's equality. As many authors (cf. Gill, 1995) have attested to, Harris and Ogelsby were outstanding researchers and professionals in sport psychology during this period of the field's development. For example, Harris was elected the first woman president of the North American Society for Psychology of Sport and Physical Activity (NASPSPA) in 1974. A few years later, Oglesby (1978) pioneered the feminist movement in sport psychology with her edited book *Women in Sport*. Similar trends at this time were beginning to take hold in Europe as well. However, in spite of these advances by women in sport psychology, the majority of research presentations and publications in sport psychology were still being conducted by men (Gill, 1995).

A Not So Quiet Challenge to North American Applied Sport Psychology Research

At the time, sport psychology research was still a largely European and North American affair, or at least it appeared to be. Some of the ethnocentric bias in the historical portrayal of sport psychology during the Cold War can be attributed to the cultural and scientific isolation that was characteristic of this period of history. Recently, researchers (e.g., Stambulova , Weisberg, & Ryba, 2006) have introduced us to what they believe was an advanced (compared to its North American counterpart) form of sport psychology research that occurred in the former Soviet Union during the 1970s. Part of the objective advancement (as measured by medal counts by Stambulova et al., 2006) was due in part to the controlled sport environment that existed in Soviet- era communism. However, the theories and research of Puni and others provide evidence for the efficacy of an alternative paradigm (i.e., one that emphasized sport psychology models of individualized performance enhancement) that until the Soviets began dominating world sport competitions was largely ignored by North American and European sport psychology researchers. One can only wonder how many other alternative paradigms lie around waiting to be rediscovered. Hopefully, efforts like that of Stambulova and colleagues (2006) representing (at least to the North American and European sport psychology audience) the contributions of Puni to Soviet sport psychology will continue to expand and include other cultural perspectives from Asia, Africa, and elsewhere, and help to alleviate sport psychology's "Western amnesia," which has excluded non-North American academic discourses.

Ongoing Issues in Sport Psychology

At this point, I want to accelerate our historical journey a bit to move us closer to the praxis focus of this book. However, before doing so I would suggest that the reader refer to Vealey (2006) for a more comprehensive chronology of sport psychology research that that includes an examination of the proliferation of sport psychology research that occurred in the 1980s and 1990s. I instead focus on some ongoing issues that continue to affect our field's development.

Problem-based Sport Psychology

Vealey (2006) provided a wake-up call for sport psychology researchers to reexamine the essence of what we research and why. As existentialism suggests, we must search for meaning in all that we do. As we progress through graduate school the calls for us to develop a concentrated (and fundable!) line of research seems to call out to us in a growing cacophony until we eventually tune out everything else but our own research area. In so doing, we often lose sight of the original research questions that led us to sport psychology in the first place. I have been guilty of this myself, as I have moved away from some of my passions and original questions in sport psychology to more practical and profitable topics. Although the recent efforts of researchers in sport psychology have moved the field closer to an inclusive, problem-focused approach, several divides continue to affect the field's development and progression. Moreover, the lack of a generally accepted paradigm (Kontos & Feltz, 2008) continues to promote these divides, although other researchers (e.g., Landers, 1983) think that doing so would expand rather than bridge current divides in sport psychology. Regardless, divides continue to persist in sport psychology. Therefore, I thought that a brief reexamination of the persisting gap between different (often divergent) hegemonies within sport psychology was warranted.

The Gap Continues: Persisting Divides in Sport Psychology

Ironically, "America's first sport psychologist" (Kroll & Lewis, 1970), Coleman Griffith, has largely (and to some degree, erroneously) been portrayed primarily as a researcher. However, early sport psychology researchers such as Griffith saw the benefit in a researcher-practitioner model (Gould & Pick, 1995). Griffith integrated the findings from his empirically driven research in the athletics laboratory at the University of Illinois into sport performance and applied work for use by coaches and athletes. The researcher-practitioner model was reflected in Griffith's focus on what he viewed as the three key aspects of sport psychology: (1) teaching, (2) adapting psychological principles and research to sport psychology, and (3) using empirical research as the basis for sport psychology practice (Griffith, 1928). Unfortunately, the current status of the research-practitioner model seems to have regressed since Griffith introduced it to sport psychology and since Martens (1987) argued for a return to this more experiential paradigm in sport psychology.

Research–practice

The rifts in sport psychology take many guises. A traditional list might include theory versus practice and academic versus applied. A more expanded, but specific list might include NASPSPA versus AASP and psychology-trained versus kinesiology-trained professionals. These rifts in sport psychology affect all aspects of the field from training (i.e., coursework) and theoretical orientations to funding and employment opportunities and respect. Although the rifts between researchers and practitioners in sport psychology may be portrayed in a more civil and politically correct light now, the divides have yet to be bridged in a discipline-wide manner. For example, many research-focused programs might encourage students to follow a path that typically entails courses in research methods and statistics; developing a concentrated, fundable line of research; publishing as much as possible in their research area; seeking extramural funding; and pursuing a career as a tenure track faculty member. In contrast, applied-focus programs might include coursework in counseling techniques and applied sport psychology geared toward AASP certification or state licensure; supervised practica and internship experiences; and a career as a consultant or mental health professional who also works with athletes. Regardless of which approach one embraces, it is typically at the exclusion of the other. Moreover, many of today's programs bill themselves to prospective students as either a research-academic or an applied-practitioner focused program. Again, here we can draw a parallel to the broader field of psychology where PsyD programs focus more on applied preparation, while PhD programs focus more on research and academic preparation. Using the paradigm of cultural praxis presented in this book, I would argue that future sport psychology training models (and psychology training models, too) need to combine applied and research foci into an integrated approach that focuses on problem solving rather than applied and research skills as distinct entities.

Sport–exercise

Another more recent (since the 1990s) schism in the field is the exercise versus sport psychology divide. Although this divide may be viewed as less contentious than the research-practice divide, it is no less apparent. An excellent analogy for the exercise-sport divide was offered by Vealey (2006), who suggested that while sport psychology was entering its adolescence in the 1980s and 1990s, exercise psychology was in its childhood. Currently, Vealey's analogy has developed into a sibling rivalry of sorts, with sport psychology as the older sibling who is constantly competing with its upstart younger sibling (i.e., exercise psychology) for attention and resources. As such, many professional research journals, textbooks, and conferences tend to now dichotomize research into exercise- or sport-focused articles, content, and programming. Academically, many courses are now divided along similar lines. In the classes that I teach, I have tended to emphasize both sport and exercise psychology research problems, although this is becoming increasingly difficult with the proliferation of potential topics and the limited time in which to cover them. Further, academic position announcements often now specify exercise-focused academicians. This trend is reflected by the current funding emphasis on obesity, physical activity, and other more health psychology-related topics that lend themselves to a broader population and impact that goes beyond sport (Kontos & Feltz, 2008; Vealey, 2006). I believe that this trend for more economic resources moving toward exercise psychology is set to continue. I also believe that researchers in exercise psychology would benefit from a more cultural praxis-based, problem and social change focus given the universal reach of physical activity and exercise.

Looking Back toward the Future of Sport and Exercise Psychology: Where are We Headed?

Throughout the history of sport psychology, researchers have conducted research and applied work in a largely convenience-based manner. The population of choice in sport psychology, which paralleled the broader field of psychology, has traditionally been college-aged white males, or in other words, as so adroitly stated in Guthrie's (1998) book on the subject, *Even the Rat Was White*. From a research perspective, this homogenization of research in sport psychology has resulted in marginalized efforts at incorporating culture, gender, age, and other factors into research paradigms. Fortunately, with the recent release of Schinke and Hanrahan's (2009) *Cultural Sport Psychology*, a multicultural model for sport psychology is gaining momentum. This book extends this momentum toward a cultural praxis wherein multicultural perspectives intersect with research and help move the field toward a less ethnocentrically biased paradigm. Three areas in sport psychology in which this movement is beginning to take shape are developmental, multicultural, and community-based research.

A Developmental Sport Psychology

In spite of the recent paradigmatic shifts in sport psychology, one aspect that has been historically omitted and continues to struggle for recognition in sport psychology is the lifespan developmental perspective. This perspective is becoming increasingly relevant, as global population trends continue to expand at the youth and older adult ends of the spectrum. As indicated by Vealey (2006), children have represented a significant focus of sport psychology since the 1980s. Researchers such as Gould (1982) and Weiss and Bredemeier (1983) have argued for a developmental focus in our field that includes youth. Institutes such as the Youth Sport Institute at Michigan State University, currently under the direction of Dan Gould, have pioneered studies aimed at researching and applying research to problems affecting youth in sport and physical activity. However, these efforts have focused solely on the youth end of the developmental lifespan spectrum, leaving the problems of middle-aged and older adult sport and physical activity participants largely unexplored by researchers. Neither the authors of this book nor Schinke and Hanrahan (2008) in *Cultural Sport Psychology* include a developmental, lifespan component to the cultural praxis approach to sport psychology that was adopted by Weiss (2004) in *Developmental Sport and Exercise Psychology*. The integrated approach adopted by Weiss and her contributing authors included common sport psychology research topics such as injury, moral development, and motivation examined from a lifespan perspective that included youths to older adults. The developmental approach to sport psychology will keep on gaining relevance as the population continues to shift and the importance of lifelong physical inactivity and its concomitant problems become more salient. I truly hope that we reinvigorate the developmental discussion in the context of our cultural praxis paradigm as we shape the field's future history.

Cultural Sport Psychology

In 2008, I, along with 37 other sport psychology researchers, contributed to Schinke and Hanrahan's *Cultural Sport Psychology*. This work represents the aggregate of a growing movement in sport psychology toward both cultural inclusion and global expansion. To this end, 11 geographic regions and their respective cultural groups are examined in the concluding applied section of the book. Many previous cultural sport psychology offerings were isolated and focused primarily on applied multicultural sport psychology strategies. For example, in 2002, Breland-Noble and I wrote an introductory multicultural sport psychology article directed at North American sport psychology professionals. Although Schinke and Hanrahan focused primarily on applied cultural sport psychology information, several of the authors concentrated on topics that go beyond applied work to frame the overarching topic. For example, McGannon and Johnson (2008) discussed reflective cultural research, where the sport psychology self is defined from post-positivist and post-modern perspectives. Gill and Kamphoff (2008) offer suggestions for researching cultural diversity in applied sport psychology, whereas McGannon and Johnson (2008) adopt a social justice perspective that emphasizes a reflexive approach to culture and self in sport psychology research. I hope that researchers in our field will continue to advocate for and expand cultural sport psychology, much as this book intends to do.

Diverse Community Approaches and Change: A Step Closer to an Inclusive Cultural Sport Psychology

As referenced above, Schinke and Hanrahan (2008) coalesced a growing movement of cultural sport psychology within their edited book, *Cultural Sport Psychology*. The logical extension of this edited work to a research cultural praxis paradigm is the premise of this book. One benefit of the proposed cultural praxis paradigm to research in sport psychology is the inclusion of marginalized groups within research such that social change can be promoted within entire social communities. An example of research that serves to improve the condition of such a community using a praxis paradigm in sport psychology research is provided by the work of Blodgett and colleagues (2008). Their work focuses on an ethnographic approach to understanding the motivations of Canadian Aboriginal athletes as they relate to improving their sport programming and increasing their physical activity. They have followed up this initial research with a collaborative research and applied effort to improve the community sport strategies used by the Aboriginal community with whom they are conducting research (Blodgett et al., in press). This example epitomizes the potential social change and problem-solving focus of the praxis paradigm. The above community-based research is an excellent example of the social benefits of the cultural praxis paradigm in sport psychology. However, this effort represents only one example of the cultural praxis paradigm, which admittedly is in its infancy in sport psychology. With that in mind, I wanted to explore the evidence for such efforts elsewhere in sport psychology.

A Snapshot from Sport Psychology Journals: Are We There Yet?

One method (albeit limited) for determining the current state of a scientific field is to examine its extant literature. Hence, I perused six current sport psychology professional journals (i.e., *Athletic Insight, International Journal of Sport Psychology, Journal of Applied Sport Psychology, Journal of Sport and Exercise Psychology, Psychology of Sport and Exercise,* and *The Sport Psychologist*) to ascertain where in fact the

Table 1. Summary of Recent Sport Psychology Professional Journals in Relation to Cultural Praxis

Journal Title	Date, Volume, Issue	# of Articles	Cultural Praxis Focus[a]	Woman First or Second Author
Athletic Insight	*2008, 10, 3*	5	0 (0%)	4 (80%)
International Journal of Sport Psychology	*2008, 39, 1*	5	2 (40%)	3 (60%)
Journal of Applied Sport Psychology	*2009, 21, 1*	9	1 (11%)	4 (44%)
Journal of Sport and Exercise Psychology	*2008, 30, 5*	7	0 (0%)	4 (57%)
Psychology of Sport and Exercise	*2009, 10, 2*	11	3 (27%)	7 (64%)
The Sport Psychologist	*2008, 22, 4*	7	0 (0%)	4 (57%)
Total	—	44	6 (14%)	26 (59%)

Note. Special topics issues were excluded from the summary.

[a] Included international, racial/ethnic, cultural, feminist, lesbian/gay/bisexual/transgendered focus in title, keyword, or abstract.

field is with regard to cultural praxis, and where it might be headed. A descriptive summary of the number of articles and their representation of the cultural praxis emphasis of the current book, and women as first or second authors, is provided in Table 1. Nearly 60% of the articles included in the current and admittedly cross-sectional and brief review had women as first or second authors. These numbers reflect a significant shift during the past decade or two, when women authors were outnumbered by men (Duda, 1991; Gill, 1992). In contrast to these positive developments for women in the field of sport psychology, little progress is evident in the way of cultural praxis. In fact, only 14% of all articles included a cultural praxis focus in the title, keywords, or abstract. However, it is important to note that both *Athletic Insight* (in 2005) and the *International Journal of Sport and Exercise Psychology* (Fall 2009) have published culture-focused sport psychology issues. Nonetheless, the need for the current book is supported by the data, which also suggest that the field of sport psychology would benefit by heading its future history in a more culturally meaningful direction.

The Move toward Cultural Praxis in Sport Psychology

Over the past decade, the dialogue for paradigmatic change in sport psychology has evolved rapidly (e.g., Ryba, 2005; Vealey, 2006). The promotion of a cultural praxis paradigm advocated in this book represents another evolutionary branch in the sport psychology paradigmatic tree. However, movement toward new paradigms in research is often bereft of action and filled with inertia. Evidence of this inertia can be seen in sport psychology's slow movement toward a recognized professional certification that has been advocated for by professionals in the field for several decades. Moreover, earlier calls to change in our field such as those from Martens (1987) spurned considerable discussion and debate, but resulted in limited changes to the construction of knowledge in sport psychology and its subsequent presentation in textbooks.

As such, the success of the premise of the current book lies with us, the sport psychology researchers, and the movement we make toward a cultural praxis. If we are to embrace a cultural praxis paradigm then we must replace the simplistic notion of the disembodied athlete with an embodied perspective that considers race, gender, culture, society, and history (Ryba, 2005). Earlier, Dzewaltowski (1997) made a similar argument for placing the athlete in context when conducting research. To do this, we must, as Ryba (2005) suggested, reconnect sport psychology to sociology, philosophy, history, and international studies (I added this last one to Ryba's suggestion). However, as Feltz and I (2008) advocated, we must also maintain, rather than abandon, connections between sport psychology and other disciplines such as exercise physiology, biomechanics, and motor learning to adopt a sincerely problem-based approach. Moreover, in contrast to Ryba's (2005) suggestion, I believe that it is important to strengthen sport psychology's ties with mainstream psychology and related disciplines rather than distance ourselves from them. Moreover, we must continue to integrate other discourses, such as critical, cultural, dialogical psychology, within the sport psychology narrative. Otherwise, we run the risk of shifting from one focus to another without broadening our research. Therefore, I challenge each of you to adopt a multidisciplinary, cultural praxis paradigm for your research line that focuses on a global sport psychology.

Conclusion

In concluding this chapter, I want to encourage you to go beyond the "white picket fence"—or "box" as Kuhn (1962) and later Vealey (2006) called it—within which the history of sport psychology has traditionally been examined. Although I agree with researchers (e.g., Vealey, 2006; Whaley, 2001) who propose that we use "multiple boxes" for framing sport psychology research, I believe that the box should be discarded altogether. Instead, I advocate that we adopt an open, cultural-praxis approach to examining sport psychology research that focuses on problem solving, as did some of the earliest pioneers in sport psychology. To accomplish this goal, we need to reframe our current lines of research to embrace gender, culture, age, and other factors as integral components in our research rather than as independent variables (e.g., Sherif, 1979). In so doing, we will increase the impact of sport psychology as a vehicle for not only personal (i.e., the athlete), but also social change that can improve lives and solve problems that are outside the traditional "white picket fence" that has framed much of sport psychology's history and research.

However, as Vealey (2006) warned, although concentrated research lines might be initially problem-driven and provide significant advances in empirical knowledge and theory, over time, even the most progressive and inclusive research can stagnate and attain dogmatic-like status that limits its contribution to the overall development of sport psychology. Hence, I hope that you will adopt the constantly evolving, problem-based approach to our field advocated by Vealey (2006) and others (e.g., Martens, 1987) that is permeated by a social change (Butryn, 2002) ethos and set upon a cultural foundation. Only then will future researchers in sport psychology be able to go beyond the decades old schisms between research-practice, academic-applied, and embrace a truly cultural praxis paradigm for research, as advocated in this book. Finally, we should in moving forward with the cultural praxis paradigm look back at the history of our field for context, direction, and awareness of the caveats of the future history of sport psychology that our research will help build.

References

Allport, G. W. (1937). *Personality: A psychological interpretation.* New York: Holt.

Allport, G. W. (1954). *The nature of prejudice.* New York: Doubleday.

Blodgett, A. T., Schinke, R. J., Fisher, L. A., George, C. W., Peltier, D., Ritchie, P. et al. (2008). From practice to praxis: Community-based strategies for Aboriginal youth sport. *Journal of Sport & Social Issues, 32,* 393–414.

Blodgett, A. T., Schinke, R. J., Fisher, L. A., Yungblut, H. E., Recollet-Saikkonen, D., Peltier, D., et al. (in press). Praxis and community-level sport programming strategies in a Canadian Aboriginal reserve. *The International Journal of Sport and Exercise Psychology.*

Brawley, R., & Martin, K. A. (1995). The interface between social and sport psychology. *The Sport Psychologist, 9,* 469–497.

Butryn, T. (2002). Critically examining White racial identity and privilege in sport psychology consulting. *The Sport Psychologist, 16,* 296–315.

Coakley, J. (2004). *Sports in society: Issues & controversies* (8th ed.) New York: McGraw Hill.

Davis, S. F., Huss, M. T., & Becker, A. H. (1995). Norman Triplett and the dawning of sport psychology. *The Sport Psychologist, 9,* 366–375.

Duda, J. (1991). Editorial comment: Perspectives on gender role in physical activity. *Journal of Applied Sport Psychology, 3,* 1–6.

Dzewaltowski, D. A. (1997). The ecology of physical activity and sport: Merging science and practice. *Journal of Applied Sport Psychology, 9,* 254–276.

Fancher, R. E. (1987). Henry Goddard and the Kallikak Family photographs: "Conscious skullduggery" or "Whig history"? *American Psychologist, 42,* 585–590.

Feltz, D. L., & Kontos, A. P. (2002). The nature of sport psychology. In T. S. Horn (Ed.), *Advances in sport psychology* (2nd ed., pp. 1–19). Champaign, IL: Human Kinetics.

Gill, D. L. (1992). Status of the *Journal of Sport & Exercise Psychology,* 1985–1990. *Journal of Sport & Exercise Psychology, 14,* 1–12.

Gill, D. L. (1995). Women's place in history of sport psychology. *The Sport Psychologist, 9,* 418–433.

Gill, D. L., (2000). Feminist sport psychology: A guide for our journey. *The Sport Psychologist, 15,* 363–372.

Gill, D. L., & Kamphoff, C. S. (2008). Cultural diversity in applied sport psychology. In R. J. Schinke & S. J. Hanrahan (Eds.) (2008). *Cultural sport psychology: From theory to practice* (pp. 45–56). Champaign, IL: Human Kinetics.

Gould, D. (1982). Sport psychology in the 1980s: Status, direction and challenge in youth sports research. *Journal of Sport Psychology, 4,* 203–218.

Gould, D., & Pick, S. (1995). Sport psychology: The Coleman Griffith era, 1920–1940. *The Sport Psychologist, 9,* 391–405.

Griffith, C.R. (1928). *Psychology of athletics.* New York: Scribners.

Guthrie, R. V. (1998). *Even the rat was white: A historical view of psychology* (2nd ed.). Boston: Allyn and Bacon.

Hothersall, D. (2004). *History of psychology* (4th ed.). New York: McGraw-Hill.

Kontos, A. P., & Breland-Noble, A. (2002). Racial/ethnic diversity in applied sport psychology: A multicultural introduction to working with athletes of color. *The Sport Psychologist, 16,* 296–315.

Kontos, A. P., & Feltz, D. L. (2008). The nature of sport psychology. In T. S. Horn (Ed.), *Advances in sport psychology* (2nd ed., pp. 1–19). Champaign, IL: Human Kinetics.

Kornspan, A. S., & MacCracken, M. J. (2001). Psychology applied to sport in the 1940s: The work of Dorothy Hazeltine Yates. *The Sport Psychologist, 15,* 342–345.

Kroll, W., & Lewis, G. (1970). America's first sport psychologist. *Quest, 3,* 1–4.

Kuhn, T. H. S. (1962). *The structure of scientific revolutions.* Chicago: University of Chicago Press.

Landers, D. (1983). Whatever happened to theory testing in sport psychology? *Journal of Sport Psychology, 5,* 135–151.

Mahoney, M. J. (1989). Sport psychology. In I. S. Cohen (Ed.), *The G. Stanley Hall lecture series* (Vol. 9, pp. 97–134). Washington, DC: American Psychological Association.

Mahoney, M. J., & Suinn, R. M. (1986). History and overview of modern sport psychology. *The Clinical Psychologist, 39*(3), 64–68.

Martens, R. (1970). A social psychology of physical activity. *Quest, 14,* 8–17.

Martens, R. (1975). *Social psychology and physical activity.* New York: Harper & Row.

Martens, R. (1987). Science, knowledge, and sport psychology. *The Sport Psychologist, 1,* 29–55.

McGannon, K. R., & Johnson, C. R. (2008). Strategies for reflective cultural sport psychology research. In R. J. Schinke & S. J. Hanrahan (Eds.), *Cultural sport psychology: From theory to practice* (pp. 57–78). Champaign, IL: Human Kinetics.

Mrozek, D. J. (1983). *Sport and American mentality, 1880–1920.* Knoxville: University of Tennessee Press.

Ogelsby, C. (Ed.) (1978). *Women in sport: From myth to reality.* Philadelphia: Lee & Febiger.

Plutarch. (1921). *Plutarch's lives* (Trans. B. Perrin). Cambridge, MA: Harvard University Press.

Poster, M. (1997). *Cultural history and postmodernity: Disciplinary readings and challenges.* New York: Columbia University Press.

Pressfield, S. (1998). *Gates of fire.* New York: Bantam.

Ryan, E. D. (1968). Reaction to "sport and personality dynamics." In *Proceedings of the National College Physical Education Association for Men* (pp. 70–75).

Ryba, T. V. (2005). Sport psychology as cultural praxis: Future trajectories and current possibilities. *Athletic Insight, 7*(3), 14–22.

Ryba, T. V. (2009). Understanding your role in cultural sport psychology. In R. J. Schinke & S. J. Hanrahan (Eds.), *Cultural sport psychology: From theory to practice* (pp. 35–44). Champaign, IL: Human Kinetics.

Ryba, T. V., Stambulova, N. B., & Wrisberg, C. A. (2005). The Russian origins of sport psychology: A translation of an early work of A. C. Puni. *Journal of Applied Sport Psychology, 17,* 157–169.

Ryba, T. V., & Wright, H. K. (2005). From mental game to cultural praxis: A cultural studies model's implications for the future of sport psychology. *Quest, 57,* 192–212.

Safrit, M. (1984). Women in research in physical education: A 1984 update. *Quest, 36,*103–114.

Schinke, R. J., & Hanrahan, S. J. (Eds.). (2009). *Cultural sport psychology: From theory to practice.* Champaign, IL: Human Kinetics.

Silva, J. M., & Weinberg, R. S. (Eds.). (1984). *Psychological foundations of sport.* Champaign, IL: Human Kinetics.

Sherif, C. W. (1979). Bias in psychology. In J. A. Sherman & E. T. Beck (Eds.), *The prism of sex: Essays in the sociology of knowledge* (pp. 93–133). Madison: University of Wisconsin Press.

Stambulova, N. B., Wrisberg, C. A., & Ryba, T. V. (2006). A tale of two traditions applied sport psychology: The heyday of Soviet sport and wake-up calls for North America. *Journal of Applied Sport Psychology, 18,* 173–184.

Triplett, N. (1898). The dynamogenic factors in pacemaking and competition. *American Journal of Psychology, 9,* 507–533.

Tutko, T. A., Lyon, L. P., & Ogilvie, B. C. (1969). *Athletic motivation inventory.* San Jose, CA: Institute for the Study of Athletic Motivation.

Vealey, R. (2006). Smocks and jocks outside the box: The paradigmatic evolution of sport and exercise psychology. *Quest, 56,* 128–159.

Weinberg, R. S., & Gould, D. (2007). *Foundations of sport and exercise psychology, 4th ed.* Champaign, IL: Human Kinetics.

Weiss, M. (2004). *Developmental sport and exercise psychology: A lifespan perspective.* Morgantown, WV: Fitness Information Technology

Weiss, M., & Bredemeier, B. J. (1983). Developmental sport psychology: A theoretical perspective for studying children in sport. *Journal of Sport Psychology, 5,* 216–230.

Whaley, D. (2001). Feminist methods and methodologies in sport and exercise psychology: Issues of identity and difference. *The Sport Psychologist, 15,* 419–430.

Williams, J. M., & Straub, W. (2007). Sport psychology: Past, present, and future. In J. M. Williams (Ed.), *Applied sport psychology* (5th ed., pp. 1–14) New York: McGraw Hill.

Wright, H. K. (1998). Dare we de-Centre Birmingham? Troubling the origins and trajectories of cultural studies. *European Journal of Cultural Studies, 1,* 33–56.

3

SPORT PSYCHOLOGY AND REPRESENTATION

Diane L. Gill and Cindra S. Kamphoff

CHAPTER SUMMARY

Sport psychology has moved away from its early emphasis on social psychology and physical activity to become narrower and more focused on elite participants since its emergence as a subdisciplinary area. Sport psychology must reclaim the social to be a representative and relevant professional discipline. The changing demographics in U.S. society and increasing globalization of sport psychology highlight issues of representation, but sport remains an exclusive space that privileges some over others. Not only are competitive athletics exclusive, but physical activity is limited by gender, race, and ethnicity; socioeconomic status; and physical attributes. Reviews of publications and programs confirm a persistent failure to include marginalized groups, with no progress over the past 20 years despite the visible growth of multicultural psychology during that same time. Research confirms persistent gender stereotypes that influence participation from earlier ages. Racial stereotypes are pervasive and stereotype threat affects behavior in sport. Sport is a particularly hostile environment for sexual minorities, and exclusion on the basis of physicality is nearly universal. Physical activity programs and professionals convey anti-fat biases that do little to promote health and well-being. To better serve professionals, participants, and the public, sport psychology must become representative and culturally competent across the full range of professional roles. Sport psychology must expand the limited multicultural scholarship; foster the development of multicultural competencies; and advocate for inclusive, empowering sport and physical activity programs that promote health and well-being for all.

Sport Psychology and Representation

This chapter covers representation, and particularly representation of cultural diversity in sport psychology. In this chapter, *sport psychology* is used broadly, to be read as sport and exercise psychology, or more inclusively as psychology of physical activity. In discussing representation in sport psychology, this chapter draws from recent papers and chapters on related issues, including the first author's recent Homans lecture on integration in kinesiology (Gill, 2007b) and 2008 McCloy lecture on social psychology and physical activity (Gill, 2009), and especially on our chapter in the cultural sport psychology text (Gill & Kamphoff, 2009).

A Note on Perspective:
Social Psychology and Physical Activity

Before moving into the main topic of representation in sport psychology, a side note to clarify our perspective is in order. The editors envisioned this book as critically examining and challenging sport psychology to better reflect our changing cultural context. The editors and chapter authors are well positioned to do that. However, neither of us is a cultural studies scholar and this chapter is not a critical analysis. We consider cultural studies and critical analysis absolutely essential to sport psychology and the larger field of kinesiology; our views are both informed and challenged by that scholarship, but follow somewhat different themes.

First, the primary scholarly base for our work and this chapter is psychology, particularly social psychology and the growing multicultural psychology scholarship. Psychology focuses on the person and behavior. Social psychology connects the person and behavior with the social environment and cultural context, but maintains a focus on the individual. Indeed, the person-environment relationship and the balancing of individual and contextual factors are key issues in psychology research and practice. This chapter relies more on psychology than cultural studies for its scholarly base.

Also, although some points in this chapter may appear critical, the chapter does not present a critical analysis. Neither of us is a critical theorist, and at least one of us (Gill) does not intentionally complicate issues, but strives for elegance with emphasis on practical theory in teaching and writing. Although we are less involved in cultural studies and critical analysis than most of the chapter authors, our views on sport psychology, described in more detail in Gill's (2009) McCloy lecture as "social psychology and physical activity" are in line with the editorial vision of this book. Moreover, Gill has been actively involved in the subdisciplinary field since the early 1970s, and thus can highlight the historical context of representation in sport psychology. As an early career scholar, co-author Kamphoff does not share this lived historical experience. She does share the social psychology and physical activity perspective, with closer connections to cultural studies and a fresher outlook on the field. The following section draws from that experience and recent lectures to provide that historical context. Then, the chapter moves into the main content, representation in sport psychology.

Historical Context of Sport Psychology

In the late 1960s and early 1970s, as Gill's academic career (and Kamphoff's life) was beginning, the subdiscipline of sport psychology emerged as *social psychology and physical activity*. That label comes from the title of my first graduate course in 1972, and the 1975 book of the same name by Rainer Martens. In that text, which served as one of the first texts and reflected the field at that time, Martens clearly looked to social psychology for content and methods, and also clearly described physical activity as encompassing varied forms of movement in a wide range of settings — and not limited to organized sport.

Since then, the academic focus has shifted away from the social to a more bio-psycho-(no social) approach, and professional attention has focused on elite athletes and exercisers. In the 1970s and into the 1980s, the field became more *sport-specific*, addressing Martens's (1979) call to move from the lab to the field. The field was the athletic field, and sport psychology began to narrow its focus and become less social. The narrowing continued through the 1980s and into the 1990s as *applied* sport psychology came to dominate the field. As Weiss (2008) noted, all sport and exercise psychology is applied, and applied need not be limited to performance outcomes. Still, the focus on narrow application with elite athletes and performance excellence made the field much narrower and less social. With that shift, sport psychology became more elite and less representative in many ways. The field expanded though the 1990s and into the 21st century, but expansion did not necessarily imply an inclusive field. In some ways the larger field of sport psychology became more diverse (e.g., including exercisers as well as athletes and a larger range of settings). However, rather than encompassing diverse participants, settings, and issues, sport psychology researchers, organizations, and programs split into separate and often intentionally separated subareas with little connection to each other.

Toward Integrative and Representative Sport Psychology

In recent years, sport psychology has made a slight (very slight) cultural turn (as in the title of this book). However, an integrative and relevant professional discipline of sport psychology could contribute more by going back to the future as social psychology and physical activity. To do that, sport psychology must move beyond dualisms and emphasize integrative scholarship that highlights the social and dynamic complexities of behavior. Kretchmar (2005) called for kinesiology researchers to look at scholarship in a new way—not as jigsaw (typical approach) where we find the pieces and fit them together; we cannot find all the pieces, and we cannot predict. Instead, think of a river—ever changing, blending together, and looking different depending on your viewpoint. Kretchmar's "river" is a perfect description of an integrative and relevant sport psychology.

Integration of sport psychology as an academic and professional discipline is clearly needed, as argued elsewhere (Gill, 2007b). Less obvious, but even more important for a representative sport psychology is integration as inclusion and social justice. Inclusion means physical activity for all, with no more left-outs. Moving beyond inclusion to social justice requires action and advocacy.

Physical activity is the key to positive health and quality of life, and thus, lifetime physical activity is the base for healthy lives. But physical activity/inactivity is not equal; physical activity disparities parallel the widely cited disparities in health. Activity levels are lower for underrepresented and minority groups—those who most need physical activity and can benefit the most. Moreover, all have a right to physical activity as a public health and social justice issue. Sport psychology as social justice and advocacy takes professional responsibility for securing that right.

Following is a summary of inclusion and social justice in sport psychology and a preview of the rest of this chapter. In terms of scholarship, research is non-inclusive and narrow in scope, methods, and paradigms. Multicultural issues are neglected, and there is little critical analysis. Professional practice is elite, and has become increasingly so in recent years. The focus is on elite (professional/collegiate athletes, physically skilled, clients in elite programs) with little attention to public, diverse participants. Education and training focuses on elite practice with little connection to wider physical activity professional areas. Generally sport psychology has a limited social/cultural scholarly base, and educational/training programs take a "tech" approach. Action in the public interest, which implies direct attention to social justice and public health, is not in the picture. Sport psychology must reclaim the *social* to truly understand the complexities of sport behavior, and to be a representative and relevant professional discipline that serves the public by promoting health and well-being for all through physical activity.

A Multicultural Psychology Framework for Representation in Sport Psychology

That overview and historical perspective sets the stage, and multicultural psychology scholarship provides a foundation and clarifies the framework for this chapter. Psychology, and particularly the American Psychological Association (APA), has moved beyond its decidedly non-multicultural past, described in Robert Guthrie's (1998) aptly titled *Even the Rat Was White*. Multicultural psychology has grown rapidly over the past 20 years, and as Trickett et al. (1994) advocated, psychology is moving from the dominant emphasis on biology, isolating basic processes, rigorous experimental designs, and a critical-realist philosophy of science, to an emphasis on *people in context*. Not only has multicultural psychology developed a scholarly base, but as Stanley Sue (2003) noted, advances in cultural competence research and guidelines (e.g., APA 2003 multicultural guidelines) have enhanced professional practice.

As described in one current text, *multicultural psychology* is the "systematic study of behavior, cognition and affect in many cultures" (Mio, Becker-Hackett, & Tumambing, 2006, p. 3). Mio et al. note that narrow definitions of culture emphasize ethnicity, but a broader definition refers to shared values, beliefs, and practices of an identifiable group of people. Thus, culture, and multicultural psychology, includes race, ethnicity, language, spirituality, sexuality, and, of particular relevance for sport psychology, *physicality* (physical characteristics and abilities).

As discussed elsewhere (Gill & Kamphoff, 2009), our framework draws on that multicultural psychology literature, and is based on the following themes:

- *Multiple, intersecting cultural identities.* All sport participants have gender, race, ethnicity, and many other cultural identities, with the mix varying across individuals, time, and contexts.
- *Power relations.* Culture relations involve power and privilege. Who makes the rules? Who is left out?

- *Action and advocacy.* Multicultural perspectives demand action for social justice. Culturally competent sport psychology professionals develop their own multicultural competencies and also promote sport psychology in the public interest.

Derald Sue (2004), in his address and article on ethnocentric monoculturalism, noted that privileged people are often unaware of power relations and that "color blindness" often denies opportunity to others. Sue argued that psychology must recognize white privilege and the culture-bound nature of our scholarship and practice to advance psychology's mission and enhance the health and well-being of all people. Sport psychology must also meet that challenge.

Moving beyond cultural boundaries and traditional approaches is no easy task. Sport psychology is explicitly context-dependent, and the sport context has many unique boundaries and limits as well as reflecting those of the larger society. As multicultural psychologists advocate, sport psychologists must pay attention to power relations and social context in sport, but also must retain concern for the individual. A balanced consideration of both the individual and cultural context is the essence of a representative and useful sport psychology that promotes inclusive and empowering sport for all.

Cultural Diversity and Representation in Sport

The changing demographics in U.S. society and increasing globalization of sport psychology highlight issues of representation. In the U.S. population, the percentage of white/Caucasians has declined over the past decade while the proportion of minorities and non-English speakers has increased (U.S. Bureau of the Census, 2001). Cultural diversity, however, is complex and goes beyond racial and ethnic categories in census reports. As Mio et al. (2006) noted, a broader definition of culture includes race and ethnicity, gender, sexual orientation, nationality, and age, as well as physical abilities and characteristics.

Despite increasing cultural diversity in the population, sport is an exclusive space that privileges some over others. More girls and women are participating in sport than ever before, but the numbers of female and male participants are not equal (Carpenter & Acosta, 2006). Richard Lapchick's annual *Racial and Gender Report Cards* on participation rates and leadership positions of women and racial/ethnic minorities in U.S. collegiate and professional sports clearly show racial and gender inequities. In the 2005 report card, Lapchick (2006) reported that 24.8% of male athletes and 15.4% of female athletes in Division I were African American, but Latino, Asian American, and Native Americans were underrepresented at very low percentages; nonresident aliens made up a higher percentage (around 4.5%) than any racial/ethnic minority group other than African Americans.

As noted earlier, it is important to go beyond participation numbers to consider power and privilege — *"who makes the rules?"* When we consider the "power" positions, diversity is nonexistent. In his discussion of ethnocentric monoculturalism and invisible privilege, Sue (2004) noted that while white males make up just 33% of the U.S. population, they make up 99% of the athletic team owners. White men dominate intercollegiate coaching, even of women's teams. In the 2004 racial report card (Lapchick, 2005) African American men coached 7.2% of men's teams and 3.4% of women's teams, African American women coached only 1.6% of women's teams, and coaches of other racial/ethnic identities could hardly be counted. The 2005 report card showed that despite some improvement, administration remains solidly white male; people of color held 13% and women 7.8% of Division I athletic director positions.

Before Title IX of the Educational Amendments Act became law in 1972 and banned sex discrimination in educational programs in the United States, more than 90% of women's athletic teams were coached by women and had a woman athletic director. Vivian Acosta and Linda Carpenter (Carpenter & Acosta, 2006) clearly documented the continuous decline in the number of women coaches since then. In their most recent 31-year update (Acosta & Carpenter, 2008), they reported the proportion of women as coaches remains low at 42.8%. The proportion of female athletic directors (21.3%), head athletic trainers (27.3%), and sports information directors (11.3%) has risen, but remains far below male numbers.

Kamphoff's (in press) research clearly shows that women coaches within collegiate athletics experience marginalization, devaluation, and homophobia. Former women coaches reported that they received fewer resources, lower salaries, more responsibilities, and less administrative support than their male counterparts. They had difficulty balancing work and family, and reported that others saw them as "distracted by motherhood" if they had children.

Within sport psychology, Krane and Barber's work (Barber & Krane, 2005; Krane, 2001; Krane & Barber, 2005) clearly points to the homophobic and exclusive nature of sport. For example, in one study with lesbian collegiate coaches, all reported that they struggled to negotiate their lesbian identity within the collegiate coaching atmosphere (Krane & Barber, 2005). The former women coaches that Kamphoff (in press) interviewed provided examples of rampant homophobia in U.S. collegiate coaching that clearly restricted their behavior, limited their ability to continue coaching, and affected all women in the collegiate system.

Not only are competitive athletics exclusive, but census data and public health reports indicate that physical activity is limited by gender, race and ethnicity, socioeconomic status, and, especially, physical attributes. Physical activity decreases across the adult lifespan, with men more active than women and racial/ethnic minorities less active across all age groups (Pratt, Macera, & Blanton, 1999; USDHHS, 2000). For example, Kimm et al. (2002) used a large national database and found that girls' physical activity levels declined dramatically across adolescence, so that at age 18–19 56% of black girls and 31% of white girls reported no regular physical activity.

Physical characteristics are key sources of exclusion, and persons with disabilities certainly are often left-outs in sport and exercise settings. Rimmer (2005) reported that people with physical disabilities are one of the most inactive segments of the population. He argued that the real barriers are organizational policies and practices, discrimination, and social attitudes rather than physical limitations.

Crespo et al. (1999), in one of the few studies looking at social class, used a national database and found greater inactivity in less privileged social classes, with females more inactive in all social class groups. Crespo (2005), in a review and discussion of physical activity in minority populations, called for professionals to consider unique needs and cultural constraints when giving advice on exercise. As Crespo argued, physical activity for cultural minorities is a public health challenge, and in line with our themes, sport psychology could address this challenge through both scholarship and social action.

Representation in Sport Psychology Scholarship

Sport psychology could follow the lead of multicultural psychology to advance multicultural scholarship and enhance cultural competence in professional practice. But, sport psychology has not done so. This section begins with an overview of representation (or lack of) in sport psychology scholarship, and then highlights the research findings on cultural influences in sport and physical activity. Unfortunately, with few exceptions, the major feature of sport psychology scholarship on cultural diversity and cultural competence is its absence.

A Void in the Literature

Nearly 20 years ago, Duda and Allison (1990) brought this issue to the forefront by identifying the dearth of research related to race and ethnicity in sport psychology. They analyzed 199 articles in the *Journal of Sport and Exercise Psychology (JSEP)* from 1979 to 1987. *JSEP* was the first, and for that time frame, the only scholarly publication specifically in sport psychology. Thus, *JSEP* reflected the major issues, research directions, and representation of the field. The results revealed a clear lack of attention to race and ethnicity, with only 1 of 13 published theoretical papers and 7 of 186 empirical papers (less than 4%) considering race and ethnicity. Moreover, none of those 7 empirical papers addressed race or ethnicity on a conceptual level, and 6 of the 7 provided only a description of the sample. More than 96% of the empirical papers in *JSEP* did not report the racial or ethnic composition of their sample, and Duda and Allison concluded that there was "no systematic attempt to deal with race and ethnicity as conceptual and meaningful categories of human experience" (p. 117).

Ram, Starek, and Johnson (2004) replicated and extended Duda and Allison's work by analyzing 982 manuscripts published in the *Journal of Applied Sport Psychology* and *The Sport Psychologist*, both of which began publishing in 1987, as well as *JSEP*, between 1987 and 2000 for inclusion of race, ethnicity, and sexual orientation. They confirmed the void in the scholarly literature, reporting that less than 20% of articles included references to race and ethnicity and just over 1% referenced sexual orientation. Only 15 papers (about 1.5%) went beyond descriptive analyses to consider race and ethnicity in a substantial and conceptual way, let alone with critical analyses. Reporting of race and ethnicity increased slightly since Duda and Allison's original paper, and there was no discussion of sexual orientation. Similar to Duda and Allison, Ram et al. concluded that there has been "no systematic attempt to include the experiences of marginalized groups in the literature" (p. 250). That is, sport psychology has not made progress; our scholarship does not address cultural diversity.

Scholarly journals may be overly restrictive and selective with a bias toward more controlled designs and "hard science" topics. One might expect that scholarly presentations at conferences such as the Association for Applied Sport Psychology (AASP) would be more open to a wider range of topics, research approaches, and professional issues. Thus, AASP conference programs might well be more representative than the journal publications. To explore this possibility, Kamphoff, Araki, and Gill (2004) surveyed the AASP conference programs from the first conference in 1986 to 2003 and coded 240 AASP conference abstracts for diversity content. Specifically, abstracts were coded for "diverse sample" (non-majority participants — females, non-Caucasian, youth under 18, adults over 50, etc.) and "diversity issue" (gender differences, roles, ethnic identity, stereotypes, etc.) as well as the first author's gender and country affiliation.

First authors of the abstracts in 1986 represented only 2 countries (United States and Canada), whereas 16 countries were represented in 2003. In 1986, 78.4% of the first authors were males and 19.6% were females; the distribution was more equitable in 2003, with 50.1% of the first authors being male and 49.9% females. Inclusion of both diverse samples and diversity issues increased from 1986 to 1995, with little change from 1995 to 2003. Diverse samples were mostly diverse by gender (including females), with some by age (youth participants), but samples were not very diverse in other ways. Diversity issues increased from 2 (4%) in 1986 to 54 (15.4%) in 2003. Nearly all those "issues" involved gender, and were comparisons of gender differences rather than more complex analyses of gender relations. AASP conference programs lacked discussion of race, ethnicity, social class, disability, older adults, and gay/lesbian issues, and did not address broader multicultural issues.

Around that same time, AASP's diversity committee, under the leadership of Ruth Hall, surveyed 192 attendees at the 2003 AASP conference about their experiences, attitudes, and skills in working with diverse clients. Hall's (2005) report revealed that the majority of respondents believed they included diverse groups in their research and discussed implications of diversity in their work. Given the reviews cited previously (Duda & Allison, 1990; Kamphoff et al., 2004; Ram et al., 2004), these beliefs do not seem to be realized.

The large majority of AASP members who responded to the survey had no specific training on diversity, and less than half indicated they would seek diversity training if offered. Most felt there were no barriers when working with diverse populations. Notably, most respondents were "majority" on most characteristics (North American, able-bodied, heterosexual, and white).

Recently, Kamphoff and colleagues (Kamphoff, Gill, Araki, & Hammond, 2009) updated and extended their analysis of AASP programs by conducting a content analysis of more than 5,000 AASP conference program abstracts from 1986 to 2007. Only 10.5% of all abstracts addressed a cultural diversity issue and 31.9% included a diverse sample. Most of the diverse samples and issues involved gender, with almost no attention to race and ethnicity, nationality, sexual orientation, social class, disability, or age. Not only did the results confirm the continuing neglect of cultural diversity, but the trend over recent years is not promising. When looking at trends over five-year blocks of time, the peak for both diverse samples and issues was 1992–1997, with slight (not significant) decreases in 1998–2002 and 2003–2007. For race/ethnicity and LGBT (lesbian/gay/bisexual/transgender), samples peaked in 1992–1997; disability peaked in the first time period, 1986–1991; and international samples peaked in 1998–2002, the same peak time for international first authors. No categories of diversity samples or issues peaked in the most recent time period, 2003–2007.

Again, the findings indicate no systematic attempt to address cultural diversity in a meaningful way. Moreover, sport psychology has not made progress over the past 20 years despite the visible growth of multicultural psychology scholarship and guidelines over that same time. Overall, multicultural perspectives are missing, and cultural diversity is marginalized in sport psychology research and practice. Our sport psychology research and programs are not representative, and professionals do not recognize that lack of representation. Our analysis of AASP programs and our observations suggest that sport psychology is *going for the gold*, with little attention to the broader public and potentially more diverse participants.

Sport Psychology Scholarship on Culture

Clearly sport psychology has not followed the lead of multicultural psychology. Nor has sport psychology drawn from the multicultural scholarship from education and public health, or adapted the social service and health-related professions' emphasis on cultural competence. However, we can draw on that broader multicultural scholarship and related work in sport studies, as well as the limited work within sport psychology. This section highlights scholarship that relates to representation in sport psychology. More detail on related research can be found in other sources (e.g., Gill, 2007a; Gill & Kamphoff, 2009).

Gender

Gender influence is clear in society, and particularly powerful in sport. Gender scholarship within psychology includes early and persistent research on sex differences, research on personality and gender roles, and more current scholarship on gender relations and social processes. Despite persistent claims to the contrary, Hyde (2005) recently reviewed 46 meta-analyses of the extensive sex differences literature and concluded that results support the *gender similarities hypothesis*. That is, males and females are more alike than different, and overstated claims of gender differences cause harm and limit opportunities.

Most psychologists have moved beyond the male-female and masculine-feminine dichotomies to developmental and social cognitive models, often taking a multicultural perspective. Psychological research confirms that how people *think* males and females differ is more important than how they actually differ. If children think that dance is for girls, boys will stand aside while girls dance. Gender stereotypes are pervasive, and particularly so in sport. Kane and Snyder (1989) confirmed gender stereotyping of sports, and identified physicality—emphasis on physical muscularity, strength, and power—as the key feature. Stereotypes are a concern because we act on them, exaggerating minimal gender differences and restricting opportunities for everyone.

Fredericks and Eccles's (2004) review of the literature on parental influence and youth sport involvement revealed that parents held gender-stereotyped beliefs about athletics and were gender-typed in their behaviors, providing more opportunities and encouragement to sons than to daughters. Fredericks and Eccles (2005) later confirmed that boys had higher perceived competence, value, and participation, despite the absence of gender differences in motor proficiency.

Race and Ethnicity

Despite the persistent void in sport psychology research, the multicultural psychology scholarship on race and ethnicity is growing, and much of that work addresses well-documented health disparities

(USDHHS, 2003). Contrada et al. (2000) summarized research indicating that racial and ethnic minorities face stress based on discrimination, stereotypes, and conformity pressures and that these stresses affect health and well-being. That health disparities work covers a wide range of underrepresented populations, and socioeconomic status is often a key factor. As Yali and Revenson (2004) suggested, with the changing population demographics, socioeconomic disparities are likely to have an even greater impact in the near future. Health disparities are particularly relevant in that physical activity is a key health behavior, and sport psychology professionals are in a position to provide guidance on promoting sport and physical activity for health and well-being.

Within psychology, the most relevant research on race and ethnicity is the extensive research on stereotypes and *stereotype threat* — the influence of negative stereotypes on performance (Steele, 1997; Steele, Spencer, & Aronson, 2002). That psychological research, primarily on gender and racial stereotypes in academic work, also indicates that the most devastating effects are on those minority group members who have abilities and are motivated to succeed. On a more positive note, research suggests that even simple manipulations that take away the stereotype threat can help. Beilock and McConnell (2004) reviewed the related sport psychology literature, concluding that negative stereotypes are common in sport and lead to performance decrements.

Negative stereotypes for racial and ethnic minorities, particularly African American athletes, are well documented. Devine and Baker (1991) found "unintelligent" and "ostentatious" associated with "black athlete," and Krueger (1996) found both black and white participants perceived black men to be more athletic than white men. Stone, Perry, & Darley (1997) had individuals listen to a college basketball game and evaluate players they believed were black or white. Black players were rated more athletic, whereas white players were perceived as having more basketball intelligence by both white and black students. Stone and colleagues (1999) later confirmed stereotype threat: black participants did worse when told a golf task was a test of sports intelligence, whereas white participants performed worse when told it was a test of natural ability.

As might be expected, most of the psychological research on stereotypes in sport involves black athletes. Little social psychology or sport psychology work has examined stereotypes or their effects for other cultural minorities. In one recent study, Fryberg et al. (2008) examined the psychological consequences of American Indian mascots. American Indian mascots are widely discussed in higher education and in sport studies scholarship, but Fryberg et al.'s study is the first to address issues within a psychological framework. Over four studies, Fryberg et al. found that American Indian students who were exposed to common images (e.g., Chief Illinwek, Pocahontas) had positive associations, but also depressed self-esteem, a lowered sense of community worth, and fewer achievement-related possible selves. Fryberg et al. suggested that even images that might be positive in some ways can have harmful effects because they highlight the limited visibility and images that others hold, thus constraining self-images.

Sexual Prejudice

Discrimination and prejudice on the basis of sexual orientation is often described as homophobia but is more appropriately termed *sexual prejudice* (Herek, 2000). Psychological research confirms persistent sexual prejudice and hostile climates faced by lesbian/gay/bisexual (LGB) individuals in society (e.g., Herek, 2000; Rivers & D'Augelli, 2001). Although scholarly research in sport psychology is limited, national reports from the National Gay and Lesbian Task Force Policy Institute (Rankin, 2003) and Human Rights Watch (2001), as well as observations and anecdotal evidence, suggest sport is a particularly hostile environment.

In one of the few empirical studies, Morrow and Gill (2003) reported that both physical education teachers and students witnessed high levels of homophobic and heterosexist behaviors in public schools, but teachers failed to confront those behaviors. More than 75% of the teachers said that they want safe, inclusive physical education, but at the same time more than 50% reported that they *never* confront homophobia. Gill et al. (2006) examined attitudes toward racial/ethnic minorities, older adults, and persons with disabilities, as well as sexual minorities, and found attitudes of pre-professional kinesiology and recreation students were markedly more negative toward both gay men and lesbians than toward other minority groups.

Physicality

Stereotypes and bias based on gender, race and ethnicity, and sexuality clearly affect perceptions and behaviors of participants and professionals in sport, and psychology research is beginning to address those issues. However, neither psychology nor sport psychology has addressed the more prominent role of physicality (physical abilities/disabilities, size, appearance). Sport involves physical activity; physical abilities and characteristics are prominent, and exclusion on the basis of physicality is nearly universal in sport and exercise. For example, Gill et al. (2005) examined the climate for minority groups (racial/ethnic minorities, gay/lesbian/bisexual people, older adults, and those with disabilities) in organized sport and exercise and recreational settings. Notably, the climate was rated as most exclusionary for those with disabilities.

Physical size, particularly obesity, is a prominent source of social stigma and oppression, and that is a particular concern for physical activity and health promotion programs. Puhl and Brownell (2001) documented clear and consistent stigmatization of obese individuals in employment, education, and health care. Although physical activity is widely promoted and justified as obesity prevention and weight management, the programs and professionals often convey biases and do little to promote health and well-being among overweight and obese people. For example, Greenleaf and Weiller (2005) found that physical education teachers held moderate anti-fat bias and strong personal weight control beliefs (obese individuals are responsible for their obesity). Similarly, Chambliss, Finley, & Blair (2004) found a strong anti-fat bias among exercise science students. Anti-fat bias and weight discrimination among professionals have important implications for health promotion. Research confirms that obese individuals are targets for teasing, are more likely to engage in unhealthy eating behaviors, and are less likely to engage in physical activity (Faith et al., 2002).

Representation in Professional Sport Psychology

As just reviewed, sport psychology research is not very representative. As a professional discipline, sport psychology should also demonstrate diversity and attention to multicultural competence in professional practice, education and training, and public service. Do our educational programs and professionals demonstrate cultural competence (e.g., use inclusive language or demonstrate diversity in resources, examples, and teaching approaches)? Do sport psychology professionals serve the public interest by promoting the health and well-being of all through sport (e.g., lobby for equal access)?

There is little direct evidence on professional activities, but observations and available evidence point to a clear answer: "No." Sport psychology research does not address diversity issues, professional practice focuses on elite sport, educational programs do not incorporate multicultural competencies, and sport psychology does not serve the public interest.

Our educational programs parallel the elite emphasis of professional practice and focus on techniques and strategies for performance enhancement, with little emphasis on the sociocultural scholarly base that might draw attention to culture and diversity issues. This elite approach to professional practice is limiting in many ways. Certainly diverse, non-elite participants can benefit from sport psychology. Professionals who target youth development programs, senior sports, or rehabilitation programs may well find their services welcomed and effective. Moreover, those efforts could support social justice through empowerment of marginalized groups.

Cultural Competence in Sport Psychology

Cultural competence takes diversity directly into professional practice. Culturally competent professionals act to empower participants and challenge restrictive social structures. Mio et al. (2006) described *multicultural competence* as referring to *the ability to work effectively with individuals who are of a different culture*. Cultural competence, or multicultural competencies, typically are described as including three general areas: *awareness* of one's own cultural values and biases, *understanding* (knowledge) of others' worldviews (in all its multicultural complexity), and *culturally appropriate intervention strategies* (Mio et al., 2006). Multicultural competence is required in psychology and many health professions, and sport psychology would do well to follow that model.

The APA is organized into four directorates reflecting the major professional roles in psychology — science, practice, education, and, of particular interest here, public interest. As stated on the website (http://www.apa.org/pi/) *The APA Public Interest Directorate supports and promotes efforts to apply the science and profession of psychology to the advancement of human welfare*. The major objectives of the Public Interest Directorate are to:

- promote those aspects of psychology that involve solutions to the fundamental problems of human justice and equitable and fair treatment of all segments of society

- encourage the utilization and dissemination of psychological knowledge to advance equal opportunity and to foster empowerment of those who do not share equitably in society's resources
- increase scientific understanding and training in regard to those aspects that pertain to, but are not limited to, culture, class, race/ethnicity, gender, sexual orientation, age, and discrimination; and to support improving educational training opportunities for all persons

The APA has recognized the key role of multicultural competencies in fulfilling psychology's mission to promote health and well-being, and APA's (2003) multicultural guidelines call for action for social justice. Sport psychology can move toward representation and cultural competence by adopting the APA PI Directorate mission and by "walking the talk" in fulfilling its objectives.

William Parham (2005), a leader in the APA's multicultural efforts and active psychology professional, offered useful guidelines for sport psychology professionals. Parham's first guiding premise, *context is everything*, implies that when working with diverse individuals (everyone in practice works with diverse individuals), history, economics, family, and social context are all relevant. Parham's second premise, that *culture, race, and ethnicity as separate indices do little to inform us*, reminds us that cultural groups are not homogeneous and that every individual has a unique cultural identity. Parham's third guiding premise is *use of paradigms reflecting differing worldviews*. Our U.S./Western worldview is culturally limited, typically emphasizing independence, competitiveness, and individual striving. Emphasis on connectedness rather than separation, deference to higher power, mind-body interrelatedness rather than control, and a sense of "spirit-driven energy" may be more prominent in another's worldview.

Conclusion: Moving toward Cultural Competence in Sport Psychology

Sport psychology must be inclusive of *all* individuals, and professionals must develop multicultural competencies to be effective and inclusive in professional practice. As this chapter indicates, scholarship addressing multicultural issues is almost nonexistent, and professionals have not embraced cultural competence. To better serve the needs of professionals, participants, and the public, sport psychology must become representative and culturally competent across the full range of professional roles, paralleling the APA's four directorates (science, practice, education, and public interest).

In terms of science, researchers must expand the limited multicultural scholarship in sport psychology, in terms of methodologies as well as content. As Sue (1999) argued in a keynote address at the first APA multicultural summit, traditional psychological research models overemphasize internal validity and hinder ethnic minority research. To move forward, sport psychology researchers might follow Sue's calls to address external validity and appreciate varied research approaches.

All sport psychology professionals must develop multicultural competencies. Cultural competence in the three often-cited general areas of awareness, understanding, and culturally appropriate interventions is essential in professional practice. Professionals would also do well to recognize and adopt Sue's (2006) more nuanced characteristics of cultural competency among service providers: *scientific mindedness*, *dynamic sizing*, and *culture-specific expertise*. Scientific-minded practitioners form hypotheses rather than make premature conclusions about culturally different clients; they test and revise hypotheses and act based on acquired data. Dynamic sizing reflects the balancing of individualizing and contextualizing. It involves knowing when to generalize and when to individualize in working with clients; those who are skilled avoid stereotyping while appreciating culture. Culture-specific expertise refers to knowledge and skills specific to the culture of the client.

Educational programs in sport psychology must include scholarship leading to a deeper understanding of the complexities or culture and diversity, as well as the development of multicultural competencies for professional practice. Graduate sport psychology programs are the logical focus for these efforts, but sport psychologists can also extend educational programs to other sport professionals (e.g., coaches, teachers, trainers), future professionals, and the wider public.

To truly demonstrate multicultural competence, sport psychologists must go beyond traditional institutions and consulting practice and advocate for inclusive, empowering sport for *all*. Sport psychologists can be advocates for diverse and underrepresented groups and individuals in our communities and in the larger sport world. Sport psychologists can extend services to a wider population, help other physical activity professionals in developing multicultural competencies, and advocate for public policies and programs that ensure that sport programs promote health and well-being for all.

References

Acosta, R. V., & Carpenter, L. J. (2008). *Women in intercollegiate sport: A 31-year update*. Retrieved May 28, 2009, from http://www.acostacarpenter.org/.

American Psychological Association. (2003). Guidelines on multicultural education, training, research, practice and organizational change for psychologists. *American Psychologist, 58*, 377–402.

Barber, H., & Krane, V. (2005). The elephant in the locker room: Opening the dialogue about sexual orientation on women's sport teams. In M. B. Anderson (Ed.), *Sport psychology in practice* (pp. 265–285). Champaign, IL: Human Kinetics.

Beilock, S. L., & McConnell, A. R. (2004). Stereotype threat and sport: Can athletic performance be threatened? *Journal of Sport & Exercise Psychology, 26*, 597–609.

Carpenter, L. J., & Acosta, R. V. (2006). *Title IX*. Champaign, IL: Human Kinetics.

Chambliss, H. O., Finley, C. E., & Blair, S. N. (2004). Attitudes toward obese individuals among exercise science students. *Medicine and Science in Sports & Exercise, 36*, 468–474.

Contrada, R. J., Ashmore, R. D., Gary, M. L., Coups, E., Egeth, J. D., Sewell, A., et al. (2000). Ethnicity-related sources of stress and their effects on well-being. *Current Directions in Psychological Science, 9*, 136–139.

Crespo, C. J. (2005). Physical activity in minority populations: Overcoming a public health challenge. *The President's Council on Physical Fitness and Sports Research Digest*, series 6, no. 2 (June).

Crespo, C. J., Ainsworth, B. E., Keteyian, S. J., Heath, G. W., & Smit, E. (1999). Prevalence of physical inactivity and its relations to social class in U.S. adults: Results from the Third National Health and Nutrition Examination Survey, 1988–1994. *Medicine & Science in Sports & Exercise, 31*, 1821–1827.

Devine, P. G., & Baker, S. M. (1991). Measurement of racial stereotype subtyping. *Personality and Social Psychology Bulletin, 17*, 44–50.

Duda, J. L., & Allison, M. T. (1990). Cross-cultural analysis in exercise and sport psychology: A void in the field. *Journal of Sport & Exercise Psychology, 12*, 114–131.

Faith, M. S., Leone, M. A., Ayers, T. S., Heo, M., & Pietrobelli, A. (2002). Weight criticism during physical activity, coping skills, and reported physical activity in children. *Pediatrics, 110*, e23.

Fredericks, J. A., & Eccles, J. S. (2004). Parental influences on youth involvement in sports. In M. R. Weiss (Ed.), *Developmental sport and exercise psychology: A lifespan perspective* (pp. 145–164). Morgantown, WV: Fitness Information Technology.

Fredericks, J. A., & Eccles, J. S. (2005). Family socialization, gender and sport motivation and involvement. *Journal of Sport & Exercise Psychology, 27*, 3–31.

Fryberg, S. A., Markus, H. R., Oysterman, D., & Stone, W. M. (2008). Of warrior chiefs and Indian princesses: The psychological consequences of American Indian mascots. *Basic and Applied Social Psychology, 30*, 208–218.

Gill, D. L. (2007a). Gender and cultural diversity. In G. Tenenbaum & R. Eklund (Eds.), *Handbook on research on sport psychology* (3rd ed., pp. 823–844). Hoboken, NJ: Wiley.

Gill, D. L. (2007b). Integration: The key

to sustaining kinesiology in higher education. *Quest, 59*, 270–286.

Gill, D. L. (2009). Social psychology and physical activity: Back to the future. *Research Quarterly for Exercise and Sports, 80*, 685–695.

Gill, D. L., & Kamphoff, C.S. (2009). Cultural diversity in applied sport psychology. In R. J. Schinke & S. J. Hanrahan (Eds.), *Cultural sport psychology* (pp. 45–56) Champaign, IL: Human Kinetics.

Gill, D. L., Morrow, R. G., Collins, K. E., Lucey, A. B., & Schultz, A. M. (2005). Climate for minorities in exercise and sport settings. *Journal of Sport & Exercise Psychology, 27*, Suppl., S68.

Gill, D. L., Morrow, R. G., Collins, K. E., Lucey, A. B., & Schultz, A. M. (2006). Attitudes and sexual prejudice in sport and physical activity. *Journal of Sport Management, 20*, 554–564.

Greenleaf, C., & Weiller, K. (2005). Perceptions of youth obesity among physical educators. *Social Psychology of Education, 8*, 407–423.

Guthrie, R. V. (1998). *Even the rat was white: A historical view of psychology* (2nd ed.). Boston: Allyn & Bacon.

Hall, R. L. (2005). In. R. Hall, D. Gill, C. Kamphoff, & E. Claspell, Where are our voices? The status of diversity in AAASP. *Association for the Advancement of Applied Sport Psychology*. Vancouver, BC, Canada.

Herek, G. M. (2000). Psychology of sexual prejudice. *Current directions in psychological science, 9*, 19–22.

Human Rights Watch. (2001). Hatred in the hallways: Violence and discrimination against lesbian, gay, bisexual, and transgender students in U.S. schools. *American Journal of Health Education, 32*, 302–306. (full report retrieved June 6, 2005, from http://www.hrw.org/reports/2001/uslgbt/toc.htm).

Hyde, J. S. (2005). The gender similarities hypothesis. *American Psychologist, 60*, 581–592.

Kamphoff, C. S. (in press). Bargaining with patriarchy: Former women coaches' experiences and their decision to leave coaching. Accepted for publication, *Research Quarterly for Exercise and Sport*.

Kamphoff, C. S., Araki, K., & Gill, D. (2004) Diversity issues in AAASP. *AAASP Newsletter*, Fall 2004, vol. 19, issue 3, pp. 26–27.

Kamphoff, C. S., Gill, D. L., Araki, K., & Hammond, C. C. (in review). A content analysis of diversity issues in the Association for Applied Sport Psychology's conference programs. Manuscript in review.

Kane, M. J., & Snyder, E. (1989). Sport typing: The social "containment" of women. *Arena Review, 13*, 77–96.

Kimm, S. Y. S., Glynn, N. W., Kriska, A. M., Barton, B. A., Kronsberg, S. S., Daniels, S. R., et al. (2002). Decline in physical activity in black girls and white girls during adolescence. *New England Journal of Medicine, 347*, 709–715.

Krane, V. (2001). We can be athletic and feminine, but do we want to? Challenging hegemonic femininity in women's sport. *Quest, 53*, 115–133.

Krane, V., & Barber, H. (2005). Identity tensions in lesbian intercollegiate coaches. *Research Quarterly for Exercise and Sport, 76*, 67–81.

Kretchmar, S. (2005). Jigsaw puzzles and riverbanks: Two ways of picturing our future. *Quest, 57*, 171–177.

Krueger, J. (1996). Personal beliefs and cultural stereotypes about racial characteristics. *Journal of Personality and Social Psychology, 71*, 536–548.

Lapchick, R. (2005). *The 2004 Racial and Gender Report Card: College sports*. (retrieved May 2009, from http://web.bus.ucf.edu/sportbusiness/).

Lapchick, R. (2006). *The 2005 Racial and Gender Report Card*: College sports. (retrieved May 2009, from http://web.bus.ucf.edu/sportbusiness/).

Martens, R. (1975). *Social psychology and*

physical activity. New York: Harper & Row.

Martens, R. (1979). From smocks to jocks. *Journal of Sport Psychology, 1*, 94–99.

Mio, J. S., Barker-Hackett, L., & Tumambing, J. (2006). *Multicultural psychology: Understanding our diverse communities*. Boston: McGraw-Hill.

Morrow, R. G., & Gill, D. L. (2003). Perceptions of homophobia and heterosexism in physical education. *Research Quarterly for Exercise and Sport, 74*, 205–214.

Parham, W. D. (2005). Raising the bar: Developing an understanding of athletes from racially, culturally, and ethnically diverse backgrounds. In M. B. Anderson (Ed.), *Sport psychology in practice* (pp. 201–215). Champaign, IL: Human Kinetics.

Pratt, M., Macera, C. A., & Blanton, C. (1999). Levels of physical activity and inactivity in children and adults in the United States: Current evidence and research issues. *Medicine and Science in Sport and Exercise, 31*, 526–533.

Puhl, R., & Brownell, K. D. (2001). Bias, discrimination, and obesity. *Obesity Research, 9*, 788–805.

Ram, N., Starek, J., & Johnson, J. (2004). Race, ethnicity, and sexual orientation: Still a void in sport and exercise psychology. *Journal of Sport & Exercise Psychology, 26*, 250–268.

Rankin, S. R. (2003). *Campus climate for gay, lesbian, bisexual, and transgender people: A national perspective*. New York: The National Gay and Lesbian Task Force Policy Institute. www.ngltf.org. Retrieved June 6, 2005, from http://www.thetaskforce.org/reslibrary.

Rimmer, J. H. (2005). The conspicuous absence of people with disabilities in public fitness and recreation facilities: Lack of interest or lack of access? *American Journal of Health Promotion, 19*, 327–329.

Rivers, I., & D'Augelli, A. R. (2001). The victimization of lesbian, gay, and bisexual youth. In A. R. D'Augelli & C. J. Patterson (Eds.), *Lesbian, gay and bisexual identities and youth: Psychological perspectives* (pp. 199–223). New York: Oxford University Press.

Steele, C. M. (1997). A threat in the air: How stereotypes shape intellectual identity and performance. *American Psychologist, 52*, 613–629.

Steele, C. M., Spencer, S. J., & Aronson, J. (2002). Contending with group image: The psychology of stereotype and social identity threat. *Advances in Experimental Social Psychology* (Vol. 34, pp. 379–440). New York: Academic.

Stone, J., Lynch, C. I., Sjomeling, M., & Darley, J. M. (1999). Stereotype threat effects on black and white athletic performance. *Journal of Personality and Social Psychology, 77*, 1213–1227.

Stone, J., Perry, Z. W., & Darley, J. M. (1997). "White men can't jump": Evidence for the perceptual confirmation of racial stereotypes following a basketball game. *Basic and Applied Social Psychology, 19*, 291–306.

Sue, D. W. (2004). Whiteness and ethnocentric monoculturalism: making the "invisible" visible. *American Psychologist, 59*, 761–769.

Sue, S. (1999). Science, ethnicity, and bias: Where have we gone wrong? *American Psychologist, 54*, 1070–1077.

Sue, S. (2003). In defense of cultural competency in psychotherapy and treatment. *American Psychologist, 57*, 964–970.

Sue, S. (2006). Cultural competence: From philosophy to research and practice. *Journal of Community Psychology, 34*, 237–245.

Trickett, E. J., Watts, R. J., & Birman, D. (Eds.). (1994). *Human diversity: Perspectives on people in context*. San Francisco: Jossey-Bass.

U.S. Bureau of Census (2001). *Census 2000, Table 4*. Retrieved on May 28, 2009, from http://www.census.gov/popu

lation/www/cen2000/briefs/phc-t1/ tables/tab04.pdf.

U.S. Department of Health and Human Services (2000). *Healthy people 2010.* Washington, DC: DHHS.

U.S. Department of Health and Human Services (2003). *National healthcare disparities report.* Washington, DC: DHHS.

Weiss, M. R. (2008). "Field of dreams:" Sport as a context for youth development. *Research Quarterly for Exercise and Sport, 79,* 434–449.

Yali, A. M., & Revenson, T. A. (2004). How changes in population demographics will impact health psychology: Incorporating a broader notion of cultural competence into the field. *Health Psychology, 23,* 147–155.

4

THE NARRATIVE TURN IN SPORT
AND EXERCISE PSYCHOLOGY

Brett Smith and Andrew Sparkes

CHAPTER SUMMARY

Narrative inquiry has recently attracted some interest within sport and exercise psychology. However, it is still embryonic within this field and much more work that is theoretically grounded, links the personal to the cultural, and is based on informed and principled decision-making processes is needed. This chapter begins with some personal reflections on why we have been inspired to turn to narrative for particular purposes. Following this, we explore the conceptual challenge of "what is narrative inquiry." Various benefits of narrative inquiry and several ways it challenges ideas within sport and exercise psychology are then pointed out. An example of sport narrative research is subsequently shown. Finally, some reflections about the future directions that narrative inquiry might take are offered.

The Narrative Turn in Sport and Exercise Psychology

Narrative inquiry, which might broadly be described as the study of stories that constitute how people experience their lives over time, has recently attracted some attention within sport and exercise psychology. Indeed, a number of scholars in this field have turned toward narrative inquiry as a way to deepen and enlarge our understandings of people's lives, cultural landscapes, and the psychosocial worlds in which we live. For example, in order to better understand the process of withdrawing from a career in golf, Carless and Douglas (2009) indicated that the stories made available to female professional golfers about this process drew on a limited cultural repertoire and highlighted how this affected their career transition experiences. In contrast, Denison and Winslade (2006) and Leahy and Harrigan (2006) considered narrative in terms of its therapeutic potential for initiating change in sporting stories that were defined as problematic. For Jowett and Frost (2007), a narrative analysis was used to understand race and ethnicity in male coach-athlete relationships, while Stelter (2007) utilized narrative theory to explore meaning making in coaching. More recently, Phoenix and Howe (in press) turned toward narrative as a way to appreciate the complex ways context shapes a traumatic injury experience.

Clearly, then, while narrative inquiry is still embryonic in sport and exercise psychology, some researchers in the field have chosen to turn to it. We have also been drawn to this approach for certain purposes. Herein, we provide some autobiographical reflections on our turn to narrative inquiry. In reflecting on our attraction to narrative forms of inquiry, we hope to signal some of their strengths and, in so doing, raise some questions for sport and exercise psychologists about how such work might be usefully integrated into an expanding methodology within this domain.

Our interest in narrative inquiry has developed sometimes by choice and sometimes by chance. That is, sometimes we have thought through an issue that then leads us to reflect on the potential of a narrative approach to explore the problem. At other times, via serendipity, we have stumbled across a book in the library or found a "gem" of a paper while flicking through a journal that provided a wonderful example of narrative as a method and/or methodology in action. Such chance encounters with the work of others continue to inspire us and encourage the ongoing sharing of these "gems" between us in our ongoing research endeavors.

Of the many currents within the field of qualitative research that have shaped our thinking regarding narrative, the ongoing *crisis of representation* (and legitimation) has also played a significant role. Linked to the linguistic and cultural turn, this crisis refers to the researcher's authority and ability to depict, describe, or portray people's experiences and sociocultural worlds (see Sparkes, 2002). The crisis addresses questions of race, gender, disability, and class and raises questions about how we write. Indeed, this crisis has stimulated scholars, including ourselves, to be more reflexive about our writing and experiment with different genres to represent data. For us, this experimentation has highlighted the analytical power of narrative work to deepen our understanding of the complexity of meaning and experience as they unfold in the personal and social fabric of people's lives. It has also emphasized the notion of the researcher as storyteller.

Another reason we have been drawn to narrative inquiry relates to its *moral* and *ethical* dimensions. For example, one moral concern emphasized in certain forms of narrative research is the relational nature of storytelling and the infusion of ethical dilemmas within this process (Bochner, 2002; Frank, 1995, 2006). Here, scholars are encouraged to consider their moral and ethical responsibility toward others, to recognize that one's life takes place not only among others, but also with and for those others. It calls upon them to act as a witness, to engage in the ethical task of dialogue, and to listen and think not just about but *with* people. It also provides a moral imperative to create spaces for marginalized stories (Bochner, 2002) and counternarratives (Randall & McKim, 2008) to be heard and acted upon that challenge the dominant discourses and offer various individuals and groups opportunities for personal and social change.

Our turn toward narrative inquiry also received a strong impetus from our experiences of *interrupted body projects*. For example, Brett's encounters with depression have often left him living in narrative wreckage, unscripted, deprived of meaningful stories, faltering in action, and stuttering in speech (see Smith, 1999). Over time, though, the embodied depressions have receded and moved into the background of his being. Of course, this is not to suggest that depression will not return into his life. However, the experiences of depression, in combination with his contact with narrative theory and different stories of illness, have taught him the crucial role that storytelling plays in living with and recovering *in* (rather than *from*) depression and other forms of interrupted body projects. It helped him find meaning in depression and learn how to live with illness, and, when fragility becomes immanent, how to tell the kind of stories that may help take care of him and others, such as friends, neighbors, and research colleagues. It also made Brett aware that it is incredibly difficult to communicate what our bodies experience to others, which raises further questions about the modes of representation we call on to accomplish the task of communication.

For Andrew, shifting forms of embodiment supported an emerging interest in narrative forms of inquiry to complement his long-term involvement in ethnographic and life history work. With regard to the latter, he had become increasingly dissatisfied with being the absent author, the silent voice, in the traditional realist tales he told about others. He was also concerned about becoming unidimensional as a researcher and as a person in terms of how he came to understand the social world around him, his place in it, and how he conveyed understandings of social life to himself and others. Against such concerns Andrew came to realize that in his "normal" academic writing he maintained tightly secured boundaries both within himself and beyond himself, keeping various identities, selves, and forms of embodiment separate, shored up, and protected from the swirling confusions he so often experience in his daily life. Various interrupted body projects have, however, collapsed these research worlds into each other and shattered the illusion of separation. For example, during his younger days Andrew engaged in elite sporting performance as a rugby union player, but acquired a chronic lower back problem at the age of 20 that terminated his involvement in top-class sport. Since then, this back problem has continued to interrupt his life and has led to numerous bouts of manipulative therapy by osteopaths and chiropractors and surgery on his lumbar spine in 1988, 1994, and 2000 to remove prolapsed discs. Acute episodes of intense back pain come without warning, and a dull aching pain in his lumbar region is a constant companion. As he puts it, he has good days and bad days (see also Sparkes, 2003).

Therefore, for both Brett and Andrew, shifting states of embodiment over time and specific interrupted embodied biographies have openly challenged the tyranny of abstraction and drawn them toward narrative inquiry as a way to hold on to the fundamental experience of bodily problems rather than allowing bodily problems to be abstracted from the needs, pains, and desires of their bodies and the bodies of others. As such, it is not surprising that some of their narrative work that has involved others has focused on interrupted embodied biographies (e.g., spinal cord injury) and the reconstruction of self over time (see Smith & Sparkes, 2005, 2008a; Sparkes & Smith, 2003, 2008a).

Having touched on some of the personal dimensions that stimulated our interest in narrative inquiry, we now turn our attention toward offering a critical overview of narrative inquiry and an analysis of the emergent field. To accomplish this task, we first consider what is meant by narrative inquiry. Next, we point out various benefits of narrative inquiry and highlight several ways it challenges ideas within sport and exercise psychology. An example of sport narrative research is then provided. Finally, some reflections about the future directions that narrative inquiry might take are offered.

What Precisely "Is" Narrative Inquiry?

Narrative inquiry may be seen as a family of approaches that all revolve around a focus on the study of stories. But, as with most families, there are differences between them. As such, any attempt to provide a singular definition of narrative inquiry or to draw a precise boundary around its meaning is problematic. That is, it is difficult to state precisely just what narrative inquiry "is" since it is an ongoing and broad field with differences, contestations, and tensions (Smith, 2007; Smith & Sparkes, 2008b). For example, there are theoretical tensions in narrative research, such as how to theorize coherence (Smith & Sparkes, 2006) and what the nature of the connections between experience and story is (Bochner, 2002). Further, there are differing theoretical lenses at play. One lens can be described as narrative constructi*vism*. Here, narrative is viewed primarily as a cognitive structure. In contrast, through the lens of narrative construction*ism* narrative is seen as a discursive action and thoroughly cultural (Sparkes & Smith, 2008b). Likewise, there are scholars who see narrative as an important, humane vehicle for conveying some of the richness, depth, and profundity of the human experience. This group of scholars is what Freeman (1993) termed narrative *expressivists*. On the other hand, there are those scholars who look toward the specific ways in which people *talk* about experience and the specific situations within which this talk takes place. Narrative, from this perspective, is not to be understood so much as a vehicle for conveying experience as a productive practice. Freeman termed this group of researchers narrative *productivists*.

Given the situation as we have described it, rather than trying to offer a precise definition of what narrative is, as we have suggested elsewhere, it is perhaps more appropriate and useful to describe what narrative inquiry *can be* (Smith & Sparkes, 2006, 2009a, b; Sparkes & Smith, 2008b). One way to do *so* involves looking at the basic assumptions that inform narrative inquiry. Another way involves highlighting how it is different from, as well as connected to, other forms of qualitative research. We turn first to the assumptions that inform narrative inquiry.

What Narrative Inquiry Can Mean: Some Assumptions

Narrative inquiry can be seen as a dynamic process founded on a set of assumptions that are at play from the first narrative imaginings of a research puzzle through to the representation and judgment of the research product (Clandinin, Pusher, & Orr, 2007; Smith & Sparkes, 2009a). These assumptions include the following.

First, for us, narrative inquiry is shaped and supported by the philosophical assumptions of interpretivism, or what some term non-foundationalism (J. Smith, 1993; J. Smith & Deemer, 2000).

Second, narrative inquiry holds that in our actions and practice we are essentially storytelling animals (MacIntryre, 1984) and/or we construct stories out of our cultural life to make our lives intelligible (Gubrium & Holstein, 2008).

Third, narrative inquiry is based on the assumption that epistemologically narrative is a way of knowing. That is, narrative is a key means by which we know and understand the world. It offers a way of knowing oneself and others.

Fourth, narrative inquiry is premised on the ontological assumption that human life is a "storied" life (Bruner, 2002; Sarbin, 1986). That is, narrative is an ontological condition of social life as it constitutes our mode of being in the world. Narrative inquirers argue that we live in, through, and out stories. Stories act on and for us. They help guide our action, structure our realities, and shape who we are, what we do, and what we might become. We also use stories to perform social actions, doing things with them that make a difference to, on, and for people.

Fifth, as indicated above, human beings are meaning-making beings. Notably, many narrative researchers add that our principal way of making meaning is narrative and that narratives are cultural resources for making sense of our experiences. Further, narratives are embodied. As Randall and McKim (2008) argued, like Stelter (2007), while underplayed in many traditions in psychology, the essence of being human is making meaning. For instance, we strive to make sense of our experiences by ascribing them with specific meanings. How, though, do we do this? For Randall and McKim, one key way is through the use of stories. That is, we go to stories *for* meaning, derive meaning *from* stories, impose meaning *onto* stories, read meaning *into* stories, and in our culture expect stories to *have* meaning. Thus, Randall and McKim noted, meaning making is an interpretive process that is "inseparable from story-making" (p. 180). Further, they stressed, this storied process of meaning construction is experienced in, on, and through the body. This storied process of meaning construction is likewise thoroughly shaped by social relations and the cultures we live in.

Sixth, stories are personal and sociocultural at the same time. People are active storytellers who have agentic capabilities to construct, personally edit, control, and resist stories. However, the stories we tell and draw on to make our experiences meaningful are not only personal. Nor are they located just in the mind, emerging from within, as if they were stored there for the telling. Rather, they are socially and culturally fashioned. As Freeman (2001) put it, "'My story' can never be wholly my mine, alone, because I define and articulate my existence with and among others through the various narrative models—including literary genres, plot structures, metaphoric themes, and so on—my culture provides" (p. 287). Thus, as McAdams (2006) noted, "Culture provides people with a menu of narrative forms and contents from which the person selectively draws in an effort to line up lived experience with the kinds of stories available to organize and express it. Indeed, the story menu goes so far as to shape lived experience itself" (p. 16). In short, while people do tell their own personal stories, they compose these stories by adopting and combining narratives that cultures make available to them across time.

Given the aforementioned six assumptions that ground the theoretical basis of narrative inquiry, and if we accept (for the moment) that we are storytellers by nature, or are constructed by stories (perhaps both), then we suggest that issues relating to narrative might be of some interest to the field of sport and exercise psychology. For example, given that narratives are a way of knowing, if we wish to know an athlete's inner world or, for example, why a person is physically (in)active, then we need to know her or his story, for that story offers a way of knowing or a way of providing meaning in relation to what one is and is not doing. Furthermore, if individuals want to know themselves, to gain insight into their own lives, then, they, too, must come to know their "own" stories (McAdams, 1993). Moreover, ontologically speaking, if narratives constitute people's lives, it therefore seems sensible that sport and exercise psychologists consider what and how narratives structure lives and the consequences these narratives have on and for people. Likewise, given we are meaning-making beings, and that a key means of making meaning is narrative, sport and exercise psychology researchers and practitioners might wish to include an exploration of the meaning systems that form athletes', coaches', and health professionals' experiences by systematically analyzing the stories they tell. Equally, because the fabric of our lives is both individual and sociocultural, sport and exercise psychologists might choose to move beyond an individualistic focus to generate a more complex exploration of people as both sociocultural and individual beings. For example, rather than focusing on only winning and individuation as the model for a successful sporting "career," a sport psychologist may also stress that our lives are relational and influenced by the social contexts and cultural settings in which we operate. This focus on the relational and sociocultural may, in turn, enhance opportunities for both athletes and sport psychologists to move beyond a focus on performance and the inner mind only and toward a focus on sport as also a source of relationships, caring, nurturing, and attachment (see Douglas, in press).

What Narrative Inquiry Can Mean: Some Differences

Building on the assumptions of narrative inquiry, another way of understanding what narrative inquiry can mean involves highlighting how it is different from, as well as connected to, other kinds of qualitative research. According to Crossley (2000), narrative psychology is premised on the assumption that human experience and behavior are meaningful and that, in order to understand ourselves and others, we need to explore the "meaning systems" and the "structures" of meaning that make up our cultural worlds and minds. To help explore meaning, she noted, researchers can turn to the narratives people tell since narrative is one of the vehicles that makes experience meaningful. Thus, for Crossley, "The basic principle of narrative psychology is that individuals understand themselves through language. . . . The focus on meaning and interpretation is of extreme importance. It is a focus which distinguishes narrative psychology from more traditional psychological approaches" (p. 10). Further, as Brockmeier and Carbaugh (2001) proposed, narrative psychologists espouse the constructedness of knowledge. Narrative inquirers also aim to examine the role of narrative as a cultural phenomenon in human life, thought, memory, and experience, and thus have a distinctive theoretical and methodological orientation.

> From early on in human development, narrative practices provide fundamental devices that give form and meaning to experience. . . . Not surprisingly, this view is distinct from, and aims to complement the traditional individualistic focus and the mentalist epistemology of psychology. How a life and, in the process, a self is constructed is a question to be examined in the

light of the narrative forms and discursive formats that are provided by culture and used by individuals in certain social events. Viewed in this way, narrative is a central hinge between culture and mind. (Brockmeier & Carbaugh, 2001, pp. 9–10)

Similarly, Day Sclater (2003) suggested some reasons narrative inquiry differs, sometimes subtly and sometimes quite radically, from other forms of scholarship and which, in turn, may make it appealing for psychologists.

For many, the need for a narrative psychology arises in order to take account of the turn to language in social science. On this view, a significance is accorded to language, at both individual and social levels, that is absent in traditional psychological paradigm. . . . For many, the attraction of narrative studies lies in its promise to enable us to think about a human subject who is socially situated and culturally fashioned, at the same time as that subject expresses a unique individuality and an agency that makes the subject, at once, quite singular but also part of more or less local and global communities. (p. 319)

More recently, Pinnegar and Daynes (2007) pointed out the following:

What distinguishes narrative inquiry is the understanding that all research is based on language whether in the language of numbers or the discourse of researchers and those being researched. Rather than imposing the antiseptic, narrow, and confining definition of scientific discourse heralded as necessary for "normal" social science (Kuhn, 1970), narrative inquirers embrace the metaphoric quality of language and the connectedness and coherence of the extended discourse of the story entwined with exposition, argumentation, and description. (p. 29)

Pinnegar and Daynes (2007) also contended that what "distinguishes the narrative turn from 'scientific' objectivity is understanding that knowing people and their interactions is a relational process that ultimately involves caring for, curiosity, interest, passion, and change" (p. 29). Likewise, Holloway and Freshwater (2007) suggested that a hallmark of much narrative research is its relational dimension, including its concern with power relations. "The relationship and collaboration between researcher and researched is also different from other types of inquiry. Although there is an equality of relationship between the two protagonists in all qualitative inquiry—or at least that is one of its aims—in narrative research the participants have more power as they control the story to a large extent, and it is not guided by the researcher as it would in a semi-structured interview" (p. 21).

Finally, according to Riessman (2008), narrative research often differs from much qualitative research given its efforts to detail the contexts of language production, the structural features of narrative, and the dialogic or co-constructed nature of narratives.

> Attention to sequences of action distinguishes narrative analysis—the investigator focuses on "particular actors, in particular social places, at particular social times." As a general field, narrative inquiry "is grounded in the study of the particular"; the analyst is interested in how a speaker or writer assembles and sequences events and uses language and/or visual images to communicate meaning, that is, make particular points to an audience. Narrative analysts interrogate intention and language— *how* and *why* incidents are storied, not simply the content to which language refers. For whom was *this* story constructed, and for what purpose? Why is the succession of events configured that way? What cultural resources does the story draw on, or take for granted? What storehouse of plots does it call up? What does the story accomplish? Are there gaps and inconsistencies that might suggest preferred, alternative, or counter-narratives? (p. 11)

In sum, therefore, narrative inquiry is the study of stories that shape how people live and experience their lives over time in different sets of circumstance. It is informed and justified on an ongoing list of assumptions that shape both its process and product in such a way as to make it different, and sometimes very different, from other kinds of research done within sport and exercise psychology. These differences, in turn, provide narrative inquiry with its own particular strengths, and thus justifications for choosing it. It is to these strengths and justifications that we now turn our attention.

Why Might Narrative be Relevant to Sport and Exercise Psychology?: Some Benefits

Narrative inquiry holds numerous benefits and has various strengths for sport and exercise psychology that may make it an attractive and appealing way to do research. While not exhaustive, they include the following strengths in relation to the sociocultural fabric of human lives, humanness and the complexity of our lives, and the writing practices of researchers (see also Smith & Sparkes, 2009a, b).

Narrative Illuminates the Sociocultural Fabric of Human Lives

Narratives can reveal much about the richness, depth, and profundity of experience and meaning (Freeman, 2003; Smith & Sparkes, 2009a), but notably they are also useful for what they tell us about the *sociocultural fabric of our lives*. As Smith and Sparkes (2009b) have argued within sport and exercise psychology, personal narratives can contribute to the understanding of individual experience as part of general social relations and cultural values, making them useful as social psychological and cultural data in general. This is because while stories people tell are intensely personal, they are thoroughly shaped by cultural conventions and derived from society. Hence, as Riessman (2008) noted, "Stories are social artifacts, telling us as much about society and culture as they do about a person or group" (p. 105). For example, the stories a young athlete tells about his or her expectations of growing old can tell us a great deal about how certain cultures regard and deal with aging (Phoenix, Smith, & Sparkes, 2007). That is, athletes' stories can illuminate the ways their aging bodies are constructed within certain cultures in terms of a process of bodily decline that needs to be combated (e.g., as in many Western cultures) or as an opportunity for personal progress that is to be embraced and cherished (as in some Asian cultures).

Further, an exercise psychologist interested in physical activity may find narrative useful as a way to deepen our understandings of the ways society and culture shape people's experiences of being and having a physically (in)active body. Indeed, narratives may tell them much about how culture frames what activities and health behaviors people take up, ignore, or reject in relation to gender, ethnicity, race, sexuality, age, and disability. They may reveal the distribution of which physically (in)active people are caught up in which stories, where those stories come from, what different stories do to the lives of those who are caught up in them, and with what reverberating effects others may experience. Equally, what people notice about their physically (in)active bodies and other bodies, how they act on what they notice, what they worry about and what they take satisfaction from, and which activities are taken seriously and what sense is made of them depend partly on which stories "out there" in culture they have access to. Thus, much may be revealed about such issues through an analysis of the stories available to people. In so doing, "solutions," "responsibilities," and "problems" are placed not simply at the door of the individual. Rather, society and culture is implicated, too, thereby leading exercise psychologists to confront, rather than sidestep, how and in what ways sociocultural practices shape, constrain, and enable a person's ability to do physical activity.

Narrative Illuminates Our Humanness and the Complexity of Our Lives

Narratives may be of value and relevance for sport and exercise psychologists who strive to understand people in all their complexity over time and in different situations. A great deal of contemporary sport and exercise psychology, supposedly an area devoted to the study of human beings, has, we feel, largely become a "lifeless" and "disembodied" field of engagement. Often it has sapped people of their humanness, embodiment, and complexity. Narrative inquiry, however, seeks to understand people and reveal the richness and complexity of human lives. As Freeman (2003) noted, narrative researchers "share an abiding respect for real human persons" (p. 345). Narrative researchers seek a different kind of psychology, one that is not only largely qualitative in its orientation but that seeks to practice a deep fidelity to embodied lived experience in all of its intricacy, variousness, and messiness. Thus, for Freeman, like others (e.g., Carless & Douglas, 2009; Crossley, 2000; McAdams, 1993; Smith & Sparkes, 2009b), narrative psychology can act as a much needed counterweight to the forms of psychology that tend to wash out complexity and obscure the very human beings they supposedly wish to understand.

For example, interviews for narrative researchers are opportunities and spaces for people to often tell long, in-depth, rich, and messy stories about their thoughts, emotions, and lives in ways they may not have done previously and in a way that quicker and cleaner qualitative methods, like a "one shot" 20-minute interview, can suppress. As such, some of the complexity of an individual life or group can be illuminated. Further, this complexity can tell us a great deal about how lives are shaped in complex ways by culture and in ways that enable or constrain what we can do, including taking on board physical activity.

Narrative Inquiry Focuses Attention on Writing Practices

According to Atkinson and Delamont (2006), "The narrative turn has had an important impact not only on *what* social scientists study, but also how they *represent* themselves and their work" (p. xl). For example, by foregrounding the idea that how we write is an analytical, political, and moral issue, work done in the field of narrative inquiry has influenced some sport and exercise researchers to see writing as something more than a mopping-up activity at the end of the research project. It has helped inspire a number of scholars to also seek to widen the range of representational strategies beyond the traditional scientific and realist tales to include, among others, ethnodrama, poetic representations, and autoethnography (see Sparkes, 2002). Thus, narrative inquiry is beneficial because it foregrounds the idea that writing is a means of knowing. It expands the choices sport and exercise psychologists have regarding how they might represent their research "findings." Further, it presents a more nuanced, varied, and complex view of representation than most other forms of qualitative research in sport and exercise psychology. For instance, writing is not seen by narrative researchers as an objective or transparent medium for presenting research findings. It is instead viewed as a subjective process and product that communicates stories researchers have co-constructed. Further, for narrative researchers, research stories are co-constructed. For example, they are shaped by both the writers' and readers' history, and the cultures they inhabit. In addition to the benefits of narrative inquiry we have outlined above, we would suggest that narrative inquiry also has an important role in sport and exercise psychology inasmuch as it problematizes and poses some interesting challenges for the field.

Some Problems and Challenges for Sport and Exercise Psychology

Given space limitations, we have chosen to focus our attention on three problems and challenges that narrative inquiry throws up for sport and exercise psychology in relation to post-positivistic thinking, theories of the self, and what we as researchers or applied practitioners believe we get from interviews.

Post-positivistic Thinking:
Some Challenges and Potential Problems

Narrative inquiry problematizes and challenges some core assumptions of post-positivism. As Brustand (2008), Sparkes (1998), and Sparkes and Smith (2009b) have pointed out, much sport and exercise psychology research, either implicitly or explicitly, holds to post-positivism. At the core of post-positivist thinking is the belief that there is a real world "out there" independent of our interest in or knowledge of it and that we can gain access to that world and know it as it really is through method. That is, because methods properly applied are believed to be neutral/objective, they can be used to establish contact with an external reality beyond ourselves. One implication of this, which many sport and exercise psychologists have taken up, is the idea that methods can give researchers direct access to reality in a way that will allow them to claim reality can be accurately or objectively depicted. Another implication is that method is a marker of quality research. In other words, if methods can get at the reality and truth, then in principle methods can sort out good research from bad research. Accordingly, sport and exercise psychology has in many respects become a methodically driven inquiry.

However, the advancement of a central role for method within sport and exercise psychology as the way to establish contact with a reality independent of us and sort out quality from less quality research has been problematized and challenged by, among others, narrative researchers. For example, as Bochner (2002), Gubrium and Holstein (2008), Richardson (2000), and Sparkes and Smith (2009a, b) have argued, given there can be no separation between the researcher-researched or the observer-observed, all observation is theory-laden and there is no possibility of theory-free knowledge. That is, who we are is crucial to how we see the world around us and we cannot cut ourselves loose from our own cultural, social, and historical standpoint. Thus, the problem is that there is no way to "get at" the reality as it really is or to know if the reality has been mirrored correctly independent of us. But, so the story goes for many scholars within sport and exercise psychology, this problem can be overcome by turning to method(s). However, as Smith and Deemer (2000) argued, the problem of "getting at" the reality as it really is and knowing if the reality has been mirrored correctly independent of us cannot be overcome or done, as methods are not neutral or discovered, and cannot secure a procedural objectivity. Methods are, they argued, something people have constructed in line with particular interests, purposes, and political/ideological commitments. Thus, if these lines of reasoning make sense, then gaining access to a real world independent of our interests, purposes, and languages used via methods is problematic. Further, if we are intimately entangled with any claim we make to knowledge or to what counts as knowledge, then, by extension, this means we are intimately a part of any understanding we have of what counts as quality in research. All this is eloquently emphasized by J. Smith:

> There can be no theory-free knowledge or observation and we do not have a language, and have not the foggiest idea how to get a language, that would allow us to express the result of a theory-free observation. Those methods that have been and still are honored because they supposedly allow us to obtain the "clear-eyed gaze," to take a view from nowhere in particular, to keep our Cartesian mirror of the mind well-polished, or however one wishes to put it, are methods that people have constructed in line with their particular interests, purposes, political/ ideological commitments, and so on. And, if this line of reasoning makes sense, then it is pointless to talk in terms of criteria, cut loose from particular times and particular places, for judging the quality of research studies. Research methods and the judgments about the quality of research studies always have been and likely always will be, contingent on who we are and what we think we can accomplish. (in press)

In making these claims, however, some may argue that sport and exercise psychologists are left in a position where they are unable to speak to policy makers and influence them for better social good. That is, if there is no way to sort out knowledge claims by calling on something outside of us (reality itself), we enter the very dangerous territory of power deciding everything, including policies informed by sport and exercise psychology work. The claim that psychologists could "speak truth to power" of sporting governing bodies, politicians, policy makers, and interest groups would become meaningless in that all researchers could do is offer an "opinion to power" (J. Smith, 1993). At one level, a narrative researcher might respond, "So what's new?" as power has always been an issue regardless of the post-positivist claims to having made a contact with reality (J. Smith & Hodkinson, 2005). At another level, Hazelrigg (1995) argued that to fear power in this way is to engage in some sort of "intellectualist flight from power" (p. 202). Because nothing can happen for good or bad without power, power itself is not the issue. Rather, the issue is how power is exercised. Since narrative researchers hold that it is not possible to challenge others by making an appeal to an independent reality or truth that can be discovered through methods, the task, as J. Smith and Hodkinson (2005) suggested, is to distinguish between the responsible/beneficial versus the excessive/damaging uses of power. Significantly, such decisions are moral choices and not scientific, technical, or instrumentalist ones (J. Smith & Hodkinson, 2005).

"The Self": Some Challenges and Potential Problems

Narrative inquiry problematizes and challenges traditional theories of the self used within sport and exercise psychology. To date, through theories of self-esteem, personality, and, for example, motivation, sport and exercise psychologists have tended to view the self as a "thing" and "entity" that an individual "has" and that can be "found" "inside" someone's "head." Here, the self is variously depicted as something extremely personal; as coherent; as a preformed substratum possessing a more or less stable set of qualities and attributes; as a manifestation of an inner essence unmoored from culture; and as a innate substance, residing inside a person, that we can somehow grab hold of and place before our very eyes. As a result, the traditional concept of self within sport and exercise psychology suggests a certain "inwardness" or "interiority" that incorporates assumptions about the authentic, objective, invariant, and unitary status of selfhood detached from culture. It tends to promote a view of the self, either implicitly or explicitly, as existing internally within us, and objects in the world as existing externally, on the outside.

A narrative perspective, however, challenges and problematizes these ideas. For example, as Andrews (2000) contended, "the self" is not some monolithic invariant entity that springs from an individual's mind. Rather, stories "out there" within culture "are one of the primary means through which we constitute our very selves. . . . We become who we are through telling stories about our lives and living the stories we tell" (pp. 77–78). Likewise, Elliot (2005) argued that our selves are structured through narratives provided by culture and formed in relation to other people. As such, for example, individuals cannot be simply understood as having a fixed narrative self that is ontologically prior to their position in the social world. The self is not singular, but plural in its origins and subsequent formation. Moreover, noted Elliot, our selves are not things to be found inside a person (like a kernel within a nut shell) but rather are relational and inhere in the social interactions a person has with others. Therefore, together these views represent a radical shift in viewpoint since they run counter to traditional, deeply entrenched views of self within sport and exercise psychology as coterminous with and "belonging" to the individual person, residing inside him or her, and as a static entity we can somehow grab hold of and place before our very eyes.

Of course, the relationship between self and narrative is multifaceted and complex. For example, suggesting that selves are constituted through narratives provided by the cultures we live in and created in social relationships, the view of a "unified and real self inside us" still remains one of the central means by which many people justify themselves to both themselves and others. However, as Hall (1992) pointed out, should we feel that we do have a unified and real self, this is because we construct a comforting narrative of self about ourselves and appropriate already established ways of talking from Western culture that promote an individualistic self. Adding more complexity to the relationship between self and narrative, some narrative researchers suggest that the self *is* a narrative (see Smith & Sparkes, 2008b). Others, however, suggest that our selves cannot be reduced simply to the textual resources of narrative that culture supplies us. For instance, as Eakin (2008) argued, to claim selves are identical to narrative or that they are solely made though narratives would be a mistake, as it would deny any possible neurological, cognitive, and corporeal basis to our selves. Despite this complexity and the multifaceted nature of selves, he was quick to point out that narratives do play an important part in our construction of selves, but this process has largely been undervalued or ignored within psychology.

Interviewing: Some Challenges and Potential Problems

Narrative inquiry problematizes and poses a challenge for sport and exercise psychology in terms of interviewing. Qualitative research done by sport and exercise psychologists has tended to rely heavily on interviews to generate data (Brustand, 2008; Culver, Gilbert, & Trudel, 2003). Often, built into this reliance is the assumption or implicit claim that the narratives generated from interviews provide an analyst with a transparent window into personal experiences and/or a clear route into the "truth" of reported events. However, for various researchers (e.g., Gubrium & Holstein, 2008; Richardson, 2000; Ryba, 2008; Smith & Sparkes, 2009b) such assumptions are problematic. For example, to assume to be able to gain access to the real truth or private experience through narratives yielded from interviews is to commit to the view that we can establish contact with a reality independent of our interests, purposes, and languages used. Yet, as noted earlier, this view is problematic given that methods, like interviews, are not discovered or objective/neutral, but are developed in line with particular goals, values, and political/ideological commitments. Likewise, no matter how hard we try we cannot achieve theory-free observation or knowledge. To suggest one can gain unmediated access to the truth or personal experience through narrative is further problematic since, as Richardson (2000) articulated, "Language does not 'reflect' social reality, but produces meaning, creates social reality" (p. 928).

Another problem is that by focusing on the interiority of experience or searching for the truth, too much sport and exercise psychology research lacks a thoroughgoing sense of the social and culture, so that an interview and the narratives that it can yield seem to float in a social and cultural vacuum. For example, by focusing simply on the "inner experiences" of an athlete, a sport psychologist may ignore or push into the background the ways in which "inner experiences" are shaped by culture, including the narrative resources "out there" in culture people have access to. Thus, sport and exercise psychology is in danger of the "personalizing of cultur[e]" (Behar, 1996, p. 25) and producing research in which there is "an extraordinary absence of social context, social action, and social interaction" (Atkinson, 1997, p. 339). This is particularly problematic since any narrative as a form of communication is influenced by the cultural conventions of telling, the motivations of the teller, the audience, and the social context. As such, narratives should be analyzed also as a sociocultural phenomenon, not as simply the vehicle for personal experience.

It would seem, therefore, that narrative inquiry poses some interesting problems and challenges for sport and exercise psychology. With these in mind, along with all the above talk about narrative inquiry, let us now turn to an example of empirical work done within sport and exercise psychology.

Narrative Inquiry in Action: The Example of Flow

The flow experience has been of interest to sport psychologists for a number of years. Within this research Sparkes and Partington (2003) identified a number of tensions. One of these relates to the problem of defining just *what* flow actually is. Here, they noted that research in the search for what flow is continually highlights inconsistencies in both measurement and response. Thus different articulations of the flow experience between groups, sports, and individuals are seen as a problem when a researcher strives to find out just what flow really is.

In contrast, Sparkes and Partington (2003) drew on the work of Holstein and Gubrium (2000) and their notion of narrative practice to ask a different kind of question about the flow experience. That is, not *what* flow is, but *how* flow is constructed. In so doing, for them, movement experiences like flow, and descriptions of that experience do not exist in any transparent, linear, one-to-one, relationship. Rather, as the experience of movement is translated into language, to become shared with others, and to become the object of analysis by researchers, a process of construction and transformation takes place that is socially and culturally mediated. Accordingly, different articulations of the flow experience between groups, sports, and individuals are not seen as a problem but taken as a resource for understanding the artful construction of a specific movement-related experience.

To illustrate how a focus on narrative practice might add to our understanding of flow, Sparkes and Partington (2003) proceeded to describe *how* the flow experience was articulated within a university-based, white water canoeing club in southwest England. Their analysis of narrative practice in action highlighted *how* the language of flow as a storytelling activity was embedded within, and constrained by, the narrative resources available within the context of the canoeing club. Specifically, their findings revealed how the organization and structure of the club influenced *who* got to tell stories within it. That is, the hierarchical structure of the canoeing club, dominated by men, provided a framework for storytelling, in terms of who got to tell certain kinds of stories and who got to listen, as part of a process of identity construction and confirmation.

With regard to the process of storytelling within the canoe club, Sparkes and Partington (2003) argued that the telling of stories served a range of needs and was particularly important for both the construction and confirmation of a desired and acceptable identity, as well as for teaching newcomers about and reinforcing to those already in the club its cultural norms and values. Their interpretations of the stories they witnessed suggested that not only was the telling of stories an integral part of the canoe club culture, but certain people within the club were designated as central storytellers. That is, within the canoeing club as a social organization were those that "told" stories and those that "listened" to them. In the telling, the male leaders, otherwise known as "Gods," conveyed messages about the significance and organization of selected canoeing experiences and also provided an acceptable vocabulary for describing them. Further, by consistently telling stories about some experiences rather than others, they conveyed to the listeners which experiences were not only reportable, but deemed worthy of attention. By creating a particular rendition of an experience, these central reality definers within the canoe club showed what the component events were, how they were related, and what was important about them.

Furthermore, the acceptance of this differential right to tell and listen acted to maintain various identity claims within the group and reinforced particular relationships of domination and subordination. For example, in the act of telling the male leaders engaged in an ongoing process of remaking and confirming their reputations and identities as "Gods." By listening and responding to these stories in appropriate ways, other members of the club simultaneously confirmed their own identity and status in relation to that of the "Gods."

Importantly, while everyone in the canoe club had a story to tell not everyone was provided with the space or opportunity to voice their story in public. Some were, quite literally, silenced. This was particularly so with regard to the opportunities available for women within the club to tell their stories and the vocabulary deemed appropriate in the telling. For example, the epic and hero tales that dominated the canoe club were gendered in relation to specific forms of masculinity. This had a number of implications for identity construction and confirmation within the club that were most evident in the ability and willingness to acknowledge fear. The "Gods" in the club were expected to display an air of indifference toward risk taking and the possibilities of death. These men were skilled canoeists and due to their level of expertise expected to be able to control their performances. They did not need luck to survive. This bravado, the notion of controllability, and narrative silence surrounding fear, was displayed in the kinds of stories they told and the language they used.

In contrast, the women in the canoe club, while having limited access to the dominant themes associated with the epic and hero tales, were allowed to express fear, acknowledge a lack of control, and admit to luck in their stories about performance. They were also able to decline tasks that they defined as dangerous, an option that was not open to the males within the club. Clearly, the narrative silences within the stories told by the male members of the canoeing club had health implications with regard to their propensity to deny fear and take unnecessary risks. At the same time, the women had greater freedom within this storytelling process to acknowledge fear and to walk away from danger. However, this narrative freedom came at a cost, in that this limited the kind of identity the women could construct within the group and it maintained their low-status position in the canoeing hierarchy.

Having also considered the narrative structure of the canoeing club and examined in detail the stories of flow told within it, Sparkes and Partington (2003) concluded that telling a story about flow is socially and culturally mediated and a communicative and relational act. It is a performance that requires narrative skills in terms of, for example, the strategic selection of narrative topics, the use of particular metaphors, and the ability to work to a particular plot in a way that maintains dramatic tension. Within the white water canoeing club they focused on, the evidence suggests that both the form and the content of the stories told by its members were shaped and constrained by a number of narrative resources and auspices. Specifically, the male-dominated, hierarchical structure of the club provided a context that defined who got to tell selected stories and who got to listen to them. Those designated as central storytellers operated as critical reality definers and in choosing to tell stories about certain experiences rather than others, they conveyed to the listener which experiences within the club were deemed worthy of attention. These central storytellers also provided club members with an appropriate vocabulary to describe their experiences of flow. This vocabulary was then utilized within the structures provided by the epic and hero narratives that influenced what should be included, and excluded, in the tale being told.

In closing, Sparkes and Partington (2003) pointed out that in emphasizing the need to understand the reporting of experiences in sport as a form of narrative practice in terms of how this is accomplished, they were not seeking to analytically privilege this approach or to demean research that focuses on the *whats* of storytelling. Rather, Sparkes and Partington argued that a focus on the *hows* of flow adds a *complementary* dimension to understanding the complexity of this phenomenon in sport by, for example, explaining why descriptions of flow as a subjective experience can both be consistent within a given sports group and vary between individuals over time, and between different groups and subcultures. Thus, quantitative researchers who utilize questionnaires and qualitative researchers who subject interview data to a content analysis have an important role to play in exploring the *whats* of storytelling. Likewise, qualitative researchers interested in narrative forms of analyses have an equally important role to play in exploring the *hows* of interaction in sport. The two approaches complement each other and can be developed in tandem.

Conclusion and Future Directions

In this chapter, we have provided some thought about the nature of narrative inquiry and the potential it has for research in sport and exercise psychology. In closing we would now like to offer some reflections on but two of the many future directions that narrative inquiry might take.

First, although realist and scientific tales dominate sport and exercise psychology, as noted, the ways we can represent our research findings have grown to include a variety of tales and performance genres. These include poetic representations, ethnodrama, and autoethnography. However, with the enthusiastic rush toward experimentation for its own sake rather than in the more deliberate process of making informed, responsible, principled, and strategic decisions about the use of any given genre comes the danger of superficiality. Such unprincipled adoption would contribute to a fetishizing of form and run the risk of elevating style, or panache, over content. However, as Wolcott (1995) pointed out, no amount of style can cover for or substitute for a problem with focus. Certainly, style is necessary but it is not sufficient in and of itself. For Wolcott, a concern for wordsmithing should not take over, "so that style becomes a preoccupation, leading to 'slick description' instead of 'thick.' Efforts at good writing need to be coupled with having something worthwhile to say" (p. 218). We could not agree more.

Furthermore, when thinking about using new genres to represent the findings of narrative studies, researchers need to be honest with themselves about their abilities to work in different areas. For example, most sport and exercise psychologists do not possess the skills or have the experience to transform interview data subjected to a narrative analysis into a play. To do so might require a considerable investment of time by an individual researcher or, equally involve the investment of working collaboratively with scholars from other disciplines who do have the necessary skills. Not to recognize our limitations but to proceed none the less with experimental genres can lead to the production of clichéd, boring, apolitical, self-indulgent, and theoretically vacuous performance pieces that make little, if any, substantive contribution to the field, lacking as they do characteristics such as theoretical points, verisimilitude, evocation, fidelity, impact, and a connection with society and culture. Naïve attempts to pass off "bad" theater or poetic representation as "good" qualitative or narrative research is a high-risk strategy and should be challenged on all occasions. In short, as Richardson and St. Pierre (2005) emphasized, novel forms of inquiry and representation should be held "to high and difficult standards: mere novelty does not suffice" (p. 960). Again, we could not agree more.

Second, for narrative inquiry to develop within sport and exercise psychology, we need to resist the loose talk about narrative that is common these days. For example, when someone speaks for a few minutes during a research interview, the outcome is often now called "narrative" by some qualitative researchers. However, on close inspection these researchers are often not generating narratives or doing this kind of inquiry. Likewise, some researchers have been quick to appropriate the idea that narratives give us insights into private experiences of sport or exercise, and then only concentrate on the personal. Yet in so doing, narratives are reduced to the individual or "inside/interior" level. This means we lose sight of the ways personal experience is significantly shaped by society and culture via structures that lie outside the individual. Thus, future research should be systematically directed to both the personal *and* the sociocultural.

In closing, while we do not want to claim that narrative is or can do everything, we would suggest that narrative inquiry holds great potential for qualitative researchers within the field of sport and exercise psychology. Narrative plays a key role in people's lives and can be one among a number of viable ways of doing research in sport and exercise psychology. The stories that surround and envelop us, which are woven into the fabric of our research and applied landscapes, can enrich our understandings and are ripe with possibilities for inquiry.

References

Andrews, M. (2000). Introduction. In M. Andrews, S. Day Sclater, C. Squire, & A. Treacher (Eds.), *Lines of narrative* (pp. 77–80). London: Routledge.

Anshel, M., & Sutarso, T. (in press). Effect of a storyboarding technique on selected measures of fitness among university employees. *Research Quarterly for Exercise and Sport.*

Atkinson, P. (1997). Narrative turn or blind alley? *Qualitative Health Research, 7,* 325–343.

Atkinson, P., & Delamont, S. (2006). Editors' introduction. In P. Atkinson & S. Delamont (Eds.), *Narrative methods* (Vol. 1, pp. xviii–liii). London: Sage.

Behr, R. (1996). *The vulnerable observer.* Boston: Beacon.

Bochner, A. (2002). Perspectives on inquiry III: The moral of stories. In M. Knapp & J. Daley (Eds.), *The handbook of interpersonal communication* (3rd ed., pp. 73–101). London: Sage.

Brockmeier, J., & Carbaugh, D. (Eds.) 2001. *Narrative and identity.* Amsterdam: John Benjamins.

Brockmeier, J., & Harré, R. (2001). Narrative: Problems and promises of an alternative paradigm. In J. Brockmeier & D. Carbaugh (Eds.), *Narrative and identity* (pp. 39–58). Amsterdam: John Benjamins.

Bruner, J. (2002). *Making stories.* Cambridge, MA: Harvard University Press.

Brustand, J. (2008). Qualitative research approaches. In. T. Horn (Ed.), *Advances in sport psychology* (3rd ed., pp. 31–43). Champaign, IL: Human Kinetics.

Carless, D., & Douglas, K. (2009) "We haven't got a seat on the bus for you" or "All the seats are mine": Narratives and

career transition in professional golf. *Qualitative Research in Sport & Exercise, 1,* 53–68.

Clandinin, J., Pusher, D., & Orr, A. (2007). Navigating sites for narrative inquiry. *Journal of Teacher Education, 58,* 21–35.

Crossley, M. (2000). *Introducing narrative psychology.* Buckingham, UK: Open University Press.

Culver, D., Gilbert, W., & Trudel, P. (2003). A decade of qualitative research in sport psychology journals: 1990–1999. *The Sport Psychologist, 17,* 1–15.

Day Sclater, S. (2003) What is the subject? *Narrative Inquiry, 13,* 317–330.

Denison, J., & Winslade, J. (2006). Understanding problematic sporting stories: Narrative therapy and applied sport psychology. *Junctures, 6,* 99–105.

Douglas, K. (in-press). Storying my self: Negotiating a relational identity in professional sport. *Qualitative Research in Sport & Exercise.*

Douglas, K., & Carless, D. (2008). Using stories in coach education. *International Journal of Sports Science and Coaching, 3,* 33–49.

Eakin, P. (2008). *Living autobiographically.* London: Cornell University Press.,

Elliott, J. (2005). *Using narrative in social research.* London: Sage.

Frank, A. (1995). *The wounded storyteller.* Chicago: University of Chicago Press.

Frank, A. (2006). Health stories as connectors and subjectifiers. *Health, 10,* 421–440.

Freeman, M. (2003). From substance to story: Narrative, identity, and the reconstruction of self. In J. Brockmeier & D. Carbaugh (Eds.), *Narrative and identity* (pp. 283–298). Amsterdam: John Benjamins.

Freeman, M. (2003). Identity and difference in narrative inquiry: A commentary. *Narrative Inquiry, 13*, 331–346.

Gubrium, J., & Holstein, J. (2008). *Analysing narrative reality*. London: Sage.

Hall, S. (1992). The question of cultural identity. In S. Hall, D. Hell, & T. Mc-Grew (Eds.), *Modernity and its futures* (pp. 342–374). Cambridge: Polity.

Hazelrigg, L. (1995). *Cultures of nature*. Tallahassee: Florida State University Press.

Holloway, I., & Freshwater, D. (2007). *Narrative research in nursing*. Oxford: Blackwell.

Holstein, J., & Gubrium, J. (2000). *The self we live by*. New York: Oxford University Press.

Jowett, S. (2008). Outgrowing the familial coach-athlete relationship. *International Journal of Sport Psychology, 39*, 20–40.

Jowett, S., & Frost, T. (2007). Race/Ethnicity in the all male coach-athlete relationship: Black footballers' narratives. *International Journal of Sport and Exercise Psychology, 3*, 255–269.

Leahy, T., & Harrigan, R., (2006). Using narrative therapy in sport psychology: Application to healthy body image among elite young women athletes. *The Sport Psychologist, 20*, 480–494

MacIntyre, A. (1981). *After virtue*. Notre Dame, IN: Notre Dame University Press.

McAdams, D. (1993). *The stories we live by*. New York: Morrow.

McAdams, D. (2006). The role of narrative in personal psychology today. *Narrative Inquiry, 16*, 11–18.

Parker, I. (2005). *Qualitative psychology*. Buckingham, UK: Open University Press.

Phoenix, C., & Howe, A. (in press). Working the when, where, and who of

social context: The case of a traumatic injury narrative. *Qualitative Research in Psychology*.

Phoenix, C., Smith, B., & Sparkes, A. (2007). Experiences and expectations of biographical time among young athletes: A life course perspective. *Time & Society, 16*, 231–252.

Pinnegar, S., & Daynes, G. (2007). Locating narrative inquiry historically. In D. J. Clandinin (Ed.), *Handbook of narrative inquiry* (pp. 3–34). London: Sage.

Randall, W., & McKim, E. (2008). *Reading our lives*. Oxford: Oxford University Press.

Richardson, L. (2000). Writing: A method of inquiry. In N. K. Denzin, & Y. S. Lincoln (Eds.), *Handbook of qualitative research* (2nd ed., pp. 923–948). London: Sage.

Richardson, L., & St. Pierre, E. (2005). Writing: A method of inquiry. In N. K. Denzin & Y. S. Lincoln (Eds.), *Handbook of qualitative research* (3rd ed., pp. 959–978). London: Sage.

Riessman, C. (2008). *Narrative methods for the human sciences*. London: Sage.

Ryba, T.V. (2008). Researching children in sport: Methodological reflections. *Journal of Applied Sport Psychology, 20*, 334–348.

Sarbin, T. (Ed.). (1986). *Narrative psychology*. New York: Praeger.

Smith, B. (1999). The Abyss: Exploring depression through a narrative of the self. *Qualitative Inquiry, 5*, 264–279.

Smith, B. (2007). The state of the art in narrative inquiry: Some reflections. *Narrative Inquiry, 17*, 391–398.

Smith, B., & Sparkes, A. (2005). Men, sport, spinal cord injury, and narratives of hope. *Social Science and Medicine, 61*, 1095–1105.

Smith, B., & Sparkes, A. (2006). Narrative inquiry in psychology: Exploring the tensions within. *Qualitative Research in Psychology, 3*, 169–192.

Smith, B., & Sparkes, A. (2008a). Changing bodies, changing narratives and the consequences of tellability: A case study of becoming disabled through sport. *Sociology of Health and Illness, 30*, 217–236.

Smith, B., & Sparkes, A. C. (2008b). Contrasting perspectives on narrating selves and identities: An invitation to dialogue. *Qualitative Research, 8*, 5–35.

Smith, B., & Sparkes, A. (2009a). Narrative inquiry in sport and exercise psychology: What can it mean, and why might we do it? *Psychology of Sport and Exercise, 10*, 1–11.

Smith, B., & Sparkes, A. (2009b). Narrative analysis and sport and exercise psychology: Understanding stories in diverse ways. *Psychology of Sport and Exercise, 10*, 279–288.

Smith, J. (1993). *After the demise of empiricism: The problem of judging social and educational inquiry.* Norwood, NJ: Ablex.

Smith, J. (in-press). Judging research quality: From certainty to contingency. *Qualitative Research in Sport & Exercise.*

Smith, J., & Deemer, D. (2000). The problem of criteria in the age of relativism. In N. K. Denzin & Y. S. Lincoln (Eds.), *Handbook of qualitative research* (2nd ed., pp. 877–896). London: Sage.

Smith, J., & Hodkinson, P. (2005). Relativism, criteria, and politics. In N. K. Denzin, & Y. S. Lincoln (Eds.), *Handbook of qualitative research* (3rd ed., pp. 915–932). London: Sage.

Sparkes, A. (1998). Validity in qualitative inquiry and the problem of criteria: Implications for sport psychology. *The Sport Psychologist, 12*, 363–386.

Sparkes, A. (2002). *Telling tales in sport and physical activity: A qualitative journey.* Champaign, IL: Human Kinetics Press.

Sparkes, A. C. (2003). From performance to impairment: A patchwork of embodied memories. In J. Evans, B. Davies, & J. Wright (Eds.), *Body knowledge and control* (pp. 157–172). London: Routledge.

Sparkes, A., & Partington, S. (1993). Narrative practice and its potential contri-

bution to sport psychology: The example of flow. *The Sport Psychologist, 17*, 292–317.

Sparkes, A., & Smith, B. (2003). Men, sport, spinal cord injury and narrative time. *Qualitative Research, 3*, 295–320.

Sparkes, A., & Smith, B. (2008a). Men, spinal cord injury, memories, and the narrative performance of pain. *Disability & Society, 23*, 679–690.

Sparkes, A., & Smith, B. (2008b). Narrative constructionist inquiry. In J. Holstein & J. Gubrium (Eds.), *Handbook of constructionist research* (pp. 295–314). London: Guilford.

Sparkes, A., & Smith, B. (in press). Judging the quality of qualitative inquiry: Criteriology and relativism in action. *Psychology of Sport and Exercise.*

Stelter, R. (2007). Coaching: A process of personal and social meaning making. *International Coaching Psychology Review, 2*, 191–201.

Wolcott, H. (1995). *The art of fieldwork.* London: Sage.

5

CRITICALLY ENGAGING WITH SPORT PSYCHOLOGY ETHICS THROUGH CULTURAL STUDIES: FOUR COMMITMENTS

Leslee A. Fisher and Allison Daniel Anders

CHAPTER SUMMARY

Could an engagement with cultural studies' ethics play a role in the ethics of sport psychology? That is the central question we address in this chapter. We explore this question through an analysis of particular political, moral, and ethical preferences in cultural studies as well as ethics related to sport psychology. First, we engage with the cultural sport psychology challenge to mainstream sport/exercise psychology discourse. Next, we include a review of the ethical guidelines that govern the practice of applied sport psychology according to the Association for Applied Sport Psychology (AASP, 2009). We then provide a critical overview of cultural studies scholarship related to such situated ethical considerations. Implicit in both reviews is the examination of power and social justice. Integrated within each section are arguments related to how the cultural turn could help us make more central the critical examination of moral aspects of sport psychology practice. We base our analysis on four commitments we make in our work.[1]

Critically Engaging with Sport Psychology Ethics through Cultural Studies

What role could an engagement with cultural studies' ethics play in the ethics of sport psychology? As Kellner (2008) suggested, some cultural studies theorists like bell hooks (1991, 1994) have integrated concerns about race, class, and gender with ethical values in their work. Other cultural studies theorists have also represented and produced discourses that challenge the hegemony of market values and the ideologies and media that perpetuate them. Scholars in cultural studies position preferences through discourses to challenge the status quo. Using research traditions that critique the domination of ideologies, which support capitalist society and the material, political, and social stratification that accompanies it, many critique the manifestations and consequences of physical and symbolic vio-lence (Bourdieu, 1977) that targeted[2] groups suffer. As such, the navigation of research positions in cultural studies—which are po-litical and moral—are qualitatively different from ethics as an area of study in disciplines like psychology, philosophy, political theory, and sport psychology. Whereas ethics may *precede* an analysis of power and discourse in the above mentioned disciplines, in cultural studies power and discourse are always already situated culturally, historically, and politically (Althusser, 1971; Heidegger, 1927/2008). Ethics is situated as well. This situatedness adjoins debates about ethics in cultural studies in ways that it does not in psychology, phi-losophy, political theory, and sport psychology.

The Cultural Sport Psychology Challenge

Fisher, Roper, and Butryn (in press), among others (see Ryba, 2009, for example), recently took up the challenge of engaging cultural studies with the discipline of sport psychology in an introductory chapter of a new book titled *Cultural Sport Psychology* by Schinke and Hanrahan (2009). Fisher and colleagues described a point of view the editors called "the cultural studies perspective" as against a "sport psychology perspective" that was also included in the intro-ductory section (see Peters & Williams, 2009; Schinke & Hanrahan, 2009, p.vii). Fisher and colleagues endeavored to integrate cultural studies and sport psychology in six areas with the use of postmodern theory and a critique of the theories and methods, typical research questions, and dominant underpinnings of "traditional" sport psy-chology. They also recommended a new way of looking at sport psy-chology personality research from a position that recognizes con-structions and locations of identity, particularly examining how identities develop with relational power matrices.

This ideal reconstruction and envisioning of sport psychology as *cultural sport psychology* (CSP) had the following emphases:

A focus on athlete identities as multiple, fragmented, and de-pendent upon location rather than fixed or unchangeable; a choice of academic methods and theories based on an intellec-tual sensibility revolving around a certain theoretical orienta-tion or critical stance versus strict interdisciplinary boundaries; an emphasis on seeing the developing athlete in a web of power dynamics and relationships that advantage some selves while disadvantaging others; an interrogation of the institution of sport and how and when it has influenced athlete identities; a critical examination of the politics of race and class and how they affect athletes and consultants; an addressing of embedded politics and unacknowledged contributions in sport related to potentially exploitative relationships and damaging long-term consequences for health. (Fisher et al., 2009, p. 30)

Expanding upon their earlier stance (Fisher, Butryn, & Butryn, 2003; Fisher et al., 2005), Fisher and colleagues (2009) also examined privilege and how it related to the practice of sport psychology. Borrowing from Heldke and O'Connor (2004), they defined privilege as part of an interlocking system of oppression,[3] privilege, and resistance that includes three major tenets: "(a) oppression is most powerfully defined as the systematic and unfair marginalization of some members of a society; (b) privilege is the flipside of oppression, in that if some members are marginalized, then other members are given an unfair advantage; and (c) oppression (and privilege) can be resisted against" (Fisher et al., 2009, p. 7). Following Heldke and O'Connor (2004), they also believed that the most effective way to create change in any oppressive system—organized sport being one—was to educate stakeholders about how "social change requires collective action working *against* existing *systems*" (p.vii, as cited in Fisher et al., 2009, p. 7).

The ethical ramifications of envisioning oppression, privilege, and resistance this way for sport psychology scholars are numerous. For example, Fisher and colleagues (2009) suggested that research theories and methods in sport psychology could include a critical intellectual sensibility toward athlete oppression, privilege, and resistance. Multiple theories such as postmodern theory, critical race theory, and queer theory could be coupled with multiple methodologies (e.g., autoethnography, critical ethnography, postcritical ethnography, semi-structured interview studies) to examine the myriad of ways that athlete identities are fragmented, multiple, and dependent upon location in matrices of power as opposed to being framed as unchangeable, fixed, or essentialized. Therefore, research questions informed by a cultural sport psychology and focused on oppression/privilege/resistance could include: How/in what ways are athletes *both oppressed and privileged* at the same time? In *which* sports are privilege and oppression occurring and *why?* Who is *resisting* oppression/

who is resisting privilege/in what ways? Are athletes and consultants even *aware* of their own oppression and privilege? Why/why
not/when? Who does it serve if they are *not* aware of it? And, most
important, are sport psychology theorists, practitioners, and athletes
interested in *taking action* against their own oppression and privilege? (Fisher et al., 2009). Like the interrogation of sport that is necessary, a concomitant interrogation of sport psychology ethics and
practices and their embedded policies/politics/contributions (although
perhaps unconscious) to athlete exploitation is also critical to cultural
studies-informed sport psychology scholarship. This is because focusing on those who embody and reproduce privilege enables us to
understand that those with privilege consciously create cosmologies
or a nexus of mutually reinforcing ideologies[4] — including those related to sport psychology ethics — to sustain arguments for entitlement, the embodiment of privilege, and the reproduction of privilege.

"Traditional" Sport Psychology Ethical Considerations

A recent special edition of *Athletic Insight* — the online journal of sport
psychology — focused entirely on ethics in the field of sport psychology (*Athletic Insight*, December, 2008, Vol. 10, Issue 4). Authors highlighted ethical issues related to multiple role relationships such as
sport psychology consultant-coach/teacher/researcher (Watson &
Clement, 2008), working with differences in college student-athletes
(Loughran & Etzel, 2008), consulting with Olympic athletes and
coaches (Werthner & Coleman, 2008), and professional boxers
(Lane, 2008). However, ethical principles and standards were first
developed and adopted for the Association for Applied Sport Psychology (AASP; previously AAASP) during the 1990s. They were
almost entirely based on the American Psychological Association's
(APA) ethical principles and code of conduct for psychologists (see
American Psychologist, 1992, *V47*, #12, pp. 1597–1611).

    As AASP's website (http://www.appliedsportpsych.org/about/
ethics) suggests, AASP is committed to "the professionalization and
advancement of the field of sport and exercise psychology. Consistent with this commitment, all AASP members must recognize their
work-related professional privileges and associated responsibilities. . . . The AASP Ethical Code is an important component of our
professional responsibilities. AASP members and visitors should become familiar with the Code."

    The above quote focuses on how practitioners should be concerned with the *privileges* that are associated with the profession as well as their *responsibilities* to the profession. *Privileges* are said to "originate in society's recognition of AASP members as trained persons possessing specialized knowledge and skills," whose responsibilities stem from "society's belief that AASP members will (a) self-regulate our work-related conduct; (b) do no harm to people we work with and serve; (c) protect the dignity and welfare of people we work with and serve; and (d) respect the autonomy and independence of people we work with and serve" (AASP, 2009). Inherent in such a definition is the "hope" that AASP's code of ethical principles serves as a "set of self-regulatory guidelines"; these guidelines also serve as a practice/legal standard for which "a reasonable person" would hold practitioners (and their behavior) accountable to (AASP, 2009). Further, membership in AASP is said to automatically commit members to adherence to the code.

There are 6 AASP general ethical principles and 25 standards. The six general principles are: (a) *competence*; (b) *integrity*; (c) *professional and scientific responsibility*; (d) *respect for people's rights and dignity*; (e) *concern for others' welfare*; and (f) *social responsibility*. The 25 standards cut across all sport psychology practitioner roles, communications, and interactions and can be found on AASP's website (AASP, 2009). The six general principles are described next as they relate to scholarly work.

Principle A: Competence

Recognizing the boundaries of one's competence — what one ethically can and cannot do — is the emphasis for Principle A. As the code states:

> AASP members maintain the highest standards of competence in their work. They recognize the *boundaries* of their professional competencies and the limitations of their expertise . . . AASP members make appropriate use of scientific, professional, technical, and administrative resources. AASP members are cognizant of the fact that the competencies required in serving, teaching, and/or studying groups of people vary with the distinctive characteristics of those groups. (AASP, 2009; emphasis added)

Of interest to those of us who are informed by a cultural sport psychology (Fisher et al., 2009; Ryba & Wright, 2005; Schinke & Hanrahan, 2009) are questions such as: *Which* knowledges is the code speaking about? In other words, *which* professional knowledges are *privileged* over which other professional knowledges? What does "making appropriate use of scientific, professional, technical and administrative resources" mean? For example, is it enough of an ethical commitment to have had the "appropriate" educational training without a concomitant examination of one's own value system related to oppression/privilege/resistance? And, where are/who determines the *boundaries* of one's competence? These and other similar questions are explored further in our four commitments presented later in the chapter.

Principle B: Integrity

AASP's second ethical principle has to do with being fair and honest, and with role relationships such as when one is both a researcher and a practitioner. As the principle reads:

> AASP members promote integrity in the science, teaching, and practice of their profession. In these activities AASP members are *honest and fair*. When describing or reporting their qualifications, services, products, fees, research, or teaching, they do not make statements that are false, misleading, or deceptive. They clarify for relevant parties the roles they are performing and the obligations they adopt. They function appropriately in accordance with those roles and obligations. AASP members avoid improper and potentially harmful *dual relationships*. (AASP, 2009; emphasis added)

As previously mentioned, sport psychology dual relationships and their ethical implications were most recently described by Watson and Clemente (2008). Several potential dual-relationships exist — including sport psychology researcher-practitioner and sport psychology researcher-professor — and were reviewed with both the pros and cons highlighted. In the coach-sport psychology practitioner section, for example, Watson and Clemente suggested that one of the disadvantages in such a multiple-role relationship is the potential for "excessive emotional involvement" (on the practitioner's side) that "may hinder his/her ability to remain calm and objective while performing psychological work" (p. 5). We believe that their analysis is incomplete and potentially dangerous.

For example, those of us committed to a scholarly cultural sport psychology are immediately suspicious of terms such as being "honest and fair," "excessive[ly] emotional[ly] involved," and "objective" in sport psychology research and practice. We reject the notion that there is a universal acceptance of what these terms mean and would push Watson and Clemente to unpack them. For instance, consider that the word *objective* is a culturally informed term that appears to mean different things in different cultures (Schinke & Hanrahan, 2009). Further, we contend that emotional connection is central to the cultural studies-informed sport psychology commitments we make later.

We believe that having an ethical standard of being "objective" and not emotionally involved as Watson and Clemente (2008) suggested may *not* be in the best interest of our research participants or our clients.

Principle C: Professional and Scientific Responsibility

AASP's third general ethical principle relates to professional conduct. As it states:

> AASP members are responsible for safeguarding the public and AASP from members who are deficient in ethical conduct. They uphold professional standards of conduct and accept appropriate responsibility for their behavior. AASP members consult with, refer to, or cooperate with other professionals and institutions to the extent needed to serve the best interests of the recipients of their services. *AASP members' moral standards and conduct are personal matters* to the same degree as is true for any other person, except as their conduct may compromise their professional responsibilities or reduce the public's trust in the profession and the organization. AASP members are concerned about the ethical compliance of their colleagues' scientific and professional conduct. When appropriate, they consult with colleagues in order to prevent, avoid, or terminate unethical conduct. (AASP, 2009; emphasis added)

We are fascinated by the italicized sentence, "*AASP members' moral standards and conduct are personal matters.*" This should not be surprising, however, since most of our foundational theories about justice are individualistic. As Young (2004) suggested, such a model privileges the "authentic" self as "autonomous, unified, free, and self-made, standing apart from history and affiliations, choosing its life plan for itself" (p. 42).

Cultural theorists, postmodernists, and post-structuralists challenge this conception of an autonomous self that functions outside political, social, and cultural histories. Framing the self instead as that which does not exist pre-linguistically, these theorists argue that issues like "morality" are contextualized through language. *Language* may mean words, text, or discourse (Gee, 1996) and this language is always already situated by political, social, and cultural histories. These histories are not without power and affect the material and the social through institutions and practices (Scott, 1990).

As such, the "personal" is laden with consequences of language and position. Personal choices for cultural theorists about morality are always already embedded in these discursive relationships. As we look at sport psychology praxis, we echo Young's (2004) argument that oppression is rooted in the often unconscious everyday assumptions, habits, symbols and norms within *institutional* rules that are carried out by well-meaning people. Further, Young suggested that people usually do not understand that they themselves are the "agents" of oppression.

Since relationships of language enact relationships of privilege, framing the multidirectionality of both power and discourse is essential. Referencing Michel Foucault, Young (2004) cautions against binary conceptions of power (e.g., polemic, either/or, conceptions of power that posit one either has power or one does not) toward work that moves to the analysis of the exercise of power. Foucault (1990) framed power as that which "comes from below; that is, there is no binary and all-encompassing opposition between rulers and ruled at the root of power relations, and serving as a general matrix" (p. 94). He argued, "power is exercised from innumerable points in the interplay of nonegalitarian and mobile relations" (p. 94). For sport psychology researchers we caution against reifying those conceptions of self that extract one's morality or professional commitments from the institutions and practices in which they live.

Principle D: Respect for People's Rights and Dignity

The fourth general ethical principle focuses on fundamental rights for all people. It reads:

AASP members accord appropriate respect to the fundamental rights, dignity, and worth of all people. They respect the rights of individuals to privacy, confidentiality, self-determination, and autonomy, mindful that legal and other obligations may lead to inconsistency and conflict with the exercise of these rights. *AASP members are aware of cultural, individual, and role differences, including those due to age, gender, race, ethnicity, national origin, religion, sexual orientation, disability, language, and socioeconomic status.* AASP members try to eliminate the effect on their work of biases based on those factors, and they do not knowingly participate in or condone unfair discriminatory practices. (AASP, 2009; emphasis added)

We wonder: Is it enough to be "aware of" cultural differences as a scholar? Does "awareness" alone equate with true understanding? How does an "awareness" of cultural differences translate into research paradigms? We believe that social justice involves respect, reproduction, and even celebration of group differences without oppression (Young, 2004). Such a stance or positionality requires critical self-examination prior to conceptualization of research or scholarly activity.

Principle E: Concern for Others' Welfare

The fifth ethical principles relates to clients' welfare. As it says:

AASP members seek to contribute to the welfare of those with whom they interact professionally. When conflicts occur among AASP members' obligations or concerns, they attempt to resolve those conflicts and to perform those roles in a responsible fashion that avoids or minimizes harm. AASP members *are sensitive to real and ascribed differences in power between themselves and others.* They do not exploit or mislead other people during or after professional relationships. (AASP, 2009; emphasis added)

Again, we believe it is necessary but not sufficient for sport psychology scholars to be "sensitive to" power differentials between themselves and those with whom they co-construct their research. A more comprehensive and thorough understanding of power dynamics inherent in sport studies research is required. For example, Fisher et al. (2009) described how power is a concept frequently interrogated in cultural studies and sport sociology but until recently not so much in sport psychology. Sport psychology researchers are just beginning to devote serious attention to the role that power/power dynamics play within applied sport settings (Fasting, Brackenridge, & Walseth, 2007; Fisher et al., 2009; Roper, 2008; Schinke & Hanrahan, 2009; Schinke et al., 2008). Fisher and colleagues (2009) suggested that privilege is also related to power in important and complex ways. For example, power dynamics not only affect athletes in sport contexts but researchers and consultants as well. As Fisher and colleagues (2009) noted in their previous work (Fisher et al., 2003), issues of race, class, gender, and sexual orientation should be "viewed not as simple categories, but as relations of power, as spaces where individuals negotiate for greater agency within the existing power structure" (p. 396). This included sport psychology scholars who, they argued, should be cultural studies-informed, able to identify and "acknowledge gender-biased and homophobic behaviors within the hyper-masculine structure of many sports, as well as to confront ways that [they], whether male or female, have the potential to be both perpetrators and victims of discriminatory practices themselves" (p. 393).

Recently, at their national conference AASP professionals were challenged by Celia Brackenridge (2008) to incorporate such an analysis of the ways that they themselves might be complicit in athlete abuse both through research and consultancy. This type of understanding via critical self- and scholarly analysis could provide a deeper and more meaningful interrogation of relations of power and the impact they have on researchers, athletes, and consultants.

Principle F: Social Responsibility

The last principle relates to community ethics. As it states:

> AASP members are aware of their professional and scientific responsibilities to the community and the society in which they work and live. They apply and make public their knowledge in order to contribute to human welfare. When undertaking research, *AASP members strive to advance human welfare and their profession while always protecting the rights of the participants*. AASP members try to avoid misuse of their work, and they comply with the law. (AASP, 2009; emphasis added)

In this section, we have explored the AASP ethical code and made some suggestions related to how a cultural sport psychology could help sport psychology researchers incorporate an analysis of power and a concern for social justice. What is described next is a more explicit discussion of the implicit relationship between ethics and cultural studies. Following are four commitments we make related to a cultural studies-informed sport psychology research ethic.

Cultural Studies: Ethics Implicit

As previously mentioned, cultural studies scholars re-represent[5] and produce discourses that challenge the hegemony of exploitive market systems. They also critically examine the ideologies, media, and institutions — religious, political, social, and sport — that perpetuate them. In cultural studies scholarship, navigating political and moral preferences is qualitatively different from ethics as an area of study in disciplines like sport psychology. Whereas a discourse on ethics in sport psychology may precede a discussion on moral imperatives, ethics through discourse is always already situated in cultural studies scholarship. This situatedness adjoins debates about ethics in cultural studies in ways that it does not in sport psychology, until now.

Cultural studies scholarship includes research and theory on power, discourse, and representation. For some scholars, the work focuses on the study of popular culture, including sport. However, historically, cultural theorists engaged Marxism and neo-Marxism confronting the material and advocating for commitments to social justice. They critiqued inequities, structures, and the discourses that perpetuated them, making the ethics of and moral commitments in cultural studies work both implicit and explicit. As cultural studies scholarship continues to flourish across critical, feminist, postcolonial, and post-structuralist work, scholars frame everyday practices in discourse, codes, and signs as a way to interrogate relationships of power (Baudrillard, 1983; Foucault, 1995; deCerteau, 2002). Together, we agree with cultural theorist Zylinska's (2005) argument that such investments, among other commitments in cultural studies, constitute an ethics of cultural studies from which we believe scholars in sport psychology can benefit.

Cultural studies scholars address the embodiment of experience, the violence of inequity, the institutionalization of power and discourse, and the re-representation of the political. Similarly, our interests cradle faithfully a commitment to reducing suffering — psychological, physical, and social — and to confronting through practice institutions and discourses that perpetrate violence against the security and dignity of being. This moral position and ontological understanding rests easily within cultural studies scholarship and in some ways the newly emerging cultural sport psychology scholarship. To work on research that addresses issues of suffering and confronts the failures of civil and political rights (that neo-liberal and neo-conservatives splinter from economic, social, and cultural rights) intones an implicit commitment toward re-representing inequities, transgressing dominant discourses, and reducing suffering.

Such an orientation in cultural studies scholarship may not exist outside our or other scholars' ontological experiences, for the experience of being is always already situated. Moral and ethical commitments in experience emerge intertextually across language — words, text, or discourse — and the enactment of discourse in institutions and practices. For those scholars who understand the discursive turn (Laclau & Mouffe, 1985) as constitutive, ethics exists within the discursive meanings of lived experience. Therefore, research or academic queries become problematic if the role of discourse is not acknowledged. When discourse instantiates social relations and social relations are imbued with power, and cultural studies scholars interrogate power such as hegemony, a discussion of ethics presupposes a positioning of ethics within discursive experience and practices.

Work in cultural studies, much like work with narrative, provides understanding of experience, welcomes tensions that emerge across scholarship, reshapes discourse, and disrupts with research in the particular (Abu-Lughod, 1991; Foucault; 1990; Noblit, 1999). In cultural studies scholarship — and in some emerging cultural sport psychology scholarship — theorists, educators, and activists who work for social justice use research, narrative, curricula, and pedagogy to produce a specific kind of culture. That culture often emphasizes, among other things, the deconstruction of institutionalized oppressions. Cultural studies provides scholars with the opportunity to interrogate the status quo, re-represent dissonant performances, and use detournement-to turn a perspective through a new representation (Debord, 1995) — to challenge claims that reify, for example, neo-conservative ideology.[6] The question remains whether future sport psychology scholars will take up this use of cultural studies theories and methods.

As previously mentioned, the focus of much cultural studies scholarship is on those structures, discourses, and embodiments that reproduce privilege. This work enables us to understand that those with privilege consciously create cosmologies or a nexus of mutually reinforcing ideologies[7] to sustain arguments for entitlement, the embodiment of privilege, and the reproduction of privilege. Such cosmologies order justifications for privilege or the redirection of challenges to privilege. Manifestations of privilege include affluence, able-bodiedness, whiteness, heterosexism, patriarchy, and economic and cultural imperialism. One way to challenge the status quo, specifically inequities between privileged and targeted individuals and groups, is to cultivate the production of a culture that promotes advocacy and action for social justice through scholarship and reflexive and participatory research in the particular.

Cultural theorist Paul Willis (1977) in his groundbreaking ethnographic work, *Learning to Labor*, reminded us that culture is produced as well as consumed: "there are deep disjunctions and desperate tensions within social and cultural reproduction. Social agents are not passive bearers of ideology, but active appropriators who reproduce existing structures only through struggle, contestation and a partial penetration of those structures" (p. 175). This activity, though saturated by market effects and consumer media, harnesses the potential to evoke change. This change via cultural studies scholarship often leads to work toward economic, social, cultural, and racial justice and is imbued with a moral imperative.

As Zylinska (2005) mused, the engagement with ethical issues in cultural studies — and we argue by extension in a cultural sport psychology — is ceaseless as absolute understandings are an impossibility. She posited that "the ethical moment in cultural studies arises out of an encounter with incalculable difference" (p. 34). To frame the ceaselessness of consideration, in this chapter, we present four commitments that we envisage as imbued ethics in a cultural sport psychology: (1) a commitment to generative meanings of violence and suffering among targeted groups and individuals; (2) a commitment to working in the particular; (3) a commitment to the intersectionality of identity; and (4) a commitment to arduous, grace-full, and sanctioned re-representations (Anders & Diem, 2008) in theoretical and empirical work. All of these commitments require recurrent unfolding.

Four Ethical Commitments in a Cultural Sport Psychology

Commitment #1: Meaning in violence and suffering

Stuart Hall (1996) named the work in cultural studies as a place to generate meaning about the antihumaneness of society: "The work that cultural studies has to do is to mobilize everything that it can find in terms of intellectual resources in order to understand what keeps making the lives we live, and the societies we live in, profoundly and deeply antihumane in their capacity to live with difference" (p. 343). Often, in the place where privilege attacks difference, bodies bleed. By extension, we believe an argument could be made that one context in which this rings particularly true is organized sport.

In the moments of violent assault, being is not performance but a body politic without freedom from agony or violation. For although discursive, institutional, and corporal assault may nest in cultural scripts — imperial colonization, economic exploitation, male domination, white supremacy — the moments of violation, the visceral blast to the body and shattering of security do not. In cultural studies, metaphors often position new understandings (Noblit, 1999). However, Fine, Tuck, and Zeller-Berkman (2007) warned us that some things cannot "serve as metaphor" (p. 495) when one undertakes the pursuit of understanding violence and suffering. For us the visceral blast to the body is not a metaphor. Such ripping violence ought to shout from stomach to throat, not toggle about under headings of "oppression" or "imperialism" or dally only in the rhetoric of discourse. On the sport field, on the court, and along the course, scholars ought to re-represent the fracturing of bodies and spirit in the terms and descriptions that wield coherence for the athlete or the abused, because the moment of injury is not "simulation" (Baudrillard, 1983).

A recent article on boxing (Lane, 2008) in the aforementioned *Athletic Insight* online journal issue devoted entirely to sport psychology ethics serves as a perfect illustration of how corporal assault nests in sport (and sport psychology) cultural scripts. In it, Lane — a former boxer and current sport psychology consultant — tried to explain why it is ethically justifiable to work as a sport psychology consultant with boxers whose primary goal is to injure their opponents. Lane relied on being an "insider" in his research/practice as a former boxer. Because of this, however, his acceptance of boxing's dominant cultural scripts related to masculinity, the "sport ethic," economic exploitation, male domination, and ideas related to the appropriateness of violence go unquestioned.

In fact, Lane justified sport psychology consultants' work with boxers—literally the promotion of bodily violence—by arguing that there is a "subtly different" mindset that a boxer must have to justify his use of bodily force; sport psychology consultants can, therefore, help a boxer reframe his behavior from violence to just "good" sport strategy. While Lane recognized that such promotion of the use of bodily force would be legally prosecutable in other contexts (e.g., "a boxer can kill his/her opponent as part of competition," p. 2), he suggested that what is "ethically more acceptable" is for sport psychology consultants to help "a boxer, therefore . . . be prepared to inflict injury on their opponent and show no mercy doing so" (p. 3). In this way, consultants could help a boxer reframe intent to injure to not "letting his opponent control the tempo of the game" (p. 4). Further, Lane stated: "In boxing . . . seeing an opponent wince after receiving a body punch acts in a motivating way, and boxers who allow their opponent time to recover are not likely to be successful. Boxers must capitalize on weaknesses of their opponents and any sign of weakness is indicative that victory is possible" (p.4). These moments of purposeful violation and visceral blasts to the body are, therefore, reframed as acceptable and the status quo in boxing.

Although such perpetration of sport violence may evoke cultural scripts of masculinity and the "sport ethic," for example, and at times even the responses, the moment of bodily assault annihilates words. A boxer's (or ice hockey player's or rugby player's) trauma cannot be controlled—when a (masculinity) script demands the damming of tears in the name of social propriety and instead against will, the body convulses against all coded performance, ribs crack against held breath and tears fall forth without bidding, scripted pages fall away from the scene if only momentarily and only the surviving or dying (visceral) breath remains. As sport psychology scholars and researchers like Lane engage in work that strives to understand violent experiences in sport, in culture, in politics, and in histories of generational suffering, as they work toward the production of institutions, practices, and discourse that celebrate the security and dignity of being, in their re-representations the words they use only, therefore, approximate what scripts and codes have failed to name.

Commitment #2: Working in the particular

Honoring the particular is important if researchers are interested in and paramount if they are committed to challenging grand narratives, dominant discourses, and the status quo. If the particular is not considered—either a particular story amidst grand narratives, or a particular experience by an always already culturally and historically situated individual—if the particular is named in these cases only as "different" or "an exception," researchers in the academy risk re-inscribing the dynamics of power already present. This re-inscription and re-representation of power is challenged on myriad fronts in cultural studies scholarship and could be in a cultural sport psychology scholarship as well. Lila Abu-Lughod (1991) provides a way for scholars and, in particular, qualitative researchers to navigate the re-inscription of power in research methodology. She argued that "one powerful tool for unsettling the culture concept and subverting the process of 'othering' it entails is to write 'ethnographies of the particular'" (p. 149). Abu-Lughod (1991) submitted:

> By focusing closely on particular individuals and their changing relationships, one would necessarily subvert the most problematic connotations of culture: Homogeneity, coherence, and timelessness. Individuals are confronted with choices, struggle with others, make conflicting statements, argue about points of view on the same events, undergo ups and down in various relationships and changes in their circumstances and desires, face new pressures, and fail to predict what will happen to them or those around them. (p. 154)

Work "in the particular" challenges hollow applications of "generalizability" that truncate and obliterate, where the claim is used to flatten difference. This work in the particular provides opportunities to use the imagination to reshape and rename experience so that a different understanding, a different story, and a different politic may emerge. This difference is not simply a critical reflection on what is already known, but a discernable alteration in the pastiche of what was already present in the story told and the alternate story or new story.

Commitment #3: The intersectionality of identity

Leslie Feinberg, an activist for transgender and social justice work who identifies as a masculine lesbian female "cross-dresser and transgenderist," constantly navigates cultural discourses through hir (one pronoun Feinberg adopts) movement from place to place. Hir asserted that the experience of identity is dependent on location and the identity of others. In cultural studies scholarship, specificity and locatedness[8] temporarily moor the fluidity of experience and the naming of identity. For Feinberg, for example, naming shifts in context. When in a transgender setting referring to Feinberg as "he" honors her "gender expression." As Feinberg disclosed, "Outside the trans communities many people refer to me as 'she,' which is . . . correct. Using that pronoun to describe me challenges generalizations about how 'all women' act and express themselves" (1998, p. 19). However, Feinberg further explained, "In a non-trans setting, calling me 'he' renders my transgender invisible" (p. 19). Feinberg's experience of identity is irreducibly contingent, as may be identities for participants in our research.

The practice of naming in our own work and across cultural studies scholarship stems from a position of privilege. "He," "She," "Straight," "Queer," "Trans," "African American," "Physically Challenged" are deployed to order another — an other — through discourse, a process of categorization through naming. What Feinberg has reminded us is that as the "other" shifts, the context shifts. This shifting is present in postcolonial research as well. Mbembe (2001) argued that people in the postcolony require several identities: "Subjects in the postcolony also have to have marked ability to manage not just a single identity, but several — flexible enough to negotiate as and when necessary" (p. 104). Mbembe explained that in postcolony subjects "splinter their identities" and "represent themselves as always changing their persona; they are constantly undergoing mitosis" (p. 104). As such, he argued that to analyze postcolonial relationships in traditional Western dualisms is not useful. Understanding the fluidity and malleability of developing contexts and the trans-performance of identity is crucial in cultural studies scholarship and in the newly emerging cultural sport psychology scholarship; moreover, recognizing the consequences of identity in institutionality is critical.

This concept of intersectionality of identity is found among critical legal and critical race scholars as well. Kimberlé Crenshaw (1994) is generally recognized as the first person to use the term *intersectionality*. Crenshaw introduced her concept of intersectionality to address the inadequacies of framing discrimination along a "single-category axis." She used the term when she applied the intersections of race and gender to her analysis of anti-discrimination cases in legal theory. Crenshaw analyzed cases that required plaintiffs to make their arguments regarding discrimination along a single categorical axis of identity. Specifically, she criticized the courts for forcing black women to present their cases on the basis of either race discrimination or gender discrimination. The courts refused to allow women to allege discrimination based on both race and gender. In doing so, they denied the multiple intersections of discrimination. Crenshaw (1990) asserted that forcing a one-dimensional lens upon the discrimination black women plaintiffs suffered oversimplified issues of discrimination: "Because the intersectional experience is greater than the sum of racism and sexism, any analysis that does not take intersectionality into account cannot sufficiently address the particular manner in which Black women are subordinated" (p. 58).

Crenshaw's (1994) emphasis on intersectionality "highlights the need to account for multiple grounds of identity when considering how the social world is constructed" (p. 94). This same emphasis could be used in cultural sport psychology research. Because intersectionality "shapes experiences" (p. 95), Crenshaw's analysis demanded that any interrogation of oppression include a framework that acknowledges the interrelationships among multiple dimensions of identity. We agree with Crenshaw's argument and invite cultural sport psychology scholars to take seriously "intersectional experience" as it relates to institutionalized sport discrimination and oppression.

Crenshaw believed that acknowledging intersectionality may be one way to recognize difference in experience and still organize politically to influence change. Inasmuch as designs in cultural studies research are capable of accounting for contradiction and ambiguity, intersectionality is useful in understanding how one tells a story and how one re-represents identity. In a recent U.S. study by Withycombe (2009), it was suggested that National Collegiate Athletic Association (NCAA) Division I African American female athletes' experiences of identity and media representation cannot be sufficiently described as either being related to gender or to race but to the experience of living intersectional lives as raced, gendered, and institutionalized athletes. More research like hers needs to be undertaken.

Commitment #4: Arduous, grace-full, sanctioned re-representations

Our fourth commitment is about researching and writing carefully, thoughtfully, and tenderly with local knowledge and sanctioned re-representations of people, communities, experience, and place in our work. Reflexivity is an essential and consistent element of such work and is required by anyone engaged in research. Much like educators who Ellsworth (1997) argued are never disinterested mediators simply seeking emancipation for their students, researchers are never disinterested analysts seeking the re-representations of their participants' experiences. Researchers and educators bring their own partial, multiple, and contradictory subjectivities to their experiences. When they invite dialogue — either through their writing or in the classroom — the invitation is a political act with its own set of rules and expectations. We — as researchers and educators — carry Ellsworth's concerns with us to spaces of inquiry in the field including the locker room.

As qualitative researchers, we recognize that when we invite another to share, we extend an invitation to vulnerability. Acknowledging both the privilege of our position and the vulnerability we invite requires those of us who work with participants and the stories they share to do so with grace. Here, the use of "grace" is a call for tenderness in working with data. As the invitation of vulnerability is extended from the researcher's privilege, careful, thoughtful, grace-full interpretation and analysis of data must accompany re-representations (Anders & Diem, 2008). As researchers traverse space, thought, and place from fieldwork back to their homes, their journey ought to be difficult, and not easily overcome, for they carry with them experiences of self and experiences not their own and then transform them into re-representations, metaphor, and, often in cultural studies scholarship, counter-narrative. This process demands responsibility, commitment to understanding, and integrity. Finally, the work that researchers produce ought to be sanctioned by those who accepted the researchers' invitation to vulnerability. As in cultural studies scholarship, cultural sport psychology researchers must work to member check, create opportunities for critique or collaboration of interpretation and analysis, and explicitly seek permission to re-represent participants in the ways they have in their work. In cultural sport psychology in particular, arduous, grace-full, and sanctioned re-representations are essential for athletes who perform so close to power, many to violence, and all in the embodied lived experience of sport.

Conclusion

We see four commitments as being central to a cultural sport psychology-informed scholarship. And, we have reviewed the six major ethical principles of the Association of Applied Sport Psychology (2009): (a) *competence*; (b) *integrity*; (c) *professional and scientific responsibility*; (d) *respect for people's rights and dignity*; (e) *concern for others' welfare*; and (f) *social responsibility* as a starting point for discussion about current sport psychology ethical cultural scripts. Although valued in consequential ways at conferences, in scholarly work, and in collegial relationships, we believe at least two of the six standards of current sport psychology ethics—*competence* and *integrity*—must be reframed relationally in work in cultural sport psychology. Embodying competence and integrity in relation to one's work but also to one's relationships on the field, on the court, in session, and in research means opening space for complex understandings. Embracing ambiguity and pursuing questions regarding the manifestations of power across place and performance means securing a space for an ethics in sport psychology always already situated in a culture that privileges the status quo. As such, these new spaces require commitments scholars may embody to support the rights, dignity, and welfare of those we research, teach, coach, consult, re-represent, and serve. Our endeavor was to introduce four of them to you here and to invite your consideration of others.

References

Abu-Lughod, L. (1991). Writing against culture. In R. G. Fox (Ed.), *Recapturing anthropology: Working in the present.* (pp. 137–162). Santa Fe, NM: School of American Research Press.

Anders, A. D., & Diem, J. (2008) Rejecting the claim of collaboration and learning to follow the unnamable. Paper presented at the American Education Research Association (AERA) Conference, New York.

Association for Applied Sport Psychology (AASP). (2009). *AASP ethical principles and standards.* Retrieved from http://appliedsportpsychology.org/about/ethics.

Althusser, L. (1971). *Lenin and philosophy and other essays.* New York: Monthly Review.

Baudrillard, J. (2001). Simulacra and simulations. In M. Poster (Ed.), *Jean Baudrillard: Selected writings* (pp. 166–184). Stanford, CA: Stanford University Press.

Baudrillard, J. (1983). *Simulations.* New York: Semiotext(e).

Bourdieu, P. (1977). *Outline of a theory of*

practice. Cambridge: Cambridge University Press.

Brackenridge, C. (2008). Sex, lies, shock, and role: Sport psychologists as agents of athlete welfare. Presentation at the Association for Applied Sport Psychology (AASP) conference, St. Louis, MO.

Collins, P. H. (1991). *Black feminist thought: Knowledge, consciousness, and the politics of empowerment*. New York: Routledge.

Crenshaw, K. (1994). Mapping the margins: Intersectionality, identity politics, and violence against women of color. In M. Albertson Fineman & R. Mykitiuk (Eds.), *The public nature of private violence* (pp. 93–118). New York: Routledge.

Debord, G. (1995). *The society of the spectacle*. Cambridge, MA: Zone.

De Certeau, M. (2002). *The practice of everyday life*. Berkeley, CA: University of California Press.

Ellsworth, E. (1997). *Teaching positions: Difference, pedagogy, and the power of address*. New York: Teachers College.

Fasting, K., Brackenridge, C., & Walseth, K. (2007). Women athletes' personal responses to sexual harassment. *Journal of Applied Sport Psychology, 19*, 419–433.

Feinberg, L. (1998). *Transliberation: Beyond pink and blue*. Boston: Beacon.

Fine, M., Tuck, E., & Zeller-Berkman, S. (2007). Do you believe in Geneva? In C. McCarthy, A. Durham, L. Engel, A. Filmer, & M. Giardina (Eds.), *Globalizing cultural studies*. New York: Peter Lang Publications.

Fisher, L. A., Butryn, T. M., & Roper, E. A. (2003). Diversifying (and politicizing) sport psychology through cultural studies: A promising perspective. *The Sport Psychologist, 17*, 391–405.

Fisher, L. A., Butryn, T. M., & Roper, E. A. (2005). Diversifying (and politicizing) sport psychology through cultural studies: A promising perspective revisited. *Athletic Insight*, Vol. 7, Issue 3 (www.athleticinsight.com).

Fisher, L. A., Roper, E. A., & Butryn, T. M. (in press). Revisiting diversity and politics in sport psychology through cultural studies: Where are we five years later? In R. J. Schinke (Ed.), *Contemporary sport psychology*. Hauppenage, NY: Nova Science.

Foucault, M. (1990). *The history of sexuality Volume 1: An introduction*. New York: Vintage.

Foucault, M. (1995). *Discipline and punish: The birth of the prison*. New York: Vintage.

Gee, J. (1996). *Social linguistics and literacies: Ideology in discourses*. New York: Taylor and Francis.

Hall, S. (1996). Looking backwards and forwards at cultural studies. In T. Miller (Ed.), *Companion to cultural studies* (pp. 331–401). Oxford: Blackwell.

Heidegger, M. (2008). *Being and time* (Trans. J. Macquarrie & E. Robinson). New York: Harper Perennial Modern Classics (Original work published 1927).

Heldke, L., & O'Connor, P. (2004). *Oppression, privilege and resistance*. Boston: McGraw Hill.

hooks, b. (1991). *Yearning: Race, gender, and cultural politics*. Cambridge, MA: Southend.

hooks, b. (1994). *Outlaw culture: Resisting representations*. New York: Routledge.

Kellner, D. (2008). *Cultural studies and ethics*. Retrieved on 10/21/09 from philpapers: online research in philosophy web site: http://philpapers.org/rec/JAMTPO-9

Laclau, E., & Mouffe, C. (1985). *Hegemony and socialist strategy*. London: Verso.

Lane, A. M. (2008). "I try to catch them right on the tip of his nose, because I try to punch the bone into the brain": Ethical issues working in professional boxing. *Athletic Insight*, Vol. 10, Issue 4. Retrieved from http://www.athleticinsight.com/Vol10Iss4/104IssueHome.htm.

Loughran, M. J., & E. F. Etzel (2008). Ethical practice in a diverse world: The challenges of working with differences in the psychological treatment of college student-athletes. *Athletic Insight*, Vol. 10,

Issue 4. Retrieved from http://www. ath leticinsight.com/Vol10Iss4/104Issue Home.htm.

Mbembe, A. (2001). *On the postcolony*. Berkeley: University of California Press.

Noblit, G. W. (1999.) *Particularities: Collected essays on ethnography and education*. New York: Peter Lang Publications.

Peters, H. J., & Williams, J. M. (2009). Rationale for developing a cultural sport psychology. In R. Schinke & S. J. Hanrahan (Eds.), *Cultural sport psychology* (pp.13–22). Champaign, IL: Human Kinetics.

Roper, E. A. (2008). Women's career experiences in applied sport psychology. *Journal of Applied Sport Psychology, 20*, 408–424.

Ryba, T. V. (2009). Understanding your role in cultural sport psychology. In R. J. Schinke & S. J. Hanrahan (Eds.), *Cultural sport psychology* (pp. 35–44). Champaign, IL: Human Kinetics.

Ryba, T. V., & Wright, H. K. (2005). From mental game to cultural praxis: Implications of a cultural studies model for future trajectories of sport psychology. *Quest, 57*, 192–212.

Schinke, R. J. (2008). Ethics in sport psychology (Special Edition). *Athletic Insight*, Volume 10, Number 4. Retrieved from http://www.athleticinsight.com/ Vol10Iss4/104IssueHome.htm.

Schinke, R. J., & Hanrahan, S. J. (2009). *Cultural sport psychology*. Champaign, IL: Human Kinetics.

Schinke, R. J., Hanrahan, S. J., Eys, M. A., Blodgett, A., Peltier, D., Ritchie, S. D., Pheasant, C., & Enosse, L. (2008). The development of cross-cultural relations with a Canadian Aboriginal community through sport research. *Quest, 60*, 357–369.

Scott, J. (1990). *Domination and the arts of resistance: Hidden transcripts*. New Haven, CT: Yale University Press.

Warren, J. T. (2001). Doing whiteness: On the performative dimensions of race in the classroom. *Communication Education, 50*, 91–108.

Watson, J. C., & Clement, D. (2008). Ethical and practical issues related to multiple role relationships in sport psychology. *Athletic Insight*, Volume 10, Number 4. Retrieved from http://www.athleticin sight.com/Vol10Iss4/104IssueHome.htm.

Werthner, P., & Coleman, J. (2008). Sport psychology consulting with Canadian Olympic athletes and coaches: Values and ethical considerations. *Athletic Insight*, Volume 10, Number 4. Retrieved from http://www.athleticinsight.com/ Vol10Iss4/104IssueHome.htm.

Winant, H. (2001). White racial projects. In B. B. Rasmussen, E. Klinenburg, I. J. Nexica, & M. Wray (Eds.), *The making and unmaking of whiteness* (p. 97–112). Durham, NC: Duke University Press.

Willis, P. (1977). *Learning to labor: How working class kids get working class jobs*. New York: Columbia University Press.

Withycombe, J. L. (2009). "Sometimes we are smart and athletic": A qualitative investigation of the social construction and psychological impact of media representations on African American intercollegiate female athletes. Unpublished doctoral dissertation, University of Tennessee.

Young, I. (2004). Five faces of oppression. In L. Heldke & P. O'Connor (Eds.), *Oppression, privilege and resistance* (pp. 37–63). Boston: McGraw Hill.

Zylinska, J. (2005). *The ethics of cultural studies*. London: Continuum International.

Notes

1. The authors would like to thank the editors for their invitation to participate in this book and for their thoughtful feedback on this chapter.

2. Whereas cultural theorists position domination and oppression in acts of discourse and practice, and institutionalized in structure, we position the stigmatization of marginalized peoples and communities, exploited groups, and vulnerable populations as an active process that requires the targeting of bodies and communities by others — often others in positions of privilege and power. The targeting of individuals and groups generates the experience of marginalization. Privilege provides the power to name and to target. Disenfranchisement occurs through an active process of discrimination by the privileged and the power they reproduce through language and institution. Using the language of "targeted" groups emphasizes the act of naming the "other" by those with privileged positions and questions the idea of individuals and communities simply emerging on the margin without others positioning them there in structured political and cultural practices.

3. Later, we expand this definition of oppression to suggest a more direct link to being targeted.

4. Patricia Hill Collins (1991) argued that "race, class and gender oppression could not continue without powerful ideological justifications for their existence" (p. 67). As a part of a dominant ideology, oppressors use markers, images, and symbols to name the "other." This media are deployed "to make racism, sexism, and poverty appear to be natural, normal, and an inevitable part of everyday life" (p. 68).

5. The use of "re-representation" acknowledges the performativity of lived experience (Warren, 2001) as well as Jean Baudrillard's (2001) assertion that "representation starts from the principle that the sign and the real are equivalent" (p. 173). We start with an acknowledgment of performance and of representation and thus employ the use of re-representation to capture both acknowledgments.

6. We use neo-conservatism as an example of the conservative right in U.S. politics reifying the concepts of individualism, meritocracy, and equality in attempts to redirect issues of equity away from contemporary movements for economic, social, cultural, and racial justice. Following the civil rights movement, neo-conservatism "attempted to frame the new post-civil rights meaning of race as a type of ethnicity, a largely cultural difference. . . . Many whites came to support a conservative and individualistic form of egalitarianism, thus upholding a supposedly 'color-blind' (but actually deeply race-conscious) position. The neo-conservative project eventually consolidated as a strategy to conserve white advantages through the denial of racial difference" (Winant, 2001, pp. 102–103).

7. See note 4.

8. For the authors and perhaps many other scholars engaged in cultural studies, both specificity and locatedness rest in discursive space.

PART II

EMERGENT FIELDS

6

INTERROGATING WHITENESS IN SPORT PSYCHOLOGY

Ted M. Butryn

CHAPTER SUMMARY

Over the past 15 years, there has been a dramatic increase in work on whiteness studies within academia. Numerous sport studies scholars have also examined the ways that whiteness relates to various sport contexts. However, few authors have discussed the role that whiteness plays in sport and exercise psychology research and practice. The purpose of this chapter is to first briefly outline some of the theoretical work on whiteness studies, including several critiques of whiteness studies as a viable progressive academic project. Following a discussion of whiteness studies, scholarship in sport studies, and the minimal research on whiteness in sport and exercise psychology, the chapter provides general comments and recommendations regarding the potential for further research on whiteness, while laying out the inherent limitations of this work.

Interrogating Whiteness in Sport Psychology

Following the election of Barack Obama as the new president of the United States in November 2008, numerous major-market newspapers and national television commentators addressed the possible implications of a leader, whose mother was white and whose father was black, for the racial politics and everyday racial discourse in a nation built on the oppressive foundation of slavery. Would Obama's victory at the polls signify the end of overt racism in the United States? Did the ultimate nonexistence of the so-called Bradley Effect, a phenomenon in which black candidates' poll numbers exceed actual votes, mean that whites are somehow "over" race? In contrast, would Obama's win trigger some sort of racist backlash? Or, would having a president of color mean relatively little to the populace given ongoing financial woes, international conflicts, race, gender, and class-based inequities, and so on? (Kristof, 2008; Swarns, 2008) As several authors have suggested, whatever the eventual effects that Obama's election may have on U.S. race relations, discussions of racial politics, and politics in general, have not been a central part of many athletes' lives over the past few decades (Coakley, 2009). Indeed, the "rebel" or "activist" athletes of the late 1960s eventually gave way to a far more depoliticized sporting space, at least where athlete voices were concerned (Butryn, 2002). However, during the hotly contested Democratic primaries leading up to the 2008 U.S. elections, and throughout the entire presidential election cycle, the era of the depoliticized athlete came to a resounding end. Many college and professional athletes received news coverage for their open and vocal support of Republican candidate John McCain (e.g., Cleveland Brown's quarterback Brady Quinn) and Democratic candidate Barack Obama (e.g., NBA all-star LeBron James). Numerous African American male athletes campaigned for Obama prior to the election, and weighed in on what they felt Obama's presence in the presidential race meant for racial identity (Gelston, 2008).

Yet, the conservative social institution of sport is still dogged by accusations of racism and the presence of white privileges in areas such as administration and, in particular, coaching (Thamel, 2008). For example, the NCAA Division I football has seen a drop in the number of African American coaches, and those who do gain access at both the college and pro levels are more likely to have been players than their white counterparts (Fish, 2006; Hohler, 2006). Further, given the long history of backlash in the United States among many conservatives during times of progressive social change (e.g., the rise of Rush Limbaugh in the early 1990s), it will not be surprising to see a resurgence of white backlash among some whites, especially white men, in the opening months of Obama's presidency.

Having written articles and presented numerous papers related to whiteness over the past several years, I began to reflect on the role of whiteness studies in the field of sport and exercise psychology, and what might be done to critically engage with issues related to whiteness and privilege in ways that go beyond mere rhetoric. How can whiteness studies, as part of a larger cultural turn in sport and exercise psychology, have a direct impact on the field, the professionals that call sport and exercise psychology home, the athletes and exercisers that many professionals work with, the students they teach, and, perhaps most important, the often conservative institution of sport and its affiliated physical cultures that many professionals rely on for employment? Therefore, I begin this chapter by outlining some of the complex theoretical work on whiteness and white privilege. The tensions within whiteness studies make any claim to a coherent definition, project, or trajectory impossible. So, I will attempt to highlight several ways that whiteness has been discussed and treated within the academic literature, and assess the projects that follow (or do not follow) from these often divergent articulations of whiteness. My point in doing this, aside from an attempt to recognize the complexity of whiteness, is to illustrate how the implications for whiteness studies in sport and exercise psychology may be vastly different depending on how whiteness is located within the larger discussion. I then highlight some of the relevant work on whiteness that sport studies scholars, including those in sport and exercise psychology, have conducted over the past 15 years. Next, I briefly reexamine, extend, and in some cases critique some of the previous, often overly optimistic, recommendations pertaining to whiteness in sport psychology, and provide some necessary steps that are needed if the field is to align itself with progressive racial politics and larger battles for social justice in the United States and globally. Finally, I interrupt the "academic voice" of the chapter from time to time with brief autoethnographic notations (i.e., my own critical commentary on the contents of the chapter) (Ellis & Boucher, 2006; Sparkes, 2000) in an effort to reflect on the implications of some of the points I make in the chapter. These short vignettes are not meant to follow any set form — or any rules of technical writing, for that matter. They are simply meant to put the process of reflexivity in the open for the reader to see, and to evoke a level of emotional or intellectual response from the reader.

One final important element of this chapter relates to the continuation of a whiteness studies project in sport and exercise psychology that amounts to more than an academic exercise. Specifically, the tension between the process of writing about whiteness studies as a means to a progressive end versus a politically flawed project that is incapable of doing anything but recentering whiteness and empowering white academics via the tenure process is one that I have taken seriously here, and I owe the anonymous reviewer of this chapter for prompting me to more clearly outline my position. As Riggs (2004) and others have argued, "one of the most important legacies that research in the area of critical race and whiteness studies draws upon is the notion of reflexivity" (p. 3). Indeed, I am not altogether certain that this chapter amounts to much more than an exercise in reflexivity, but I leave it to the reader to determine the ultimate utility of this project.

An Overview of Whiteness Studies

The interdisciplinary scholarship on whiteness studies, and critical race theory more generally, has grown significantly since the early 1990s (Bonilla-Silva, 2003; Doane, 2003; Hill, 2004; Roediger, 2002). When discussing race in this chapter, I draw from Omi and Winant's (1994) often-cited definition of race as "a concept which signifies and symbolizes social conflicts and interests by referring to different types of human bodies" (p. 55). Further, race is to be understood not as a biological construct, because the collection of features that are grouped together to signify a certain race are always socially and historically contingent (Omi & Winant, 1994). In other words, "the constructions of race and ethnicity are constantly in flux, and closely tied to the political and social dynamics of the times" (Walton & Butryn, 2006, p. 4). For example, some ethnic groups we now readily recognize as "white" (e.g., Irish, Italian, etc.) were, in fact, not considered as such before a complex process of becoming read as white (Allen, 1997; Roediger, 1999). I will discuss the social construction of whiteness in greater length later in the chapter.

Whiteness, then, does not refer simply to skin color or any fixed set of physical characteristics, but the power dynamics related to what we consider to be "white" in a particular social space. As opposed to the problematic practice of examining the experiences of minority groups, or the racial "other," from a supposedly color-blind perspective, whiteness studies "reverses the traditional focus of research on race relations by concentrating attention on the socially constructed nature of white identity and the impact of whiteness on intergroup relations" (Doane, 2003, p. 3). Whiteness studies, then, acknowledges that what we mean by "white" is contingent on sociohistorical and political contexts, and recognizes the need to mark or designate whiteness as an "organizing principle in social and cultural relations" (Lipsitz, 1998, p. 1).

As a way of categorizing the copious amount of whiteness studies scholarship that has been produced since the mid-1990s, Wiegman (1999) identified three trajectories of work that characterize the bulk of the work on whiteness studies. The "race traitor" school centers on the complete dismantling of whiteness and a disaffiliation from white racial identity and privilege. As the race traitor credo states, "Treason to whiteness is loyalty to humanity." Further, as Roediger (2002) noted, the process by which white immigrants in the 20th century were coerced into accepting the "wages of whiteness" in exchange for low-paying jobs could be repeated in the 21st century if new immigrants see "crossing over" to whiteness as a means of upward mobility. The "white trash" school centers on the relationship between whiteness and poor whites, and the discourses by which poor whites are "othered" within larger notions of white identity. Finally the "class solidarity" school examines how historical and contemporary working-class struggles can contribute to new coalitions across racial and ethnic boundaries. While there is not space to elaborate here, I see many applications of all three of these veins of whiteness studies to sport and exercise domains, and I touch on some possible avenues of research and intervention later.

Before continuing, it is important to recognize that whiteness studies did not emerge out of thin air in the late 1980s and early 1990s. Rather, the origins of whiteness studies and writings about white privilege can be traced to numerous African American authors, such as W. E. B. DuBois, Langston Hughes, and Ralph Ellison, who in 1970 wrote, "Since the beginning of the nation, white Americans have suffered from a deep uncertainty as to who they really are" (Ellison, 1998, p. 165). Part of this uncertainty relates to the supposed transparency, or invisibility, of white racial identity. As bell hooks (1998) wrote: "In white supremacist society, white people can 'safely' imagine that they are invisible to black people since the power they have historically asserted, and even now collectively assert over black people, accorded them the right to control the black gaze. As fantastic as it may seem, racist white people find it easy to imagine that black people cannot see them if within their desire they do not want to be seen by the dark Other" (p. 41).

Whiteness as an invisible norm has been a prominent theme of the whiteness studies literature (Andersen, 2003; Gabriel, 1998), and although it is not without limitations that I will deal with later, it is necessary to discuss it here if only to give the reader a more complete understanding of the current state of whiteness studies. Lipsitz (1998), for example, noted that while whiteness is almost omnipresent in various U.S. social spheres, it is difficult to identify. When whiteness is both invisible and normative, it also works to reinforce hegemonic racial ideologies that centralize whiteness and marginalize the racial "other" (Gabriel, 1998). However, other scholars have argued that whiteness was never anything *but* glaringly visible to black writers in the United States for more than 200 years (cf. Roediger, 1998). Some groups associated with right-wing forms of white racial identity have made whiteness visible as a neo-conservative political force (Hill, 2004). As the anonymous review of this chapter noted, even a cursory glimpse at U.S. popular culture reveals how distinctly visible whiteness is. For example, whether it be the comedy sketches of the African American comedian Dave Chappelle, or the white "redneck" routines of the Blue Collar Comedy Tour veterans like Larry the Cable Guy, it is difficult to credibly say that whiteness and white racial identities are invisible.

This caveat aside, according to much of the work in whiteness studies, a central goal of critical work *should* be to make whiteness visible to whites in spaces where they may not see the impact of whiteness, and decentralize its status as the unacknowledged normative status. As Walton and Butryn (2006) stated: "The issues of race and racism, rather than being inscribed singularly on non-Whites, needs to be considered in the context of how Whites construct whiteness most often through strategically diverting attention away from white racial identity. It is this process through which white remains an ambiguous concept, and that allows whiteness to remain the norm and standard, that without conscious deconstruction, remains unnoticed" (p. 5).

An important component of whiteness studies, then, involves the process by which the transparency of white identity, and the privileges associated with whiteness, are foregrounded, made visible and tangible, and thus more immediately subject to critical analysis (Dyer, 1997). One means of making whiteness visible is to engage in what McIntosh (1988) called the unpacking of the "invisible knapsack of white privilege." McIntosh proposed that whites (and white men in particular) carry with them a host of unexamined, unearned privileges across many social spheres simply because they are considered "white." In addition, these privileges must be analyzed within the larger context of a system of privilege (Andersen, 2003) that bestows "rewards" upon whites in myriad ways. Importantly, in addition to benefiting whites, the privileges McIntosh wrote about also necessarily oppress people of color, and thus we can say that white privileges are both unearned and antithetical to racial equality. The literal listing of these privileges, McIntosh suggested, is potentially effective method by which to *begin* to confront, denounce, and ultimately eliminate these privileges that would otherwise continue to exist (McIntosh, 1988). However, as numerous scholars have argued, simply identifying one's own privileges and even denouncing one's own white identity will never be an adequate or sufficient means of addressing the larger systematic nature by which whiteness, and white racism specifically, operates (Andersen, 2003).

Another of the more prominent themes in whiteness studies has been the "crisis of whiteness" and the rise of a backlash of whiteness. According to Graham (1997), among others, the worldviews of some whites have been disrupted by the slow realization that they are not the only players on the world's stage, and that the normative status of whiteness in the United States has been, and continues to be, challenged. Writing specifically of the growing discourse on whiteness and privilege in the 1990s, Giroux (1997) further stated that "As Whiteness came under scrutiny by various social groups — such as black and Latina feminists, radical multiculturalists, critical race theorists, and others — as an oppressive, invisible center against which all else is measured, many whites began to identify with the 'new racism' epitomized by right-wing conservatives" (p. 2).

hooks (1998) noted that other whites developed a less overtly racist, yet sill problematic sense of white guilt characterized by a defensive attitude toward critical discussions of what whiteness has meant in U.S. society. Both of these conservative strategies, backlash and guilt, ultimately reify whiteness and further solidify the entrenched nature of white privilege and racial inequality.

Finally, it is important to recognize that privileges associated with white racial identity and larger systems of white supremacy are always and already woven into the existing power dynamics of other lines of identity besides class, including gender and sexuality in particular. Indeed, the early work by Peggy McIntosh (1988) on white male privilege was crucial in showing how many forms of white privilege are intimately connected with male privilege as well. Thus, as Wray and Newitz (1997) stated, there is a "need for developing our understanding of how the construction of whiteness varies across lines of class, gender, sexuality, and how these constructions vary according to the politics of place and region" (p. 4).

Within sport and exercise psychology, we might take the experience of an academic conference as an opportunity to consider how the phenomenology of whiteness intersects with other lines of social identity, including class and gender:

Have you ever asked yourself what it feels like at a conference? Like what vibe the conference has? Do you feel "at home" or more like an outsider? When you scan over the crowd at the opening reception, who do you look for, and do you see your-self represented among the conference attendees? Does the AASP [Association for Applied Sport Psychology] conference feel upper-class, heterosexual, and white? It sort of does to me, but what exactly feels upper-class, or straight, or white about it? But maybe . . . maybe this is just about me, and my own in-securities? Maybe I'm not okay being the "whiteness guy" or the "culture guy" in the field? What do I crave about just being an applied sport psych guy who feels cool in khakis?

Critiques of the Growth of Whiteness Studies

While much of the literature in the 1990s was aimed at this well-mean-ing project of making the invisible visible, thereby dislodging white-ness and the entrenched system of white privilege from its central and normative position, scholars have critiqued the usefulness and political implications of whiteness studies, especially as it has come to exist as an area of specialization within the academy (Giroux, 1997, Hill, 2004; Wiegman, 1999). For example, several authors have argued that while the notion of describing whiteness as somehow transparent or invisible may have been compelling at one point, re-cent trends in racial politics and media discourse involving race make claims of transparency or invisibility seem odd at best and highly suspect at worst. Indeed, the work of Hill (2004) and others clearly demonstrates that whiteness has not only become visible and tangi-ble for many whites, it has also served as a galvanizing force for right-wing racist projects (Hill, 2004). Thus, McIntosh's (1988) metaphor of the "invisible knapsack" of white privileges, while perhaps still useful as a start point for individual progressive racial projects, has lost much of its epistemological validity.

Another criticism of some of the whiteness studies work in the 1990s centered on the essentialization of whiteness and the framing of white racial identity as a less diverse collection of projects than it really is. As Wiegman (1999) stated, "To consecrate the study of white racial identity and power as a field formation called whiteness studies (as opposed to its earlier operation within ethnic studies) is not to divest whiteness of its authority and power but to articulate the locus of its identity claims from the universal to the particular" (p. 149). Further, the existence, and a healthy one at that, of a field of whiteness studies does not call into question the frameworks and structures by which most knowledge is produced in the academy or the epistemological status of the white scholars who do research in whiteness studies (Wiegman, 1999). Wiegman wrote that the white subject may simultaneously seek to disaffiliate itself from white supremacist practices and movements on the right to empower a conservative form of white identity and benefit from it. Wiegman argued that a central consequence of white disaffiliation has been the formation of a liberal white identity, which he described as a "color-blind moral sameness whose reinvestment in 'America' rehabilitates the national narrative of democratic progress in the aftermath of social dissent and crisis" (p. 121). In other words, whether on the individual level or as a now recognized area of scholarship called "whiteness studies" within academia, "seldom has whiteness been so widely represented as attuned to racial equality and justice while so aggressively solidifying its advantage" (p. 121). Any understanding of whiteness and its relationship to sport and exercise psychology, then, must recognize and clearly outline not only the promising outcomes of an engagement with whiteness, but also the inherent and perhaps even debilitating limitations of that same engagement.

Giroux (1997) also expressed concerns over the tendency of some scholars to frame whiteness as a monolithic experiential identity that is part of a larger system of white supremacist practices. As he stated, "whiteness needs to be theorized carefully in terms of its potential to provide students with a racial identity that can play a crucial role in refashioning an anti-racist politics that informs broader, radical, democratic projects and coalitions" (p. 384). For sport and exercise psychology, this need to show students different trajectories of white identity has very important implications, because not allowing white graduate students, for instance, a space to critically come to terms with how whiteness relates to their own identities and to their own ambitions in and outside of academia necessarily sets up a zero-sum pedagogical situation that will yield no real change. Finally, Giroux (1997) called upon scholars to more clearly articulate the ways that whiteness is not simply a signifier of exploitation and domination, but a "form of identity and cultural practice" (p. 383). In other words, whiteness is not only about the racial identities of white people in a particular place and social location. Rather, it may also be embedded in, and a constituent part of, social practices such as sporting events and spaces.

To summarize this section, whiteness studies has become increasingly popular in academic circles, starting in the mid-1990s and continuing to the present. Most of the work has centered on white racial identity and the notion of white privileges, and its collective aim has often been to make whiteness visible, and thus more available for critique, critical engagement, and ultimately a more progressive racial project. However, this trajectory within whiteness studies has come under a great deal of scrutiny by scholars who charge that while perhaps better than nothing, much of the whiteness studies work is characterized by several flaws, including the now outdated and always problematic focus on making whiteness visible, and a tendency to de-emphasize the fact that whiteness studies have, at times, bordered on a self-referenced and essentialized understandings of whiteness that leave little room for progressive forms of white racial identity. Further, while the eventual usefulness of whiteness studies remains uncertain, what is certain is that much of the work seems to be generated by and for other white academics.

Whiteness and Sport Studies

As one of the major social institutions in the United States and elsewhere, sport has much to do with racial formation, racial ideology, and whiteness. As Lipsitz (1998) noted, "cultural practices and products have often played crucial roles in prefiguring, presenting, and preserving political coalitions grounded in an identification with the fictions of whiteness" (p. 99). The social institution of sport and the sports media that have the power to frame issues of race in a way that normalizes whiteness and condemns "problematic" forms of black expression have certainly played such a role. Indeed, much as the mainstream whiteness studies literature by white scholars was preceded by a large body of work by scholars of color; the contemporary research on whiteness and sport is only the latest in a long history of such work. As McDonald (2005) noted, for instance, several sport sociologists, including Harry Edwards in his groundbreaking text *The Revolt of the Black Athlete* (1969), elaborated on early 20th-century writings by black authors that criticized the simplistic and erroneous claims made by the white scientific establishment concerning black-white racial binaries and physical attributes related to performance. McDonald also observed that "subaltern perspectives" (p. 247) that feature the histories, voices, and perspectives of authors of color, as well as feminist writers, have too often been missing from the reference pages of the mainstream whiteness studies works in the 1990s and 2000s.

Within the past decade, the increasing amount of interest in whiteness in sport has reflected the larger phenomenon of the proliferation of whiteness studies scholarship in academia (King, Leonard, & Kusz, 2007; McDonald, 2005). More specifically, numerous sport studies scholars have written about the many ways that white backlash has manifested itself in various sporting spaces, many of them at least somewhat conservative politically, including NASCAR (Kusz, 2007; Newman & Giardina, 2008), BMX bike racing (Kusz, 2003), women's tennis (Douglas, 2005), U.S. distance running (Walton & Butryn, 2006), and others. Fusco (2005) even examined how exercise spaces that might seem commonplace or mundane, such as fitness center locker rooms, relate to whiteness, bodies, and aesthetics. Finally, while it was beyond the scope of this essay to fully address the geopolitical dimensions of whiteness studies and how they might play out in sport and exercise psychology, I recognize the work by Gunew (2004) and others that has problematized the use of the term *whiteness* in ways that do not account for differences in how white racial identity is defined in different geopolitical spaces. Indeed, several sport studies scholars have examined the intersections between national identity, gender, and whiteness in non-U.S. contexts. Cosgrove and Bruce (2005), for example, examined the ways in which the death of New Zealand sailor and adventurer Sir Peter Blake was represented in the media in ways that served to recenter the white, male national hero as a point in time when globalization and immigration forces posed threats to taken-for-granted notions of who counts as a "true" New Zealand sporting hero.

Despite the U.S.-centered nature of my discussion here, most of the work across geopolitical contexts on whiteness in sport has taken the discourse well past the individual renunciation of white privileges and toward the ways that racial inequality and racism are reproduced and experienced in what Bonilla-Silva called the "new racism" (2003, p. 272). Bonilla-Silva argued that while ideas about race in U.S. society have certainly progressed a great deal since the Jim Crow period, when segregation was a legal institution, new strategies have emerged that are equally as effective in perpetuating inequality and racism. These elements include, for example, a more covert discourse on race, an avoidance of racial terminology, claims of reverse racism by whites, and the incorporation of "safe minorities" such as Colin Powell and Michael Jordan, all of which are designed to show how race really is less important than it was in the past.

Some scholars have done work, though not directly related to sport and exercise psychology, that has also begun to qualitatively examine not only the experiences of whites and their own understanding of their racial identities and privileges, but the experiences of those who encounter marginalization and discrimination that is partly a result of whiteness and white racism. For example, Burden, Harrison, & Hodge (2005) examined the perceptions and experiences of nine African American faculty members in predominately white kinesiology departments. One of the themes in their results dealt with the presence of double standards in the retention, tenure, and promotion process; the marginalization of faculty of color as scholars, particularly where mentoring; and perceived biases against "black" scholarly work. While the authors did not draw directly from the work of whiteness studies scholars, they clearly found evidence of "new racism" in kinesiology, at least at the institutions their participants worked in. The marginalization of scholarly work dealing with issues related to people of color is especially troubling given the aforementioned study on the lack of research on minorities in sport and exercise psychology.

The work by Burden et al. (2005) has posed problems for whiteness studies scholars who see the inclusion of faculty of color within sport and exercise psychology as a means of promoting racial equity within the fields. In this excerpt, I discuss how sessions on "diversity" might (and I stress might) be little more than window dressing:

> Last year, cultural studies scholar Handel Wright gave an invited keynote at AASP, and in his presentation mentioned the whiteness of the conference. I was close to the front, and I remember wanting to turn around to see the reactions of people in the crowded room. I also recall having a self-serving, narcissistic sense that he was not talking about my type of whiteness. Anyway, Handel then joked that his presence at the conference, and the entire keynote session, could perhaps be seen as "mere tokenism." Maybe it wasn't totally a joke? I laughed, but others laughed a bit too heartily. The room was full though, with a lot of young, white grad students. Maybe that's a really good sign? Maybe people felt good about themselves?

As a response to the growth of whiteness studies work within sport studies, two special editions of sport sociology journals devoted to whiteness and sport (*Sociology of Sport Journal*, 2005, no. 3) and white power and sport (*Journal of Sport & Social Issues*, 2007, no. 1) were published, both of which included pieces that offered pointed critiques of the sport studies work on whiteness and white racism. King (2005), for example, drew from much of the work discussed earlier in this chapter, and pointed to several themes in the whiteness studies research both within and outside of sport that he argued could be antithetical to antiracist sport studies work. He questioned whether whiteness studies work would really alter any lives or account for individuals' racialized daily lives, outside the ivory tower, and expressed doubts about the ability of the individual unpacking of privileges as a means of enabling any real redistribution of power in sport on a micro or macro level. Finally, he raised the question of whether whiteness studies can actually contribute to, and reassert, the privileges it seeks to disrupt. In the end, King offered what might be called the "worst-case" scenario of a whiteness studies that fails to keeps its ground in social justice and antiracist aims:

> Within and beyond the sport studies classroom, there is grave danger that whiteness studies will be whitewashed. Absorbed by white studies, I fear it will become a white-centered, white-dominated, and white-identified social field, a context in which white perspectives and practices (ways of thinking and learning) shape the organization and dissemination of knowledge about largely white actors and authors within spaces marked by white-centered norms of civility and sociality. (p. 403)

Further, Wiegman (1999) noted claims of an antiracist white subject are suspect, because "the desire to combat white privilege seems unable to generate a political project against racism articulated from the site of whiteness itself" (p. 139). It is perhaps impossible, in other words, to talk of an antiracist trajectory in sport and exercise psychology given that whiteness cannot be extricated from the very context — in this case contemporary sport and physical cultures and some of the organizations that study them — that often confer privileges based on whiteness.

Another problem with the sport studies scholarship on whiteness studies is that, as Crosset (2007) argued, some of the work allows the theoretical framework to drive the analysis, and thus "whiteness research risks reifying whiteness" (p. 175). Crosset also noted there has been a lack of historical context as a weakness of whiteness studies research in sport, and demonstrated how, at times, scholars have perhaps glossed over arguably important issues in their attempts to focus on race. The challenge of whiteness scholarship, he stated, "is to make concrete connections between racial framings and racial inequality" (p. 176). Crosset (2007) also stated that in order to understand whiteness and racism in sport, it is "imperative to examine the practices of those involved in the creation and consumption of sport that inform the racial projects that operate in and around sport" (p. 174). This begs the question: What role does sport and exercise psychology play in contributing to different racial projects in sport, and how do professionals in sport and exercise psychology contribute to or benefit from whiteness and white racial identity? I argue that it is possible that by not understanding how whiteness relates to our work in sport and exercise psychology, we may be complicit in the perpetuation of white privilege and racism in ways that remain unexamined. This is not to say that a predominately white field can somehow immediately divest itself from whiteness, even if it wanted to, or that the confrontation of whiteness would not be confounded by encounters with other forms of privilege related to gender, class, and sexual orientation. I will return to the possibilities and, importantly, the limitations and possible pitfalls of whiteness studies in sport and exercise psychology in the following sections.

Whiteness and Sport and Exercise Psychology

Over the past decade a growing number of scholars have begun to sketch out what a more critically informed and culturally centered sport and exercise psychology might look like (Fisher, Butryn, & Roper, 2003; Ryba & Wright, 2005; Schinke & Hanrahan, 2009), and although they have taken different theoretical and methodological approaches, they have all addressed the issue of race, and other lines of social identity, in their work. For example, Ryba and Wright (2005) wrote that "Sport psychologists [and all sport and exercise psychology professionals] must confront the fact that athletes have fragmented identities and identifications within various discourses of class, gender, race, sexual orientation, region, etc., that athletics is a subculture within a larger culture, and that the institutions within which athletes are located attempt to control and mold their behavior" (p. 205).

While much of the work in the sociology of sport on whiteness has taken the form of theoretical articles or media analysis research, the scholarship on whiteness in sport and exercise psychology has been more applied in nature, with its roots in mainstream counseling psychology and the need to examine racial awareness among white counselors (Pedersen, 1997; Sue, 2004). As Dana (1998) suggested, the racial identity of counselors affects how clients of color perceive them, and thus consultants should explore as thoroughly and as critically as possible their own racial identities, especially if they are white. The overall competency and efficacy of white consultants dealing with different racial and ethnic populations is related to an understanding and awareness of the counselor's own racial and cultural identity, as well as that of the client (Dana, 1998). Psychologist Derald Wing Sue has also written on multicultural issues in psychology, and pointed out that while many of his white colleagues in the field of psychology may perceive the field to have made significant inroads in the area of multicultural issues, "people of color continue to see 'cultural malpractice' and the growing obsolescence of psychology" (Sue, 2004, p. 762). In addition, as Sue (2004) and cultural studies scholar bell hooks (1999) have noted, many white professionals are not aware that they bring their whiteness and associated norms, belief systems, and perhaps even judgmental attitudes into classrooms, and in the case of sport and exercise psychology, applied settings, with them.

Despite the inroads into incorporating the whiteness studies literature into mainstream psychology, however, much of the research in sport and exercise psychology has not only failed to account for the potential salience of racial and ethnic identities, it has been profoundly and problematically color-blind. Indeed, while counseling psychology in particular began to actively address issues related to whiteness and white racial identity in the 1990s, sport and exercise psychology continues to do a poor job of accounting for race, in any form, in the research (Peters & Williams, 2006; Ram, Starek, & Johnson, 2004). While a thorough discussion of the reasons for the lack of research that centralizes cultural and identity issues is not possible here, I suggest that various forms of privilege, including privileges of whiteness, could be, unconsciously, at play. Of course, there have been several notable encouraging exceptions, including the 1991 special issue of *The Sport Psychologist* on "working with special populations." However, as Ram and colleagues (2004) found in their investigation of the inclusion of race, ethnicity, and sexual orientation in 3 sport psychology journals over a 14-year period, "In all, only 15 papers published in the last decade looked at race/ethnicity in a substantial way" (p. 262). Peters and Williams (2006) concluded that, "Given the relevance of an individual's cultural background, the void of cultural research within the sport psychology literature is alarming and in direct conflict with the ideals of scientific inquiry and the need to explore the generalizibility of research findings across different populations" (p. 248). The color-blindness and unnamed whiteness of the sport and exercise psychology research, whether conscious or unconscious, intentional or unintentional, has also served to obscure any differences among racial and ethnic groups as they relate to the plethora of social and psychological phenomena scholars choose to investigate and perhaps to marginalize the experiences of racial, ethnic, and/or cultural minorities.

A small number of sport psychology scholars have qualitatively investigated whiteness in sport. For example, Veri (1999) interviewed white female administrators in NCAA Division I athletic departments about how they viewed themselves in relation to race, how they constructed notions of blackness, and how they made sense of race, in general. Following Oglesby's (1993) work that examined issues related to white racial identity and privilege in intercollegiate sport, Veri (1999) discovered that many of these white administrators often did not view themselves as being affiliated with any specific race, although they tended to attribute characteristics of fear and "otherness" to black athletes. Veri (1999) also noted that further work in the area of whiteness and race privilege in sport was needed, "especially when we consider the disproportionate numbers of white (male) staff members who supervise racially diverse groups of student-athletes" (pp. 219–220).

In 2002, *The Sport Psychologist* published a pair of articles in the professional practice section of the journal that dealt with racial and ethnic diversity. The first drew from the aforementioned work in counseling psychology on working with multicultural populations (Kontos & Breland-Noble, 2002), and the other addressed the issue of whiteness in the applied domain of sport psychology (Butryn, 2002). In the latter piece, I attempted (albeit with limited success, upon further reflection) to qualitatively examine how different individuals perceive whiteness within sport and exercise psychology, via a three-way discussion between myself, at the time a second-year doctoral student; Ron, an African American master's student in sport psychology; and Andrew, a prominent, white, male sport psychology professor and consultant in his early 50s. Among the main themes that emerged were Andrew's shifting experiences of white racial identity over the course of his career, especially with respect to his own academic department, our overall thoughts regarding racial and ethnic diversity in sport psychology, and what we felt the future may hold with respect to whiteness and the applied field, in particular.

Andrew's comments regarding the makeup of kinesiology departments in which sport and exercise psychology programs are often housed were very interesting. Andrew stated that his own thinking about race, and his first education on whiteness and privilege, came as a result of his department's move from a human performance perspective to one that centered on a cultural studies approach that integrated issues of race, and other lines of social identity, into the curriculum. He also noted that it was in the newly developed cultural studies program that he was first confronted with what his own white racial identity meant. Importantly, his comments on why his previous department did not openly discuss issues such as race and whiteness clearly speak to precisely why the aforementioned work by Ram and colleagues (2004) found such a dearth of any mention of racial or cultural identity in the sport and exercise psychology literature: "Human performance and sport studies operated out of a science-type model. We didn't talk about issues of race and gender. It was more a matter of the human performer. It's not that the department was racist; its members just didn't address those issues" (Butryn, 2002, p. 326). Andrew's perceptions of the traditional pedagogical and epistemological approach are certainly valid. However, they also reveal the problematic color-blind "liberal whiteness" that has been roundly criticized by most critical race scholars, including those in whiteness studies.

In the conclusion of the paper, I listed several white privileges that the participants of the study and myself felt were present in the field, at least at that time (Butryn, 2002). A few of these privileges included: (1) if I need to take up an issue with a head coach or administrator, I will usually be meeting with someone of my own race; (2) when applying for jobs, I will probably not be viewed as an exception to the perspective employer's notion of "white people;" and (3) because I am not confronted by my race every day, I can comfortably advocate a color-blind sporting and consulting environment.

I mention these three privileges specifically because as I reread the article for the first time in a few years, an article I felt so proud of when it was published, I realized how little effect it has had, at least visibly. There are still very few Division I coaches of color in the NCAA; there are still very few grad students of color in AASP, at least from my observations at conferences; and the cultural turn in sport and exercise psychology has yet to firmly take hold, let alone become a driving, central perspective. As an anonymous reviewer of this chapter pointed out, the very act of writing about whiteness as a white scholar can take one tenuously close to a narcissistic project, rather than a progressive one. I published an article, naively, and perhaps even self-absorbedly I thought it would serve as a whiteness wake-up call, and I eventually continued writing about whiteness in other articles and book chapters. In one sense, then, I had done what the critics of whiteness studies had suggested would happen. I re-centered whiteness even as I aimed at doing the opposite. Perhaps more people read the work than would have otherwise, but on a personal level, I was rewarded in the tenure process for my work on whiteness. I had colleagues in my department comment favorably on my work in "diversity" in sport and exercise psychology. Meanwhile, the African American scholars who were participants in the study by Burden and colleagues (2005) were often *dissuaded* from bringing their race into their work. They were *relying* on race as a topic of research. This double standard, of sorts, is obviously unjust, and it is a tension that I cannot seem to resolve. And still, I sometimes fall back to thinking like this:

> "I don't want to be known as the 'cultural studies' or 'race theory' guy," I've thought, many, many times. "I want to be respected by the 'young guns' of the field for my sport psychology research, not the diversity stuff," I recently told another close female colleague. I'm writing about oppression and I don't think I've ever felt or been oppressed based on my race, class, gender, or sexual orientation. Why am I insecure, and even defensive? Where does my desire to do "pure" sport psychology work, and have it validated by other younger white men, come from? Can I disregard the hand that I wish to pat me on the back?

Recommendations for Continued Work on Whiteness Studies and Sport and Exercise Psychology

In this section I lay out a few recommendations that follow from the discussion of whiteness studies and sport and exercise psychology presented in this chapter. I also attempt to recognize the potential potholes that may line the path to bringing any of these recommendations to fruition. First, I have argued that, along with making multicultural education a core feature of graduate and undergraduate training (Martens, Mobley, & Zizzi, 2000), sport and exercise psychology professionals committed to antiracism should openly confront their "taken-for-granted" notions of race and "name" their white racial identities. As I have previously argued (Butryn, 2002), the recent dialogue surrounding the incorporation of models of multicultural training into sport and exercise psychology is highly encouraging (e.g., Martens et al., 2000), but there is also a need to engage in the difficult task of examining one's own whiteness while recognizing the inherent limits of this project.

Regarding applied sport psychology, I also maintain that the AASP guidelines for certified consultants do not require enough background in areas of culture, broadly defined, and racial and ethnic identities and experiences, specifically. Concerns over standards and competencies related to race, ethnicity, and culture are shared by counseling psychology scholars. For example, Sue (2004), an award-winning member of the American Psychological Association, has questioned why the APA accreditation process has not done a better job of enforcing "multicultural standards" (p. 762). Therefore, I argue for a reexamination of the AASP certification standards, and if appropriate, a more thoughtful, yet aggressive attempt at ensuring that AASP-certified consultants have the training not simply to work more competently with athletes of color, as the issue has often been framed, but to ensure that professionals in our field who go out into increasingly diverse settings have a solid understanding of the social, cultural, historical, and political meanings of whiteness and how whiteness relates to sport and exercise psychology. Merely listing the privileges of whiteness is not enough, nor has it ever been. As a first step in becoming aware of one's privileges, this suffices, but if sport and exercise psychology is to claim any level of cultural competency, and perhaps any relevance, in a multicultural global landscape, a nuanced understanding of whiteness will be necessary.

More work is also warranted on how whiteness, as a form of "embodied racial power," will remain relevant in a changing U.S. and global racial landscape characterized by "new racism" (Bonilla-Silva, 2003, p. 271). New racism involves several elements, including: (1) an increasingly open racial discourse in which ideas, preconceptions, and biases about race are no longer taboo; (2) the avoidance of racial terminology altogether, and accompanying claims of "reverse racism" by whites; (3) the invisibility of the mechanisms (i.e., institutional practices) by which racial inequalities are reproduced; (4) a growth in so-called safe minorities who, according to critical race scholars, may do little to promote progressive racial change; and (5) a rearticulation of some racial practices that harkens back to a past era (Bonilla-Silva, 2003). While several sport studies scholars have begun to examine the existence of "new racism" in sport subcultures, it is unclear how these often subtle forms of racism relate to sport and exercise psychology. We have little *psychological* research on the stressors faced by African American, Latina/o, and Asian athletes in predominately white sporting and/or social environments, or the perceptions of white athletes in predominately white sports as "their" sporting spaces reflect the changing racial and ethnic demographics of many Western nation-states. Within the rapidly expanding research on coaching psychology, there is a serious need to understand how athletes, coaches, and parents make sense of racial and ethnic differences, and in what ways whiteness continues to maintain its normative, unacknowledged position. While sport sociologists have conducted some work along these lines, the theoretical frameworks and conceptual models (e.g., self-fulfilling prophecy; leadership theories; Hall, Mack, Pavio, and Hausenblas's model of imagery use, etc.) used by sport and exercise psychology professionals would be useful in investigating how racial identities, including whiteness, manifest themselves in contemporary sporting cultures.

In addition, sport and exercise psychology organizations should actively promote the growth of a more racially and ethnically diverse professional landscape, but not merely to satisfy a mission statement, or as part of a "diversity initiative," or as Handel Wright phrased it, tokenism. Importantly, the field must, as McDonald (2005) argued, recognize the work of black, Latina/o, and feminist writers who have written about whiteness and the continued effects of white racism in the United States and in other international contexts. As Roediger (2002) stated, the canonization of certain white whiteness scholars "represents both a continued insistence on placing whites at the center of everything and a continuing refusal to take seriously the insights into whiteness that people of color offer" (p. 20). King (2005) further contended that the cultivation of a nonwhite sport studies, which "not only empathizes with and expresses a commitment to alternative, marginalized sporting experiences and identities but also makes spaces for people of color to speak as equals" (p. 405), is essential. Methodologically, scholars might employ innovative qualitative research designs to more thoroughly understand the motivations, experiences, and behaviors of athletes and exercisers from previously marginalized racial and ethnic groups. Indeed, King (2005) stated that there is a need for work "on indigenous peoples and sport, sport in a global context, and racialization in sport outside the confines of Black/White binaries" (p. 405). Future research by sport and exercise psychology professionals outside of the United States is needed to examine how whiteness is represented and how race, in general, is negotiated in other national and cultural landscapes. As Bonnett (1996) stated, "One of the reasons it is necessary to understand the American 'race' debate is because it has such wide international repercussions" (p. 152). Because this chapter is centered on whiteness studies in the context of the United States, it may have limited application to other geopolitical contexts where definitions of race, and conceptualizations of whiteness, vary greatly.

Finally, I suggest a more in-depth examination of the tensions between a sport and exercise psychology community committed to a critical engagement with whiteness, and the college and professional sporting environments, as well as exercise and fitness settings that many professionals work in. I began this chapter with mention of the institutionalized racism within the coaching profession. In addition, notable sport studies scholars such as Eitzen and Sage (2003) have labeled the many structured inequities experienced by black athletes in major college programs as a kind of "college sport plantation" (pp. 120–121). In what ways does working within organizations where racism exists, and where particular versions of whiteness are still prominent, compromise the ability of sport and exercise psychology professionals to claim that they are in any way aligned with social justice? Do those in applied spaces have the ability to challenge the racial thinking of coaches, administrators, or fitness facility owners, or are they somehow silenced and forced into being complicit in the maintenance of the racial status quo? At the present time, we have few research-based answers to these sorts of questions.

Conclusion

When writing about or discussing my thoughts on where sport and exercise psychology should go in the future, I often make reference to the comments of the late athlete-activist Jack Scott, who was a vocal advocate of athletes' rights and social justice in the United States in the late 1960s (Fisher et al., 2003; Fisher, Butryn, & Roper, 2005). In his 1971 book, *The Athletic Revolution*, Scott strongly articulated the need for "sport psychologists" to consider how their work related to the larger social issues of the time, and asserted that those in the field could work toward social justice in a variety of ways. In fact, he suggested that sport psychology professionals were "in a prime position from which to work with insensitive, racist, sexist, homophobic, xenophobic coaches, and help them become more open, tolerant and understanding individuals" (cited in Fisher et al., 2003, p. 400). Scott openly discussed how racial politics and the white male power structure operated in politics of race in sport and academia, and he felt compelled to do what he could to work for equity and justice in both of these domains. Thus, before we set about any of the possible paths toward confronting and decentralizing whiteness in the field, I suggest that we first remember what I have called the "spirit of Jack Scott," and then begin to set about situating whiteness studies work in sport and exercise sport psychology as part of a larger attempt at building a "cultural praxis version" of sport and exercise psychology (Ryba, 2009). As Ryba stated, in a cultural praxis model, "our role shifts from being the expert who shapes minority athletes' [and exercisers'] responses to hegemonic normative systems in the name of athletic success to being a co-participant in the collaborative process of learning, reflection, critical awareness, and intervention" (pp. 43–44).

I agree with sport studies scholars when they argue that "the ultimate focus and payoff in studying whiteness should not be on the structure and meaning of white culture and identity but rather on how whiteness, a whole set of ideologies, discourses, and identities, serves to produce and perpetuate existing racial hierarchies and white domination more specifically" (Hartmann, 2007, p. 56). So, hopefully this chapter stimulates readers to introduce some of the whiteness studies literature, including the work in sport and exercise psychology, into their classrooms. As the autoethnographic vignettes have hopefully illustrated, it is often (and even intermittently) difficult, awkward, scary, pretentious, off-putting, and frustrating to identify and come to terms with how whiteness operates in sport and exercise psychology, including our journals, our organizations, our departments, and the relationships with athletes and coaches we work with and are employed by. There is space within sport and ex-

ercise psychology for a progressive contingent of scholars and practitioners to bridge the gap between the scholarship on critical whiteness studies and our own scholarly and applied endeavors.

In conclusion, I continue to struggle with the usefulness of any further whiteness studies scholarship in the domain of sport and exercise
psychology. If the audience is merely a group of other white scholars
and practitioners, and the dialogue never leads to any real ruptures in
the ways that whiteness is embedded in the very institution of sport
and notions of the fit, disciplined body, then what good does it really
do? If all whiteness studies in sport and exercise psychology amounts
to is an individual project of unpacking one's own privileges, then the
critiques discussed in this chapter will continue to ring true. If, on the
other hand, whiteness studies work prompts white scholars and practitioners to do the difficult, even incendiary, work of actively and
openly taking the dominant power structure and ideological frameworks to task in ways that build coalitions across racial, ethnic, gender, and class identities, then whiteness studies may make a difference outside of the relatively safe confines of the academy.

I began this chapter with a few brief thoughts on the 2008 election of U.S. President Barack Obama, and it seemed fitting to end
with a final note, as well. The results of the election and the first few
months of the Obama administration have clearly revealed the presence of a range of projects, both national and international, related
to whiteness. Clearly, the appeals of the McCain campaign to "Joe
the plumber" as a stand-in for white, working-class men did not lead
to the kind of overwhelming support the Republicans had anticipated, and even when Obama failed to gain support from white vot-
ers, he did no worse than his predecessors, Al Gore and John Kerry,
in the previous two elections (Zernike & Sussman, 2008). And yet,
it did not take long for the inevitable backlash, some of it subtle and
some quite blatant, to begin (e.g., Egan, 2009). This sort of tenuous
progress is, perhaps, all that might ever be expected from the cultural turn in sport and exercise psychology.

References

Allen, T. (1997). *The invention of the white race: The origin of racial oppression in Anglo-America*. New York: Verso.

Andersen, M. L. (2003). Whitewashing race: A critical perspective on white-ness. In W. Doane & E. Bonilla-Silva (Eds.), *White out: The continuing significance of racism* (pp. 21–34). New York: Routledge.

Bonilla-Silva, E. (2003). "New racism," color-blind racism, and the future of whiteness in America. In W. Doane &

E. Bonilla-Silva (Eds.), *White out: The continuing significance of racism* (pp. 271–284). New York: Routledge.

Bonnett, A. (1996). White Studies: The problems and projects of a new research agenda. *Theory, Culture, & Society, 13,* 145–155.

Butryn, T. M. (2002). Critically examining White racial identity and privilege in sport psychology consulting. *The Sport Psychologist, 16,* 316–336.

Burden, J. W., Harrison, L., & Hodge, S. R. (2005). Perceptions of African American faculty in kinesiology-based programs at predominately White American institutions of higher education. *Research Quarterly for Exercise and Sport, 76,* 224–237.

Chan, S., & Peters, J. W. (2009, February 18). Chimp-stimulus cartoon raises racism concerns. *The New York Times.* Retrieved from http://cityroom.blogs.nytimes.com/2009/02/18/chimp-stimulus-cartoon-raises-racism-concerns/.

Coakley, J. J. (2009). *Sport in society: Issues and controversies* (10th ed.). Boston: McGraw-Hill.

Cosgrove, A. & Bruce, T. (2005). The way New Zealanders would like to see themselves: Reading white masculinity via media coverage of the death of Sir Peter Blake. *Sociology of Sport Journal, 22,* 336–355.

Crosset, T. (2007). Capturing racism: An analysis of racial projects within the Lisa Simpson vs. University of Colorado football rape case. *International Journal of the History of Sport, 24,* 172–196.

Dana, R. H. (1998). *Understanding cultural identity in intervention and assessment.* Thousand Oaks, CA: Sage.

Doane, W. (2003). Rethinking whiteness studies. In W. Doane & E. Bonilla-Silva (Eds.), *White out: The continuing significance of racism* (pp. 3–20). New York: Routledge.

Douglas, D. D. (2005). Venus, Serena, and the women's tennis association:

When and where "race" enters. *Sociology of Sport Journal, 22,* 256–283.

Dyer, R. (1997). White. New York: Routledge.

Edwards, H. (1969). *The revolt of the black athlete.* New York: The Free Press.

Egan, T. (2009, March 4). Fears of a clown. *The New York Times.* Retrieved from http://egan.blogs.nytimes.com/2009/03/04/fears-of-a-clown/?scp=10&sq=obama%20backlash&st=cse.

Eitzen, S. D., & Sage, G. H. (2003). *Sociology of North American sport* (7th ed.). Boston: McGraw-Hill.

Ellis, C. S., & Bochner, A. P. (2006). Analyzing analytic autoethnography: An autopsy. *Journal of Contemporary Ethnography, 35,* 429–449.

Ellison, R. (1998). What America would be like without Blacks. In D. Roediger (Ed.), *Black on white: Black writers on what it means to be white* (pp. 160–167). New York: Schocken.

Fish, M. (2006). Colorado, others barely made the minority grade. Retrieved from http://sports.espn.go.com/espn/blackhistory/news/story?id=2325630.

Fisher, L.A., Butryn, T. M., & E. A. Roper (2003). Diversifying (and politicizing) sport psychology through cultural studies: A promising perspective. *The Sport Psychologist, 71,* pp. 391–406.

Fisher, L. A., Butryn, T. M., & Roper, E. A. (2005). Diversifying (and politicizing) sport psychology through Cultural Studies: A promising perspective revisited. *Athletic Insight, 7*(3). Retrieved from http://www.athleticinsight.com/Vol7Iss3/DiversifyingPoliticizing.htm.

Fisher, L. A., Roper, E. A., & Butryn, T. M. (2009). Engaging cultural studies and traditional sport psychology. In R. Schinke & S. J. Hanrahan (Eds.), *Cultural sport psychology* (pp. 23–34). Champaign, IL: Human Kinetics.

Fusco, C. (2005). Cultural landscapes of purification: Sports spaces and discourses of whiteness. *Sociology of Sport Journal, 22,* 283–310.

Gabriel, J. (1998). *Whitewash: Racialized politics and the media*. New York: Routledge.

Gelston, D. (2008, November 5th). Sports world pauses to talk about Obama's win. Retrieved from http://abcnews.go.com/Sports/wireStory?id=6193355.

Giroux, H. A. (1997). White squall: Resistance and the pedagogy of whiteness. *Cultural Studies, 11*, 376–389.

Graham, J. R. (1997). The end of the great white male. In R. Delgado & J. Stefancic (Eds.), *Critical white studies: Looking behind the mirror* (pp. 3–5). Philadelphia: Temple University Press.

Gunew, S. (2004). *Haunted nations: The colonial dimensions of multicuturalisms*. New York: Routledge.

Hall, C. R., Mack, D., Paivio, A. & Hausenblas, H. (1998). Imagery use by athletes: Development of the sport imagery questionnaire. *International Journal of Sport Psychology, 29*, 73–89.

Hartmann, D. (2007). Rush Limbaugh, Donovan McNabb, and "a little social concern." *Journal of Sport & Social Issues, 31*, 45–60.

Hill, M. (2004). *After Whiteness: Unmaking an American majority*. New York: New York University Press.

Hohler, B. (2006, September 21). Few minorities get the reins in college football. Retrieved from http://www.boston.com/sports/colleges/football/articles/2006/09/21/few_minorities_get_the_reins_in_college_football/.

hooks, b. (1998). Representing whiteness in the black imagination. In D. Roediger (Ed.), *Black on white: Black writers on what it means to be white* (pp. 38–53). New York: Schocken.

King, C. R. (2005). Cautionary notes on whiteness and sport studies. *Sociology of Sport Journal, 22*, 397–408.

King, C. R., Leonard, D. J., & Kusz, K. W. (2007). An introduction. *Journal of Sport & Social Issues, 31*, 3–10.

Kontos, A. P., & Breland-Noble, A. M. (2002). Racial/ethnic diversity in applied sport psychology: A multicultural introduction to working with athletes of color. *The Sport Psychologist, 16*(3), 296–315.

Kristof, N. The Wilder effect. (2008, October 29) Retrieved from http://kristof.blogs.nytimes.com/2008/10/29/the-wilder-effect/?scp=18&sq=whites%20obama%20effect&st=cse.

Kusz, K. (2003). BMX, extreme sports, and the white male backlash. In R. E. Rinehart & S. Sydnor (Eds.), *To the extreme: Alternative sports, inside and out* (pp. 153–175). Albany: State University of New York Press.

Kusz, K. (2007). From NASCAR to Pat Tillman: Notes on sport and the politics of white cultural nationalism in Post-9/11 America. *Journal of Sport and Social Issues, 31*, 77–88.

Lipsitz, G. (1998). *The possessive investment in Whiteness: How White people profit from identity politics*. Philadelphia: Temple University Press.

Martens, M. P., Mobley, M., & Zizzi, S. J. (2000). Multicultural training in applied sport psychology. *The Sport Psychologist, 14*, 81–97.

McDonald, M. (2005). Mapping whiteness and sport: An introduction. *Sociology of Sport Journal, 22*, 245–255.

McIntosh, P. (1988). White privilege and male privilege: A personal account of coming to see correspondences through work in women's studies. Paper presented at the meeting of the American Educational Research Association, Boston.

Newman, J. I., & Giardina, M. D. (2008). NASCAR and the "Southernization" of America: Spectatorship, subjectivity, and the confederation of identity. *Cultural Studies/Critical Methodologies, 8*, 479–506.

Oglesby, C. (1993). Issues of sport and racism: Where is the white in the rainbow coalition? In D. D. Brooks & R. C. Althouse (Eds.), *Racism in college athletics* (pp. 252–267). Morgantown, WV:

Fitness Information Technology, Inc.

Omi, M., & Winant, H. (1994). *Racial formation in the United States: From the 1960s to the 1980s* (2nd ed.). New York: Routledge.

Pedersen. P. B. (1997). *Culture-centered counseling interventions: Striving for accuracy.* Thousand Oaks, CA: Sage.

Peters, H. J., & Williams, J. M. (2006). Moving cultural background to the foreground: An investigation of self-talk, performance, and persistence following feedback. *Journal of Applied Sport Psychology, 18,* 240–253.

Ram, N., Starek, J., & Johnson, J. (2004). Race, ethnicity, and sexual orientation: Still a void in sport and exercise psychology. *Journal of Sport & Exercise Psychology, 26,* 250–268.

Riggs, D. M. (2004). "We don't talk about race anymore": Power, privilege, and critical whiteness studies. *Borderlands e-journal, 3*(2).

Roediger, D. (1999). *The wages of whiteness.* London and New York: Verso.

Roediger, D. (2002). *Colored white: Transcending the racial past.* Berkeley: University of California Press.

Ryba, T. V. (2009). Understanding your role in cultural sport psychology. In R. Schinke & S. J. Hanrahan (Eds.), *Cultural sport psychology* (pp. 35–44). Champaign, IL: Human Kinetics.

Ryba, T. V., & Wright, H. K. (2005). From mental game to cultural praxis: A cultural studies model's implications for the future of sport psychology. *Quest, 57,* 192–212.

Scott, J. (1971). *The athletic revolution.* New York: The Free Press.

Schinke, R. J., & Hanrahan, S. J. (Eds.) (2009). *Cultural sport psychology.* Champaign, IL: Human Kinetics.

Sparkes, A. C. (2000). Autoethnography and narratives of self: Reflections on criteria in action. *Sociology of Sport Journal, 17,* 21–43.

Sparkes, A. C. (2002). *Telling tales in sport and physical activity: A qualitative journey.* Champaign, IL: Human Kinetics.

Sue, D. W. (2004). Whiteness and ethnocentric monoculturalism: Making the "invisible" visible. *American Psychologist, 59,* 761–769.

Swarns. R. L. (2008, August 25). Blacks debate civil rights risk in Obama's rise. *The New York Times.* Retrieved from http://www.nytimes.com/2008/08/25/us/politics/25race.html?_r=1&scp=10&sq=whites%20obama&st=cse.

Thamel, P. (2008, December 20). Blacks find few offers for top college football coaching jobs. *The New York Times.* Retrieved from http://www.nytimes.com/2008/12/21/sports/ncaafootball/21coaches.html?scp=6&sq=.

Veri, M. J. (1999). Race discourse among white women in intercollegiate athletics. Unpublished doctoral dissertation, University of Tennessee.

Walton, T. A., & Butryn, T. M. (2006). Policing the race: United States men's distance running and the crisis of whiteness. *Sociology of Sport Journal, 23,* 1–28.

Wiegman, R. (1999). Whiteness studies and the paradox of particularity. *Boundary, 226*(3), 115–150.

Wray, M. & Newitz, A. (1997). *White trash: Race and class in America.* London and New York: Routledge.

Zernike, K., & Sussman, D. (2008, November 6). For pollsters, the radial effect that wasn't. *The New York Times.* Retrieved from http://www.nytimes.com/2008/11/06/us/politics/06poll.html?_r=1&scp=3&sq=2008%20elections%20and%20white%20vote&st=cse.

7

QUEERING SPORT PSYCHOLOGY

Vikki Krane, Jennifer J. Waldron, Kerrie J. Kauer, and Tamar Z. Semerjian

CHAPTER SUMMARY

To queer sport psychology is to destabilize heteronormativity while recognizing the existence of lesbian, gay, bisexual, and transgender (LGBT) identities in sport. In a queer sport psychology, researchers confront dominant practices that privilege heterosexuality and establish alternative practices and structures that value all sexual and gender identities. We approach the queering of the field by merging a queer feminist foundation (Krane, 2001; Waldron, Semerjian, & Kauer, 2009) with critical pedagogy (Markula & Pringle, 2006) and cultural praxis (Ryba & Wright, 2005); this framework embraces a commitment to social justice and inclusion, which then compels compassionate and inclusive practice. In this chapter, we trace the history of research on LGBT issues in sport psychology, which has been hampered by the dominant positivist view of science and the persistent heterosexism and homonegativism initially endemic in early physical education and athletic programs. Consequently, until the early 1990s, limited examination of LGBT issues occurred in the sport psychology literature. To advance queer research in sport psychology, we advocate for the broadening of our epistemological and methodological frameworks as well as filling in gaps in our knowledge. Further, a queer sport psychology has the potential to generate practices that restructure sport by reducing heterosexism, homonegativism, and transphobia; change how we practice sport psychology; and mainstream the importance of creating productive and healthy sport environments by countering heteronormativity in sport.

Queering Sport Psychology

So what exactly is *queering* sport psychology[1]? Simply by using the term *queer* in our title, we have begun the process of queering sport psychology, which is the process of destabilizing heteronormativity while recognizing the existence of LGBT identities in sport. The use of a term previously considered derogatory can empower people who identify within the queer umbrella; naming queerness acknowledges LGBT people in, and by, the field. We should note that not all LGBT people identify as queer. Yet we use this term as a political expression as well as an identity marker (cf. Krane & Waldron, 2000). By using the term *queer*, we intentionally subvert heteronormativity as well as impugn the expectation that everyone in sport is heterosexual (Krane & Waldron, 2000). Confronting heteronormativity includes not only being inclusive of LGBT people, but also resists the privileging of heterosexuality. Accordingly, queering is much more than simply adding sexuality to the compendium of social identities athletes may have. As Butler (1990) explained, identities only exist in the presence of what they are not; to consider being queer as not typical (i.e., not heterosexual) merely reinforces LGBT people's marginalized status by their continued consideration as "other than" normal. Rather, queering is "a cultural and social process of change of a dominant practice in a context—for example on how to act sexually, or how to behave as women or as men—away from strictly heteronormative expectations, to more multiple, diverse practices" (Eng, 2006, p. 23).

To queer sport psychology is to confront dominant practices that privilege heterosexuality and to establish alternative practices and structures that value all sexual and gender identities. Recognizing queer existence then serves to challenge and ultimately change heteronormative structures, behaviors, identities, and discourses (Eng, 2006). We aim to situate issues such as homonegativism, transphobia, and heterosexism as problems for all athletes, not only as challenges for gender and sexual minority sport participants. Eng argued that queering sport should take place from the inside, such as via policy or rule changes; making queer existence visible within the dominant structure of sport can dismantle the heteronormative foundation of sport. And, as Johnson and Kivel (2007) asserted, queering can, and should, be done by heterosexuals as well as LGBT individuals. Being queer in sport includes all people acting in ways that reshape sport experiences by disrupting the existing power structure and creating social change. Queering sport psychology encourages acting "in ways that do more than create 'virtual equality' by creating an equality that resonates in us through our celebration of difference" (Johnson & Kivel, 2007, p. 104). As we have argued elsewhere, sport psychologists are ideally positioned to challenge

sporting norms and inspire participants to re-envision sport practices (e.g., Barber & Krane, 2005).

A Queer Feminist View of Sport

We approach the queering of sport psychology broadly from a queer
feminist foundation (Krane, 2001; Waldron et al., 2009) and more
specifically by combining critical pedagogy (Markula & Pringle,
2006) and cultural praxis perspectives (Ryba & Wright, 2005). Our
conceptual foundation joins queer, trans, and feminist approaches.
These complementary perspectives all challenge dominant notions of
gender and sexuality while also providing nuanced theorizing specific to gender and sexual identities. This hybrid framework also
embraces the strong praxis and social justice themes embedded
within each of these approaches. Altogether, this queer feminist approach provides a strategy for broadening how we view sport psychology research and practice.

Our queer feminist perspective deconstructs the ways in which
sport reinforces and reproduces dichotomous and hegemonic constructs of gender and sexuality (Travers, 2006). When referring to
dichotomous gender, or the gender binary, we invoke the perception
that there are two genders (i.e., female and male) that are socially
constructed as very different from each other, often treated as polar
opposites. Our queer feminist perspective is heavily grounded in Ju-
dith Butler's (1990, 2004) theorizing about queer identities, which
contends that identities are fluid and that is inclusive of all sexual
and gender identities. Butler described gender as a performance —
individuals act in a manner that creates the impression of maleness
(masculinity) or femaleness (femininity). The iterative process of
continuous gender performances reinforces the social acceptability
of "correct" gender performances. Butler's (1990) concept of gender
performance negates the notion of an "essential" or innate gender of
woman or man. Rather, individuals perform hegemonic femininity
or hegemonic masculinity to conform to social norms and reap the
rewards accrued when one performs gender correctly. Gender becomes something that is enacted unconsciously, making gender not
the expression of who we are but what we do performatively. Thus,
equating maleness with masculinity and femaleness with femininity
is delegitimized.

Although gender performance is volitional, it also is constrained
by the social structure that privileges and rewards appropriate per-

formances while also punishing undesirable gender performances. Consider how a young male gymnast is treated by his peers or the social perception of adult female rugby players as lesbian. As Namaste (1994) argued, people are a part of a complex network of social relations that "determine which subjects can appear where, and in what capacity" (p. 221). For example, every time a coach disparages a male athlete by calling him a "fag" or saying he is "acting like a girl," boys on the team learn to fear and avoid acting like a fag or a girl, resulting in the coach's behavior being copied. This example illustrates how sport becomes a cultural site where binary gender categories are reinforced, heteronormativity is perpetuated, and some identities are rendered nonexistent.

Further, performances of gender are negotiated as individuals are embedded in a dominant discourse that perpetuates the iterative process of performing gender correctly. What this means is that our common language shapes how we view and interpret the world (Rose, 2007); in this case, language perpetuates what is considered an acceptable gender performance. As a whole, discourse is a system of language comingled with social practices. Language contains omissions that can erase some identities from our consciousness. For instance, within existing heteronormative discourse in sport, gay men largely are invisible. Discourse creates a social structure that reinforces existing social norms, beliefs, and thoughts. Yet within this discourse and social structure, people simultaneously are subjected to and have agency to negotiate particular gender performances depending on historical and social contexts. Individuals can conform to traditional notions of discourse of gender, but individuals also can resist, reject, or challenge dominant discursive practices (Namaste, 1994). A visible queer presence in sport can disrupt social practices and discourse that support hegemonic notions of masculinity and femininity.

Drawing on a queer feminist theory exposes the power and privilege operating within the discourse of sexuality, gender, and the body (Waldron et al., 2009). The body is socially constructed within a heterosexual conceptualization (e.g., Bordo, 1993, 2000). Male bodies are to be large and muscular, whereas female bodies should be thin and small; such bodies are glorified as ideal, heterosexual, sexy, and marketable. Feminists have long questioned the role of the media in normalizing and reinforcing the feminine female and masculine male bodies as heterosexual and desirable (Bordo, 1993, 2000).

People with such bodies gain social privilege and approval. Sport further perpetuates this cultural perspective every time, for example, an attractive female athlete gains a lucrative endorsement or a highly masculine male receives a multimillion-dollar contract, especially if these athletes have not achieved great athletic success. Our queer feminist framework challenges the normative assumptions of non-hegemonic bodies as deviant (Waldron et al., 2009).

Our queer feminist approach also embraces theorizing about transgender people. We overtly question adherence to a gender binary perpetuated and reinforced through sport. The *gender binary* refers to the belief that there are two genders and all people nicely fit into the male category or the female category. Mayer et al. (2008) defined *transgender* as "an inclusive term to describe people who have gender identities, expressions, or behaviors not traditionally associated with their birth sex" (p. 990). Transgender is an identity distinct from female and male identities and may include a combination of femaleness and maleness or what is excluded by femaleness and maleness (Cromwell, 2006). Youth are identifying as transgender, genderqueer, and the like at early ages (Grossman & D'Augelli, 2006). Some of these children are going to want to participate in sport. Similarly, athletes already in sport may begin to openly identify as trans and change their gender presentation. Within our queer approach, sport psychologists ought to be prepared to not only work with these individuals, but also to create sport environments that support and embrace them.

Conceptual Implications for Sport Psychology Practice

Messner (2002) provided a fascinating model about how the culture of sport is preserved. This model situates those with the most power in sport as the "center of sport." As his theorizing focused on male sport, typically the most traditionally masculine males are positioned as leaders at the center of sport. These also are the males who are most privileged (e.g., through social approval, exceptionally high salaries, etc.). Surrounding these privileged males is the "audience" who overtly supports the leaders and emulates their behaviors. Finally, the "marginals" are quietly complicit males who may not want to be like the leaders, yet they fear confronting or contradicting them since that likely will result in some sort of retribution (e.g., they may be ridiculed by peers, or worse). Waldron and Krane (2005) extended this model to also include women's sport. Messner's model,

and the Waldron and Krane extension, explains how homonegativism, heterosexism, and sexism in sport are sustained and perpetuated. As long as the people at the center of sport (i.e., leaders in
sport) act in derogatory, complicit, or traditional manners, these
gender performances will be replicated, reinforced, and perpetuated. The implication for sport psychologists is that we can challenge those individuals at the center of sport while also empowering
the marginal participants to voice dissent. Queering sport psychology is one avenue to do so. Both cultural praxis and critical pedagogy
are educational models that provide direction on how to engage in
the queering of sport psychology. These approaches also emphasize
the responsibility of practitioners to question socially unjust customs.

A cultural praxis perspective combines cultural studies and practical outreach with service learning for social justice as its primary
focus (Ryba & Wright, 2005). "What Wright conceptualizes locally
as 'cultural studies as praxis' blends the theory and literature of cultural studies, service learning as an activist/practice component, and
empirical research as mediator between theory and practice, with
the various components held together with a progressive politics that
focuses on social difference, equity, and justice" (Ryba & Wright,
2005, p. 201).

As long as people in sport, regardless of sexual and gender identity, are part of an institution that sustains a system of fear, heteronormativity, and oppression, effective sport psychology consulting
will be stifled and, possibly, be futile for sexual and gender minorities in athletics. Therefore, we believe it is advantageous to frame
sport psychology within a cultural studies praxis model (Ryba &
Wright, 2005), which embraces social justice and pursues social
change to make sport a productive and safe environment for all participants. In the cultural praxis model of sport psychology, education "goes beyond teaching athletes to develop psychological skills
and beyond the notions of performance enhancement as neutral and
an end in and of itself" (Ryba & Wright, 2005, p. 27). In other words,
social justice issues are infused into our consulting. Teaching athletes to be open-minded and appreciative of diversity is as important
as teaching mental skills for peak performance. An essential component of a cultural praxis approach is to encourage athletes to critically explore their experiences as gendered, raced, sexualized,
classed, and potentially exploited or oppressed athletes. How they
perform their identities, the power and oppression associated with

these identities, and how they negotiate power in sport and beyond can be broached within sport psychology consulting. Our goals can encourage personal growth beyond the playing fields, opening athletes' eyes to the broad culture outside of sport and leading them toward creating more positive climates within sport. As Ryba and Wright stated,

> performance enhancement is taken up as political and a potential tool for individual empowerment and social justice rather than neutral and an end in itself. Thus, it is sport enhancement for sport enhancement sake that is eschewed in favor of the notion of sport enhancement in the context of athletes' general self-awareness and empowerment (in terms of their sociocultural identities, identifications and relationships, and the like). (2005, p. 205)

In their application of Foucault's theorizing to sport, Markula and Pringle (2006) engaged a discussion about critical pedagogy that complements the cultural praxis model and that also has strong implications for sport psychologists. In particular, they considered questioning dominant, marginalizing social practices as an ethical responsibility. As Foucault (1978) explained, dominant ways of knowing divide people into inflexible categories, which are closely connected to contemporary problems, including sexism, heterosexism, and homonegativism. Ample evidence supports that as a whole, sport reifies hegemonic masculinity and femininity (Choi, 2000; Connell & Messerschmidt, 2005) and the concomitant denigration of LGBT participants (Griffin, 1998; Messner, 2002). Hegemonic conceptions of masculinity and femininity include that strong, muscular, independent, and assertive males are idealized in our society, as are thin, vulnerable, and demure females. That these forms of masculinity and femininity are most valued exemplifies the connection between idealized and privileged forms of gender performance with social rewards and power. The sport environment implicitly and explicitly requires men and women to behave in ways that reflect these hegemonic discourses. Although multiple forms of masculinity and femininity exist, most sport settings encourage a narrow range of "acceptable" characteristics: men must be tough and strong and women must be sexy and toned. And, of course, all athletes must be heterosexual. When athletes do not perform their gender correctly, they often are accused of being lesbian or gay or called harmful and destructive names. This encompassing climate is unlikely to change, unless sport psychologists adopt a critical approach to how we view sport, and then share this approach with coaches, administrators, and athletes.

Using critical pedagogy, or teaching queerly, as explained by Sears (1999) "embodies educators who model honesty, civility, authenticity, fairness, and respect. Queering . . . is creating classrooms that challenge categorical thinking, promote interpersonal intelligence, and foster critical awareness" (pp. 4–5). Teaching queerly engages a holistic perspective of diversity, deconstructing and negating binary perspectives, and treating all students with dignity. In addition, in her research in education, Capper (1999) argued that "the significance of studying queerness in education . . . has less to do with numbers, and more to do with what such study can reveal about the 'normal' state of affairs in schools, which affects all people" (p. 5). This critical pedagogy approach can be used to understand the role of sport psychology consultants within the larger institution of sport, and to examine the ways that queer research can unearth the insidious power dynamics that inhibit everyone. Thus, the focus is not entirely on sport participants with diverse sexual and gender identities, but on how sexuality and gender are used to create hierarchical relations in an institution such as sport.

This critical pedagogy approach easily can be adopted in sport and be reflected in our research, teaching, and consulting. We believe that it is our responsibility to engage sport participants to reflect upon common social practices in sport that privilege and oppress different people. Sport psychologists can provide innovative insight about these practices, disrupt normalized truths, and ultimately challenge coaches' and athletes' understandings about common sport practices. For example, stereotypes (i.e., normalized truths) about LGBT participants can be acknowledged, discussed, and challenged. Also, consider how common language in sport is used as a form of power and domination. It is not uncommon for coaches to use homonegative language to disparage athletes or for athletes to use terms such as *that's so gay*, *faggot*, or *dyke* to establish a hierarchy among team members (Krane, 2008; Messner, 2002). In a critical pedagogy approach, the role of the sport psychologist is to provide alternative perspectives to the stereotypes and challenge athletes to consider how greater acceptance of LGBTs can make sport a better place. This process easily can be focused on the level of an individual team or a whole league (cf. Kauer & Krane, in press). The goal of this critical pedagogy approach is to "help promote transformative possibilities by allowing individuals to develop a sense of community or collective identity; in other words, develop a new way of viewing themselves" (Markula & Pringle, 2006, p. 204). This collective view can reflect appreciation for all team members and the recognition that every person on a team plays an important role in team success.

The reciprocal relationships among theory, research, and practice are at the heart of a queer sport psychology. Queer sport psychology research compels implications for critical pedagogy and cultural praxis. Research and practice are inherently interconnected. Our research provides a foundation for how to encourage affirming and productive sport experiences, whereas the political implications of practical experiences can become a starting point for further theorizing and research.

LGBT Research in American Sport Psychology[2]

The evolution of research about LGBT athletes and issues in the field of sport psychology has been strongly influenced by the paradigmatic foundations and shifts in the field.[3] That sport and exercise psychology is steeped in positivistic traditions (what Martens, 1987, called "orthodox science") has impeded progress toward a queer understanding of sport. The emphasis on objective, value-free, and quantifiable research steered scholars away from studying social issues and cultural topics (Krane, 1994), such as sexual orientation and race. The goal of such a focus in the 1960s and 1970s was to garner respect for our developing field from the broader areas of kinesiology and psychology (Vealey, 2006). Yet, positivism determined "acceptable" areas of study and what was published (or not) in our literature. Additionally, the heterosexism and homonegativism that plagued physical education and athletics historically, carried over into the new subdisciplines, such as sport psychology, that were growing out of physical education and kinesiology. Consequently, until the early 1990s, many sport psychology scholars and educators were fearful of publishing, discussing, or presenting material that centered on sexuality (Guthrie & Kauer, 2009).

The interminably slow acceptance of diverse epistemologies, methodologies, and methods in sport psychology further curbed research on LGBT issues. Perhaps the first resistance to positivism came through the courageous writings of early feminists, such as Dorothy Harris and Carole Oglesby. While feminist writings began to chip away at the cloak of positivism, feminist scholars tended to publish their work in sport sociology journals, where there was much more acceptance of it. Sport psychology continued to marginalize research on any diverse population until recently. Textbooks and conferences that included discussion about women, LGBTs, race, or other minority social identities included ubiquitous chapters or sessions on "diversity" or "special populations." Still, rarely were these topics included in mainstream publications or during "prime time" at conferences. As Gill (1994) noted, "Indeed, sport psychology is silent on most diversity issues" (p. 419). Only after feminist approaches, qualitative methods, and, more recently, cultural studies frameworks appeared in our literature did research on LGBT issues emerge in the sport and exercise psychology literature. Even then, these articles were sporadic and did not lead to sustained lines of research by sport psychologists until the 1990s.

One of the earliest known studies on *homosexual athletes* appeared in the *Journal of Sex Research* in 1977. In response to Dave Kopay, a former professional football player, coming out in 1975, Garner and Smith examined the degree to which 25 male collegiate athletes participated in a variety of sexual activities, including *homosexual acts*. The paper made it clear that the authors were shocked and surprised by the number of athletes who reported engaging in these homosexual acts and they assured the readers that the majority of the participants only engaged in heterosexual acts.

A more sensitive approach emerged during the 1970s, when feminists began an important movement in sport research. At this time, most studies did not include women as participants and women's sporting experiences were rendered mostly invisible. To address this void in the literature, publications from the Division of Girls and Women in Sport (Harris, 1971, 1973) highlighted stereotypes affecting women in sport. Ellen Gerber, Jan Felshin, Pearl Berlin, and Waneen Wyrick (1974) provided a comprehensive overview of women in sport in their book, *The American Woman in Sport*. "Berlin authored the section on psychological perspectives, including chapters on personality, motivation, and other psychological characteristics" (Gill, 1995, p. 426). Although focused on women, it was the foundational works of Dorothy Harris (1972) and Carole Oglesby (1978) that introduced an explicitly feminist perspective into sport psychology. Harris "brought women's issues to the forefront of sport psychology and paved the way for women scholars who followed" (Gill, 1995, p. 419). Oglesby, in her book, *Women's Sport: Myth, Reality, and Social Change*, overtly challenged positivism as she questioned whether research can be value-free and went on to suggest that "unconscious sexism has pervaded that which appeared to be value-free" (p. 255). Notwithstanding the significance of the texts, these feminist treatises were published as books, circumventing the review process of journals in the field, reflecting the lack of acceptance of this work in publication outlets in sport psychology.

Though these early writings did not expressly address issues such as heterosexism or homonegativism, they did examine gendered sex roles (e.g., Hoferek, 1978) and the female apologetic (Felshin, 1974), which we consider to be an early incarnation of what would become queer research. For example, Harris (1971) noted that "the artifacts of femininity assist in reducing the threat of sports participation to the revered feminine image" (p. 1). Grounded in the language of sex roles, these early studies situated female athletes as atypical or deviant, compared to nonathletic women, due to their masculine or androgynous mannerisms (Sheriff, 1971) and laid the foundation for subsequent research on the lesbian label and stereotyping (e.g., Blinde & Taub, 1992; Kauer & Krane, 2006).

The 1983 New Agenda for Women and Sport Conference, sponsored by the Women's Sport Foundation (WSF) and the U.S. Olympic Committee, further pushed the boundaries of discussions of LGBT issues in sport. This conference focused on education, advocacy, and research on girls' and women's sport. Carole Oglesby was the conference director, and with other scholars such as Pat Griffin and Christine Shelton, deliberately included workshops about homophobia in sport (Oglesby, February 13, 2009, personal communication). The WSF Executive Board banned use of the word *lesbian* in promotional materials (Griffin, 1998). Still, Oglesby expressly discussed lesbians in sport during her keynote presentation (Oglesby, February 13, 2009, personal communication). Some other presenters also discussed lesbians and homophobia in sport (e.g., Pat Griffin) and resolutions about addressing homophobia were put into the accepted advocacy agenda emerging from the conference (Oglesby, February 13, 2009, personal communication). The word *lesbian* was not written into the conference resolution, however (Griffin, 1998).

Expanding upon this early feminist foundation, a few researchers specifically began exploring homophobia[4] in sport. Pat Griffin was a pioneer in this area of research, explicitly discussing homophobia in sport and the experiences of lesbian and gay athletes (e.g., Griffin, 1988). A small number of other researchers also wrote about issues such as the lesbian stigma that kept girls and women from participating in sport, manifestations of homophobia, and strategies to break the pattern of homophobia (Gondola, 1988; Gondola & Fitzpatrick, 1988). The publication of sport sociologist Helen Lenskyj's (1987a) book, *Out of Bounds: Women, Sport & Sexuality*, provided another turning point in LGBT research. Through her historical examination of women's participation in physical activity and the "frailty myth," Lenskyj confronted compulsory heterosexuality in women's sport. At the same time, the *Women's Studies International Forum* published a special edition containing articles focused on the experiences of women in sport from a feminist perspective. Articles by Roberta Bennett, Gail Whitaker, Nina Jo Woolley Smith, and Anne Sablove (1987) and Helen Lenskyj (1987b) specifically discussed homophobia, "lesbian-baiting," and the negative effect of these issues on females in sport. Unlike sport psychology, women's studies and sport sociology continued to support and encourage this genre of research.

To the best of our knowledge, a few early conference presentations provided significant momentum, albeit slow-moving, toward LGBT research in sport psychology. At the 1987 American Psychological Association conference, Pat Griffin implored sport psychologists to explore their own homophobia; consider how homophobia affects clinical sport psychology work; educate sport participants on issues of diversity and social justice, including sexual orientation; and conduct research on lesbians and gay men in sport. Also at that conference, Steven Heyman presented *Gay and Lesbian Athletes and Sport Participation: Special Issues*. That same year Pat Griffin organized a session entitled, *Homophobia and Homosexuality in Physical Education and Sport: Issues in Conducting Controversial Research*, at the American Alliance for Health, Physical Education, Recreation, and Dance (AAHPERD) conference. This session included presentations by Jim Genasci, Sherry Woods, and Don Sabo as well as by Griffin. That the session was framed as an issue of conducting contentious research and not focused on the experiences of physical education and sport participants was telling. Very likely, the authors felt that examining research issues would be more acceptable to program reviewers than a session explicitly on lesbians and gay men in sport.

Likewise, conference organizers obviously considered this a tangential topic of little interest to conference attendees. This was evidenced by scheduling the session at the last time slot on the last day of the conference and the hard to find room in which the session was scheduled. By the time Pat Griffin introduced her groundbreaking presentation, the standing-room only crowd had overflowed into the hallway.

Similarly, when Vikki Krane and Robin Vealey presented *Breaking the Silence: Gays and Lesbians in Sport* at the Association for the Advancement of Applied Sport Psychology (AAASP; now known as the Association of Applied Sport Psychology, or AASP) in 1994, their Sunday morning session also was better attended than most sessions in the last hours of the conference. We believe that this was the first empirical research on lesbians presented at a North American sport psychology conference. Large audiences, despite the marginal scheduling, showed support for the researchers as well as the desire to understand and discuss heterosexism and homonegativism in sport. Another significant conference presentation previously was described by Krane (2001) as "an impromptu conference session at the 1989 AAASP conference by Dorothy Harris and Bruce Ogilvie. . . . In what may be best depicted as a 'fireside chat,' they openly addressed a broad range of issues related to sexuality in sport (e.g., sexual attraction, sexual harassment, sexual orientation, homophobia)" (p. 401). It is this session that Krane attributes to inspiring and initiating her line of queer research.

Beginning in the 1990s, a number of feminist researchers have continued to research and write about issues affecting LGBT athletes as well as ways to create more inclusive sport climates. In 1991, Brenda Bredemeier, Gloria Desertrain (Solomon), Leslee Fisher, Deborah Getty, Nancy Slocum, Dawn Stephens, and Jaime Warren included a sample of athletes from a lesbian softball league in their study, published in the *Journal of Applied Sport Psychology (JASP)*, "Epistemological Perspectives Among Women Who Participate in Physical Activity." Bob Rotella and Mi Mi Murry, in a 1991 article in *The Sport Psychologist*, argued that if consultants want to be successful in developing human potential, they should be concerned about homophobia in sport. The authors, while being sensitive to concerns facing the *homosexual athlete* (the authors' term), remained silent on the importance of identity to that individual. For example, Rotella and Murry noted, "most of the time the sexual preference of an athlete or team member is not apparent or *of concern* when working on performance enhancement" (p. 361; emphasis added). Stating that sexual identity is irrelevant perpetuates heteronormativity by the continued invisibility of LGBT athletes and their needs in sport. Furthermore, the authors' use of the term *sexual preference* infers that athletes consciously choose their sexuality. The use of this term also signifies LGBT as deviant behavior because being gay is a preference. Although ground-breaking in acknowledging homophobia in sport psychology, this piece was anecdotal, cited no references, and was largely the authors' opinions (Andersen, Butki, & Heyman, 1997).

A 1992 special issue of *Quest* focused on women in sport. In that issue, Pat Griffin (1992) exposed the roots of homophobia in women's sport and highlighted the problems associated with homophobia. Krane, in a 1996 *Journal of Sport and Exercise Psychology (JSEP)* article, proposed a heuristic model for examining lesbian experiences in sport.[5] Subsequently, a groundbreaking special issue of the *Women in Sport and Physical Activity Journal* (1997) explored *Sexualities, Culture, and Sport*. This issue included qualitative studies relevant to sport psychology. Krane (1997) interviewed lesbian collegiate athletes about their experiences with homonegativism. Interviewed athletes shared that gender role nonconformity resulted in stigmatization; that female athletes, as whole, often were perceived to be lesbian; and that the lesbian label was used as a means to intimidate female athletes. Through interviews with female coaches, Wellman and Blinde (1997) revealed how the lesbian label influenced coaching careers by narrowing career choices, shaping the *image* of programs, and affecting recruiting. In her study, Brenda Riemer (1997) interviewed lesbian, recreational softball players who reported that a healthy, lesbian identity was formed or maintained when exposed to positive role models and social support within the softball league.

In 1996, Brian Butki, Mark Andersen, and Steve Heyman published "Knowledge of AIDS and Risky Sexual Behavior among Athletes," which appeared in the *Academic Athletic Journal*. This is one of the still very few studies about HIV and AIDS written by sport psychologists. Their article was followed by "Homophobia and Sport Experience: A Survey of College Students," also published in the *Academic Athletic Journal* (Andersen, Butki, & Heyman, 1997). Pushing the boundaries of the social psychology of sport, Andersen et al. noted, "The problems of lesbian and gay male athletes usually have less to do with their sexual orientation and more to do with the homophobic environment in which they find themselves" (p. 36). Steve Heyman's role as a pioneer regarding issues related to gay men must be acknowledged. As a clinical psychologist, his work in community psychology included teaching one of the first courses on AIDS (at the University of Wyoming). His untimely death in 1993, the horrific outcome of gay-bashing, cut short the long-term impact his research would have had in sport psychology.

Another important advancement toward queering sport psychology research was the 2001 publication of a special issue of *The Sport Psychologist (TSP)*, edited by Diane Gill, on feminist sport psychology. The issue included works from established scholars in the field as well as from scholars who were at the beginning of their careers. Throughout the issue, the authors challenged sport and exercise psychology researchers to broaden our methodological approaches (Whaley, 2001); investigated the intersections of gender, race, and social class (Hall, 2001); and integrated cultural studies and queer theory into our conceptualizations (Krane, 2001). The issue also highlighted the lack of recognition of women's contributions to the field (Oglesby, 2001) and the struggles of early career feminist scholars using feminist approaches in sport psychology (Greenleaf & Collins, 2001; Roper, 2001; Semerjian & Waldron, 2001). Bredemeier (2001) encouraged readers "to transform the power and privilege differentials based on social structures and practices that deny or diminish the full humanity of all peoples" (p. 412). The stance that feminist perspectives were viable and vital to the field of sport and exercise psychology was an important stepping-stone allowing for continued investigation of queer athletes in exercise and sport.

The need to address unhealthy sport climates and study and discuss the status of LGBTs in sport was made clear in 2003 when the National Gay & Lesbian Athletics Foundation held its first conference, which was attended by close to 300 athletes, sport practitioners, activists, and scholars. Described as the "first ever national conference on homophobia in sports" (GLAAD, 2003), the conference sought to increase visibility and dispel stereotypes of LGBT athletes, offer strategies to develop inclusive and supportive sport environments, and provide an avenue for networking and mentoring relationships. While several sport psychologists were in attendance, research presentations were conducted primarily by sport sociologists.

The above chronology may seem to be an overview of literature on lesbians in sport. With the exception of sport sociologist Brian

Pronger's 1990 book, *The Arena of Masculinity: Sports, Homosexuality, and the Meaning of Sex*, there is virtually no early scholarly literature on gay men in sport. It wasn't until 2002 that Eric Anderson, also a sport sociologist, published "Openly Gay Athletes: Contesting Hegemonic Masculinity in a Homophobic Environment" in *Gender & Society*, which was followed by his 2005 book *In the Game: Gay Athletes and the Cult of Masculinity*. The majority of queer-focused research has been on the experiences of lesbians in sport and there continues to be a dire need to understand better the experiences of other queer individuals, including gay men, bisexuals, and trans athletes.

We began this section of the chapter by noting the limiting impact the positivist foundations of sport psychology have had for queer research. Early research on gender and sexual orientation typically was published in sport sociology or women's studies journals, suggesting the field of sport psychology was slow to accept the importance of these topics in sport and perhaps even devalued this knowledge. The long-term implication of this state of affairs was documented in 2004, when Ram, Starek, & Johnson (2004) reported that only 1.22% of all articles published in the top North American sport psychology journals (*JSEP, TSP, JASP*) between 1987 and 2000 mentioned sexual orientation. In all, they found 12 articles that noted the sexual orientation of athletes, yet only 4 of them did so in what was considered a substantial manner (i.e., grounded theoretically or empirically). They concluded that one "explanation for the absence of substantial literature on diverse populations is that the field is apathetic about the necessity of conducting research on non-White, nonheterosexual individuals" (p. 263).

Still, we are optimistic. The acceptance of feminist, cultural studies, and qualitative research has allowed sport psychology scholars to continue examining queer topics. For example, Krane and Barber have a line of research examining experiences of lesbians in sport that is grounded in social identity theory (e.g., Krane & Barber, 2003, 2005). Tamar Semerjian has instituted research examining transgender athletes (e.g., Semerjian & Cohen, 2006). Ron Morrow and Diane Gill's ongoing research examines heterosexism and homonegativism in physical education (e.g., Morrow & Gill, 2003). Moreover, queer-feminist approaches are appearing in sport and exercise psychology writings (Lucas, 2009; Sandler & Kauer, 2009; Waldron et al., 2009). We are hopeful that young scholars will see this literature and realize that it is a viable avenue for research.

Queering Our Research

Suggestions for how to queer sport psychology research can be summed up quite simply: include research on gender and sexual identities in our literature. While the small body of knowledge is growing, these studies are most likely to appear in interdisciplinary or sport sociology journals. Gatekeepers in sport psychology can become more open to this area of study. Such progress entails encouraging research on LGBTs, being supportive of scholars doing this research, and considering queer research a fundamental component of sport psychology knowledge. More specifically, queering sport psychology research requires a paradigmatic shift away from how sport psychology training, research, and sporting practices traditionally have been conducted. Queering our research requires a discussion of topics that have, until quite recently, been silenced in our field. Advancing queer research in sport psychology necessitates broadening the epistemological foundations of sport psychology and employing a broader range of methodological frameworks as well as filling in gaps in our knowledge.

A first step in applying a queer feminist perspective in sport psychology research can be to move away from our view of gender as a dichotomous variable. The simple act of asking participants to identify as female or male sustains heteronormativity and forces participants to categorize themselves as only male or female. For transgender or genderqueer athletes, this requirement to identify as male or female does not allow them to report their gender identity accurately. Forcing individuals to mark one of two genders sustains the erasure of diverse gender identities from our literature and consciousness. Just as there is increasing awareness that asking participants to check one box for their race or ethnicity denies the possibility of multiple ethnic and/or racial identities, fitting gender into a dichotomous choice also is limiting.

Currently, information about sexuality and gender identity typically only is considered when it is the central focus of the study, yet as we have pointed out, such studies are rare in sport psychology. In a queer sport psychology, we would question the common implication that sexual and gender identities are not related to central concepts in sport psychology, such as motivation, anxiety, or confidence. Assuming that gender and sexuality are not relevant to most research in sport psychology is problematic because sexual identity is presumed to be private and irrelevant. However, discriminatory sport climates will interfere with, for example, productive confidence, anxiety, and motivation. Athletes can become distracted by homonegativism or demotivated by hostile teammates. It is shortsighted of the field not to acknowledge how gender and sexuality influence our major constructs of interest. As long as we treat sexual and gender identities as taboo, greater acceptance of the diversity of sport participants will be encumbered. Simply being more inclusive in our descriptions of participants, gender identity and sexuality will begin to move from the margins of our awareness to being seen as a central component of athlete identity.

While there has been some research on lesbian athletes and coaches, there is a considerable lack of discussion of gay, bisexual, or transgender athletes. Feminist sport psychology provided the space and support for investigations into homonegative team climates and the experiences of lesbian sport participants. However, a parallel supportive foundation did not exist for research on gay males, until the recent emergence of masculinity studies and the infusion of cultural studies into sport psychology. Still, we know very little about gay men in sport. One potential beginning would be to investigate the homonegative atmosphere that pervades many men's sporting environments and makes it challenging for gay men to come out, and in some cases to even participate.

Investigations of transgender sport experiences not only will fill an obvious void in our knowledge, it can broaden our overall conceptualization of sport and gender. To date there has been no research in the sport psychology literature that overtly has included transgender athletes even though there has been increasing media attention given to trans athletes. Because of the strict gender binary in sport, the presence of trans participants is disruptive to strongly held beliefs about boys' and girls' participation in sport. Investigations into the experiences of transgender athletes and interrogating the sport environments they encounter are critical to queering sport psychology research. Similarly, examination of bisexuals and sport also will extend our understanding of sexual identities in sport. Queer spaces in sport do exist (Jarvis, 2006; Wellard, 2006); an understanding of the emergence and cultivation of these spaces, as well as the meanings given to them by their participants, would be valuable.

Up to now, the majority of research regarding queer athletes has focused on identity and the experiences of the athletes (Brackenridge, Alldred, Jarvis, Maddocks, & Rivers, 2008). In early stages of research, an understanding of the experiences of queer athletes is important; however, as the field develops, research that goes beyond reporting experiences will be warranted. For example, researchers in the United Kingdom have begun examining homophobic bullying in sport (e.g., Brackenridge, Rivers, Gough, & Llewellyn, 2007). This line of research puts the focus on the systemic heteronormativity and homonegativism in sport. It also removes the stigma from LGBT participants by highlighting institutionalized prejudice and intolerance. Within this epistemological shift from individual experiences to a deconstruction of heteronormative sport environments, disruptions within the dominant discourse become possible. By continuing to ignore this pervasive aspect of sport, sport psychologists are complicit in sustaining heteronormativity, potentially negating positive experiences and optimal performances in sport.

Another important avenue for future research is to examine interventions and educational programs aimed at reducing heterosexism and homonegativism in sport. For example, *It Takes a Team* is an educational program, available on the Women's Sport Foundation website, aimed at "eliminating homophobia as a barrier to all women and men participating in sport;" disseminating educational information for parents, coaches, administrators, and athletes; and making "sport safe and welcoming for all" (WSF, 2008a, ¶ 1). Preliminary research, reported on the WSF website, supports the efficacy of the program (WSF, 2008b). However, additional research on this and other educational programs would be helpful in determining what types of interventions could create more hospitable atmospheres for queer athletes and allies.

Queering our literature also requires an awareness that lines of oppression and power do not operate in isolation, but rather intersect with one another (Anzaldua, 1987; Collins, 2007). Gender identity and sexuality do not exist in a vacuum, but rather understandings of gender and sexuality are significantly influenced by cultural practices that vary among, for example, ethnic, social class, and religious groups. Future research regarding gender and sexuality necessitates acknowledgment of these social, political, and ethnic environments. Persistent reliance on mainstream, white experiences limits our understandings of sport environments and queer athletes. Queer scholars consciously and intentionally include diverse populations in research studies.

While investigations on the preceding topics are important, a dismantling of the fundamental epistemological foundations of sport psychology research is essential in their attainment. There needs to be a broadened understanding and acceptance of the forms that this valuable research might take. It is unlikely for this research to occur within a positivist epistemology and more likely to be based in feminist, queer, trans, cultural studies, postmodern, or post-structural perspectives. Inclusion of future queer research in the sport psychology literature is dependent upon gatekeepers (e.g., editors, graduate advisors) being familiar with foundational assumptions, suitable methodologies, and appropriate evaluation criteria within diverse epistemologies. Lining up qualified reviewers also is essential for this work to receive appropriate evaluation. Gatekeepers also may want to broaden what are considered acceptable formats for research reports. Creative analytical and writing practices (Ely, Vinz, Downing, & Anzul, 1997; Richardson, 2000) are appearing in postmodern and queer research; findings are being presented as narratives, anecdotes, vignettes, layered stories, or some combination of these. Recognition and appropriate evaluation of these innovative styles will lead to more inclusiveness and a queering of the sport psychology literature.

Conclusion: A Queer Sport Psychology

Within a queer feminist approach to sport psychology, researchers and consultants attempt to understand the athlete in relation to his or her environment. Unlike traditional epistemological foci that separate out the political from the social from the psychological, queer thinking integrates these interrelated components of sport. Within this ontological shift, no longer would athletes be considered as if they exist in a vacuum, detached from the social world. Instead, social and cultural forces such as racism, sexism, classism, and heterosexism become ethical considerations guiding theory, research, and consulting practice (Ryba & Wright, 2005). Queer infers an overarching commitment to social justice and inclusion, which then compels compassionate and inclusive practice. Our view of a queer sport psychology connects a queer feminist lens with praxis (i.e., consulting practice). Epistemology, theory, research, and practice are inextricably interconnected.

A queer sport psychology will avoid essentializing identities; there are no innate social psychological components of being an athlete. Gender, sexuality, ethnicity, and other social identities are socially constructed and reinforced through social discourse and related social practices. As long as sport psychologists consider social identities as categorical variables, a functionalist approach to mental skills will be sustained (Ingham, Blissmer, & Davidson, 1999). A functionalist approach maintains the status quo and allows institutions, such as sport, to continue working in the same manner that historically has been privileged. In sport, this means that heteronormativity will be sustained because those people privileged by this social system will continue to support it, implicitly and explicitly. A queer approach will question institutionalized heteronormativity and consider who is hurt by this discourse and social structure.

Queering sport psychology research brings issues that surround the social climate into the professional discourse in sport psychology, which then can influence how consultants approach mental skills training. Rather than making athletes responsible for adjusting their mental states or accommodating the attitudes and behaviors of others, queer practice will assess the team social climate as well as individual mental states. For example, an athlete's confidence in sport often is attributed to the individual and treated as something that individual controls (e.g., use positive thinking to be more confident). Such functionalist, performance-enhancing discourse reinforces the status quo; reproduces systems of domination; and does not take into consideration issues of inclusion, social justice, and equality. Now imagine that the low-confident athlete identifies as genderqueer and that the low confidence stems from the excessive ridicule from teammates this athlete receives in response to making mistakes. Without addressing the transphobic climate of the team, teaching this individual skills to enhance confidence likely will be ineffective.

Hegemonic discourses in sport psychology that support heteronormativity will be challenged in a queer sport psychology. Within this framework, research moves from a neutral or objective endeavor to one that engenders social change (Broad, 2001; Sykes, 1998). By its nature, queer research is inherently political; queer sport psychology researchers are compelled toward an ethical responsibility to transform sport through inquiry. Queer praxis attempts to use theory as action to effect social change by understanding the ways in which the dominant discourse in sport proclaims and reinforces "normalcy" (e.g., heterosexuality) and "deviance" (e.g., queer identities), and how these dominant proclivities can be interrogated and challenged by sport psychology interventions. The ultimate goal of queer research may be to promote social justice or to problematize accepted understandings of gender, sexual orientation, gender identities, and, more broadly, the ways that the body is viewed, constructed, and understood. Each of these aims will lead to questioning how we *do* applied sport psychology.

To achieve an ideal queer sport environment, queering sport psychology needs to occur within all aspects of the field, including training, research, consulting, and sporting practices. Specifically, our training, consulting, and sporting practices can be informed by critical theory and queer research. For example, the early feminist work by Harris (1972) and Oglesby (1978) helped reform sport, research, and practice. Using feminist theory, both Harris and Oglesby led the way for women scholars, and for research examining gender and how gender influences sport participation. In a similar manner, the use of queer theory and research has the potential to generate practices that restructure sport by reducing heteronormativity, homonegativism, and transphobia. When approaching sport psychology from a queer perspective, we will make progressive changes and create best practices so sport will be a safe and inclusive place for all participants. We argue that to remain current and relevant, sport psychologists need to broaden our vision. Because there has been relatively little work in this area, there is tremendous potential for future research. Queering sport psychology research can be beneficial to all sport participants as it has the potential for educating future generations of leaders in sport, changing how we practice sport psychology, and mainstreaming the importance of creating productive and healthy sport environments by countering heteronormativity in sport.

References

Andersen, M. B., Butki, B. D., & Heyman, S. R. (1997). Homophobia among athletes: A survey from the heartland. *Academic Athletic Journal, 12*, 27–38.

Anderson, E. (2002). Openly gay athletes: Contesting hegemonic masculinity in a homophobic environment. *Gender & Society, 16*, 860–877.

Anderson, E. (2005). *In the game: Gay athletes and the cult of masculinity.* Albany: State University of New York Press.

Anzaldua, G. (1987). *Borderlands/La frontera: The new mestiza.* San Francisco: Spinsters/Aunt Lute.

Barber, H., & Krane, V. (2005). The elephant in the lockerroom: Opening the dialogue about sexual orientation on women's sport teams. In M. B. Andersen (Ed.), *Sport psychology in practice* (pp. 259–279). Champaign, IL: Human Kinetics.

Bennett, R. S., Whitaker, K. G., Smith, N. J. W., & Sablove, A. (1987). Changing the rules of the game: Reflections toward a feminist analysis of sport. *Women's Studies International Forum, 10,* 369–379.

Blinde, E. M., & Taub, D. E. (1992). Women athletes as falsely accused deviants: Managing the lesbian stigma. *Sociological Quarterly, 33,* 521–533.

Bordo, S. (1993). *Unbearable weight: Feminism, Western culture, and the body.* Berkeley: University of California Press.

Bordo, S. (2000). *The male body: A new look at men in public and in private.* New York: Farrar, Straus and Giroux.

Brackenridge, C., Alldred, P., Jarvis, A., Maddocks, K., & Rivers, I. (2008). *A review of sexual orientation in sport.* Retrieved December 22, 2008, from the Sportscotland website, http://www.sportscotland.org.uk/ChannelNavigation/Resource+Library/Publications/A+Literature+Review+of+Sexual+Orientation+in+Sport.htm.

Brackenridge, C. H., Rivers. I., Gough, B., & Llewellyn, K. (2007). Driving down participation: Homophobic bullying as a deterrent to participation. In C. C. Aitchison (Ed.), *Sports and gender identities: Masculinities, femininities, and sexualities* (pp. 122–139). London: Routledge.

Bredemeier, B. L. (2001). Feminist praxis in sport psychology research. *The Sport Psychologist, 15,* 412–418.

Bredemeier, B. J. L., Desertrain, G. S., Fisher, L. A., Getty, D., Slocum, N. E., Stephens, D. E., & Warren, J. M., (1991). Epistemological perspectives among women who participate in physical activity. *Journal of Applied Sport Psychology, 3,* 87–107.

Broad, K. L. (2001). The gendered unapologetic: Queer resistance in women's sport. *Sociology of Sport Journal, 18,* 181–204.

Butki, B. D., Andersen, M. B., & Heyman, S. R. (1996). Athletes' knowledge and risky sexual behaviors related to acquired immunodeficiency syndrome. *Academic Athletic Journal, 11,* 29–36.

Butler, J. (1990). *Gender trouble: Feminism and the subversion of identity.* New York: Routledge.

Butler, J. (2004). *Undoing gender.* New York: Routledge.

Capper, C. A. (1995). (Homo) sexualities; organizations, and administration: Possibilities for In(queer)y. *Educational Researcher, 28,* 4–11.

Choi, P. Y. L. (2000). *Femininity and the physically active woman.* London: Routledge.

Collins, P. H. (2007). *Black feminist thought: Knowledge, consciousness, and the politics of empowerment* (10th Anniversary, 2nd ed.). New York: Taylor & Francis.

Connell, R. W., & Messerschmidt, J. W. (2005). Hegemonic masculinity: Rethinking the concept. *Gender & Society, 19,* 829–859.

Cromwell, J. (2006). Queering the binaries: Transsituated identities, bodies, and sexualities. In S. Stryker & S. Whittle (Eds.), *The Transgender studies reader* (pp. 509–520). New York: Routledge.

Ely, M., Vinz, R., Downing, M., & Anzul, M. (1997). *On writing qualitative research: Living by words.* New York: RoutledgeFalmer.

Eng, H. (2006). We are moving up like a hard-on!": Doing sex/uality in sport. *Nordic Journal of Women's Studies, 14,* 12–26.

Felshin, J. (1974). The triple option for women in sport. *Quest, 21,* 36–40.

Foucault, M. (1978). *The history of sexuality, volume 1: An introduction.* London: Penguin.

Garner, B., & Smith, R. W. (1977). Are there really any gay athletes: An empirical survey. *Journal of Sex Research, 13,* 22–34.

Gay & Lesbian Alliance Against Defamation (GLAAD). (2003). Boston conference first to address homophobia in sports. Retrieved February 2, 2009, from the GLAAD website, http://www.glaad.org/media/newspops_detail.php?id =3234.

Gerber, E. W., Felshin, J., Berlin, P., & Wyrick, W. (1974). *The American woman in sport*. Reading, MA: Addison-Wesley.

Gill, D. L. (1994). A feminist perspective on sport psychology practice. *The Sport Psychologist, 8*, 411–426.

Gill, D. L. (1995). Women's place in the history of sport psychology. *The Sport Psychologist, 9*, 418–433.

Gill, D. L. (2001). Feminist sport psychology: A guide for our journey. *The Sport Psychologist, 15*, 363–372.

Gondola, J. C. (1988). Homophobia: The red herring in girls' and women's sports. In M. J. Adrian (Ed.), *National coaching institute applied research papers* (pp. 30–33). Reston, VA: American Association for Health, Physical Education, Recreation, and Dance.

Gondola, J. C., & Fitzpatrick, T. (1988). Homophobia in girls' sports: 'Names' that can hurt us . . . all of us. In M. J. Adrian (Ed.), *National coaching institute applied research papers* (pp. 36–38). Reston, VA: American Association for Health, Physical Education, Recreation, and Dance.

Greenleaf, C., & Collins, K. (2001). In search of our place: An experiential look at the struggles of young sport and exercise psychology feminists. *The Sport Psychologist, 15*, 431–437.

Griffin, P. (1987, August). *Homophobia, lesbians, and women's sports: An exploratory analysis*. Paper presented at the American Psychological Association convention. New York.

Griffin, P. (1988). How to identify homophobia in women's athletic programs. In M. J. Adrian (Ed.), *National coaching institute applied research papers* (pp. 33–36). Reston, VA: American Association for Health, Physical Education, Recreation, and Dance.

Griffin, P. (1992). Changing the game: Homophobia, sexism, and lesbians in sport. *Quest, 44*, 251–265.

Griffin, P. (1998). *Strong women, deep closets: Lesbians and homophobia in sport*. Champaign, IL: Human Kinetics.

Griffin, P., Genasci, J., Woods, S., & Sabo, D. (1987). *Homophobia and homosexuality in physical education and sport: Issues in conducting controversial research*. Symposium at American Association for Health, Physical Education, Recreation, and Dance, Las Vegas.

Grossman, A. H., & D'Augelli, A. R. (2006). Transgender youth: Invisible and vulnerable. *Journal of Homosexuality, 51*, 111–128.

Guthrie, S., & Kauer, K. (2009). The ongoing saga of homophobia in women's sport. In S. Guthrie, T. M. Magyar, A. F. Maliszewski, & A. Wrynn, *Women, sport & physical activity: Challenges and triumphs* (2nd ed., pp. 161–174). Dubuque, IA: Kendall-Hunt.

Hall, R.L. (2001). Shaking the foundation: Women of color in sport. *The Sport Psychologist, 15*, 386–400.

Harris, D. V. (Ed.) (1971). *DGWS research reports: Women in sports*. Washington, DC: American Association for Health, Physical Education, Recreation, and Dance.

Harris, D. V. (Ed.) (1972). *Women and sport: A national research conference*. Pennsylvania State University, University Park.

Harris, D. V. (Ed.) (1973). *DGWS research reports: Women in sports* (Vol. 2). Washington, DC: American Association for Health, Physical Education, Recreation, and Dance.

Heyman, S. R. (1987, August). *Gay and lesbian athletes and sports participation: Special issues*. Presentation at the annual meeting of the American Psychological Association. New York.

Hoferek, M. J. (1978). Toward wider vistas: Societal sex-role models and their relationships to the sports world. In W. F. Straub (Ed.), *Sport psychology: An analysis of athlete behavior* (pp. 293–299). Ithaca, NY: Mouvement.

Ingham, A. G., Blissmer, B. J., & Davidson, K. W. (1999). The expendable prolympic self: Going beyond the boundaries of sociology and psychology of sport. *Sociology of Sport Journal, 16,* 236–285.

Jarvis, N. (2006). Ten men out: Gay sporting masculinities in softball. In J. Caudwell (Ed.), *Sport, sexuality, and queer/theory* (pp. 62–75). New York: Routledge.

Johnson, C. W., & Kivel, B. (2007). Gender, sexuality, and queer theory in sport. In C. C. Aitchison (Ed.), *Sport & gender identities: Masculinities, femininities, and sexualities* (pp. 93–105). New York: Routledge.

Kauer, K. J., & Krane, V. (2006). "Scary dykes" and "feminine queens": Stereotypes and female collegiate athletes. *Women in Sport and Physical Activity Journal, 15*(1), 43–55.

Kauer, K. J., & Krane, V. (in press). Inclusive excellence: Advancing diverse sexual and gender identities in sport. In S. J. Hanrahan & M. B. Andersen (Eds.), *Handbook of applied sport psychology.* New York: Routledge.

Krane, V. (1994). A feminist perspective of contemporary sport psychology research. *The Sport Psychologist, 8,* 393–410.

Krane, V. (1996). Lesbians in sport: Towards acknowledgment, understanding, and theory. *Journal of Sport and Exercise Psychology, 18,* 237–246.

Krane, V. (1997). Homonegativism experienced by lesbian collegiate athletes. *Women in Sport and Physical Activity Journal, 6*(2), 141–164.

Krane, V. (2001). One lesbian feminist epistemology: Integrating feminist standpoint, queer theory, and feminist cultural studies. *The Sport Psychologist, 15,* 401–411.

Krane, V. (2008). Gendered social dynamics in sport. In M. Beauchamp & M. Eys (Eds.), *Group dynamics advances in sport and exercise psychology: Contempo-rary themes* (pp. 159–176). New York: Routledge.

Krane, V., & Barber, H. (2003). Lesbian experiences in sport: A social identity perspective. *Quest, 55,* 328–346.

Krane, V., & Barber, H. (2005). Identity tensions in lesbian college coaches. *Research Quarterly for Exercise and Sport, 76,* 67–81.

Krane, V., & Vealey, R. (October 8, 1994). *Breaking the silence: Gays and lesbians in sport.* Paper presented at the meeting of the Association for the Advancement of Applied Sport Psychology, Lake Tahoe, NV.

Krane, V., & Waldron, J. (2000). The Gay Games: Creating our own culture. In K. Schaffer & S. Smith (Eds.), *The Olympics at the millennium: Power, politics, and the Olympic Games* (pp. 147–164). Piscataway, NJ: Rutgers University Press.

Lenskyj, H. (1987a). *Out of bounds: Women, sport, and sexuality.* Toronto: The Women's Press.

Lenskyj, H. (1987b). Female sexuality and women's sport. *Women's Studies International Forum, 10,* 381–386.

Lucas, C. B. (2009). *Transgender athletes: Re-imagining the sport terrain.* Presentation at the Sexuality, Culture, & Sport Conference, Ithaca College, NY.

Markula, P., & Pringle, R. (2006). *Foucault, sport and exercise: Power, knowledge and transforming the self.* New York: Routledge.

Martens, R. (1987). Science, knowledge, and sport psychology. *The Sport Psychologist, 1,* 29–55.

Mayer, K. H., Bradford, J. B., Makadon, H. K., Stall, R., Goldhammer, H., & Landers, S. (2008). Sexual and gender minority health: What we know and what needs to be done. *American Journal of Public Health, 98,* 989–995.

Messner, M. A. (2002). *Taking the field: Women, men, and sports.* Minneapolis: University of Minnesota Press.

Morrow, R. G., & Gill, D. L. (2003). Perceptions of homophobia and heterosexism in physical education. *Research Quarterly for Exercise and Sport, 74*, 205–214.

Namaste, K. (1994). The politics of inside/out: Queer theory, poststructuralism, and a sociological approach to sexuality. *Sociological Theory, 12*, 220–231.

Oglesby, C. (1978). *Women and sport: From myth to reality*. Philadelphia: Lea & Febiger.

Oglesby, C. A., (2001). To unearth the legacy. *The Sport Psychologist, 15*, 373–385.

Pronger B. (1990). *The arena of masculinity: Sports, homosexuality, and the meaning of sex*. New York: St. Martin's.

Ram, N., Starek, J., & Johnson, J. (2004). Race, ethnicity, and sexual orientation: Still a void in sport and exercise psychology? *Journal of Sport & Exercise Psychology, 26*, 250–268.

Richardson, L. (2000). Writing: A method of inquiry. In N. K. Denzin & Y. S. Lincoln (Eds.), *Handbook of qualitative research* (pp. 923–948). Thousand Oaks, CA: Sage.

Riemer, B. (1997). Lesbian identity formation and the sport environment. *Women Sport and Physical Activity Journal, 6*(2), 83–108.

Roper, E. A. (2001). The personal becomes political: Exploring the potential of feminist sport psychology. *The Sport Psychologist, 15*, 445–449.

Rose, G. (2007). *Visual methodologies: An introduction to the interpretation of visual materials*. (2nd ed.). Los Angeles: Sage.

Rotella, R. J., & Murray, M. M. (1991). Homophobia, the world of sport, and sport psychology consulting. *The Sport Psychologist, 5*, 355–364.

Ryba, T. V., & Wright, H. K., (2005). From mental game to cultural praxis: Implications for a cultural studies heuristic "model" for future trajectories of sport psychology. *Quest, 57*, 192–212.

Sandler, A., & Kauer, K. (2009). *Out/standing success: Female coaches on lesbian identity disclosure*. Presentation at the Sexuality, Culture, & Sport conference, Ithaca College, NY.

Sears, J. T. (1999). Teaching queerly: Some elementary propositions. In W. J. Letts IV & J.T. Sears (Eds.), *Queering elementary education: Advancing the dialogue about sexualities and schooling* (pp. 3–14). Lanham, MA: Rowman & Littlefield.

Semerjian, T. Z., & Cohen, J. H. (2006). "FTM means female to me": Transgender athletes performing gender. *Women in Sport and Physical Activity Journal, 15*(2), 28–43.

Semerjian, T. Z., & Waldron, J. J. (2001). The journey through feminism: Theory, research, and dilemmas from the field. *The Sport Psychologist, 15*, 438–444.

Sheriff, M. (1971). Girls compete??? In D. V. Harris (Ed.), *DGWS research reports: Women in sports* (pp. 31–35). Washington, DC: American Association for Health, Physical Education, Recreation, and Dance.

Sykes, H. (1998). Turning the closets inside/out: Towards a queer-feminist theory in women's physical education. *Sociology of Sport Journal, 15*, 154–173.

Travers, A. (2006). Queering sport lesbian softball leagues and the transgender challenge. *International Review for the Sociology of Sport, 41*, 431–446.

Vealey, R. S. (2006). Smocks and jocks outside the box: The paradigmatic evolution of sport and exercise psychology. *Quest, 58*, 128–159.

Waldron, J. J., & Krane, V. (2005). Whatever it takes: Health compromising behaviors in female athletes. *Quest, 57*, 315–329.

Waldron, J. J., Semerjian, T. Z., & Kauer, K. (2009). Doing "drag": Applying queer-feminist theory to the body image and eating disorders across sexual orientation and gender identity. In J. J. Reel & K. A. Beals (Eds.), *Beyond sorority sisters and gymnasts: Body image and eating disorders in diverse populations* (pp. 63–82). Reston, VA: National Association for Girls and Women in Sport.

Wellard, I. (2006). Exploring the limits of queer and sport: Gay men playing tennis. In J. Caudwell (Ed.), *Sport, sexuality, and queer/theory* (pp. 76–89). New York: Routledge.

Wellman, S., & Blinde, E. (1997). Homophobia in women's collegiate basketball. *Women in Sport and Physical Activity Journal, 6*(2), 63–82.

Whaley, D. E. (2001). Feminist methods and methodologies. *The Sport Psychologist, 15*, 419–430.

Women's Sport Foundation. (2008a). *About It Takes a Team!* Retrieved February 23, 2009, from WSF website, http://www.womenssportsfoundation.org/Issues-And-Research/Homophobia/About-It-Takes-A-Team.aspx.

Women's Sport Foundation. (2008b). *It Takes a Team! Video evaluation executive summary 2005–2006.* Retrieved February 23, 2009, from WSF website, http://www.womenssportsfoundation.org/Content/Articles/Issues/Homophobia/I/It-Takes-A-Team-Video-Evaluation-Executive-Summary-2005-2006.aspx.

Notes

1. We recognize and appreciate that the larger field is inclusive of exercise (i.e., sport and exercise psychology); however, our focus, in this chapter, is on the sport environment. Certainly many of our ideas pertain to exercise contexts as well.

2. We appreciate Carole Oglesby's contribution toward developing a complete and accurate historical overview of LGBT research in sport psychology.

3. While our focus in on sport psychology in the United States, see Brackenridge et al. (2008), who provide a thorough review of the research in the United Kingdom.

4. While we prefer to use the term *homonegativism*, throughout the chapter we will use the term used by specific authors. Historically, *homophobia* was the commonly used term when referring to discrimination against LGBTs.

5. Contrary to published critiques of this model, it is not a linear model of coming out (cf. Iannotta & Kane, 2002; King, 2008). Rather it is a heuristic or "a conceptual model for studying lesbians in sport" (Krane, 1996, p. 239) that identifies social factors that may influence the development of a positive lesbian identity in sport.

8

INDIGENOUS RESEARCH AND DECOLONIZING METHODOLOGIES

Janice Forsyth and Michael Heine

CHAPTER SUMMARY

In this chapter, we provide an overview of theoretical and applied perspectives on indigenous research and decolonizing methodologies. The chapter is divided into five sections. (1) In the introduction, we identify the social and political significance of the emergence of indigenous research and decolonizing methodologies. (2) The analysis of the field constitutes the second section. It is guided by two main questions: What is the cultural turn in the social sciences and humanities? How is the cultural turn related to indigenous research and decolonizing methodologies? (3) The third section outlines key issues and debates in the literature. Topics related to power, complexity, voice, the commodification of knowledge, and ethics are discussed. (4) Fourth, we consider an applied understanding of the subject. Here, we examine some of the questions outlined in the second and third sections through a case study approach, drawing on our experience of conducting a research project involving Aboriginal youth in an impoverished area of Winnipeg, Manitoba. Our main purpose with the case study is to call attention to the potential benefits and drawbacks of using indigenous and decolonizing research in conjunction with a participatory action research (PAR) approach. (5) In the fifth and final section we provide some thoughts on possible avenues for exploration, including the value of a multidisciplinary approach for methodological development. Our argument here emphasizes the need for a deeper and a more sustained engagement with PAR when conducting research with Aboriginal people.

Indigenous Research and Decolonizing Methodologies

Research is a site of contestation not simply at the level of epistemology or methodology but also in its broadest sense as an organized scholarly activity that is deeply connected to power. That resistance to research, however, is changing ever so

slightly as more indigenous and minority scholars have engaged in research methodologies and debates about research
with communities.

—Linda Tuhiwai Smith, 2005, p. 87

Scholarly disciplines are often centered on highly influential texts
that fundamentally change the way researchers understand and operate within their field. Every now and again, a text will come along
that is so timely and of such consequence that its impact does not remain limited to a single area of inquiry. For academics engaged in
research with groups that have historically been excluded from post-
secondary education and often exploited through academic knowledge production — such as indigenous people in Canada, the United
States, and Australia — arguably such a text is Linda Tuhiwai Smith's
Decolonizing Methodologies: Research and Indigenous Peoples. Published in
1999, *Decolonizing Methodologies* signaled to the broader academic community the coming of age and mainstream acceptance of indigenous
methods and methodologies as rational and legitimate strategies for
conducting scholarly investigations. While previous assessments,
such as *Natives and Academics: Researching and Writing About American
Indians* (Mihesuah, 1998), dissected traditional institutionalized research practices and their impacts on indigenous people, it was
Smith's sustained consideration of the complexities and interconnect-
edness of modern colonial and capitalist forces with university-based
research that marked a decisive turning point in methodological history. It moved methodological discussions to a point that unified the
scattered accounts into a coherent voice and vision for what indigenous research represented and had the potential to be, and it provided a social and political platform for critique and action.

What followed in the wake of *Decolonizing Methodologies* was a surge
in critical analysis and reflection on indigenous research, with indigenous scholars themselves advancing thorough and thought-pro-
voking arguments on the problematic. Three prominent examples in
recent years include *Research as Resistance: Critical, Indigenous & Anti-
Oppressive Approaches* (Brown & Strega, 2005), a collection of theoretically informed articles that focus on and incorporate issues important to indigenous people; *For Indigenous Eyes Only: A Decolonizing
Handbook* (Wilson & Yellow Bird, 2005), a generalist reader aimed
at community activists who are interested in researching for social
change; and *Handbook of Critical and Indigenous Methodologies* (Denzin,

Lincoln, & Smith, 2008), an extensive anthology of contributions that examine indigenous research and indigenous inquiries from multiple perspectives, including indigenous research as an archetype of the performative turn in the social sciences and humanities.

The performative turn in indigenous research is based on assumptions about both the constitution of social and cultural identity and the process of academic knowledge production. This approach rejects the notion that the position and identity of individuals is characterized by social and cultural fixity; rather, it is argued that identity is fluid and constantly produced, reproduced, and changed through the way people act—perform—in their lives. Culture is thus produced in and through performance; the constitution of identity qua performance shifts the focus away from function or fixed position to contingent fluidity (Burke, 2005). Likewise, the narratives created in indigenous knowledge production are themselves understood as textual performances of the experiences of others; the text seeks to capture the performativity of others' experiences from their point of view. The text's meanings themselves therefore must be as "contextual, improvised and performative" (Denzin, 2001, p. 25) as the experiences it seeks to capture. Such an approach can contribute to "radical social change, to economic justice, to a utopian cultural politics that extends localized critical (race) theory and the principles of a radical democracy to all aspects of decolonizing, indigenous societies" (Denzin et al., 2008, p. xi).

In this chapter, we aim to build on the existing literature on indigenous research and decolonizing methodologies, in part, by offering a concise overview and assessment of current writings and critiques. Appraisals of this nature are important for gauging the energy and robustness of any field of inquiry. In addition to appraising the field, this chapter makes another contribution: within the extensive body of literature currently available on sport history, sociology, anthropology, and psychology, it represents one of the few stand-alone segments on indigenous research and decolonizing methodologies in a major anthology on Canadian sport. In most instances, discussions about indigenous research are limited to method or methodology sections. Indeed, thus far it appears only in sport psychology that an approach referred to as cultural sport psychology (CSP) has been developed that offers the potential to be compatible with the application of indigenous methodology in sport (cf. Schinke et al., 2009; Schinke et al., 2006a; Schinke et al., 2006b; Ryba & Wright, 2005). While there is a small but growing number of scholars who are beginning to explore the contours of CSP (e.g., Schinke & Hanrahan, 2009), the fact remains that it is not yet an integral part of investigations in sport more generally, and this limitation makes it difficult to assess the contributions of CSP to research informed by indigenous and decolonizing methodologies.

To outline the contours of current writings and critiques, several questions must first be addressed. What is the cultural turn? What gave rise to this thinking? How is it linked to indigenous research and decolonizing methodologies? Further, what is indigenous research? What is a decolonizing methodology? What are the similarities and differences between the two approaches? Responding to these questions will help elucidate Linda Tuhiwai Smith's quote prefacing this chapter, that is, her challenge to researchers — both Aboriginal and non-Aboriginal — to be more conscientious and reflexive when considering the power relations embedded in the research process.

Analysis of the Field

It's not sticking to the old ways that's important. It's being us, using all the new knowledge our way. Everything new belongs to us too.

— Patricia Grace, cited in Johnson, 2008, p. 129

The Cultural Turn

We begin with a brief overview of the cultural turn in the social sciences and humanities. This intellectual movement was initiated by Richard Hoggart, Stewart Hall, and their contemporaries at the Birmingham Centre for Contemporary Culture Studies in Britain in the 1960s. It signaled a shift away from traditional understandings of culture as a social form of organization, toward an understanding of culture as a social process whereby people create meaning from everyday life and construct identities for themselves based on their lived experiences. Influenced by this movement, scholars throughout the world began examining such issues as the intersection of globalization, colonialism, and capitalism with race, gender, and sexuality. Furthermore, the cultural turn's focus on popular culture opened up new vistas by broadening the areas of scholarly inquiry to include examinations about sports, with the result that sports studies, once considered a trivial pursuit in academe, gained legitimacy as an area of serious scholarly investigation.

Of course, the cultural turn also shaped the type of scholarship on sport. For example, in sport history, the emphasis shifted from writing chronological narratives of particular sports, personalities, or events to studies of the past infused with sociological questions about how race, gender, or class shaped people's experiences in, and understandings of, sport (Booth, 2005). Today, the areas of application in sports studies are as varied as they are engaging. For instance, scholars have explored how modern technologies of surveillance affect the physically active body (e.g., Markula & Pringle, 2006). They have also shed light on the intersection of sporting landscapes with ideas about gender and sexuality (e.g., Bale & Vertinsky, 2004). And still others have considered the role of sports films as global mediums that transmit powerful social messages about the racialized and gendered dimensions of cultural identity (e.g., King & Leonhard, 2006). The range of cultural studies is remarkable for its vastness.

It was within this broader scholarly shift that indigenous research is positioned. In terms of methodological history, the cultural turn contributed to what Denzin and Lincoln (2005) have referred to as the "blurred genres" of the 1970s and 1980s. It was a major turning point for indigenous research in that it was a time "when local knowledge and lived realities became important, when a diversity of paradigms and methods developed, and when a theoretical and methodological blurring across boundaries occurred" (Smith, 2005, p. 90), thus helping to legitimize indigenous forms of inquiry. Evidence of institutional acceptance of indigenous research is signaled by the publications mentioned above, as well as by new nontraditional funding in Canada, as demonstrated by the Social Sciences and Humanities Research Council (SSHRC) Aboriginal Research Grants program, which "supports university-based researchers and Aboriginal community organizations to conduct research on issues of concern to Aboriginal peoples" (SSHRC, 2009, Strategic Research Grants, Aboriginal Research). However, at the point of writing, this program is stalled, having been under review since December 2006. This lack of movement indicates the significant political challenges still faced by this type of program in the mainstream of institutionalized academic research.

As with the development of other intellectual approaches, threads of vibrant dialogue arose in the literature about what constitutes in-

digenous and decolonizing research, as well as the possibilities and
challenges that exist for these approaches in university settings. For
example, Paraschak, Heine, & McAra, (1995) argued that academic
and indigenous knowledge had significant structural and philosophical issues to address before they could identify meaningful intersections and points of articulation.

Another voice was Rigney's (1999), who made a case for greater
indigenous intellectual theorizing about "race," so that a more nuanced approach to indigenous research—what he viewed as a race-
based research epistemology—could better be understood and
applied as a liberation methodology. At the time of Rigney's intervention, Warrior (1999) also argued the need for a more candid and
purposeful dialogue about the place and importance of indigenous
intellectual theorizing in the academy. Working toward a synthesis
with mainstream contemporary theory, he maintained, would effect
a better understanding of indigenous research as an intellectual
journey, and not simply as a set of principles setting out how data
should be collected from indigenous participants.

We will return to these issues in the subsequent section. At his
point, it is important to outline how the terms *indigenous research* and
decolonizing methodology are used in this chapter. Setting these parameters is necessary if we are to understand these approaches individu-
ally and in relation to each other. There remains one problem: delin-
eating these boundaries is a challenging and political act, due in part
to the wide range of expressions that are often used to refer to indigenous research and decolonizing methodologies, as well as the
lack of clarity around the indigenous and decolonizing research lexi-
con in general. For example, the terms *indigenous research* and *decolonizing methodology* are often used interchangeably in the literature;
they are also variously referred to as *critical indigenous research, decolonizing research, red pedagogy*, as well as *American Indian, anti-oppressive*,
or *anti-colonial* research. Inconsistent terminological usage can be a
hindrance to the development of research methodologies. How can
researchers contribute to our knowledge and practice of specific approaches when terms are understood and applied in a variety of
ways? How can researchers have a meaningful discussion about
methodological issues when the field is flooded with vague terminology? A more stable ground on which to pursue these discussions
is needed.

Indigenous Research and Decolonizing Methodology

We begin with a brief discussion about indigenous research. Developing a coherent description is complicated, and doing so means traversing highly contested terrain. There have been few serious attempts to establish a consistent approach to what indigenous research is, the principles surrounding it, and the desired outcomes. In the absence of this groundwork, indigenous research can be taken to mean many different things — from investigations conducted by indigenous people on indigenous issues, to descriptions of specific research methods and protocols, to (less frequently) detailed analyses of indigenous epistemological standpoints. This should not be taken to mean that indigenous research is less rigorous than more established approaches but that setting some boundaries for what constitutes indigenous research would strengthen this area of inquiry.

In view of such a diffuse range of understandings, we need to lend some precision to the term *indigenous research* so that there exists some agreement about what the expression means. To be sure, though, the plethora of interpretations about "how to" do indigenous research should remain a productive part of the conversation. Some of the most radical challenges to the established order happen on the margins, where critical interventions are most likely to flourish (hooks, 1999). Still, it is necessary to tease out the intellectual and political strands that distinguish this approach from others, in this case, decolonizing approaches.

To do so, we return to Linda Tuhiwai Smith (1999), who discussed indigenous research within a decolonizing framework. By intent and definition, indigenous research is informed by, and must respond to, indigenous political struggles for liberation from colonialism and imperialism and the concrete manifestations that flow from those oppressions, including racism, sexism, and poverty — and their link to capitalist exploitation. A good example of such research is provided by Castleden, Garvin, & Huu-ay-aht First Nation (2007), whose use of community-based participatory research is a model well worth exploring. Their questions and outcomes helped to address local indigenous concerns about health while still meeting institutional requirements for scholarly output — a highly significant control mechanism that shapes the way university-community research collaborations can be structured. Given that analyses of this relationship exist elsewhere (e.g., Giles & Forsyth, 2007; Paraschak et al., 1995), and various organizations have outlined what presently constitutes an ethical research relationship with indigenous people (e.g., McNaughton & Rock, 2004; Inuit Tapiriit Kanatami, 2003), we need not dwell on that issue here. Our main point is that indigenous research must engage the "struggle for development, for rebuilding leadership and governance structures, for strengthening social and cultural institutions, for protecting and restoring environments, and for revitalizing language and culture" (Smith, 1999, p. 89). Indigenous research is first and foremost a political project aimed at addressing historical inequities that have impacted indigenous people worldwide, and it approaches its subject from the perspective of contemporary indigenous needs and interests (Wilson, 2001). It is research that responds to the questions and issues that indigenous people identify as being relevant to them and worthy of serious scholarly investigation.

This approach serves to define indigenous participants as intellectual subjects rather than research objects, yet it also firmly positions them within the realm of academic practice with its delimited options for making specific types of contributions to research. This pattern is analogous to the positioning of indigenous literary authors that has too often led us to think of them as "artists and not enough as intellectuals" (Warrior, 1999, p. 50). Furthermore, this ghettoization of indigenous intellectual work has led some scholars to challenge and critique the role of indigenous knowledge in the academy, calling for and sometimes planting the foundations of a methodology that takes into account the politics of indigenous lived experiences. For these reasons, Smith (2005) has referred to indigenous research as "tricky" because it proposes fundamental shifts in institutionalized research practices: research must traverse "the spaces between research methodologies, ethical principles, institutional regulations, and human subjects as individuals and socially organized actors and communities" (p. 85).

An associated approach is decolonizing methodology, also sometimes known as a methodology of the margins or empowerment research. Tuhiwai Smith (1995) has described decolonizing methodology as an approach that aims to transform the site of knowledge production in that it is "not simply about challenging or making refinements to qualitative research. It is a much broader but still purposeful agenda for transforming the institution of research, the deep underlying structures and taken-for-granted ways of organizing, conducting, and disseminating research and knowledge" (p. 88).

Though Smith is not the only scholar to speak of decolonizing research — a glance through the literature on feminist and queer theory
will show a rich and diverse understanding of what decolonization is
and how it can be carried out within a research context — hers is one
of the few analyses to provide a thorough, thoughtful, and sustained
examination of research as an institutional practice, of the impact of
research on the lives of indigenous people, and the efforts by some
indigenous people to "research themselves back to life."

Without a doubt, both approaches are political projects linked in
their endeavor to create space for alternative knowledges and practices in the academy; however, indigenous research is more direct in
its attempt to make academic research useful and accessible to indigenous people. Both approaches also aim to give voice, empower,
and redistribute existing human and financial resources, while indigenous research aims to achieve the same outcomes specifically for
indigenous people. The parallels are such that when the two are used
in tandem, the outcome can be "a transformative project that is active in pursuit of social and institutional change, that makes space
for indigenous knowledge, and that has a critical view of power relations and inequality" (Smith, 1995, p. 89). It can also enable "peoples and communities to reclaim and tell their stories in their own
ways and to give testimony to their collective histories and struggles"
(Smith, 1995, p. 89). And by remaining focused on indigenous experiences, needs, and interests, research can actively contribute to community capacity development by shifting the focus of attention to
community needs and interests while also developing "a critique of
the 'rules of practice' regarding research, the way research projects
are funded, and the development of strategies that address community concerns about the assumptions, ethics, purposes, procedures,
and outcomes of research" (Smith, 1995, p. 90). Indigenous research,
when it is anchored by decolonizing methodology, can be a powerful
vehicle for progressive social change for indigenous people and people in the academy.

A number of important questions emerge from the definition of
these boundaries. Who can "do" indigenous research? Must indigenous research always be decolonizing? Is indigenous research the
only approach that is decolonizing? Is it possible to do indigenous
research employing the conventionally established forms of authorization of "traditional" research approaches? How are we to understand the challenges faced by indigenous research and indigenous

knowledge in our increasingly commodified world? A brief discussion of these issues and debates follows in the following section.

Key Issues and Debates

If we are going to *decolonize* research let us also *aboriginalize* it
As aboriginal scholars let us honour our own knowings first
Lest we colonize ourselves by prioritizing the knowing and
    practices of those
Who have taken our land perverted our knowledges felonized
    the speaking
Of our languages and outlawed the practicing of our cultures

Nonaboriginal Indian experts cannot decolonize they cannot
    aboriginalize
They can only do another white rewrite
                                    — Peter Cole, 2004, p. 27

Political positions on academic knowledge production, such as the one quoted above, reflect the long history of colonial exploitation, unauthorized use and misuse of indigenous knowledge that has occurred in North America, and throughout the world, over a long period of time. Current key issues and debates over the application of indigenous research can be understood only when the historical background is taken into account. A number of considerations will then follow: discussions of the impacts brought about by the exploitation of indigenous knowledge; the constitution of such knowledge itself, that is to say, theories of indigenous knowledge; issues of ethics in indigenous research; questions related to the authorization to conduct such research; and lastly, a consideration of the control and ownership rights to the results of research with indigenous communities.

Exploitation of Indigenous Knowledge

For a long period of time, university-based academic (Western) research has entered indigenous communities without consideration for the impact or consequences of research, very often without consultation, and almost always without authorization by community-based groups or organizations. Indigenous communities therefore had little control over or input into any part of the research process. The definition of questions, research programs, methods, and theories exclusively within the frame of relevance of academic knowledge production tends to elide the existence of alternative ways of knowing. What is more, the outcomes and results of research are then typically presented in non-indigenous language and categories, making access to such information by members of the indigenous community exceedingly difficult.

Since indigenous communities have been excluded from the determination of relevant and meaningful research questions, even well-meaning researchers often tend to emphasize in their research "the application of a pathologizing lens" (Ermine, Sinclair, & Jeffrey, 2004, p. 12), focusing on negative social issues. Such a preoccupation tends to exert a debilitating effect in that it deprives the indigenous community of the opportunity to undertake, through research, a consideration of its own strengths. What is more, the devaluation of indigenous knowledge as "non-scientific" (Witt, 2007, p. 226) has not aided in the formulation of research projects that focus on potentially existing strengths rather than pathologizing social or cultural marginalization. The overall effect has been the wide-ranging exclusion of indigenous communities from all aspects of research that was conducted about or on them, or that referenced their knowledge and traditions in some way. Inasmuch as academic research was the only site for authorized and validated knowledge production, indigenous knowledge remained excluded from this site.

More recently, these issues have acquired added urgency through the wide-ranging expropriation and commodification of indigenous biological and environmental knowledge by biotechnological and pharmaceutical corporations that transform such knowledge into medical-industrial products (Battiste & Henderson, 2000; Ellen, Parks, & Bicker, 2000). It is this series of expropriations, in particular, that has rendered visible the problematic link between indigenous knowledge and its commodification in academic and industrial contexts. The aspirations of indigenous societies to retain control over their traditional knowledge, now re-presented to, and alienated from, them in legal discourses as "intellectual property," often run counter to those processes. In this context, the danger emerges that the process of collaborative, participatory research, through which indigenous communities seek to exert a degree of authority and control, may itself be co-opted in the interest of such commodified knowledge production, such that even "participatory research models are being subjected to the processes of commodification for the purposes of supporting and reproducing the social relations of accumulation in their multifarious forms" (Jordan, 2003, p. 195). The issue at the core of these political contestations involves a consideration of the nature of indigenous knowledge itself. Is it possible to speak of an academic theory of, or on, indigenous knowledge?

Complexity and Theory: The Site of Traditional Knowledge

Somewhat paradoxically, perhaps, the fundamental unifying element of indigenous knowledges is the great diversity of their frames of relevance, their local and dispersed sites of authorization and range of meanings, and the embeddedness of their procedures of empirical or experiential validation into social and cultural networks of authority. Such a concept of indigenous knowledge "acknowledges diverse ways of knowing and respects pluralism of knowledge" (Martin-Hill, 2008, p. 7). In the understanding of indigenous knowledge producers working in universities, then, indigenous knowledge has multiple sources that can be positioned in traditional, empirical, and spiritual dimensions, respectively (Martin-Hill, 2008, p. 7). The diversity of knowledges that emanates from locally specific attachments to language, landscape, and culture serves to circumscribe these knowledges and their localized range of authorizations (cf. Castellano, 2000). Inasmuch as the validity and authority of indigenous knowledge tends to be tied to specific cultural and geographical sites, conceptualizations of a theory of indigenous knowledge as a theoretical project of the academy have proven difficult to effect. The relevant question remains, however, as to how indigenous research — as a theoretical project — can contribute to a broader understanding of indigenous ways of knowing and to their potential to intersect with existing bodies of knowledge conducted from multiple lived and theoretical points of view.

Ethics of Research Participation

The redefinition of the site of traditional knowledge also serves to shift the locus of authority over the process of knowledge production to a large extent away from the academy and to indigenous spaces. This has implications for the ethics of participation of collaborative university-based researchers in indigenous research. These implications are addressed in more detail below, in our considerations of a case study of community-based participatory research. Here, a brief overview of some of the main considerations will suffice.

It is important, first, to consider that participation in research with indigenous communities involves building, enhancing, and committing to a set of personal and research relationships whose development requires a significant amount of time, energy, and often resources. In this sense, research ethics represent more than a mere proscriptive code of conduct; rather, it is a way of thinking about research relationships as an attempt to even out the power relations between researcher and indigenous community to the widest extent possible (Manzo & Brightbill, 2007). Research carried out ethically in this sense tends considerably to extend the requirements for acceptable practice laid out by institutional ethics review boards (Ermine et al., 2004). It also demands of the researcher a considerably greater personal commitment to the research process.

Furthermore, even though there may be agreement on the need to act ethically, the community's interpretation of what that means may differ from that of the researcher. Both the indigenous community and the researcher have standards for assessing conduct, but these may not be commensurable (Smith, 2005; Wax, 1991). Where this often emerges very clearly is during the determination of potential benefits that the research is designed to deliver. Preexisting unequal power relations may be replicated here and lead to the unequal distribution of benefits, such that disadvantaged groups may be unable to access the benefits of research outcomes. This has become particularly evident in the course of the recent intensified commodification of indigenous environmental and biological knowledge (Smith, 2005) referred to previously, but it is a concern in indigenous research in general. The resolution of such potential imbalances must therefore be addressed in the overall research design and the definition of desirable outcomes.

Applied Understanding

Using our experience of conducting research with Aboriginal youth in Winnipeg, Manitoba, we will discuss how PAR, when linked to indigenous research and decolonizing methodology, can be a potentially useful way to build strong research relationships with Aboriginal people, and through this process, help mediate some of the issues and concerns identified above. We do so with the understanding that the research question normally determines the framework for data collection, analysis, and dissemination. In other words, PAR

should not be the default approach for conducting research on indigenous issues or with indigenous people, though it is well suited
for research that is politically motivated.

Our experience is drawn from a three-year program of activities
funded by the Social Sciences and Humanities Research Council
(SSHRC). Our overall goal for this program was to explore how
the positive potential in sport and recreation could be organized to
provide Aboriginal youth with opportunities to participate in meaningful physical activity programs that improve their overall health
and well-being and expand their leadership skills in ways that respect
and enhance their cultural identities. The program consisted of three
mutually supporting facets: a youth mentorship program, an after-
school recreation program, and a social mapping project. We will
discuss the social mapping project in detail here, because we see it as
a prime example of the growing relevance of PAR within indigenous
settings. What follows is a description of how we used PAR within
the context of our research project.

Linking Theory and Practice: Principles in Action

The overall scope of the three-year program, including the three sets
of activities and our commitment to using research for social justice,
led the research team to generate a set of operating principles to
guide our decision making. With more than 30 people working on
various aspects of the project over the 3-year period, we needed common reference points to unite our actions. The research team was
comprised of undergraduate and graduate research assistants; community leaders, including high school principals, teachers, and students: the vast majority self-identified as Aboriginal. Given the size
of the team and range of activities being offered, our research principles formed the basis for how we would carry out our research program in a way that addressed local Aboriginal needs and interests
while also building research capacity.

One main principle was to decolonize the research process by de-
mocratizing it from the outset. This meant that our Aboriginal collaborators and participants had to be able to derive direct benefits
from the research relationship. Through the project, we had to give
back in meaningful and concrete ways to the community in which
we were researching. We operationalized this principle by involving
community members in the development, implementation, and evaluation of the research in order to help ensure the project had local rel-

evance. We also focused on research capacity development, in particular among the youth, so as to familiarize them with university research protocols in the hopes of encouraging higher education by alleviating some of the fear associated with entering an environment that has historically been viewed as hostile and foreign to indigenous people. Additionally, we worked on projects that would have immediate and long-term positive impacts for our research participants and partner organizations.

A second principle was to position and explain research as an activity that has the potential for beneficial and remedial effects when founded on local Aboriginal needs and perspectives. From this outlook, scholarly investigations can be viewed as an opportunity for participants to "research themselves back to life." This approach helped our Aboriginal and non-Aboriginal research team members stay focused on matters related to the process and outcomes. It also served as a reminder of the extent to which Aboriginal and non-Aboriginal lives are intertwined in everyday practices, and how research can be used to help address the various inequities that exist between those two groups. For example, in 2001, Winnipeg had more Aboriginal people living in the inner city than any other urban center in Canada; the number given ranged from 30% to 50%, depending on the data source used (Silver, 2006, p. 16). The growing concentration of Aboriginal people in the inner city is worth noting in particular because of the extreme poverty that characterizes this area. While we understand that poverty is not confined to Aboriginal people alone, we cannot fail to recognize that a disproportionate number of Aboriginal people in the inner city are poor. In 1996, while more than 50% of all inner-city households had incomes below the poverty line, more than 80% of Aboriginal inner-city households were living in poverty (Silver, 2000, p. 39).

We also used a "strength's perspective" approach (Weick, Charles, Sullivan, & Kirstardt, 1989). It is a concept borrowed from social work and begins with the premise that disadvantaged or at-risk groups have existing positive features — strengths — that often go unrecognized and are underutilized by researchers engaged in community development research on account of having been trained to think from a deficit remediation paradigm (Saleebey, 1996). The practical implications can be problematic for the intended recipients of even well-meaning research. For instance, in their review of health and wellness programs in urban Aboriginal communities in Canada,

Davidson, Brasfield, Quressette, and Demerais (1997) concluded that projects initiated from a deficit perspective "failed to provide holistic and culturally appropriate solutions" (p. 38) because they tended to emphasize individual pathologies while neglecting the various ways that Aboriginal people have attempted to address health issues, thereby portraying Aboriginal people as responsible for their own limiting conditions. The negative implications of such perspectives should not be underestimated. As Chapin (1995) pointed out, the findings of research projects founded on deficits are regularly translated into social policies that directly affect people's lives. When the strength's perspectives is applied to research, the emphasis shifts to focus on existing capacities and local agency, thus helping to avoid the double victimization of participants, first through their actual marginalization in society and again through the research process.

Fourth, and finally, is our belief that research should be a cooperative learning endeavor. This meant that our project was to foster a deeper understanding of issues founded on a complex interplay of knowledge and experiences of both Aboriginal and non-Aboriginal people involved in the project. From this perspective, research is a two-way learning process wherein the researchers, collaborators, and participants contribute to, and derive benefits from, the knowledge that is produced. Altogether, these principles aligned with our own understanding of how research should be conducted with Aboriginal people so as to mediate the exploitative nature of traditional paradigms that view participants as the objects — versus active agents — of the research enterprise.

Participatory Methods: Creating a Collaborative Environment

To turn our principles into action, we used social mapping techniques to collect data. The methods included thematic mapping, sketch mapping, biographical writing, and photo elicitation. These approaches have shown to be effective in the context of marginalized populations where the intent is to identify and discuss issues important for everyday social practices. When the contours of these practices are delineated and presented back to the participants for their review and commentary, the possibility for producing a more honest assessment of their experiences, as well as an awareness of their own options for agency, can be created. Such an approach can be an effective tool in the struggle for social justice, a critical element in PAR research.

There are a number of different ways to do social mapping. The methods vary depending on the desired outcomes. In our project, we used social mapping to visually demonstrate, from Aboriginal youth perspectives, where urban Aboriginal students spend their time engaged in healthy leisure activities. The overall goal of the project was to improve access to those spaces, so as to encourage greater physical activity among this population. In total, 18 Aboriginal youth took part in the project. Additionally, six people assisted with the development and implementation of the project and contributed to the data analysis. This group included the two authors, two project coordinators, and two research assistants (university students). Specifically, the youth were asked to construct a social topography and pictorial map of their school and neighborhood environment that (1) identified areas where they are physically active, (2) explained the type of physical activities that happen in those places, and (3) discussed the enabling and constraining elements associated with those spaces. Social mapping provided us and the students with a deeper understanding of the day-to-day recreational preferences of Aboriginal youth in inner-city Winnipeg.

We began with thematic mapping, using large- and small-scale maps of Winnipeg to plot the physical spaces where the youth participants engaged in healthy physical activities, including sport and recreation. We used Post-it notes to mark healthy spaces on each map. We purposefully defined physical activity broadly to include leisure activities, that is, walking to the mall to go shopping or hanging out with friends, to account for the fact that inner-city youth generally do not have regular opportunities to participate in organized sport and recreation. The reasons for this deficiency include socioeconomic factors, as well as issues related to gender (e.g., girls are usually the babysitters or caregivers for younger siblings) and/or race (e.g., aspiring participants are not made to feel welcome in organized settings). As such, when the youth identified sport and recreation as part of their daily life, it was usually within the context of meeting curricular requirements of high school attendance (e.g., gym class).

We also used a sketch mapping technique to plot their personal sport and recreation biographies in map form, as well as biographical writing (brief narrative accounts) and photo elicitation (participant research photos) to obtain relevant information at a very personal level.

In each case, the participant controls how the discursive fragment

Simkin Park: "Where I take my dog to run around and I also play baseball here. You can't see it, but it takes about 5 minutes from my house."

in question is framed. In addition to identifying the active spaces inhabited by youth, the maps call attention to the symbology of empty spaces, those areas youth cannot access for a variety of reasons (e.g., costs, safety, family responsibilities, fear of racism, etc.). When these methods are used together, a coherent image of lived experience emerges.

By using these techniques, we were able to develop visual representations of community use patterns and social dynamics in an urban setting employing cartographic metaphors. The link between the way in which we interpreted indigenous research and PAR was provided by the political intent of the project. Maps can be used visibly and visually to communicate important social information among marginalized groups who may not have the mastery to employ officially sanctioned forms of discourse. In this study, we used social mapping to communicate important social information in an effort to "reclaim the commons" and depict "strategies of resistance" (Aberly, 1993, p. 4). In our case, mapping was used as an effective method to visualize barriers, enabling a deeper analysis of the misalignments between the conditions surrounding the allocation and distribution of sport and recreation facilities and aboriginal youth community use patterns. Researchers who seek to help local populations reclaim communal spaces and to offer alternative visions for

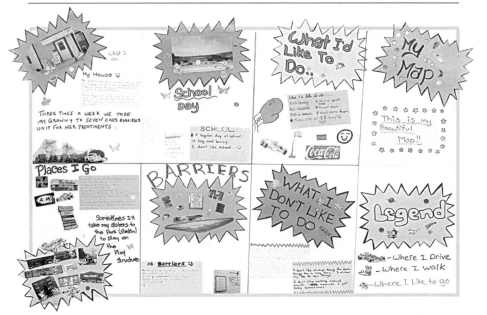

the possibilities of public policy development might find social mapping of benefit.

Conclusion

In this final section, we return to our work with inner-city Aboriginal youth in Winnipeg, Manitoba, and what we have learned about the links between indigenous research, decolonizing methodology and PAR. Our most salient learnings are as follows:

- PAR may be a tool for advocacy and change, if the necessary groundwork for articulating the core principles of indigenous and decolonizing research has been carried out ahead of time and is maintained throughout the project.
- When paired with social mapping techniques, PAR can offer researchers and participants a useful visioning of a space as it presently is structured, thereby helping residents to find a way to reclaim that space in cases of dispossession and marginalization.

Linking indigenous and decolonizing research with social mapping techniques and PAR can potentially lead to productive and mutually beneficial outcomes by overcoming the cartographic silences that exist and continue to limit Aboriginal communities' ability to realize their own goals for sport and recreation, and by giving voice to the research participants, turning ideas, thoughts, and experiences into a reality visible to themselves and to others. Rendering the topography of their marginalization visible to Aboriginal participants themselves in this way can have a strong enabling effect for their capacity for self-generated political intervention. It is the creation of enabling effects that often extend beyond the duration of a specific project that defines PAR's potential to effect progressive change.

As methodologies that seek to make visible the social experiences of marginalized groups and individuals, PAR and applications such as social mapping are closely related to the cultural turn's focus on narratives of individual experience. While some aspects of the cultural turn do not share the explicitly political orientation of indigenous and decolonizing research, they are both now part of the mainstream; there is now significant interest in these approaches and their legitimization. In view of their epistemic assumptions relative to the fluid and performative nature of social existence, however, they remain experimental in a principal sense, in that the authorization of knowledge cannot occur without validation of the entire research process by the indigenous community involved. The situatedness of a research process in the process of academic knowledge production alone can no longer serve as the sole criterion of validation. This creative contingency is also reflected in the necessity to demonstrate the political relevancy of a project for indigenous participants, every time over.

There is thus much to be learned from a multitude of fields, where thoughtful and provocative discussions are taking place: researchers need to continue to engage with indigenous research and decolonizing methodologies more critically, and our practice needs to take place within a broader awareness of the work of scholars in other fields. In doing so we can help bridge what are often disparate but informed discussions, raising our level of awareness and understanding of these alternative. And while fuzzy terminology might be expected from an emergent field, and perhaps even encouraged to support new and experimental forms of inquiry, there remains an ongoing need to articulate and examine the intellectual practices underlying such thinking if these approaches are to develop any further.

References

Aberly, D. (1993). *Boundaries of home: Mapping for local empowerment*. Gabriola Island, BC: New Society.

Bale, J., & Vertinsky, P. (Eds.). (2004). *Sites of sport: Space, place, experience*. London and New York: Routledge.

Battiste, M., & Youngblood Henderson, J. (2000). *Protecting indigenous knowledge and heritage: A global challenge*. Saskatoon, SK: Purich.

Booth, D. (2005). *The field: Truth and fiction in sport history*. London: Routledge.

Brown, L., & Strega, S. (Eds.). (2005). *Research as resistance: Critical, indigenous & anti-oppressive approaches*. Toronto, ON: Canadian Scholars' Press.

Burke, P. (2005). Performing history: The importance of occasions. *Rethinking History, 9*(1), 35–52.

Castellano, M. (2000). Updating Aboriginal traditions of knowledge. In G. J. Sefa De, B. L. Hall, & D. G. Rosenberg (Eds.), *Indigenous knowledges in global contexts: Multiple readings of our world* (pp. 21–36). Toronto, ON: OISE & University of Toronto Press.

Castleden, H., Garvin, T., & Huu-ay-aht First Nation. (2008). Modifying photo voice for community-based participatory Indigenous research. *Social Science & Medicine, 66*, 1393–1405.

Chapin, R. K. (1995). Social policy development: The strength's perspective. *Social Work, 40*, 506–515.

Cole, P. (2004). Trick(sters) of Aboriginal research: Or how to use ethical review strategies to perpetuate cultural genocide. *Native Studies Review, 15*(2), 7–30.

Davidson, S., Brasfield, C., Quressette, S., & Demerais, L. (1997). What makes us strong: Urban Aboriginal perspectives on wellness and strength. *Canadian Journal of Mental Health, 16*(2), 37–50.

Denzin, N. K. (2001). The reflexive interview and a performative social science. *Qualitative Research, 1*, 23–46.

Denzin, N., & Lincoln, Y. S. (Eds.). (2005). *The Sage handbook of qualitative research (3rd ed.)*. Thousand Oaks, CA: Sage Publications.

Denzin, N. K., Lincoln, Y. S., & Smith, L. T. (Eds.). (2008). *Handbook of critical and indigenous methodologies*. Thousand Oaks, CA: Sage.

Ellen, R., Parkes, P., & Bicker, A. (Eds.). (2000). *Indigenous environmental knowledge and its transformations: Critical anthropological perspectives*. Amsterdam: Harwood Academic.

Ermine, W., Sinclair, R., & Jeffery, B. (2004). *The ethics of research involving indigenous peoples. Report of the Indigenous Peoples' Health Research Centre to the Interagency Advisory Panel on Research Ethics*. Regina, SK: Indigenous Peoples' Health Research Centre.

Giles, A., & Forsyth, J. (2007). On common ground: Power, knowledge, and practice in the study of Aboriginal sport and recreation. *Journal of Sports and Leisure, 1*, 1–20.

hooks, b. (1999). *Yearning: Race, gender, and cultural politics*. Toronto, ON: Between the Lines.

Inuit Tapiriit Kanatami. (2003). Negotiating research relationships: A guide for communities. *Pimatziwin: A Journal of Aboriginal and Indigenous Community Health, 1*(1), 17–25.

Johnson, J. T. (2008). Kitchen table discourse: Negotiating the "tricky ground" of indigenous research. *American Indian Culture and Research Journal, 32*(3), 127–137.

Jordan, S. (2003). Who stole my methodology? Co-opting PAR. *Globalisation, Societies and Education, 1*, 185–200.

King, C. R., & Leonhard, D. L. (Eds.). (2006). *Visual economies of/in motion: Sport and film*. New York: Peter Lang.

McNaughton, C., & Rock, D. (2004). Opportunities in Aboriginal research: Results of SSHRC's dialogue on research and Aboriginal peoples. *Native Studies Review, 15*(2), 37–60.

Manzo, L. C., & Brightbill, N. (2007). Toward a participatory ethics. In S. Kindon, R. Pain, & M. Kesby (Eds.), *Participatory action research approaches and methods: Connecting people, participation and place* (pp. 33–40). London: Routledge.

Markula, P., & Pringle, R. (2006). *Foucault, sport and exercise: Power, knowledge and transforming the self*. London: Routledge.

Martin-Hill, D. (2008). *The Lubicon Lake Nation. Indigenous knowledge and power.* Toronto, ON: University of Toronto Press.

Mihesuah, D. A. (Ed.). (1998). *Natives and academics: Researching and writing about American Indians.* Lincoln and London: University of Nebraska Press.

Paraschak, V., Heine, M., & McAra, J. (1995). Native and academic knowledge interests: A dilemma. In K. Wamsley (Ed.), *Method and methodology in sport and cultural history* (pp. 62–68). Dubuque, IA: Brown and Benchmark.

Rigney, L. (1999). Internationalization of an indigenous anticolonial cultural critique of research methodologies. A guide to indigenist research methodology and its principles. *Wicazo SA Journal of Native American Studies Review, 14*(2), 109–121.

Ryba, T. V., & Wright, H. K. (2005). From mental game to cultural praxis: A cultural studies model's implications for the future of sport psychology. *Quest, 57,* 192–212.

Saleebey, D. (1996). The strength's perspective in social work practice: Extensions and cautions. *Social Work, 41,* 296–306.

Schinke, R. J., Blodgett, A., Ritchie, C., Pickard, P., Michel, G., Peltier, D., et al. (2009). Entering the community of Canadian indigenous athletes. In R. J. Schinke & S. J. Hanrahan (Eds.), *Cultural sport psychology: From theory to practice* (pp. 91–102). Champaign, IL: Human Kinetics.

Schinke, R. J., Eys, M. A., Danielson, R., Michel, G., Peltier, D., Pheasant, C., et al. (2006a). Cultural social support for Canadian Aboriginal elite athletes during their sport development. *International Journal of Sport Psychology, 37,* 1–19.

Schinke, R. J., & Hanrahan, S. J. (Eds.). (2009). *Cultural sport psychology: From theory to practice.* Champaign, IL: Human Kinetics.

Schinke, R. J., Michel, G., Gauthier, A.,

Danielson, R., Pickard, P., Peltier, D., et al. (2006b). Adaptation to the mainstream in elite sport: A Canadian Aboriginal perspective. *The Sport Psychologist, 20,* 435–448.

Silver, J. (Ed.). (2000). *Solutions that work: Fighting poverty in Winnipeg.* Winnipeg and Halifax: Canadian Centre for Policy Alternatives, Manitoba and Fernwood.

Silver, J. (2006). *In their own voices: Building urban Aboriginal communities.* Halifax, NS: Fernwood.

Social Sciences and Humanities Research Council. (2009). Applying for Funding, Strategic Research Grants. Retrieved March 17, 2009, from http://www.sshrc.ca/site/apply-demande/faculty-profes seurs-eng.aspx.

Smith, L. T. (1999). *Decolonizing methodologies: Research and indigenous peoples.* London: Zed Books Ltd.

Smith, L. T. (2005). On tricky ground: Researching the Native in the age of uncertainty. In N. K. Denzin & Y. S. Lincoln (Eds.), *The Sage handbook of qualitative research* (3rd ed., pp. 85–107). Thousand Oaks, CA: Sage.

Wax, M. L. (1991). The ethics of research in American Indian communities. *American Indian Quarterly, 15*(4), 431–457.

Warrior, R. (1999). The Native American scholar: Towards a new intellectual agenda. *Wicaso Sa Review, 14*(2), 46–54.

Weick, A., Charles, R., Sullivan, P., & Kisthardt, W. (1989). A strength's perspective for social work practice. *Social Work, 34,* 350–354.

Wilson, S. (2001). What is indigenous research methodology? *Canadian Journal of Native Education, 25,* 175–179.

Wilson, W. A., & Yellow Bird, M. (Eds.). (2005). *For indigenous eyes only: A decolonization handbook.* Santa Fe, NM: School of American Research.

Witt, N. (2007). What if indigenous knowledge contradicts accepted scientific findings? *Educational Research and Review, 2,* 225–235.

9

RETHINKING SUBJECTIVITY IN SPORT AND EXERCISE PSYCHOLOGY: A FEMINIST POST-STRUCTURALIST PERSPECTIVE ON WOMEN'S EMBODIED PHYSICAL ACTIVITY

Kerry R. McGannon and Rebecca Busanich

CHAPTER SUMMARY

There is great power in the limited way(s) that female bodies and physical activity are represented because such representations become commonsense ways of relating to ourselves as embodied beings. Neither a neutral nor a benign process, these commonsense representations of the body and physical activity — whether at the level of culture or the individual — are connected to dominant discourses that perpetuate a theme of thinness conflated with an ideal where it is suggested that thin is healthy and fit, regardless of how (or even if) it can be attained. Researchers in psychology, public health, cultural studies, and sport and exercise psychology problematize the foregoing because when women's bodies do not meet appearance ideals they experience their physical selves as flawed. In this chapter, we explore feminist post-structuralism as a way to extend the above scholarship by theorizing women's physical selves (i.e., subjectivities) as *constructed* within discourses. We conclude by discussing how a post-structuralist approach to subjectivity contributes toward feminist consciousness and the implications for behavior change and physical activity promotion. The purpose is to ultimately show that feminist post-structuralism is a useful theoretical tool to add to existing forms of feminist analysis in sport and exercise psychology by advancing nuanced forms of critical analysis of women's physical activity promotion within health and fitness discourses.

Rethinking Subjectivity in Sport and Exercise Psychology

Do you have to be strong-armed into training your upper body? Many of us do, especially women. Most of us tend to focus on our lower bodies, while men tend to favor developing their upper bodies. Which gender has the winning strategy for a strong, sexy body?

—*Cedar Rapids Gazette*, Health Section 3E, February 21, 2005

When promoting physical activity, popular culture sources (e.g., newspapers, magazines) often invoke stereotypical images and ideals concerning gender (Bordo, 1993; Choi, 2000; Markula, 1995, 2001, 2003; Markula, Burns, & Riley, 2008; Mutrie & Choi, 2000). In turn, women's physical activity narratives tend to rely upon narrowly defined images of femininity, which are linked to the ideologies[1] of individualism, consumerism, and heteronormativity (Bordo, 1993; Markula et al., 2008). To begin to illustrate these points, consider the following personal narrative of author Kerry McGannon about her physical self and physical activity experiences:

"As a physically active woman, the journey of understanding my physical self has spanned over 20 years. I have drawn upon weight loss and appearance discourses to make sense of, and experience, my body as fat and unfit, fat and fit, lean and fit, and lean and unfit. By objective appearance standards I was (and am) neither too fat, too thin nor too muscular—the images and associated meanings tied to such standards mirrored back to me by popular cultural discourses "tell" me so. By drawing upon such discourses, I engaged in dietary and exercise practices such as counting calories, doing particular exercises (e.g., aerobics, abdominal/sit-up exercises), and avoiding particular exercises (e.g., lifting heavy weights) in order to make my body smaller and a particular shape. I have experienced a paradox of feelings in relation to my body and physical activity, such as guilt, anxiety, happiness, enjoyment, frustration, elation, a sense of freedom and control, and a loss of control. The result has been a sense of subjectivity that is shifting and contradictory; on the one hand I have experienced my physical self as flawed and in need of fixing via exercise. On the other hand I have experienced my physical self as strong because of liberating features of my exercise (Brabazon, 2006; Haravon Collins, 2002; Krane, Choi, Baird, Aimar, & Kauer, 2004; Markula, 1995, 2003; Markula & Pringle, 2006).

"During my nine years (1994–2002) as a group fitness leader, I witnessed female exercise participants of all shapes and sizes draw upon weight loss and appearance discourses to ask questions about their bodies; "how can I get rid of THIS?" (pointing at: abdominals or thighs), "how many calories did we burn?" or "I've been doing this exercise for a year, why isn't the weight coming off?" And many of us—participants and fitness leaders alike—despite trying to attain a particular version of fitness via the gendered practice of aerobics, also recognized the futility of obtaining the socially constructed ideal fit female body (Markula, 1995, 2003; McGannon, 2003, 2004; Mutrie & Choi, 2000). Some of my fitness participants and fitness instructor colleagues went further than verbal acknowledgment and irritation at the socially constructed ideal fit female body, and openly challenged and transgressed the ideal. For example, one of my instructor friends taught boxing and saw her muscularity and athleticism as a tool for her sport and recreational endeavors. She strove to be strong and imparted that knowledge to fitness participants through how she structured her boxing classes with women (e.g., emphasizing skill and correct form; deemphasizing body-shaping motives and practices). Another group of participants I taught in a class for overweight women reclaimed the term *fit and fat* and openly appreciated their curvier fleshier bodies.

"When I left teaching group exercise in 2003 and took up recreational running, I continued to draw upon weight management and appearance discourses to experience my running as a body management tool and familiar experiences followed (e.g., I felt guilty when I didn't run; I felt fat if I ate too much and/or if I didn't run far enough). Contradictory experiences continued when I resisted weight loss and appearance discourses by framing my physical activity within health and wellness discourses (Duncan, 1994; Foucault, 1977; Markula, 2001) to experience my running as empowering and my body as fit apart from how it looked. Healthy psychological experiences (e.g., enjoyment, a sense of accomplishment) and behavioral practices (e.g., not using running as a punishment but as a tool for energy and well-being) followed when I drew upon alternative discourses."

What we hope further to show with Kerry's brief self-reflexive narrative is the power and complexity in the way(s) that female bodies and physical activity are (re)presented and experienced. Such representations have power and complexity because they become commonsense ways of understanding and relating to ourselves as embodied beings, which is further linked to health and well-being (Wiggins, 2008). Neither a neutral nor a benign process, commonsense representations of the female body and physical activity—whether at the level of culture or the individual—are connected to weight loss and appearance discourses perpetuating a pervasive theme of thinness conflated with an ideal suggesting that a thin body is healthy and fit (Bordo, 1993; Choi, 2000; Markula, 1995, 2001, 2003; Markula et al., 2008; Mutrie & Choi, 2000; Wiggins, 2008).

Researchers in sport and exercise psychology and cultural studies have problematized the notion that "thin is fit and healthy" because when women's bodies do not meet appearance ideals—and the ideal cannot be attained (Bordo, 1993; Choi, 2000; Markula, 2001; Mutrie & Choi, 2000) women feel dissatisfied with their bodies (Grogan, 1999, 2008; Krane et al., 2004; Markula, 1995, 2003; Prichard & Tiggemann, 2005; Raedeke, Focht, & Scales, 2007). Feeling dissatisfied with one's body is linked to unhealthy behaviors for female recreational exercisers and athletes. Behaviors include avoidance of public places to be active (Eriksson, Baigi, Marklund, & Lindgren, 2008), avoidance of particular forms of physical activity (e.g., weight training) or over-exercising (Prichard & Tiggemann, 2008), withdrawal from exercise when appearance-related motives are not attained (Segar, Spruijt-Metz, & Nolen-Hoeksema, 2006), and athletic performance concerns related to appearance concerns (e.g., toned but not too muscular) (Krane, Waldron, Michaelnok, & Stiles-Shipley, 2001). Exercisers and athletes who experience the perception that others are judging their bodies (i.e., social physique anxiety) (Hart, Leary, & Rejeski, 1989) are also vulnerable for disordered eating and disordered exercise patterns (Hausenblas, Brewer, & Van Raalte, 2004; Krane et al., 2004; Krane, Stiles-Shipley, Waldron, & Michaelnok, 2001; Levine & Piran, 2004; Stice, 2002).

Kerry's personal physical activity experiences echo the preceding pessimistic literature findings that women do not always experience the positive self-related benefits of physical activity promoted by sport and exercise psychologists. However, her narrative also illustrates that weight loss and appearance discourses and associated meanings (e.g., thin is fit, exercise leads to weight loss) and practices (e.g., disordered eating, avoiding particular forms of exercise) can be actively challenged/resisted to experience one's self as strong and healthy apart from appearance aspirations (Haravon Collins, 2002; Markula, 1995, 2003; Markula & Pringle, 2006). How can women begin and continue to challenge/resist gendered regimes surrounding their physically active bodies to make physical activity experiences more liberating and healthy and more frequently connected to positive self-related views?

Researchers in exercise psychology and cultural studies agree that answering the above question is difficult because the self and physical activity is associated with sociocultural influences (e.g., media, fitness industry, peers, and family). It has been further acknowledged that self-related concerns (e.g., body image) are public health issues that need to be addressed as social and cultural issues (Bordo, 1993; Grogan, 2008; Krane et al., 2001b; Krane et al., 2004; Mutrie & Choi, 2000; Markula et al., 2008). Despite this acknowledgment, the intricate relationship between sociocultural influences, the physical self, and women's physical activity participation remains poorly understood. Following the call for alternative theoretical perspectives to understand the self and physical activity in sport and exercise psychology that locate the impact of sociocultural influences within larger frameworks of power (Fisher, Butryn, & Roper, 2003; Fisher, Roper, & Butryn, 2009; McGannon & Johnson, 2009; McGannon & Mauws, 2002), we explore the potential of a theoretical perspective on the margins of sport and exercise psychology: feminist post-structuralism (Gavey, 1997; Henriques, Holloway, Urwin, Venn, & Walkerdine, 1998; Hollway, 1989; Weedon, 1997).

To accomplish our purpose, the central assumptions of feminist post-structuralism and the implications for conceptualizing and understanding the self and women's physical activity participation will be discussed. The ways in which a feminist post-structuralist approach to the self and subjectivity further contributes toward raising feminist consciousness so that physical activity promotion and participation can lead to empowering psychological and emotional experiences for women will then be outlined. The ultimate goal is to show how feminist post-structuralism adds to existing forms of critical analysis in sport and exercise psychology (e.g., critical feminist approaches of Krane, 1994, 2001b) by advancing more nuanced forms of critical analysis of the self and women's physical activity participation.

Post-structuralism and the Self

In the recently edited book *Cultural Sport Psychology* (Schinke & Hanrahan, 2009), Kerry McGannon and Christina Johnson outlined how post-structuralism (Henriques et al., 1984; Hollway, 1989; Weedon, 1987) can be used to contribute toward carrying out reflexive cultural sport psychology research. As the term is used here, *reflexive* pertains to issues relating to the self and identity of the researcher;

reflexive researchers acknowledge their own experiences and how such experiences influence the research process, thus questioning the possibility of collecting and evaluating data with complete objectivity (McGannon & Johnson, 2009). While McGannon and Johnson focused on the self of the researcher, they also noted the implications of post-structuralism for how female athletes make sense of their embodied physical selves. The contribution of post-structuralism to understanding the self and physical activity participation within exercise psychology was also outlined in an earlier paper by McGannon and Mauws (2002). In the present section we draw upon the information presented by McGannon and Johnson and McGannon and Mauws to briefly outline post-structuralism and the implications for the self. The sections that follow also extend the two previous articles by further developing the features of feminist post- structuralism we see relevant for advancing feminist understandings of the self and women's physical activity participation. Where appropriate, empirical research examples will be integrated into the discussion.

In general the term *post-structuralism* refers to a collection of diverse theoretical positions (e.g., Derridean deconstruction, Lacanian psychoanalysis, and Foucauldian analysis of power and discourses) related to a body of literature exploring the ambiguity inherent in language, meaning, and subjectivity (Gavey, 1997; McGannon & Mauws, 2002; Weedon, 1997). All of these theoretical positions give primacy to the process and outcome of language, as opposed to the content, and how language is tied to discursive and social practices. Understanding discourses as competing ways of giving meaning to the world makes language a site of exploration and struggle. These ideas reinforce the notion that language *structures* reality rather than *reflects* a pre-given reality (McGannon & Mauws, 2000, 2002). Therefore language and discourse are key in the (re)production of what people hold as true and factual and the (re)production of power (Gavey, 1997; Weedon, 1997).

Because language is regarded as constitutive of reality, from a post-structuralist perspective self-related phenomena is regarded as constituted and brought into being in social activity, particularly in *discourse* (Harré & Gillett, 2004; Potter & Wetherell, 1987). From a post-structuralist perspective, language does not result from the self, reflect self-related views, or provide transparent access to the self (McGannon & Mauws, 2000, 2002). Instead, the self is a discursive accomplishment that is simultaneously local, social, cultural, and political (Gavey, 1997; Weedon, 1997). Knowledge and conceptualizations of the self are therefore further contextualized in social practice and webs of power (Weedon, 1997), making language *the* means by which "social organization and power are defined and contested and the place where one's sense of self—one's subjectivity—is constructed" (Richardson & St. Pierre, 2005, p. 961).

Feminism and Feminist Cultural Studies

While more will be said about the above ideas and how they can be extended into feminist post-structuralism to understand the self and women's physical activity participation, it is important to first outline what is meant by the term *feminism*. Defining feminism is important because feminist post-structuralism adheres to its basic tenets and understanding these tenets is important to further articulate the contribution feminist post-structuralism makes to sport and exercise psychology. Additionally, while no empirical studies exist within sport and exercise psychology employing feminist post-structuralism, some researchers in sport and exercise psychology have used a critical cultural studies perspective grounded in feminism[2] to understand women's sport and exercise participation in the context of ideal femininity. These studies provide an important foundation and excellent starting point to introduce feminist post-structuralism and the potential contributions to sport and exercise psychology.

Feminism is a broad term with multiple meanings that implies multiple perspectives rather than one theoretical framework (Crotty, 1998; Gill, 2001). While feminism used to be marked by the distinct categories of liberal, Marxist, radical, psychoanalytic, socialist, existentialist, and postmodern feminism (Tong, 1995), contemporary feminist theories are conceived of in the plural (Birrell, 2000; Krane, 1994). As a set of theories constantly undergoing change, feminism adheres to the central assumption that gender is a primary and productive category of experience (Birrell, 2000). Hall and Stevens (1991) noted three basic principles inherent in all feminisms: (1) a valuing of women and attaching validity to their experiences, ideas, and needs; (2) a recognition of the conditions that oppress women; and (3) a desire to bring about social change through criticisms and political action. Additionally, Striegel-Moore (1994) noted that all feminist scholarship aims to recognize bias as an inherent aspect of human inquiry, maintain a stance of self-conscious reflexivity, and emphasize context as essential for understanding human behavior.

Contemporary feminist psychologists (e.g., Gavey, 1997; Gergen, 2001; Hollway, 1989; Wiggins, 2008) most closely align with either post-structuralism or critical cultural studies perspectives. In addition to being used in feminist psychology, critical perspectives have also been used within the cultural studies of sport (see Birrell, 2000). In a shift away from gender as the only category of oppression, a feminist cultural studies approach recognizes the intersection of gender, race, class, sexuality, religion, age, and other categories of difference as "the interconnected matrix of relations of power" (Birrell, 2000, p. 65). The main agenda of a feminist cultural studies approach is to identify the ways in which power is produced, reproduced, and resisted, often through an understated existing ideology (Birrell, 2000). As the term is used here, *ideology* refers to a set of ideas that privilege a dominant group yet are adopted as common sense by an entire society, including those who are disempowered by them (Theberge & Birell, 1994). In addition to looking at the (re)production of ideologies, the area of feminist cultural studies is increasingly informed by Gramscian hegemony theory, with hegemony referring to ideologies that are so entrenched within a society that they are no longer questioned and are assumed as the truth (Birrell, 2000; see Pringle, 2005 for an in-depth discussion of Gramscian theoretical tools in sport).

As a site of ideological contestation and negotiation and powerful hegemonic discourses, sport has emerged as a domain for critical feminist scholarship (Birrell, 2000). Birrell (1988) identified four themes inherent in feminist cultural studies scholarship we see as pertinent to understanding athletes' and exercisers' embodied experiences: "(1) the production of an ideology of masculinity and male power through sport, (2) the media practices through which dominant notions of women are reproduced, (3) physicality, sexuality and the body as sites for defining gender relations, and (4) the resistance of women to dominant sport practices" (Birrell, 2000, p. 67).

Feminist Sport and Exercise Psychology Research

Feminism has been noted as an important theoretical framework within sport and exercise psychology because women's experiences are placed at the center of analysis and it challenges assumptions of traditional psychological research (e.g., value-free objective researcher, the promotion of physical activity as neutral and accessible to everyone), allowing for new forms of knowledge to be considered and used to advance understandings of women's experiences in sport and exercise (Gill, 2001; Krane, 1994). Researchers in sport and exercise psychology have taken on some of the above themes, recognizing the ways in which a feminist paradigm extends our understanding of physical activity behavior from a psychological perspective (Choi, 2000; Gill, 2001; Krane, 1994, 2001b; Mutrie & Choi, 2000). In a special issue of *The Sport Psychologist*, intellectual space was created for feminist perspectives in sport and exercise psychology (e.g., Gill, 2001; Krane, 2001b). Consistent with feminist tenets, articles in the issue focused upon an action oriented view of feminism, seeking to end sexism and the oppression of women. Further, gender was viewed as socially and culturally constructed and thus linked to race, class, and social identities within the context of power issues.

While little empirical research has been done exploring the self and women's physical activity participation from a critical feminist perspective, examples of research using a feminist cultural studies approach come from Vikki Krane's work. Krane (2001a) used the concept of hegemonic femininity[3] to understand how female athletes experience and negotiate their physical selves and the social psychological implications. Drawing upon the work of sport studies scholars such as Cole (1993), Hall (1996), and Lenskyi (1990, 1994), Krane (2001a) noted that because femininity is historically and socially constructed rather than naturally given, there are multiple femininities in Western culture. However, there is a privileged or hegemonic form of femininity, which emphasizes a white, heterosexual, thin, and toned ideal, with gendered physical activities (e.g., aerobics, lifting light weights, aesthetic sports) promoted as the means to achieve the ideal. Improper bodies, even when physically active, transgress ideal femininity by being too fat, too muscular, too thin, and/or not white and heterosexual. Hegemonic femininity was further outlined as connecting the physically active female body to self-policing/self-surveillance, self-transformation, and moral responsibility, with research in cultural studies of sport supporting these notions (Duncan, 1994; Maguire & Mansfield, 1998; Markula, 1995). When female bodies in sport and exercise conform either through how they look and/or how they move, they are viewed as normal and morally superior. In contrast to what is normal, good and moral, improper bodies along with associated improper physical activities (e.g., contact sport such as rugby, lifting heavy weights) are judged as abnormal, morally inferior and/or bad (Krane, 2001a; Krane et al., 2004).

Krane (2001a) further noted that "women's psychological well-being requires that women form new modes of perceiving their bodies, unrestrained by hegemonic femininity. They must learn to enjoy and appreciate their bodies rather than focus on how to mold them into some semblance of the feminine ideal body" (p. 129). As a means of improving self-regard and body image apart from ideal femininity, a suggested solution from a feminist cultural studies perspective is for women to participate in sport activities that allow them to feel strong and powerful. Further, women must receive social support for engaging in feminist sport practices (e.g., improving skills, working toward noncompetitive goals, improving mental and physical fitness) rather than reinforcement from coaches and teammates about how they look, to make positive self-related experiences lasting. Finally, Krane proposed that muscular and physically assertive female athletes (i.e., rugby and ice hockey players, boxers) and lesbian athletes all directly resist/challenge notions of hegemonic femininity.

In a qualitative study, Krane et al. (2001b) used the concept of hegemonic femininity to understand how women in sport versus exercise perceive their bodies. It was found that female athletes experienced body (dis)satisfaction depending on the social context and their multidimensional body image, which includes an internalized cultural ideal body image (i.e., appearance body) and an internalized athletic body image (i.e., performance body) (Krane et al., 2001b). Exercisers were shown to experience positive and negative effects in relation to body image that were also tied to cultural female body ideals; when body image was viewed positively, self-assurance resulted and when body image was negative, disconcerting mental states (e.g., guilt, anxiety) were experienced and self-presentation concerns resulted.

More recently, Krane et al. (2004) used a feminist cultural studies approach to explore the link between hegemonic femininity and how the effects of ideal femininity are exercised ideologically in a qualitative study of 21 female athletes and body image. It was found that in negotiating femininity with athleticism, female athletes developed two contrasting internal self-identities of "woman" and "athlete" and experienced positive and negative effects from their activity in the form of a paradox. This paradox, in brief, was that athletic women were proud of their trained bodies, but at the same time, were conflicted about their muscular bodies within the context of the culturally defined ideal body (Krane et al., 2004). Unfortunately, athletic women's empowerment from their physical activity and muscular bodies was shown to be undermined by body dissatisfaction as a result of their immersion in broader cultural expectations surrounding ideal female bodies.

Together, from the research findings in the above studies, there is indication that as long as appearance and weight loss are emphasized in women's physical activity promotion and participation, self-esteem and body image will be entwined with culturally defined ideal femininity and unhealthy effects may result (e.g., disordered eating, compulsive exercising, anxiety). These findings are consistent with work in cultural studies of physical activity where it has been found that while female exercise participants are empowered by their activity and aware that media messages are unrealistic, they may still feel dissatisfied with their bodies (Brabazon, 2006; Maguire & Mansfield, 1998; Markula, 1995, 2003; Markula & Pringle, 2006). Practical strategies that could eradicate pressures in sport and exercise settings that reinforce negative body image and body dissatisfaction perceptions include the minimization of social influences' (e.g., coaches, exercise leaders, administrators) discussion of weight and body shape, instead focusing on fitness and athletic skill improvement. Finally, broader social and cultural change (e.g., advertising in fitness centers, media treatment of female athletes) needs to occur if social and individual-level change are to be internalized and lasting (Krane, 2001a; Krane et al., 2001b; Krane et al., 2004). Mutrie and Choi (2000) and Choi (2000) have also highlighted the importance of promoting physically active lifestyles at the social and cultural level within health and exercise psychology using a feminist sensibility to encourage more physically active lifestyles based on intrinsic (e.g., enjoyment) rather than extrinsic (e.g., body beautiful ideals) motivations.

The sport and exercise psychology literature from a feminist cultural studies perspective has taught us a great deal about how gender is experienced and negotiated by female athletes and exercisers and the psychological and behavioral effects. Such research is important because it raises awareness about what is taken for granted about physical activity and the female body (e.g., being thin is fit and healthy, being muscular and athletic is not feminine, physical activity should be promoted as a weight loss tool). Raising such awareness has led to studying and understanding why ideal femi-

ninity in sport and exercise can be problematic, how ideal femininity can be transgressed, and the practical implications for individual
and sociocultural change. Despite the knowledge generated from
studies grounded in feminist cultural studies approaches, such research remains on the margins of sport and exercise psychology to
explore the self and physical activity participation.

More research using feminist cultural studies perspectives is
clearly needed in sport and exercise psychology to better understand the self and women's physical activity participation. In addition to future work employing a feminist cultural studies perspective, two points recently raised by cultural studies scholars can also
contribute toward advancing feminist research in sport and exercise
psychology. Markula et al. (2008) and Markula and Pringle (2006)
have challenged some feminist researchers' work grounded in critical perspectives and psychology's adherence to a neoliberal view of
the self to study women's physical activity. These scholars have also
pointed out the implications of how critical perspectives focusing on
the study of hegemonic relations conceptualize power and how that
impacts understandings of the self in the context of body management (e.g., exercise, dieting) practices in one way, as opposed to another (Markula et al., 2008; Markula & Pringle, 2006)[4].

Markula et al.'s (2008) and Markula and Pringle's (2006) critique
of the neoliberal self is in line with feminist post-structuralist psychologists' critiques of an essentialist view of the self, where it is assumed that people share a unique essence of human nature known
as "the self," which is an entity that can be accessed (Gavey, 1997;
Henriques et al., 1998; Hollway, 1983, 1989). An essentialist view of
the self further emphasizes a *natural* and *obvious* separation of self
and society (Harré & Gillett, 1994), viewing the self as a structure or
process residing within the mind, or as a social property of culture
that is internalized into the mind (Cerulo, 1997). For example, the
previously reviewed feminist research revealed that "disconcerting
mental states," "body image," "identities," and "self-esteem" within
the individual were impacted by separate and distinct social (e.g.,
coaches, teammates) and cultural (e.g., feminine ideals from the media and fitness industry) influences. Solutions that lead toward more
healthy self-related views and behaviors focused upon how internal
problematic self-perceptions within the individual can be changed
by impacting sociocultural influences (e.g., social support, what

coaches do or say) or by resisting externally imposed feminine "gender roles" (e.g., participating in non-feminine sports).

While largely unchallenged by sport and exercise psychology researchers (exceptions are Faulkner & Finlay, 2002; Locke, 2004; McGannon & Mauws, 2000, 2002; Smith & Sparkes, 2005), empirical research in cultural studies has challenged psychology's focus on the interiority of the person because it has resulted in a decontextualized understanding of the sociocultural realm within which embodiment and body management practices (i.e., exercise) take place (e.g., Markula, 2001; Markula & Pringle, 2006; Thorpe, 2008). In addition to adhering to an essentialist view of the self, feminist research conducted in sport psychology studying female embodiment and body management practices conceptualizes power as coming from the top down, which means that dominant groups (e.g., heterosexist media, the fitness industry) oppress marginalized groups (e.g., overweight women, lesbian sporting women, muscular women). As mentioned, power within the context of Krane's research has been shown to exert influence over how women think and feel about themselves in sport and exercise contexts through ideological constructions of femininity (i.e., ideal femininity). Thus, feminist perspectives as used in sport and exercise psychology research to date have conceptualized power as working *on* people (i.e., power is effectively held by the dominant over the dominated, but exercised ideologically rather than through force or threat of force). At the same time, hegemonic relations are thought to be unstable because subordinated women possess agency by taking control over their bodies and self-related views through the various ways outlined by Krane (2001a) and Krane and colleagues. Such a conception of how power works in relation to the self is but one fruitful way to understand the self and women's physical activity participation.

To conclude this section we reiterate that research grounded in feminist cultural studies is extremely informative and provides an excellent starting point to understand the complex relationship between sociocultural influences, the self, and women's physical activity participation in sport and exercise psychology. We advocate that more work be done in sport and exercise psychology employing a feminist cultural studies approach. What should also be clear is that there is still much to be learned from a feminist perspective about the self and women's physical activity participation, and the psychological and behavioral implications. Feminist cultural studies perspectives, as used by researchers in sport and exercise psychology to date, are but one way accomplish feminist research. A feminist post-structuralist perspective is another useful theoretical tool to expand a feminist understanding of sociocultural influences on the self and women's physical activity in light of its differential view of power, ideology, and the self.

Feminist Post-structuralism and the Self

The stream of feminist post-structuralism that we draw upon to understand the self and women's physical activity participation is informed by critical cultural theorist Chris Weedon. Weedon (1997) suggested that post-structuralism provides a useful foundation for feminist practice, describing feminist post-structuralism as "a mode of knowledge production which uses post-structuralist theories of language, subjectivity, social processes and institutions to understand existing power relations and to identify areas and strategies for change" (pp. 40–41). Our earlier brief overview of post-structuralism focused upon three ideas central to feminist post-structuralism that will now be further developed: (1) the self and subjectivity are constituted in language and discourse (i.e., the self is a discursive accomplishment); (2) language and discourse are therefore of great interest in understanding what people hold to be true about themselves and others; and (3) exploring the self as a discursive accomplishment requires a consideration of how power (i.e., social processes) allows for the acceptance and validation of some forms of self-related knowledge over others. It is important to note that the foregoing conceptualization of the self is in contrast to the essentialist view of the self outlined earlier that informs critical research grounded in feminist perspectives in sport and exercise psychology.

Weedon's work is particularly influenced by Foucault's (1978) concept of discourse to help understand the relationship between socially constructed forms of truth, power, and the implications for self-related knowledge and associated behavioral practices. For Foucault, language is always located in discourse, which refers to an interrelated "system of statements that cohere around common meanings and values . . . [that] are a product of social factors, of powers and practices *rather than an individual's set of ideas*" (Hollway, 1983, p. 231; emphasis added). Further, discourse is a broad concept referring to various ways of constituting meaning, which is specific to particular groups, cultures, and historical contexts (Gavey, 1997; Markula & Pringle, 2006). While discourse can refer to verbal performances, discourse is not limited to conversations between individuals and can also be understood as providing the meanings that constitute people's everyday practices. Thus discourses not only "systematically form the objects of which they speak" (Foucault, 1978, p. 49) but they have material/concrete implications for bodies and embodiment (Markula et al., 2008). Stated differently, while discourses are resources that people can draw upon to explain and/or give meaning to who they are and what they experience, discourses also actively shape, enable, and/or constrain behavioral practices.

A study by Thomsson (1999), which used the concept of discourse as outlined above to understand women's physical activity participation, helps to illustrate the above points. Focusing upon naturally occurring talk within interviews with Swedish women, women's everyday talk about exercise and how talk organized their actions in socially specific ways were explored. How "exercise" was constructed in consistent and variable ways via the words and concepts employed, with particular effects resulting, was also explored. Findings revealed that women's "exercise talk" was linked to their lack of exercise participation, which was deeply rooted within discourses of gender-equity, womanhood, and fitness. Beyond the discourses and practices connected (e.g., performing childcare duties instead of exercise, engaging in "spot reducing exercises," withdrawing from exercise) were taken-for-granted norms in Swedish society, whose subscription to a democratic political discourse striving for gender equity kept these discourses of female subordination well-hidden. Exploring exercise as socially and discursively constructed allowed for important insights into the women's physical selves (i.e., their bodies were constructed as not measuring up to female body ideals), psychological experiences (e.g., guilt, anxiety), and subsequent lack of exercise participation. This discursive psychological study highlights the complexity of how individual women and broader society view and (re)produce exercise in particular ways (e.g., as a gendered activity linked to a particular body shape and size for women), with particular effects resulting (e.g., withdrawal from exercise, limitation of what kinds of exercise women participate in, anxiety about one's physical self).

To further illustrate the principles of discourse outlined, research on the female body and discourse is also informative. The idea that the body is a site for defining gender and power relations within particular discourses has become a critical topic among feminist psychologists who align with feminist post-structuralism. As a visible signifier of identity, the body is inscribed with meanings, depending on sex, color, shape, age, and forms of display (Henriques et al., 1998). Feminist psychologists have recognized the ways in which the body is constructed in discourse as a site for self-management, which "is exemplified in an obsession with techniques for shaping and honing the body, as in aerobics, jogging and all forms of keeping fit, tied to different regimes of dieting and medication" (Henriques et al., 199, p. xiv). The meanings and values associated with body size and body management practices (e.g., exercise) are recognized as profoundly gendered (Markula et al., 2008). As such, the body is a site for discursive self-definition, marking one's gender a socially constructed instrument of achievement (Gergen, 2001), with the thin body representing more than just beauty and health but also symbolizing competence, intelligence, and success of women (Bordo, 1993).

Feminist post-structuralists place further primacy on understanding how discourses offer competing and (potentially) contradictory ways of giving meaning to the world and how we view ourselves. Known as "subject positions" for individuals to take up (Davies & Harre, 1990; Hollway, 1989; Weedon, 1997), these positions can be thought of as conditions of possibility for constituting subjectivity (identities, understandings of the world) and vary in terms of the power they afford people (Weedon, 1997). While the site of subjectivity one occupies in a discourse carries with it particular conventions as to how one will think, feel, and behave, individuals are not passive and have some choice when positioning themselves in discourses. For example, an initiate exerciser drawing upon a patriarchal discourse of the family and occupying the position of "wife" will be enabled to make particular claims that those occupying that same position within a liberal feminist discourse are not entitled to make. As well, in occupying a subject position as "wife" within a patriarchal discourse of the family, one is also likely to attend to others' utterances in particular ways, to think in particular ways, and to have particular experiences when it comes to exercise that follow from the position of "wife." Claims such as "I cannot exercise today because I have to be home for my children" made by the "wife" in a patriarchal familial discourse will be an acceptable reason to avoid exercise because to say otherwise would breach the conventions of how one should behave and feel. Stated differently, when one's site of subjectivity is a "wife" within a patriarchal familial discourse, an excuse such as taking care of children will be deemed an acceptable reason for not exercising because the behavioral and discursive practices are such that putting one's self before one's children would be selfish. Additionally, if one positioned in the same way engages in exercise at the expense of taking care of children and the family, she will likely experience guilt and selfishness, being less likely to exercise on future occasions because of wanting to avoid such feelings.

Those same claims made by one who is positioned as a "wife" within a liberal feminist discourse would be challenged or simply not uttered when it comes to exercise. Thus a woman whose subjectivity is constructed as a "wife" within a liberal feminist discourse may utter phrases such as "when I exercise my partner will take care of the children; exercise is something liberating I do for myself." By having such a conversation from a different subject position about one's self within a different discourse, guilt or selfishness is not experienced when exercising instead of taking care of children. Such alternative experiences result because the discourse furnishes different conditions of possibility for speaking, feeling, and behaving in relation to one's self. In fact, one might further experience feelings of empowerment and a sense of accomplishment when positioned as a "wife" in a liberal feminist discourse when drawing upon such a discourse to make sense of one's exercise.

In addition to the discursive articulation of certain kinds of selves and subjectivities, as mentioned, the use of particular discourses also maintains power relations and patterns of domination and subordination (Potter & Wetherell, 1987). The view of how power works within feminist post-structuralism as contingent upon discourse and tactical usages of discourses by dominant individuals and groups is based on Foucault's assertion that power works *through* people (i.e., power is diffused throughout the body politic, held by no one, acting on everyone, and articulated or made visible in its various discursive iterations) (Markula & Pringle, 2006). Unlike the feminist sport psychology researchers we discussed before who tend to view power as dualist oppressor-oppressed relations (i.e., dominant groups hold power or arrive at their positions because they have power), Foucault's view of power is relational and "omnipresent in every relationship and working as a capillary-like network. Within this network, there are multiple points of resistance and struggle" (Markula et al., 2008, p. 11).

Markula and Pringle (2006) discussed Foucault's conception of power relations as neither positive nor negative, noting that power relations are productive in light of their ability to (re)produce subjectivities, economic systems, and social transformation. Thus, instead of trying to understand how dominant groups (e.g., the media, the fitness industry) hold power over powerless groups (e.g., overweight women, lesbian athletes), feminist post-structuralists are concerned with how power operates through discourse(s) that provides knowledge about how women understand, regulate, and experience their selves and bodies (Lupton, 1997). While Foucault was reluctant to discuss the notion of resistance in the context of self and identity transformation (a criticism of his work) (Thorpe, 2008), feminist post-structuralist scholars such as Weedon (1997) advocate that the power/discourse nexus can be confronted and resisted by taking up a new subject position within discourse, as outlined in our previous example.

Researchers in cultural studies of sport and exercise have used Foucault's concept of the technologies of the self as a way for feminist scholars to further understand how individual practices of freedom can challenge and change dominant discursive practices. Outlining the details of the complex concept of the technologies of the self is beyond the scope of the present discussion, but some scholars have noted the concept's similarity to what we outlined with respect to changing subject positions in discourse (see Markula et al., 2008). The reader is referred to Markula (2004), Markula and Pringle (2006) or Thorpe (2008) for further discussion and application of the concept to feminist research in sport and exercise. In addition to the critical feminist research and feminist post-structuralist principles outlined, research grounded in the technologies of the self also has great potential as a feminist theoretical tool to understand the self and physical activity participation in sport and exercise psychology.

Feminist Post-structuralism and Implications for Behavior Change

Since post-structuralism has implications for how people make sense of one's self, depending on the discourses and subject positions taken up within discourses, when drawing upon particular cultural discourses (e.g., discourses of ideal femininity) as opposed to other discourses (e.g., discourses of radical feminism or liberal feminism) there are particular limited possibilities for feeling and behaving. Viewed through the theoretical lens of feminist post-structuralism, we can see this process in Kerry's self-story about her body and physical activity experiences presented in the introduction. In her personal story Kerry discussed how she made sense of her physical activity (e.g., aerobics, running) by drawing primarily upon weight loss and appearance discourses. Because such discourses construct and reinforce particular views of femininity as opposed to other views of femininity, the subject position afforded Kerry within these discourses was that of a woman with a flawed body that is in need of further work/transformation via the disciplinary practice of gendered physical activity. These discourses and gendered practices were further reinforced as real and factual through the kinds of fitness classes offered, portrayals of women's bodies in the media, and the larger practices of the fitness industry (e.g., training instructors to teach "body shaping" classes, spot-reducing exercises, promoting exercise a weight loss tool). While Kerry conforms to some aspects of ideal femininity because she is white and heterosexual, her body does not conform to the discursively constructed fit and feminine ideal. Hence guilt, anxiety, and a lack of enjoyment in relation to her body and physical activity were experienced. When positioned as flawed and deviating from the fit female "norm" within these discourses, Kerry was more likely to engage in unhealthy behaviors such as avoiding particular modes of exercise, counting calories in relation to exercise, and/or exercising as a punishment for calories consumed. In short, as an effect of drawing upon these limited discourses to make sense of herself and taking up a subject position as that of a woman with a flawed body to make sense of physical activity, Kerry did not always experience the self-related benefits of her physical activity. Kerry was also exercising disciplinary power over herself and body by drawing upon these discourses and engaging in the associated behavioral practices (Markula & Pringle, 2006).

How might we intervene to help make it more likely that Kerry experiences more positive self-related views and does more healthful practices in relation to her exercise? As mentioned, traditional social psychological research and research in sport and exercise psychology grounded in feminist cultural studies locate women's lack of resistance to things or separate structures outside of themselves (e.g., cultural norms, media images of women's bodies) that then impacts something deficient within themselves (e.g., body image, self-esteem, body dissatisfaction). Intervening to change women's negative self-related feelings and unhealthy behaviors in relation to exercise thus requires an awareness of the power located in particular sociocultural influences (e.g., the fitness industry, Kerry's social network), with *internal self-related views* the ultimate focus of change.

In the context of feminist post-structuralism, women's lack of resistance is explained differently, providing further understanding as to why women do not always easily resist the ideological power of cultural norms and how we might enhance resistance. In this regard, of note is that in Kerry's narrative, there were times that she, along with her exercise participants, also recognized that the ideal fit female body was unrealistic and not possible to attain. She also had friends and fitness participants that actively resisted gendered fitness norms. Similarly Krane et al.'s (2004) research suggested that female athletes were aware that pursuit of the ideal feminine body was futile and made attempts to resist it through muscularity and/or sport participation. Yet, all of the women in these examples sometimes contradicted themselves via the discursive and behavioral practices they engaged in and still experienced guilt and shame in relation to how their bodies looked.

In the context of feminist post-structuralism and self-related views and behavior in order to understand how and why the above happens, we must remember that while women's local practices (i.e., self-talk and behavior) are chosen by them, these choices are made within a larger web of discourses. Such discourses are further held in place by larger social and institutional practices beyond their "selves." Viewed in this way, women's choices are their own (i.e., they have some agency) as in feminist perspectives employed within sport and exercise psychology, but they are not entirely free from webs and regimes of productive power (i.e., choices are limited and structured in particular ways by the conditions of possibility within the discourses drawn upon). Moreover, women's choices and the resulting behavioral effects are not due to something deficient or lacking *within* them. Instead, a possible explanation for Kerry and her fitness participants subjecting themselves to the stringent image of the fit female body is that the discourses and power relations intertwined within them are internalized and their actions/behaviors with respect to diet and physical activity are partly structured by their own fear and anxiety. From a feminist post-structuralist perspective, Kerry's conscious choices and experiences within particular discourses are therefore shaped by the social and discursive construction of what is taken for granted as feminine (e.g., the fit female body, the practices of diet and exercise) and the exercise-body beautiful complex (i.e., the wider practices within the health and fitness industry that reinforce a particular "look").

In order to change negative self-related views and associated unhealthy behavioral practices, several things need to be the focus of intervention from a feminist post-structuralist perspective. First, women need to be made aware (i.e., have their consciousness raised) as to how daily conversations (i.e., micro-level self-related talk) with themselves and others (e.g., friends, other exercise participants) within appearance and weight loss discourses are contributing to the thoughts, feelings, and behaviors they are experiencing in relation to their bodies and exercise (McGannon & Mauws, 2002). In turn, significant others may also need to expand their discursive resources so that identities of "fit female" and "female exerciser" could be constructed in ways that allow for conditions more facilitative of healthy physical activity and wellness practices. This would necessitate offering new subject positions, perhaps within a health and wellness discourse and feminist discourses, from which to make sense of one's body in relation to exercise, making alternative ways of speaking, feeling, and behaving more likely. In turn, women and their significant others could not only expand their discursive resources, but women would be made the subject of, rather than the cause of, the situation (McGannon & Mauws, 2002). The outcome would be that women experience less distress, guilt, and self-blame for how their bodies look (and do not look) in relation to their physical activity.

The potential of focusing on discourse for behavior change was evident in Kerry's narrative and Krane and colleagues' feminist research with athletes. All of these sources revealed that when drawing upon feminist discourses, exercisers and athletes are more likely to draw upon reasons for exercise other than appearance and experience positive psychological outcomes from their physical activity participation. Research from feminist perspectives grounded in Foucauldian notions of discourse and power has also shown that while women may experience the repressive forces of exercise, they can and do experience liberating features of exercise in relation to their physical selves in varying degrees by virtue of the discourses drawn upon (Brabazon, 2006; Markula, 1995, 2003; Markula & Pringle, 2006). Such research further underscores the importance of focusing on discourse(s) and subject positions to lead women toward more positive self-related views and experience their exercise as empowering.

Finally, to change behavior and make positive self-related views more likely, we also need to raise women's consciousness and awareness of the institutional and material conditions keeping particular discourses surrounding the female body and physical activity (e.g., thin is fit, muscular is unfeminine) as "facts" in place. This is so that women and their significant others can see possibilities for change to institutional arrangements rather than accepting that ideal femininity is natural and the way things are. In raising such awareness, it would be important that some of the concrete institutional practices reinforcing a narrow version of the fit female body (e.g., the social and environmental climate of sport and exercise) would begin to be changed, affording concrete conditions of possibility via various discursive and behavioral practices that can make change more likely. As an outcome of such changes, the discourses and practices constituting relations and self-identities can also begin to be changed, making it more likely that women who experience less empowerment and self-distress in relation to their exercise and bodies experience the liberating features of their exercise more often (McGannon & Mauws, 2002). Indeed, as Maguire and Mansfield (1998) noted from the findings in their study of aerobics participants, "participating in exercise is not the problem. It is the pursuit of the social body that is a negative strategy for women" (p. 135). This observation is important because it acknowledges the possibility of resistance to predominant appearance-related exercise discourses, thereby eliminating the negative effects as opposed to simply concluding that the practice of exercise in and of itself is the problem.

Conclusion

In addition to work in sport and exercise psychology grounded in feminist cultural studies to explore the relationship between ideal femininity, the self, and women's physical activity participation, feminist post-structuralism can be used to extend such work via its differential conception of subjectivity, ideology, and power. Studying the self in relation to physical activity participation from a feminist post-structuralist perspective allows for a conceptualization of the self as built up in discourse(s), which are held in place by social and institutional practices. If we want to begin to fully comprehend the ways in which women's physical selves are constituted within the sociocultural realm and the complex psychological and behavioral effects that result, then attention also needs to be given to those modes of behavior that women and society have taken on and constructed as normal (i.e., the taken-for-granted ways of speaking about exercise and the physical self). In turn, in addition to the practical suggestions afforded us from feminist research in sport psychology to date, we can further develop interventions for lasting self-transformation and behavior change that lead women to have more empowering experiences from their physical activity participation.

In closing this chapter, it should be clear that attending to women's embodied physical activity by employing feminist post-structuralism as a theoretical tool further opens up a window onto the circulating discourses and politics of the physically active body. Opening such a window and dialogue is something that both researchers and practitioners in sport and exercise psychology can benefit from in order to promote physical activity — at cultural and individual levels — in ways that lead to healthful outcomes for women and men.

References

Birrell, S. (1988). Discourses on the gender/sport relationship: From women in sport to gender relations. *Exercise & Sport Sciences Reviews, 16,* 459–502.

Birrell, S. (2000). *Feminist Theories for Sport.* In J. Coakley & E. Dunning (Eds.), *Handbook of sports studies* (pp. 61–76). Thousand Oaks, CA: Sage.

Bordo, S. (1993). *Unbearable weight: Feminism, western culture and the body.* Berkeley: University of California Press.

Brabazon, T. (2006). Fitness is a feminist issue. *Australian Feminist Studies, 21,* 65–83.

Cerulo, K. A. (1997). Identity construction: New issues, new directions. *Annual Review of Sociology, 23,* 385–409.

Choi, P. (2000). *Femininity and the physically active woman.* London: Routledge.

Cole, C. L. (1993). Resisting the cannon: Feminist cultural studies and technologies of the body. *Journal of Sport and Social Issues, 17,* 77–97.

Crotty, M. (1998). *The foundations of social research: Meaning and perspective in the re-search process.* London: Sage.

Davies, B., & Harre, R. (1990). Positioning: The discursive production of selves. *Journal for the Theory of Social Behaviour, 20,* 43–63.

Duncan, M. C. (1994). The politics of women's body images and practices: Foucault, the panopticon, and *Shape* magazine. *Journal of Sport and Social Issues, 18,* 48–65.

Eriksson, L., Baigi, A., Marklund, B., & Lindgren, E. C. (2008). Social physique anxiety and socio-cultural attitudes toward appearance impact on orthorexia test in fitness participants. *Scandinavian Journal of Medicine Science and Sports, 18,* 389–394.

Faulkner, G., & Finlay, S. J. (2002). It's not what you say, it's the way you say it! Conversation analysis: A discursive methodology for sport, exercise, and physical education. *Quest, 54,* 49–66.

Fisher, L. A., Butryn, T. M., & Roper, E. A. (2003). Diversifying (and politicizing) sport psychology through cultural studies: A promising perspective. *Sport Psychologist, 17*, 391–405.

Fisher, L. A., Roper, E. A., & Butryn, T. M. (2009). Engaging cultural studies and traditional sport psychology. In R. J. Schinke & S. J. Hanrahan (Eds.), *Cultural sport psychology* (pp. 23–31). Champaign, IL: Human Kinetics.

Foucault, M. (1977). *Discipline and punish: The birth of the prison*. London: Penguin.

Foucault, M. (1978) *The history of sexuality, volume 1: An introduction*. London: Penguin.

Gavey, N. (1997). Feminist poststructuralism and discourse analysis. In M. M. Gergen & S. N. Davis (Eds.), *Toward a new psychology of gender: A reader* (pp. 49–64). New York: Routledge.

Gergen, M. (2001). *Feminist reconstructions in psychology: Narrative, gender and performance*. Thousand Oaks, CA: Sage.

Gill, D. (2001). Feminist sport psychology: A guide for our journey. *The Sport Psychologist, 15*, 363–372.

Grogan, S. (1999). *Body image: Understanding body dissatisfaction in men, women and children*. London: Routledge.

Grogan, S. (2008). Body image and health: Contemporary perspectives. *Journal of Health Psychology, 11*, 523–530.

Hall, A. M. (1996). *Feminism and sporting bodies: Essays on theory and practice*. Champaign, IL: Human Kinetics.

Hall, J. M., & Stevens, P. E. (1991). Rigor in feminist research. *Advances in Nursing Science, 13*(3), 16–29.

Haravon Collins, L. (2002). Working out the contradictions: Feminism and aerobics. *Journal of Sport and Social Issues, 26*, 85–109.

Harré, R., & Gillett, G. (1994). *The discursive mind*. Thousand Oaks, CA: Sage.

Hart, E. H., Leary, M. R., & Rejeski, W. J. (1989). The measurement of social physique anxiety. *Journal of Sport and Exercise Psychology, 11*, 94–101.

Hausenblas, H. A., Brewer, B. W., & Van Raalte, J. L. (2004). Self-presentation and exercise. *Journal of Applied Sport Psychology, 16*, 3–18.

Henriques, J., Hollway, W., Urwin, C., Venn, C., & Walkerdine, C. (1998). *Changing the subject*. London: Methuen.

Hollway, W. (1983). Heterosexual sex: Power and desire for the other. In S. Cartledge & J. Ryan (Eds.), *Sex and love: New thoughts on old contradictions* (pp. 124–140). London: Women's Press.

Hollway, W. (1989). *Subjectivity and method in psychology: Constructing gender, meaning and science*. London: Sage.

Krane, V. (1994). A feminist perspective on contemporary sport psychology research. *The Sport Psychologist, 8*, 393–410.

Krane, V. (2001a). We can be athletic and feminine, but do we want to? Challenging hegemonic femininity in women's sport. *Quest, 53*, 115–133.

Krane, V. (2001b). One lesbian feminist epistemology: Integrating feminist standpoint, queer theory, and feminist cultural studies. *The Sport Psychologist, 15*, 401–411.

Krane, V., Choi, P. Y. L., Baird, S. M., Aimar, C. M., & Kauer, K. J. (2004). Living the paradox: Female athletes negotiate femininity and muscularity. *Sex Roles, 50*, 315–329.

Krane, V., Stiles-Shipley, J., Waldron, J., & Michaelnok, J. (2001). Relationships among body satisfaction, social physique anxiety, and eating behaviors in female athletes and exercisers. *Journal of Sport Behavior, 24*, 247–264.

Krane, V., Waldron, J., Michaelnok, J., & Stiles-Shipley, J. (2001). Body image concerns in female exercisers and athletes: A feminist cultural studies perspective. *Women in Sport and Physical Activity Journal, 10*, 17–34.

Lenskyi, H. (1990). Power and play: Gender and sexuality issues in sport and physical activity. *International Review for the Sociology of Sport, 25*, 235–245.

Lenskyi, H. (1994). Sexuality and femininity in sport contexts: Issues and alternatives. *Journal of Sport and Social Issues*, *18*, 356–376.

Levine, M. P., & Piran, N. (2004). The role of body miage in the prevention of eating disorders. *Body Image: An International Journal of Research*, *1*, 57–70.

Locke. A. (2004). Accounting for success and failure: A discursive psychological approach to sport talk. *Quest*, *56*, 302–320.

Lupton, D. (1997). Foucault and the medicalization critique. In A. Petersen & R. Bunton (Eds.), *Focault, health and medicine* (pp. 94–110). London: Routledge.

Maguire, J., & Mansfield, L. (1998). "Nobody's perfect": Women, aerobics, and the body beautiful. *Sociology of Sport Journal*, *15*, 109–137.

Markula, P. (1995). Firm but shapely, fit but sexy, strong but thin: The postmodern aerobicizing female bodies. *Sociology of Sport Journal*, *12*, 424–453.

Markula, P. (2001). Beyond the perfect body: Women's body image distortion in fitness magazine discourse. *Journal of Sport and Social Issues*, *25*, 134–155.

Markula, P. (2003). Post-modern aerobics: Contradiction and resistance. In A. Bolin & J. Granskog (Eds.), *Athletic intruders: Ethnographic research on women, culture and exercise* (pp. 53–78). Albany: State University of New York Press.

Markula, P. (2004). Turning into one's self: Foucault's technologies of the self and mindful fitness. *Sociology of Sport Journal*, *21*, 302–321.

Markula, P., Burns, M., & Riley, S. (2008). Introducing critical bodies: Representations, identities and practices of weight and body management. In S. Riley, M. Burns, H. Frith, S. Wiggins, & P. Markula (Eds.), *Critical bodies: Representations, identities and practices of weight and body management* (pp. 1–22). New York: Palgrave Macmillan.

Markula, P., & Pringle, R. (2006). *Foucault, sport and exercise: Power, knowledge and transforming the self*. New York: Routledge.

McGannon, K. R. (2003). Resistance to exercise: Questioning notions of the fit female body. *Wellspring*, *15* (1), 5–6.

McGannon, K. R. (2004). Honey, is it just me, or does this research make my AAAS(P) look fat?: An autoethnographical tale of the physical self and exercise participation. Presentation to the annual meeting of the Association for the Advancement of Applied Sport Psychology, Minneapolis, MN.

McGannon, K. R., & Johnson, C. R. (2009). Strategies for reflective cultural sport psychology research. In R. J. Schinke & S. J. Hanrahan (Eds.), *Cultural sport psychology* (pp. 57–75). Champaign, IL: Human Kinetics.

McGannon, K. R., & Mauws, M. K. (2000). Discursive psychology: An alternative approach for studying adherence to exercise and physical activity. *Quest*, *52*, 148–165.

McGannon, K. R., & Mauws, M. K. (2002). Exploring the exercise adherence problem: An integration of ethnomethodological and poststructuralist perspectives. *Sociology of Sport Journal*, *19*, 67–89.

Mutrie, N., & Choi, P. (2000). Is "fit" a feminist issue? Dilemmas for exercise psychology. *Feminism and Psychology*, *10*, 544–551.

Potter, J., & Wetherell, M. (1987). *Discourse and social psychology: Beyond attitudes and behavior*. London: Sage.

Prichard, I., & Tiggemann, M. (2005). Objectification in fitness centers: Self-objectification, body dissatisfaction, disordered eating in aerobic instructors and aerobic participants. *Sex Roles*, *53*, 19–28.

Prichard, I., & Tiggemann, M. (2008). Relations among exercise type, self-objectification, and body image in the fitness centre environment: The role of reasons for exercise. *Psychology of Sport and Exercise*, *9*, 855–866.

Pringle, R. (2005). Masculinities, sport and power: A critical comparison of Gramscian and Foucauldian inspired theoretical tools. *Journal of Sport and Social Issues, 29,* 256–278.

Raedeke, T. D., Focht, B. C., & Scales, D. (2007). Social environmental factors and psychological Responses to acute exercise for socially physique anxious females. *Psychology of Sport and Exercise, 8,* 463–476.

Richardson, L., & St. Pierre, E.A. (2005). Writing: A method of inquiry. In N. K. Denzin & Y. S. Lincoln (Eds.), *The Sage handbook of qualitative research* (3rd ed., pp. 959–978). Thousand Oaks, CA: Sage.

Schinke, R. J., & Hanrahan, S. J. (2009). *Cultural sport psychology.* Champaign, IL: Human Kinetics.

Segar, M. Spruijt-Metz, D., & Nolen-Hoeksema, S. (2006). Go figure? Body-shape motives are associated with decreased physical activity participation among midlife women. *Sex Roles, 54,* 175–187.

Stice, E. (2002). Risk and maintenance factors for eating pathology: A meta-analytic review. *Psychological Bulletin, 128,* 825–848.

Smith, B., & Sparkes, A.C. (2005). Analyzing talk in qualitative inquiry: Exploring possibilities, problems, and tensions. *Quest, 57,* 213–242.

Striegel-Moore, R. H. (1994). A feminist agenda for psychological research on eating disorders. In P. Fallon, M. A. Katzman, & S. C. Wooley (Eds.), *Feminist perspectives on eating disorders* (pp. 438–454). New York: Guilford.

Theberge, N., & Birrell, S. (1994). The sociological study of women and sport. In D. Costa & S. Guthrie (Eds.), *Women and sport: Interdisciplinary perspectives* (pp. 331–340). Champaign, IL: Human Kinetics.

Thomsson, H. (1999). Yes, I used to exercise, but — A feminist study of exercise in the life of Swedish women. *Journal of Leisure Research, 31,* 35–56.

Thorpe, H. (2008). Foucault, technologies of self, and the media: Discourses of femininity and snowboarding culture. *Journal of Sport and Social Issues, 32,* 199–229.

Tong, R. (1995). *Feminist thought: A comprehensive introduction.* London: Routledge.

Weedon, C. (1997). *Feminist practice and post-structuralist theory* (2nd ed.). Malden, MA: Blackwell.

Wiggins, S. (2008). Representations and constructions of body weight and body management. In S. Riley, M. Burns, H. Frith, S. Wiggins, & P. Markula (Eds.), *Critical bodies: Representations, identities and practices of weight and body management* (pp. 23–26). New York: Palgrave Macmillan.

Notes

1. An ideology is a set of ideas and ways of thinking that privilege dominant groups and adopted as common sense by an entire society, including those who are disempowered (Theberge & Birrell, 1994). Health and fitness narratives and the ideologies connected are further legitimized by the discourses of public health and medicine that provide a backdrop for commonsense understandings of what constitutes proper and improper bodies in the realm of physical activity and health (Markula & Pringle, 2006).

2. Within the sport studies literature the perspective is typically called "critical cultural studies" — which was pioneered by sport studies feminist scholar Susan Birrell. We have therefore opted to use the term *critical cultural studies* rather than *critical feminism.* The term *critical feminism* might be misleading for some feminist researchers, since *all* feminist work could be considered critical. Have said the foregoing, we also acknowledge that some contemporary sport studies scholars (e.g., Markula) have also used the term *critical feminism* to describe the work we draw upon.

3. We acknowledge the problems, debates, and concerns some scholars have expressed about representations of sport via a hegemonic lens. Our use of the term *hegemonic femininity* is reflected by the use of the term by prominent sport psychology researcher Vikki Krane. It has been recently suggested by Pringle (2005) that researchers be aware of how the Gramscian concept of hegemony is similar on the one hand to Foucauldian conceptions of power, but different on the other. Pringle's article concerns hegemonic masculinity and power in sport, but the same could be said of hegemonic femininity. Pringle notes that some researchers advocate that one *can* combine the two approaches (i.e., hegemony and post-structuralism), while others say "do not combine the two." Regardless, researchers should acknowledge up front that these theoretical debates exist. Our purpose is not to combine the two concepts of hegemony and discourse per say, but rather to suggest that post-structuralism can be used to help extend our understanding of the research done in sport psychology that has primarily used the concept of hegemonic femininity. Our goals are more pragmatic and in the interest of encouraging sport and exercise psychology researchers to ask new questions, think differently, and allow for the creation of new knowledge.

4. Researchers in sport studies have acknowledged that there are similarities between Gramscian and Foucauldian notions of power and have also problematized the differences (see Pringle, 2005), thus arguing against combining Gramscian and Foucauldian notions of power. Other researchers for pragmatic reasons argue that Foucault is usefully complemented by a post-structuralist reading of Gramsci (e.g., combining concepts of discourse and hegemony).

10

WORKING WITH COMMUNITY: PARTICIPATORY ACTION RESEARCH WITH/IN WIKWEMIKONG

Robert J. Schinke, Duke Peltier, Tatiana V. Ryba,
Mary Jo Wabano, and Mike Wabano

CHAPTER SUMMARY

Sudbury Ontario, Canada, and its outlying region of Manitoulin Island (the location of Wikwemikong Unceded Indian Reserve) is a community regarded as tri-cultural (Anglophone, Francophone, Canadian Aboriginal). Within the region, there are many possibilities for multicultural research teams, and also projects that forefront a blending of relevant cultural practices for the intended community. Herein, the relational experiences of a research team are considered, where some of the authors are Canadian mainstream academics and some are Canadian Aboriginal (on reserve) community co-researchers living on reserve. What follows is an overview of how the project team has evolved in their practices from those initially derived within the academy to questions, strategies, and implementations catalyzed and then guided by the Aboriginal co-researchers. The team's evolution will be situated within a more general discussion of methodological preferences that eventually manifested in participatory action research (PAR) practices. A general introduction to the project's evolution and then also to PAR will frame the chapter. Within the general framing of the chapter, the authors will also consider what has been achieved through the research, an approach regarded as "research as praxis."

Working with Community

Participatory action research (PAR) is gaining traction within sport and exercise psychology. With increasing interest in culturally reflexive research and practice, sport and exercise psychologists are now turning to research methodologies where diverse perspectives are encouraged. What follows is a detailed description of two successive collaborative efforts among academic mainstream researchers and community co-researchers from an Aboriginal reserve in Northern Ontario, Canada: Wikwemikong. Situating the projects will be a general overview of the tenets of PAR as well as two formative sport research projects where PAR methodologies were employed to varying extents. The intent from the enhanced knowledge of PAR in and through sport and activity is to excavate two projects undertaken by Laurentian University and Wikwemikong Unceded Indian Reserve. The aim is to make apparent to the reader that PAR methodologies engage community members to varying extents. The first project will briefly exemplify potential missteps, arguably serious ones that might occur at the beginning of a PAR project. Within a limited initial effort at PAR the community co-researchers were unable to fully integrate local indigenous culture within the project. The salience of what was found through the project was regarded by Wikwemikong as removed/impertinent in relation to their current community challenges. The project team's more recent work, though not perfect, is more integrative of Aboriginal perspectives and involvement from project inception to implementation (ongoing). Consequently, the project team continues to work together, with enhanced relations and more potent strategies according to those living in Wikwemikong.

Setting the Context

In the autumn of 1996, the first author began working as a sport psychology consultant with the Canadian National Boxing Team. Prior to that point it never occurred to him that athletes/clients require unique approaches based in part upon their cultural backgrounds. When one is from a mainstream culture in a given region, there really is not much awareness that one's actions and practices are culture bound (Butryn, 2002). After all, it could easily be assumed that when practices are familiar to the mainstream practitioner, they are familiar to most every client (Schinke, Hanrahan, & Catina, 2009). The first author began his work innocently enough by hanging out with the elite boxers. The dialogues between the athletes and practitioner sometimes worked, but they also sometimes were stilted. Initially, it was assumed that the exchanges were a matter of some athletes being more open and other athletes being closed off, and therefore unwilling to consider his consulting services. However, when the author now recalls who did not relate with him during that first National Boxing Team training camp, the athlete who chose not to engage was from India and lived by traditional Sikh cultural practices. The author approached that athlete as he did all of the other athletes, who happened to be white Canadians with cultural practices similar to his own (e.g., they were individualistic in goal orientation, they preferred individual over group discussions).

Fast forward to the consultant's second year with the national team. The author continued seeking meetings with each athlete, though the national team was much more multicultural. There were athletes originating from South America, North Africa, the Caribbean, and three Canadian cultures, meaning those of English, French, and Aboriginal origins (Schinke, 2007). Again, the consultant worked effectively with some clients, though an awkward exchange with one client in particular resulted in another failed attempt at sport psychology, catalyzing a journey, which later through research opportunities with the first author became a journey for his co-authors from Laurentian University (it should be noted that Tatiana Ryba considered the intersection of research and culture in a context outside of elite boxing at about the same time, independently). The athlete was quiet, averted the consultant's eye contact, and felt uncomfortable with how the author was communicating. Intuitively, there was some indication that there were problems throughout the encounter, but the author (a white Canadian mainstream researcher) did not know how to achieve/negotiate a middle ground within the exchange (also Thomason, 1991). The athlete is Aboriginal from a reserve in Western Canada and the consultant is white, mainstream, and formally educated. The athlete seemed petrified to meet the consultant's gaze. Perhaps from the athlete's response there were signs that he felt he and the first author were not on equal footing due to the author's privileged position as white, educated, and upper middle class (see also Butryn, 2002). Consequently the athlete did the only thing he could; he remained silent and avoidant, likely regarding the practitioner as suffering from some form of "white amnesia." *White amnesia* is an indigenous term, indicating a silencing approach that "allows non-Indigenous people to continue in their day to day world without seeing or involving themselves in other worldviews that would challenge their understanding of their oppressive practices" (Moeke-Pickering et al., 2006, p. 2). When the season ended, the athlete never competed in boxing again, and so he was lost to the National Team. Boxing with the National Team was also lost to the athlete.

According to Brant and colleagues (2002; see also Schinke et al., 2006), similar hardships are encountered by elite Aboriginal athletes generally when they pursue excellence within mainstream sport contexts. As Butryn (2002) observed several years ago, sport psychology consultants (SPCs) in North America are often white, middle-class, and privileged. Even when an SPC is from a race, ethnic group, or socioeconomic class other than one regarded as privileged in North America, what is garnered through sport education often reflects raced and classed values of the dominant group. As such, all but the possibility of one general template for sport psychology is subverted. Consequently, many sport psychologists approach their first experiences in the field informed by practices that are not socially and culturally situated and meaningful for all clients (Hill, 1993), but rather through a monocultural and generic series of skills (Ryba & Wright, 2005). Clearly there exists the potential for missteps when working with athletes from oppressed populations, missteps that need to be identified and addressed through research and practice. What follows before returning to a deeper delineation of two successive collaborations among the sport psychology authors herein as responses to challenges encountered by Aboriginal athletes is a more general overview of PAR followed by two case examples of PAR in sport and physical activity.

Research Practices with Oppressed Populations

In chapter 8 of this volume, Janice Forsyth and Michael Heine articulate that work with oppressed people is beginning to surface within the sport literature. The intent through such work is to make space and encourage to the fore voices that have been subverted. Those who have taken initial steps in such work have in several cases done so meaningfully through approaches loosely regarded as participatory action research (PAR) projects (Reason, 1998). It should be noted that there are many methodologies that fall within the boundaries of PAR, though within such work an overarching objective is to place social justice as the focal point (Hagey, 2002). Unlike conventional projects, where often the primary goal is to generate knowledge, PAR projects are meant to put/relinquish "research capabilities in the hands of the deprived and disenfranchised people so that they can transform their lives for themselves" (Park, 1993, p. 1). There are general criteria espoused by Hall (1981) and echoed consistently across PAR projects, including those in the sport sciences (e.g., Frisby, Crawford, & Dorer, 2005). The general tenets include the following:

1. The problem should be identified within the community from the grassroots (i.e., community) and only then brought forward

as relevant with the intended participants. The goal is to improve the lives of those involved through the research, in the
present case, the community's residents, through a form of
structural and social transformation derived during the project.

2. People from the intended community assigned to the project
   are involved with the project from its inception to its implementation. The capabilities of those previously oppressed are affirmed so that there is an appreciation among all concerned (including the community members themselves) that community
   members hold expertise that is meaningful and critical to any
   potential solution sought through the PAR project.

3. The focus of such projects is placed on those oppressed through
   racism, colonization, exploitation, and marginalization. The
   goal is to ensure that community voices and standpoints are
   placed at the center of the project, with those of academic co-
   researchers relocated to the periphery.

4. Academic researchers regarded as outsiders to the community
   need to acknowledge that they too are engaged in learning regarding research and practical strategies salient among the
   community at the forefront of PAR projects.

In summary, then, the PAR project can be defined as "a collaborative approach to research, [that] equitably involves all partners in
the research process and recognizes the unique strengths that each
brings. [PAR] begins with a research topic of importance to the community with the aim of combining knowledge and action for social
change to improve community" (Minkler & Wallerstein, 2005, p. 4).

There have been increasing numbers of projects featuring oppressed groups in the scholarly literature. Among indigenous peoples (each community can be regarded as a people; see Smith, 1999),
PAR been regarded as particularly appealing, likely as a result of indigenous peoples often having served as powerless subjects in anthropological, epidemiological, and sociological studies for some
time (Canadian Institutes of Health Research, 2007; Green & Mercer, 2001). As noted by Denzin and Lincoln (1998) such work, common in the early 20th century, tended to depict indigenous peoples
as human specimens engaged in exotic and oftentimes erratic, in-
comprehensible cultural practices. Contrasted with the indigenous
communities' practices were those of competent academic researchers.
The consequence of how such practices were featured through the
academic literature was a perpetuated form of "othering," with cul-

tural practices and human behaviors regarded as dissimilar and odd. Responding to experiences of being studied as objects, communities of indigenous peoples have blocked academic mainstream researchers' access to engage in research "on" Aboriginal peoples. Linda Smith (1999) described the negative connotation that mainstream research practices hold among indigenous peoples and within indigenous communities. Through PAR, the intent is not to study and exoticize people, but rather to study a problem salient to the community *with* the community through a long-term partnership.

There are a number of challenges posed by those engaged in PAR research, and sample reviews of such challenges are provided by Wallerstein and Duran (2006), Minkler (2000), as well as Cunningham (2008). One such concern is the matter of *power*. Within the two projects that partner Wikwemikong and Laurentian, what the reader will find is that in the initial project, more power was held by the academic researchers than by the intended community in terms of the research question, proposed methods, and subsequent applications from what was gleaned. As Khanlou and Peter (2005) aptly pointed out, "there are variations in the degrees to which studies are influenced by a PAR approach" (p. 2335). During the team's more recent work, the reader will find a shift in power away from the academic researchers and toward the community co-researchers from project inception on. When reading the two projects it becomes clear that power is dynamic within and across projects, constantly revisited with intent to increase capacity of the marginalized (Khanlou & Peter, 2005). There is also a matter of *shifting involvement*, as reflected in the modified roles of the present chapter's authors from their initial to more recent work, hopefully with increasing involvement by those previously oppressed as they gain confidence and trust in the academic researchers. As Wallerstein and Duran noted, when projects reflect capacity building as opposed to a problem orientation, skeptical community co-researchers gain enthusiasm in the project's emancipating potential, with a shift in focus toward community impact and away from dissemination of results alone. Most salient perhaps is the matter of *cultural humility*, where academic researchers can struggle to redress power imbalances through research. Pertaining to cultural humility, it is important to realize that research is socially organized and mainstream research practices are predicated on a Eurocentric vision of the world (Ryba & Schinke, 2009). When mainstream researchers engage in PAR with oppressed people, their normalized research practices must be decentered so that the community's cultural practices can be centered. Though intuitively the strategy of cultural humility is appealing as a means of facilitating social justice, it is an ambivalent site of negotiations between researchers' self-awareness, awareness of the community, and cultural reflexivity. In other words, while it is dangerous to be framing understanding through the Western worldview and, therefore, there is an urgency to implement culturally appropriate ways of doing research with cultural communities, it is equally dangerous to be romanticizing cultural members and their everyday life. To avoid a pitfall of the unreflective use of "authentic" experiences as a means of research legitimation, we need to engage critical theory to unravel issues of sociocultural difference, power, and voice that underlie these experiences. As will be explained later, at one point in time one of the academic researchers had to retract his point (and his voice) and listen to the community members as they quietly and indirectly through storytelling attempted to relay how to proceed in a community that he was visiting only through research. Though some might consider cultural humility as a means of "giving voice," the question becomes why one would need to give it. As Spivak (1988) conveyed, by pushing beyond "ventriloquism"—speaking on behalf of a community's members—multiple spaces are created. Through an appreciation of when and how missteps happen, the intent is to reverse (and correct) oppression through research instead of perpetuating past wrongs.

PAR Research Exemplars

There are a few examples within the sport and activity research where PAR projects have been attempted with minority (in terms of power) populations. Among the initial work, (beyond the Wikwemikong and Laurentian partnership), examples have been published by Frisby and colleagues (e.g., Frisby, Reid, Millar, & Hoeber, 2005, Frisby et al., 1997) and Janice Forsyth and Michael Heine (in press). A brief overview of two sample projects will be described briefly in terms of how PAR was employed.

Frisby and Colleagues' Emancipating Feminist Research

Wendy Frisby and her colleagues were among the first sport researchers to engage in PAR research. Frisby et al.'s goal was through PAR to "increase the access of women living below the poverty line and their families to local physical activity services" (Frisby et al., 1997, p. 8). Underlying Frisby et al.'s work were statistics indicating that the lowest sport and activity participation rates are among the poor, and especially among low-income women during their child bearing years (Hoffman, 1995). Consequently, when a group of low-income women identified their lack of access to sport and physical activity to a staff member at their local health unit, a PAR project was catalyzed. With the support of the low-income women and the health unit, the local municipal recreation department was approached for assistance to ameliorate the problem. They in turn contacted Frisby, an academic researcher with some background in community research, and so a link was created from the bottom up, bridging community and academy (stage one). Frisby facilitated a series of focus groups and questionnaires (stage two) as a form of needs assessment, where it was confirmed that even though low-income women desired equivalent access to sport and activity services as those in their community from higher socioeconomic strata, they were unable to access services due to limited finances and social support. Stage three was comprised of community mobilization, where community members volunteered to lead portions of the project such as serving on advisory committees, assisting with data collection and analysis, and participating in community action plans. Stage four reflected information gathering, data analysis, and the arrival at conclusions from the research. Three program designs were then implemented over the course of 18 months and each program was then evaluated in terms of success rates and also anecdotal feedback (stage five). From the project there were certain tangible signs that the methodology was a success. For example, at the beginning of projects with a marginalized group, researchers are often regarded with suspicion. When PAR is facilitated with sensitivity on the part of academic researchers, trust develops. From trust, the co-researchers slowly step forward and accept leadership roles within the project. Within Frisby's project there were indications that the women became more comfortable as the project developed and as such, they shared their views progressively. Further, there was indication that mutual learning occurred through the project, with the community researchers gaining a better appreciation of the reasons underlying their challenges as a group and how they might ameliorate physical activity barriers through effective programs. For the academics, learning also occurred, especially pertaining to contextual information and how best to relate with the community members.

Forsyth and Heine's Canadian Aboriginal Youth Based Project

Forsyth and Heine, similar to the authors of the present chapter, have engaged in PAR with Canadian Aboriginal youth through Social Sciences and Humanities Research Council (SSHRC) national funding. The researchers' goal has been to explore how Aboriginal youth could gain meaningful physical activity opportunities through sport. The research project is comprised of a youth mentorship program, an after-school recreation program, and a social mapping project. The research team is comprised of undergraduate and graduate research assistants and community representatives, including high school principals, teachers, and Aboriginal students, all from the inner city in one locale. As such, the intent has been to provide a comprehensive approach through the project whereby the youth and those who support them in sport and activity were enlisted. From the beginning, the researchers worked closely with the youth so that beyond the direct benefits derived from the programs, the youth were exposed to research opportunities and also the possibility of higher education opportunities. The researchers also employed a strength's perspective in their work, where the focus is on affirming the competencies and knowledge among the youth. It should be noted that in keeping with PAR, those who adopt a strength's perspective are far more likely to be successful in their initiatives as contrasted with a deficit remediation paradigm (Forsyth & Heine, in press). Finally, the co-authors identified cooperative learning as an integral part of their project with knowledge/insights gained by the community members and academic researchers. One facet of the project pertained to social mapping, where the Aboriginal youth were asked to visually demonstrate the types of sports and sport contexts they were most attracted to and also the sports and physical contexts that served as constraints to their sport engagement. From what was gleaned it became apparent that the youth have been constrained due to their race, socioeconomic status, and gender. The intent by the researchers and community members is to reclaim sport opportunities within the community through the development of more positive spaces in and through sport.

Commonalities among the Sport and Physical Activity Examples

When the work of Frisby and her colleagues and Forsyth and Heine are considered, both share similarities that affirm the thoughtful engagement of PAR. There is evidence that both projects are salient among their intended communities with support from the various stakeholders within the respective communities. Also, the insights gained through the projects reflect evolution among co-participants and researchers and also a power redistribution where community members and researchers are placed on equal footing. Also of note, both projects appear to be steps forward for those immersed in each community in relation to important community-driven topics, where efforts are reflected in ongoing application beyond traditional researcher benefits. Though such projects are in their infancy within the sport literature, PAR promises emancipating opportunities, assuming kinesiology researchers are willing to partner with community members, listen to what is salient among the oppressed, and then support "the" group through meaningful partnerships.

The Initial Collaboration with Wikwemikong— A Weak First Step toward PAR

What follows is a third example of PAR, evidenced through two consecutive funded research projects among the co-authors from the present chapter. The collaboration reflects an evolution toward a more meaningful topic, methodology, and application among the Wikwemikong. Worth noting, as reflected in this section's title, are the weaknesses of the team's initial research attempt. Though what follows in the present section is critical, the intent is to shed light on how PAR project teams can engage meaningfully in community-driven projects through evolving trust and communication over time.

The first author and colleagues eventually submitted a research project to one of Canada's federal granting agencies. The researchers believed, supporting Bruce Kidd's (1995) words, that

> we need to make links with those who have long been left out of Canadian sport and physical activity, to learn from their experiences, incorporate them in our way of viewing sport, and to help them develop appropriate opportunities for themselves. This will require working with the marginalized directly. . . .

Their active collaboration in research, planning, and dissemination of results will be essential if the presently marginalized are to enjoy genuine opportunities for beneficial physical activity. (p. 16)

The project was developed with endorsements from two Aboriginal communities in the local region. Once the grant was conferred, work in earnest began with community co-researchers in Wikwemikong. When the project team first met, it was in the Chamber of Commerce in Wikwemikong. The first author along with a senior colleague presented a research idea to chief and council, and there was the same stoicism as when Aboriginal athletes were encountered in practice. With the ensuing quietness the author made his presentation to the community attendees, and eventually very short, succinct questions were asked of the presenter. The questions that followed were not really questions, but points that the member wanted to discuss with the larger group.

When an agreement was struck among the academic and Wikwemikong members, work in earnest began, starting with the piloting of an interview guide. Despite what might be gleaned by asking questions of relevance to people representing another culture perspective, several pitfalls can be committed through the asking. For example, Hanrahan (2004, 2009) and Running Wolf and Rickard (2003) have recognized that when a client or participant has been socialized with a collective orientation, individual interviews can be regarded as intrusive and intimidating. Typically when working with community, especially from collective-oriented cultures, a lot of work is done in group meetings where problems are discussed collaboratively as opposed to making decision unilaterally (Hanrahan, 2004). The research team herein, however, proceeded with the aforementioned conventional style of interviewing common in many mainstream North American qualitative projects. As a consequence, they encountered varying degrees of success and also resistance in data collection, with some participants providing extensive in-depth responses and others offering one-word answers, leading to extremely short interviews. Upon reflection, the silencing the first author committed in his earlier applied experiences resurfaced though in his research as opposed to practice. Those who remained quiet throughout the interviewing did not match with the formalized protocol. Such errors were the beginnings of a research trajectory that eventually became more culturally inviting through corrected strategies.

Also, the authors consider another facet from their initial research that undermined its quality: it did not forefront relevant (in Wikwemikong) Aboriginal cultural practices sufficiently and thoughtfully. In the earlier work, there were steps taken to encourage voices from within Wikwemikong, in addition to those of the participants. For example, the Aboriginal community vetted the interview questions we devised. Also, there was assistance with the thematic analysis to enhance the likelihood that the coding was reflective of a general Canadian Aboriginal perspective. Though a consideration of more than one cultural perspective is arguably crucial in the advancement of our domain, the consideration must be inclusive in a meaningful way of those the researchers wish to learn from (Smith, 1999), and not merely as a symbolic series of superficial strategies to build the case that what we are serving up is authentic. Consequently, the addition in our work of Aboriginal co-authors enhanced the credibility of the work, though not as much as the academic authors initially believed. If one looks a little closer at the work, the efforts fell short in several critical ways that have been outlined elsewhere (Schinke et al., 2008). The academic researchers were not aware of their oversights until the lead community co-researcher asked for a meeting, and within the meeting, proposed a research project that was more relevant among those living in Wikwemikong. The proposed topic was a shift away from elite sport practices (i.e., the first author's interest) to sport and physical activity among community youth (i.e., the Wikwemikong's interest). Underpinning the request was more comfort among the Wikwemikong members to request something pressing in the daily lives of Wikwemikong's people. In retrospect, the Wikwemikong co-researchers were aware that many methodological errors were being committed in the earlier work, and they waited with patience until the academic researchers were ready to learn a little more about culturally relevant research in their community. When Wikwemikong's co-researchers voiced the need for a shift in project focus, a new grant was developed and subsequently conferred. The step was monumental to the team, as the work presented a move along the continuum to more community integration. The deeper integration of community researchers was intended as a form of research as praxis. Before returning to the team's more recent work, the authors will unpack what praxis is and how it works in and through research.

Research as Praxis

The term *praxis* refers to the cyclical relationship between academic and applied work or theory and practice, which is rooted in an overarching commitment to positive social change (Bredemeier, 2001; Ryba & Wright, 2005). The way praxis informs our fieldwork is largely shaped by Lather's (1986a, 1991) concept of research as praxis and its consequent incorporation into a cultural praxis discourse of sport psychology proposed by Ryba and Wright (chapter 1 in this volume).

In her reconceptualization of research as praxis, Lather attempted to highlight the methodological implications of critical theory, particularly in relation to issues of emancipatory research (e.g., feminist research and Freirian "empowering" research). Lather (1986b) took issue with the positivistic research norms in social sciences, arguing that scientific neutrality and objectivity "serve to mystify the inherently ideological nature of research in the human sciences and to legitimate privilege based on class, race, and gender" (p. 64). She acknowledged the importance of then emerging feminist, neo-Marxist, and Freirian research paradigms; however, she voiced a concern for the lack of clear strategies for how to do research informed by critical theory — an approach she put forward as research as praxis. The primary objective of research as praxis is to involve the researched in the empirical process of knowledge production, which is negotiated, reciprocal, and empowering.

Lather's focus on the social organization of research and research practices was not lost in Ryba and Wright's articulation of sport psychology as cultural praxis. Triggered by the cultural turn, which created the foment ground for reexamining philosophical and political assumptions of the ways that we produce knowledge, cultural praxis points to the multiplicity of sport psychological discourses contingent on a specificity of sociocultural location and historical conjuncture. The important point here is that cultural praxis offers a discursive framework to address messy and blurry issues of contested cultures, competing and often ambivalent belongingness, fragmented subjectivities, and transnational identities in and through theory, research, and practice of sport and exercise psychology. Within a cultural praxis framework, many unproblematized assumptions about empowerment, emancipation, and transformative intellectuals that underpin research as praxis, and that were subsequently troubled in Lather's later work, are approached more cautiously from the perspective of postcolonial theorizing. Research is taken up as a discursive site through which theoretical insights, psychosocial problematic, and lived culture blend together in praxis to instigate social equity and justice. Our collaborative community project is a timely reminder that cultural praxis is not a frozen monolithic formation but always already open to negotiation and change as "practice always exceeds theory's grasp" (Lather, 1994, p. 182).

A Shift in the Team's Focus and Power through More Integrated PAR

Beneath the surface, there was also a shift in power in the initiative, with community members identifying the project and thus taking over as the leaders (as opposed to serving as cultural guides). The shift in focus and also power placed the bicultural research team members on equal footing, a position they should have undoubtedly attempted more carefully earlier. What the mainstream authors have found, similar to others engaged in PAR (e.g., Frisby et al., 1997), is that good multicultural collaborations sometimes take more time than a traditional research grant allows. As such, the successive grant allowed the team to learn more regarding how to work together, how to be open about what is important, and how to express when a mainstream researcher should lead, follow, lend support, step back, and then step away. Again, such insights resembled those affirmed by others (e.g., Wallerstein & Duran, 2006).

With the project team's more recent work, again the initiative has been supported within the academic community. The authors have continued to publish extensively, because publishing is a necessary aspect when one is conferred a research grant. Each work was written to inform others interested in cultural reflexivity (McGannon & Johnston, 2009; Schinke et al., 2008). In addition, three data-informed manuscripts have been written, two of which are in press, with a third in review. The latter three manuscripts uncover topics where Wikwemikong has been seeking solutions, comprising the role of family (Schinke et al., in press) and community in enhanced youth sport and activity programming (Blodgett et al., in press), and also the challenges and effective adaptation strategies when Aboriginal youth compete off reserve in mainstream sport events (Schinke et al., submitted for publication). All such works address aspects of youth sport involvement among a Canadian population and cohort at risk (Health Council of Canada, 2007). Though it is not the focus here to consider the trends from their most recent work, the project team believes it is worth noting that the topics have provided a few tentative answers to community challenges in Wikwemikong. What has been gleaned is now informing youth leadership training through a series of week-long seminars every summer and also through educational seminars provided to coaching and sport administration staff. Throughout the work is a focus on more effective programming strategies to retain Wikwemikong youth in sport and activity programs in the years to come. The topic has been met with enthusiasm in Wikwemikong, leading to the promise of new research opportunities developed in response to community-driven questions.

There have been challenges associated with the development of culturally reflexive methods in psychology departments. When one of the academic members in the project team began her work in Wikwemikong as an undergraduate student, she proposed a research project for her thesis to faculty members from an undisclosed multidisciplinary program. The project focus was to consider the recommendations from the initial study's participants and also from Wikwemikong co-researchers. Included in the methods were community meetings, a culturally relevant consultation process among the Wikwemikong community akin to a focus group discussion, though far less structured at the outset. In community meetings at Wikwemikong, the discussions are free flowing and the topics are considered among the group, followed immediately by group discussions. The faculty members in charge of the course were dumbfounded by the proposed method of community meetings, and they threatened failing the student out of the thesis course. The belief of the mainstream academics was that the proposed work was not research, though shortly thereafter, reviewers from a well-regarded peer-reviewed journal disagreed with the faculty members and supported the method as a culturally relevant approach (Blodgett et al., 2008). The authors herein propose that what constitutes good research across cultures must be appropriately culturally informed. Part of the PAR approach employed within the evolving work with Wikwemikong has reflected extensive consultation, not only in relation to what topic matter is being pursued, but also in relation to how the mainstream authors seek out the perspectives of Wikwemikong's participants in a way that encourages voices instead of silencing them. Of the strategies integrated, the most recent published works include community discussions (Blodgett et al., 2008) and talking circles (Running Wolf

& Rickard, 2003). The community discussions have been ongoing over three years of monthly meetings. In earlier meetings, the academic co-researchers arrived in Wikwemikong with a series of items to be covered during each monthly meeting. However, in those earlier meetings, agendas would always modify within the first few minutes, leaving the academic researchers puzzled, frustrated, and grasping for a focus. Slowly, the meeting topics would unfold through the group's discussions, often with Wikwemikong's co-researchers sharing teachings along the way as subtle suggestions of how the team needed to proceed in a sensitive, collaborative, and patient way. For example, one of the two resident elders on the team (elders are regarded in Wikwemikong as wise educators able to mentor younger community members in traditional practices) shared one story early on of how a bunch of academics arrived in her school one day, when she was a young teacher. They sat in the hallway and canvassed students to fill in assessment, without even introducing themselves to the school's teaching staff. She also relayed a second story immediately afterward, in which she described how recently a research team from a large university conducted medical research in Wikwemikong, departed with many false promises, and never returned to Wikwemikong to share the findings or even to inform the medical staff on reserve of its implications. From those formative stories of mistrust (cf. Cunningham, 2008) the underlying message was that our academic researchers were expected to share findings and also to work with and listen to Wikwemikong over the long term to maintain active engagement with the community, even after the findings had been gathered, analyzed, and disseminated. Noteworthy is that the mainstream members were never formally told what Wikwemikong's expectations were. Instead, they were guided gradually through a process of non-interference (Martin-Hill & Soucy, 2007) in which the expectations surfaced indirectly through progressive teachings. And so began one community meeting where the values of Wikwemikong were imparted to the academics in a manner that Frisby and colleagues (1997) described as mutual learning.

The community meeting served as the means through which the aforementioned resident elder and the Wikwemikong co-researchers set the parameters within and across the meeting that constituted the overarching project. Community consultation was a struggle for the academic mainstream researchers, primarily because they were accustomed to directing the research through an approach that was often top-down in many ways. Much like the aforementioned early work, academics are accustomed to developing research questions and methods well in advance of a project. However, PAR in general, and its immediate derivative style, change very quickly as new questions and problems unfold through deeper discussions and better collaborations. The struggle among the academics with evolving discussions and a loose structure to the project has been the desire to lead, even within meetings. That struggle has been managed somewhat effectively by one of the academics calming the other (not always the same academic doing the calming) so that they might learn attentively what the Wikwemikong co-researchers are trying to say and teach. The shift in leadership is necessary for both parties, and it is also in a sense restorative for the Wikwemikong co-researchers as they gain footing as researchers in the world of academe, much like the co-participants who have worked with Forsyth and Heine (in press). The Aboriginal members are experts in their cultural practices, and the academic researchers are not. Through awareness among members from both cultures, the academic researchers have attempted, sometimes tediously to step back, while supporting the Wikwemikong as they step forward in and through the project (Schinke et al., in press). The dance that the researchers have engaged in is not easy, but as indicated earlier it is restorative as the Aboriginal researchers correctly are now at the forefront of the initiatives. It is also in keeping with the policies for research and ethics involving Canadian Aboriginal members (Canadian Institutes of Health Research, 2007). The community meetings that have been integrated as a data source now forefront the negotiations and tedious exchanges among the bicultural research team. The end result of each such meeting is always amazement on the part of the academic researchers, as they drive the 250 kilometers home after each meeting. The debriefing always seems to go something like this:

Rob S: What an amazing meeting. So much for the agenda, but wow.

Graduate Student: I thought we were going to cover X and Y.

Rob S: I guess Mary Jo (Wabano) or Duke (Peltier) had something else in mind, and what we covered is so much more profound than what we were expecting to cover. Back to the drawing board.

Other Graduate Student: We didn't get to discuss the upcoming conferences. I thought they were important for our plans.

Rob S: Maybe they were important to our [academic members'] plans, but they aren't all that important to the project. We need to remember that plans are loose and responsive in this project.

Though the words above are not verbatim, they capture the struggles that the academic researchers have encountered through the community discussions. Those struggles reflect a need for structure and outcome over process and collaboration. Undoubtedly, the community co-researchers have chuckled (kindly) after each meeting, as there always seems much to teach their culturally insensitive academic colleagues and friends.

Talking circles have also been integrated within the team's more recent work. The team has been told that in some local Aboriginal communities, talking circles are not allowed as a method because they are sacred cultural practices. However, in Wikwemikong, talking circles have been used for research purposes in a process where again our approach has become progressively more culturally relevant. As Running Wolf and Rikard (2003) and Picou (2000) have unpacked, there are a few important grounds rules to be followed in talking circles. Those practices include a concept that academics are not often accustomed to: circles are not bound to time, and people talk regardless of how long the talking circle takes, until nothing more is left to be said. In earlier work, Schinke and colleagues (2009) indicated that many Canadian Aboriginal communities employ event in place of clock-based time (see also Myers & Spencer, 2003, for a review). The Wikwemikong are a community of people who employ event-based time, meaning that clocks and calendars are not as important as the fact that meetings take place when they are needed, for as long as is required to address the topic/concern/problem. Recently, the first author was asked to review a research project proposed for an academic community much like Wikwemikong with talking circles, and the consent form indicated that the talking circles would last approximately 90 minutes. The omission is undoubtedly part of the hesitancy among some Aboriginal communities to contort their cultural practices to meet the academic researchers' misconceptions of how a project should be undertaken. So talking circles take as long as they need to be, and only one person at a time is allowed to speak. Also of note, the person who holds the symbolic object (e.g., stone, eagle feather, talking stick, tobacco) is the speaker for as long as she or he requires to share thoughts and reflections with the group.

The practices within the talking circles have slowly also become better, more inviting practices within Wikwemikong. From the outset, meals were served in the form of feasts with culturally relevant menu items chosen and offered in large portions, and catered by a community restaurant. The strategy was developed to respect local Aboriginal diets, and also to support the employment of local restaurant staff through the research. After meals, ice-breaking circle games of a cooperative nature were led by the youth center's staff to facilitate member comfort. Despite such culturally relevant strategies, initially the researchers tended to intervene within talking circles to use follow-up probes, in the form of clarifying, detail, and contrast questions (Patton, 2002). When such follow-up questions were posed, it seemed that the circle's flow was disrupted and that the younger members of the circle would become silent. The following month, talking circles were led in the community, though no follow-up questions were asked. Instead, the discussion brought forth by participants reflected what they thought was worth mentioning. As such, the participants' right to speak, which includes what is said with no guidance, was included as information. The academic researchers continued to step back with each series of successive talking circles to the point where in more recent ones they left the circles entirely and asked community members relevant to each age cohort to lead the circles. Within the final circles, the academics did not even sit in the room. Rather, they moved outside the room, symbolizing the extent of leadership assumed by the Wikwemikong co-researchers and those designated by the community co-researchers to lead each circle. Consequently, the academics' removal from the latter talking circles exemplified one example when they needed to step back very far into the periphery. Brought to the forefront in and through the research were community members varying in age from late teens for adolescent talking circles to elders for adult and mixed-age talking circles. Hence, participation was broadened, adding to the ownership (see also Schnarch, 2004) over what was learned.

Though other culturally sensitive methods have also been employed throughout the project, the data collection strategies alone reflect the dynamic nature of how methods were refined over time to encourage comfortable participation. Also encouraged to the forefront have been the community co-researchers, who now speak far more openly about what is needed and wanted from the academic members when assistance is sought with facets of the project and also other projects. Though some researchers might correctly point out that the academic researchers have done themselves out of a job when earlier work is compared with more recent, and correctly so, the point through the project has been to engage in research in a manner that encourages to the forefront community members from Wikwemikong who have been marginalized through residential schooling, federal policies, and sport practices in mainstream society (University of Victoria, 2003).

Inherent throughout the two projects has been a push for doing what is socially and culturally just in and through the research. One of the authors serves as the chair of the Laurentian University Research Ethics Board. Over the course of his tenure he has evaluated several projects where the term *decolonizing* has been employed as part of a project's proposed methods in relation to work with Canadian Aboriginal participants. Sadly, as Smith (1999) relayed in a well-cited passage 10 years ago regarding how research and researchers are regarded among Aboriginal peoples, mainstream researchers tend to be regarded as oppressive: "The word itself, 'research,' is probably one of the dirtiest words in the indigenous world's vocabulary. When mentioned in many indigenous contexts, it stirs up silence, it conjures up bad memories, it raises a smile that is knowing and distrustful. . . . The ways in which scientific research is implicated in the worst excesses of colonialism remains a powerful remembered history for many of the world's colonized peoples" (p. 1).

Presently, at least among some of research projects finding their way to northern Ontario, Canada, inconsiderate practices continue. The term *decolonizing* is sometimes used loosely to indicate to the reader/evaluator that the researchers are doing what is correct in their proposed research. However, beneath the veneer of research projects sometimes the methods include only light consultation, often without culturally sound methods, ample community support and resources, or community imperatives at their forefront. What our authors have tried to indicate is that working with participants and co-researchers from oppressed cultures and groups requires heightened sensitivity. Consultation can be sought in degrees, and the more academic researchers engage in meaningful research partnerships with Aboriginal co-researchers and co-participants, the better and more ethical the research becomes. Cho and Trent (2006) have spoken of the term *transformational validity* and in a similar vein Lather (1986) has considered *catalytic validity*, meaning that a project becomes valid through its intent and accomplishment as a catalytic/emancipating work among the intended population. The guidelines for evaluating good research with marginalized peoples ought to be held to a set of rigorous standards that imply something quite different from the orthodox versions of validity and trustworthiness. When one engages in ethical research with Aboriginal populations then, there are several criteria or standards to be accounted for. The first is a matter of more firsthand involvement assigned from within the intended community forefronted. As Smith (1999) articulated of less sensitive, though still common protocols, "The collective memory of imperialism has been perpetuated through the ways in which knowledge about indigenous peoples was collected, classified and then represented in various ways back to the West, and then, through the eyes of the West, back to those who have been colonized" (pp. 1–2).

The push in better research with Aboriginal peoples then is to include and promote Aboriginal voices, and in so doing, to have the more contextually knowledgeable people speaking of their own experiences. Through a more thoughtful and intuitive sensitivity among mainstream academic researchers regarding what works and what is silencing, the goal can be to encourage community expertise to the forefront so that important words and standpoints travel beyond a community such as Wikwemikong, for more people to learn and also support the vast number of standpoints available through research. Research can empower diverse groups, and the authors herein believe that good research begins with an understanding of what culture(s) are being empowered in a given project (and method) and which are being silenced and disempowered. The goal is for the appropriate culture to speak, and the one in a supportive role to listen and support.

Conclusion

In this chapter, the authors have sought to explain how PAR research develops over time into a meaningful endeavor. Community members are well aware of the challenges posed within their respective communities through living conditions, resource constraints, or both aspects combined. When academic researchers are approached to partner in work to further identify and build upon existing strengths within a community as a supportive mechanism, the potency of the research and, more important, what is achieved in terms of betterment through the project is enhanced. Conversely, when projects are developed by academic researchers and then proposed to an oppressed group, the likelihood of emancipation through the project diminishes. Within the present chapter, the authors have delineated and then situated the tenets of PAR in relation to research that partners Canadian Aboriginal youth on reserve with academic researchers from the same geographic region. What has been achieved ongoing cannot be evaluated in terms of outcome — the project's applied aspects are still ongoing in a self-governed format, with strategies that continue to unfold. What can be said, much like many other PAR projects, is that what has been achieved in terms of research has now been outweighed by what has been achieved through research. Benefits have been derived in terms of programming, though equally important, it would seem that positive relations have been achieved by co-researchers from two cultures traditionally divided through marginalization and colonization experienced on the part of the first culture and acts of racism and oppression committed on the part of the second culture. The present authors continue to work together as collaborators and as friends. The authors believe after five years of collaborations that PAR holds significant promise as a research practice in their region, though obviously in a manner that reflects a cultural turn.

Acknowledgments

The authors would like to thank the Social Sciences and Humanities Research Council of Canada for their generous support of our ongoing work (SSHRC #856-2005-0030). In addition, this project would not have been possible without the support of the Chief and Band and Council, and also the youth of the Wikwemikong Unceded First Nations Indian Reserve.

References

Blodgett, A. T., Schinke, R. J., Fisher, L. A., Wassengeso-George, C., Peltier, D., Ritchie, S., & Pickard, P. (2008). From practice to praxis: Community-based strategies for Aboriginal youth sport. *Journal of Sport and Social Issues, 32*, 393–414.

Blodgett, A., Schinke, R. J., Fisher, L. A., Yungblut, H. E., Recollet-Saikkonen, D., Peltier, D., et al. (in press). Praxis and community-level sport programming strategies in a Canadian Aboriginal reserve. *International Journal of Sport and Exercise Psychology, 7.*

Brant, R., Forsyth, J., Horn-Miller, W., Loutitt, J., Sinclair, C., Smith, M., et al. (2002). *North American Indigenous Games Sport Research Panel.* In R. Brant & J. Forsyth (Eds.), *2002 North American Indigenous Games Conference Proceedings* (pp. 67–70). Winnipeg, Canada: University of Manitoba Press.

Bredemeier, B., 2001. Feminist praxis in sport psychology research. *The Sport Psychologist, 15,* 412–418.

Butryn, T. M. (2002). Critically examining White racial identity and privilege in sport psychology. *The Sport Psychologist, 16,* 316–336.

Canadian Institutes of Health Research. (2007). *CIHR guidelines for health research involving Aboriginal people.* Ottawa, Canada: Canadian Institutes of Health Research.

Cho, J., & Trent, A. (2006). Validity in qualitative research revisited. *Qualitative Research, 6,* 319–340.

Cunningham, W. S. (2008). Voices from the field. *Action Research, 6,* 373–390.

Denzin, N. K., & Lincoln, Y. S. (1998). Entering the field of qualitative research. In N. K. Denzin & Y. S. Lincoln (Eds.), *Strategies of qualitative inquiry* (pp. 1–34). London: Sage.

Forsyth, J., & Heine, M. (in press). Indigenous research and decolonizing methodologies. In T. V. Ryba, R. J. Schinke, & G. Tenenbaum (Eds.), *The cultural turn in sport psychology.* Morgantown, WV: Fitness Information Technology.

Frisby, W., Crawford, S., & Dorer, T. (1997). Reflections on participatory action research: The case of low-income women accessing local physical activity services. *Journal of Sport Management, 11,* 8–28.

Frisby, W., Reid, C. J., Millar, S., & Hoeber, L. (2005). Putting "participatory" into participatory forms of action research. *Journal of Sport Management, 19,* 367–386.

Green, L. W., & Mercer, S. L. (2001). Can public health researchers and agencies reconcile the push from funding bodies and the pull from communities? *American Journal of Public Health, 91,* 1926–1930.

Hagey, R. S. (2002). Guest editorial: The use and abuse of participatory action research. Retrieved February 10, 2009, from http://www.phac-aspc.gc.ca/publicat/cdic-mcc/18-1/a_e.html.

Hall, B. (1981). Participatory research, popular knowledge and power: A personal reflection. *Convergence, 14*(3), 6–19.

Hanrahan, S. J. (2004). Sport psychology and indigenous performing artists. *The Sport Psychologist, 18,* 60–74.

Hanrahan, S. J. (2009). Working with Australian Aboriginal athletes. In R. J. Schinke & S. J. Hanrahan (Eds.), *Cultural sport psychology* (pp. 153–164). Champaign, IL: Human Kinetics.

Health Council of Canada. (2007). *Aboriginal Health 2006 Annual Report.* Retrieved June 10, 2008, from www.healthcouncilcanada.ca.

Hill, T. L. (1993). Sport psychology and the collegiate athlete: One size does not fit all. *The Counseling Psychologist, 21,* 436–440.

Hoffman, A. (1995). Women's access to sport and physical activity. *Avante, 1*(1), 77–92.

Khanlou, N., & Peter, E. (2005). Participatory action research: Considerations for ethical review. *Social Science & Medicine, 60,* 2333–2340.

Kidd, B. (1995). Confronting inequality in sport and physical activity. *Avante, 1*(1), 1–19.

Lather, P. (1986a). Research as praxis. *Harvard Educational Review, 56*(3), 257–277.

Lather, P. (1986b). Issues of validity in openly ideological research: Between a rock and a soft place. *Interchange, 17*(4), 63–84.

Lather, P. (1991). *Getting smart: Feminist re-*

search and pedagogy with/in the postmodern. London: Routledge.

Lather, P. (1994). Dada practice: A feminist reading: Reaction to Stephanie Kirkwood Walker's review of "Getting Smart." *Curriculum Inquiry, 24*(2), 181–187.

Martin-Hill, D., & Soucy, D. (2007). *Ethical guidelines for Aboriginal research elders and healers roundtable.* Report by the Indigenous Health Research Development Program to the Interagency Advisory Panel of Research Ethics.

McGannon, K., & Johnson, C. (2009). Strategies for reflective cultural sport psychology research. In R. J. Schinke & S. J. Hanrahan (Eds.), *Cultural sport psychology* (pp. 57–76). Champaign, IL: Human Kinetics.

Minkler, M. (2000). Using participatory action research to build healthy communities. *Public Health Reports, 115,* 191–197.

Minkler, M., & Wallerstein, N. (Eds.) (2005). *Community organizing and community building for health.* New Brunswick, NJ: Rutgers University Press.

Moeke-Pickering, T., Hardy, S., Manitowabi, S., Mawhiney, A. M., Faires, E., Gibson-van Marriwejk, K., et al. (2006). Keeping our fire alive: Towards decolonizing research in the academic setting. *World Indigenous Nations Higher Education Consortium, 2,* 1–8.

Myers, D. G., & Spencer, S. J. (2003). *Social psychology: Canadian edition.* Toronto: McGraw-Hill Ryerson.

Park, P. (1993). What is participatory research? A theoretical and methodological perspective. In P. Park, M. Brydon-Miller, B. Hall, & T. Jackson (Eds.), *Voices of change: Participatory research in the United States and Canada* (pp. 1–20). Toronto: Ontario Institute for Studies in Education.

Patton, M. Q. (2002). *Qualitative research and evaluation methods* (3rd ed.). Thousand Oaks, CA: Sage.

Picou, J. S. (2000). The "talking circle" as sociological practice: Cultural transformation of chronic disaster impacts. *Sociological Practice: A Journal of Clinical and Applied Sociology, 2,* 77–97.

Reason, P. (1998). The approaches to participatory inquiry. In N. K. Denzin & Y. S. Lincoln (Eds.), *Strategies for qualitative inquiry* (pp. 262–291). Thousand Oaks, CA: Sage.

Running Wolf, P., & Rickard, J. A. (2003). Talking circles: A Native American approach to experiential learning. *Multicultural Counseling and Development, 31,* 39–43.

Ryba, T. V., & Schinke, R. J. (2009). Methodology as a ritualized Eurocentrism: Introduction to the Special Issue. *International Journal of Sport and Exercise Psychology, 7*(3), 263–274.

Ryba, T. V., & Wright, H. K. (2005). From mental game to cultural praxis: A cultural studies model's implications for the future of sport psychology. *Quest, 57,* 192–212.

Schinke, R. J. (2007). A four-year chronology with national team boxing in Canada. *Journal of Sport Science and Medicine, 6*(CSSI-2), 1–5.

Schinke, R. J., Blodgett, A., Yungblut, H. E., Recollet-Saikkonen, D., Peltier, D., Battochio, R., et al. Understanding the adaptation process of Canadian Aboriginal Athletes leaving their cultural community. Submitted for publication.

Schinke, R. J., Hanrahan, S. J., & Catina, P. (2009). Introduction to cultural sport psychology. In R. J. Schinke & S. J. Hanrahan (Eds.), *Cultural sport psychology: From theory to practice.* Champaign, IL: Human Kinetics.

Schinke, R. J., Hanrahan, S. J., Eys, M. A., Blodgett, A., Peltier, D., Ritchie, S., et al. (2008). The development of cross-cultural relations with a Canadian Aboriginal community through sport psychology research. *Quest, 60,* 357–369.

Schinke, R. J., Michel, G., Gauthier, A.,

Danielson, R., Pickard, P., Peltier, D., et al. (2006). Adaptation to the mainstream in elite sport: An Aboriginal perspective. *The Sport Psychologist, 20,* 435–448.

Schinke, R. J., Yungblut, H. E., Blodgett, A., Peltier, D., Ritchie, S., & Recollet-Saikonnen, D. (in press). The role of families in youth sport programming within a Canadian Aboriginal community. *The Journal of Physical Activity and Health.*

Schnarch, B. (2004, January). Ownership, control, access, and permission or self-determination applied to research: A critical analysis of contemporary First Nations research and some options for First Nations communities. *Journal of Aboriginal Health,* 80–95.

Smith, L. T. (1999). *Decolonizing methodologies: Research and indigenous peoples.* Dunedin: University of Otago Press.

Spivak, G. (1988). Can the subaltern speak? In G. Nelson & L. Grossberg (Eds.), *Marxism and the interpretation of culture* (pp. 271–313). Urbana: University of Illinois Press.

Thomason, T. C. (1991). Counseling Native Americans: An introduction for non-Native American counselors. *Journal of Counseling and Development, 69,* 321–327.

University of Victoria. (2003). *Protocols & principles for conducting research in an indigenous context.* Unpublished report.

Wallerstein, N. B., & Duran, B. (2006). Using community-based participatory research to address health disparities. *Health Promotion Practice, 7,* 312–323.

PART III

APPLIED ARENAS

11

DISABILITY IN SPORT AND EXERCISE PSYCHOLOGY

Tamar Z. Semerjian

CHAPTER SUMMARY

Sport and exercise psychology researchers have begun to explore the experiences of athletes and exercisers with disabilities, and increasingly seek to understand the determinants and outcomes of exercise for individuals with disabilities. Since early calls for research in this area (Asken, 1991; Crocker, 1993) there has been growth; however, much more research that is theoretically grounded and incorporates a critical cultural studies approach is needed.

This chapter begins with a framework for defining disability and a review of previous research relating to sport and exercise among individuals with disabilities. I then discuss the significant amount of research relating to individuals with spinal cord injury as well as the research that I have conducted with individuals with spinal cord injury in an adapted exercise setting. This chapter advocates for the use of critical cultural studies, in particular a consideration of how lines of power related to race, class, gender, and sexuality intersect with the experiences of individuals with disabilities. Suggestions are made regarding how cultural studies can be incorporated into research relating to individuals with disabilities. Finally, future directions in the area of disability sport and exercise are proposed. The focus of this chapter is on adults with physical disabilities, particularly mobility impairments, and not on intellectual and developmental disabilities or children.

Disability in Sport and Exercise Psychology

"Isn't it depressing?" I was asked when talking to a colleague about the research I was conducting involving individuals with spinal cord injury. I was taken aback. In the four years that I had worked with individuals with spinal cord injuries (SCI) I had never found the work depressing. There were sad stories, but there were also stories of determination. I had met people who were funny, outgoing, and creative. I had met people who were young and old, newly injured and those who had been injured nearly 30 years prior. I had gone to plays in which participants in our study were performing, one of which was written by the performer. I had seen the majority of the study participants increase their functional abilities, and I had the joy of interviewing them at the end of their participation. Most of the participants appreciated the exercise sessions and training they received and felt that it had helped them both physically and psychologically. They felt emotionally and physically stronger; through exercise and working with student trainers they felt supported and motivated to continue exercising. Depressing? Nothing about the work that I was doing was depressing, but the comment highlighted the misperceptions of the able-bodied community that living with a disability was by definition depressing and sad.

In this chapter I will present definitions of disability and discuss previous research about sport and exercise among individuals with disabilities. In discussing such work, I will focus on research regarding individuals with spinal cord injuries. Finally, I present a critical analysis of disability research in sport and exercise psychology and make recommendations for future directions and highlight theoretical frameworks that may be useful in future work.

Defining Disability

When discussing individuals with disabilities it has been suggested that a "person first" language be used in order to focus on the individual, not the disability, and I have attempted to engage this style throughout this chapter (DePauw & Gavron, 2005). Examples of "person first" language are phrases such as "athletes with mobility impairments" or "individuals with disabilities" in contrast to phrases such as "mobility impaired athletes" or "disabled individuals."

For the purposes of this chapter *disability* is used to refer to a physical impairment that interferes with the performance of activities of daily living and limits individuals' abilities to perform physical tasks they desire to execute (Hanrahan, 2005). Although I use this definition to organize the chapter, several theorists have challenged the use of such definitions of disability. Thomas (2007) emphasized that although medical discourses on disability rely primarily on definitions highlighting the limitations of the individual, sociological definitions focus on the limitations "from the outside" (p. 13). Thomas argued that disability is constructed as a social deviance. Individuals with disabilities do not conform to notions of the normal able body, and as a result are seen as having bodies that are problematic. Rarely, however, are the social structures that limit individuals' mobility and access interrogated. Thus Thomas argued that it is the social structures that limit individuals' lives that ought to be problematized. Additionally she suggested that disability and bodily impairment are inextricably linked to oppression, psychoemotional dimensions of life, and the sociocultural world. Thomas's perspective on disability, and the use of such a definition in sport and exercise psychology, would likely result in research more in line with the cultural turn, highlighting the discursive construction of disability rather than assuming that the category of disability is fixed and easily understood. Disability is both constituted by and influences material conditions. Material conditions allow some individuals to use assistive devices that enhance their physical abilities, at times beyond those of able-bodied individuals, as will be discussed later in the case of Oscar Pistorius. However, lack of access to assistive devices can lead to diminished capacities to achieve individual goals.

In defining disability it is important to remember that disability is typically constructed in contrast to what is considered normal, or the "able body." When the able-bodied individual or athlete is considered the norm, then individuals or athletes who are differently able are seen as "other" and non-normative. For sport and exercise psychology consultants, such perceptions could limit a full understanding of the individual with a disability as a complete and complex person, resulting in an undue focus on the disability (Hanrahan, 1998, 2007). Several theorists have highlighted that even the term *able-bodied* is problematic, because everyone is susceptible to injury or physical impairments associated with aging and thus individuals without disabilities are "temporarily able-bodied" (Breckenridge & Vogler, 2001; Shakespeare, 1998). While I will use the term *able-bodied* throughout this chapter, it is with the acknowledgment that this bodily condition can be temporally unstable. I am wary, however, of the term *temporarily able-bodied* because, as Hughes (2007) has suggested, at the same time that this term universalizes disability, it can simultaneously erase disability identity. For disability activists who work toward visibility and social change, the suggestion that everyone is "in the same boat" diminishes the experiences of those with disabilities.

Another consideration in the definition of disability is that it is not a fixed category. With technological advancements disability becomes a transmutable category. If individuals can use technologies that enable them to do what they were previously unable to do (and therefore placing them in the category of "disability"), then the label no longer applies, and using the definition set forth at the beginning of the chapter, the individual no longer has a disability. With a prosthetic leg, an individual with a lower limb amputation may be able to run as well as, and at times faster and arguably better, than an individual without a prosthetic appendage. Technologies have created "cyborgs" (Haraway, 1991) among all people who engage them, and particularly among athletes. Butryn (2003) stated, "athletes have interacted with and been shaped by various technologies since birth" (p. 18). Individuals with disabilities often engage with technologies out of necessity, and it is these technologies that can enhance their exercise and sport participation, through the use of wheelchairs, prosthetics, and adapted exercise machines. When South African sprinter Oscar Pistorius, who is a double amputee, attempted to qualify for the 2008 Beijing Olympics, questions were raised about whether it was fair for him to compete against able-bodied athletes. Journalists in the mainstream media asked, "Do prosthetic legs simply level the playing field for Pistorius, compensating for his disability, or do they give him an inequitable edge via what some call techno-doping?" (Longman, 2007). The case of Pistorius highlights that definitions of disability are necessarily problematic. Disability is often defined as a condition that negatively impacts the ability of an individual to function in nearly all aspects of life, and that once acquired is permanent. However, recently philosophers have argued that there are important similarities between elite athletes and individuals with disabilities. "Both concepts of dis-ability and super-ability are based upon deviations from standards of normality" (van Hilvoodre & Landeweerde, 2008, p. 98). In one case those deviations are assumed to result in lower performances and in the other better performances than average. However, in the case of Pistorius and other athletes with disabilities, this assumption is proven false. "New technologies such as prostheses apparently help to turn disabled people into 'normal' subjects" (van Hilvoorde & Landeweerd 2008, p. 100), and therefore destabilize understood notions of "disability" and "super-ability." Edwards (2008) also applied a philosophical interrogation to the question of whether Pistorius should be allowed to participate in the Olympics, and concluded that unless it could be argued that what Pistorius does when competing is not running, the common arguments would have to be dismissed and fairness would dictate that he be allowed to compete. To limit the opportunities of athletes with disabilities because the advantages that are provided by the equipment used to allow them to move and complete "normally" is, according to these philosophers, unfair. As Edwards (2008) stated "one wonders that if OP [Pistorius] is barred from the Olympics surely it follows that he should be barred from the Paralympics. If he has an advantage on 'able-bodied' runners, then this is surely true in relation to the Paralympics too" (p. 123). As technologies advance and disability activists are successful in arguing for the integration of athletes with disabilities into mainstream sport, ethical questions regarding the fairness of using prosthetics and other technological aides are likely to arise more frequently and pose interesting questions regarding what counts as disability and an unfair advantage.

Overview of Research

Others have conducted comprehensive reviews of the literature pertaining to sport and physical activity participation among individuals with disabilities (Hanrahan, 2007; Martin, 1996). In this overview I will discuss some of the trends in sport and exercise psychology disability research, specifically early work on comparison studies, instrument assessment, psychological skill development and consultation with athletes, and determinants of exercise and sport participation. Initial calls to conduct research on individuals with disabilities were made by researchers such as Asken (1991) and Crocker (1993). Both of these papers can be seen as the beginning of sport psychology's foray into discussions of disability in the sport and exercise context and influencing much of the research described in this section.

Comparison Studies

Researchers in the field of sport psychology have historically relied primarily on positivistic and post-positivistic paradigms, and valued scientific, empirical, and quantitative studies (Sparkes, 1998). As a result, it is no surprise that initial research on individuals with disabilities employed quantitative studies and the use of measures that were deemed valid and reliable among the able-bodied population, such as the Profile of Mood States and measures of self-efficacy. Determining if athletes with disabilities were in some way different from those without disabilities was seen as important, because it would establish if research findings with athletes without disabilities are applicable to those with disabilities. In general, researchers found that athletes with disabilities were similar to able-bodied athletes and demonstrated similar psychological and mood profiles (Asken, 1991; Greenwood, Dzewaltowski, & French, 1990; Paulsen, French, & Sherrill, 1991). Henschen, Horvat, and Roswal (1992) identified differences in psychological profiles between those who qualified for the United States Wheelchair Basketball Paralympics Team and those who did not. They found that athletes selected for the team had significantly lower scores on tension and anger than those not selected. In addition to comparing disabled athletes and able-bodied athletes, researchers have compared athletes with disabilities to those who are non-athletes. Roeder and Aufsesser (1986) found that wheelchair athletes had higher levels of self-esteem and physical orientation than disabled non-athletes. These comparison studies presupposed that there could be differences between athletes with and without disabilities, but did not consider the cultural contexts in which athletes participated and the sociocultural reasons for why differences may have been found.

Instrument Assessment

Once it was established that athletes with disabilities were not dissimilar when compared to athletes without disabilities, the next area of research focused on issues of measurement and instrument assessment. Martin et al. (1997) and Tasiemski, Kennedy, Gardner, and Blaikley (2004) examined the factor structure of the Athletic Identity Measurement Scale (AIMS; Brewer, Van Raalte, & Lindner, 1993) with athletes with disabilities. While Martin et al. confirmed a four-factor structure that had been previously identified with another population of athletes with disabilities, Tasiemski et al. did not validate this multifactor structure of the AIMS.

More recently, Ferreira and Fox (2008) sought to establish the reliability, validity, and factor structure of the Portuguese version of the Physical Self-Perception Profile with elite basketball players with and without disabilities. The factor structure for the able-bodied athletes was consistent with previous findings, but the factor structure was quite different for athletes with disabilities and led the researchers to conclude that "the pattern found for Physical self and Global Self-esteem in this group may be understood as a particular characteristic or may be determined by the difference provided by dealing and living with physical disability in a competitive sport environment" (p. 43).

In general, measures used with able-bodied athletes have been useful in working with athletes with disabilities. Unfortunately the sample sizes used in these studies are often relatively small and focus on a particular type of disability, further limiting the generalizability of the findings. Studies assessing instrumentation are important, in that they provide a foundation for further work with individuals with disabilities and some visibility to their experiences. However, there is no critical consideration of how disability is defined, or how the settings in which individuals with disabilities participate in sport might be influenced by social and cultural ideas regarding the body and ability.

Determinants of Sport and Physical Activity Participation

While early work in sport psychology focused on athletes with disabilities, there has been a significant increase in the exercise psychology literature related to individuals with disabilities. These researchers (Martin et al., 2002; Swanson, Colwell, & Zhaor, 2008; Warms, Belga, Whitney, Mitchell, & Steins, 2004; Wetterhahn, Hanson, & Levy, 2002) acknowledged the importance that exercise can have in increasing self-esteem, self-efficacy, quality of life, and other aspects of psychological well-being. They sought to identify the barriers and determinants of exercise and physical activity participation. Heimer and Relac (1998) argued for the importance of sport in the lives of individuals with disabilities and that there should be state-sponsored support for accessible sport programs. They advocated for sport on the basis that sport participation will enhance the physical and mental health and well-being of individuals with disabilities.

Reasons identified for engaging in exercise and sport for individuals with disabilities have been a desire to maintain or increase physical conditioning, strength, and ability, as well as perceived positive psychological outcomes such as increased social contacts and support and improvements in general psychological well-being (Martin et al., 2002; Tasiemski et al., 2004). Major barriers to participation in both sport and physical activity have been a lack of access and knowledge about available programs (Martin et al., 2002). Arbour and Martin Ginis (2007) found that the environment had a significant effect on the physical activity levels of individuals with spinal cord injuries and the availability of ramps, attractive environments, and sidewalk maintenance were among the factors that predicted moderate intensity wheelchair use.

Swanson et al. (2008) assessed sources of motivation and social support that influenced the physical activity participation of individuals with disabilities. They found that the motives of males and females differed and that the type of social support that was important varied based on level of participation. Increasing one's sense of competence may be particularly important for athletes with disabilities. Researchers have found a positive relationship between body image and physical activity participation among individuals with amputations, and this may also be related to enhanced self-esteem (Wetterhahn et al., 2002).

Warms et al. (2004) and Kosma, Ellis, Cardinal, Bauer, and Mc-Cubbin (2007) have used the transtheoretical model (TTM) to better understand exercise behaviors among individuals with disabilities. Warms et al. found that their intervention based on TTM resulted in increased physical activity, lower levels of perceived barriers to exercise, progression in stage of change, and increased perceptions of self-efficacy and health. Kosma et al. found that stage of change, intention to exercise, and perceived behavioral control were all significant predictors of physical activity.

The majority of the researchers discussed above highlighted the positive psychological benefits associated with exercise, and advocated that individuals with disabilities have the right to have access to physical activity. While researchers of exercise and physical activity participation may not actively call for social justice and change, their recommendations for increased accessibility for individuals with disabilities begins to approach the intentions of the cultural turn.

Providing Psychological Skills Training and Consulting Services

There is evidence that athletes with disabilities are able to effectively use psychological skills and benefit from psychological skills training and working with sport psychology consultants (Cox & Davis, 1992; Hanrahan, 1998, Hanrahan, Grove, & Lockwood, 1990). Asken (1991) and Hanrahan (1998, 2007) both discussed providing psychological skills training and sport psychology consulting to individuals with disabilities and emphasized the need for competence when working with athletes with disabilities. They suggested that consultants educate themselves on disabilities and the impact that disability and the trauma that may have led to the disability could have on the athlete.

Hanrahan et al. (1990) used psychological skills training with athletes with visual impairments. They found that with minor modifications much of the skills traditionally used by sport psychology consultants were effective for athletes with visual impairments. Athletes with disabilities can certainly benefit from working with sport and exercise psychology consultants and developing their psychological skills, just as has been demonstrated among able-bodied athletes. Often sport psychology consultants are interested in performance enhancement among the most elite of athletes. Sport psychology consultants may have limited information regarding athletes with disabilities, and may require education regarding how athletes with disabilities are largely similar to other athletic populations as well as some of the unique aspects of working with this population. Attention to the experiences of athletes with disabilities and their interests, needs, and desires for sport participation can bring their voices to the forefront and lead to more effective population relevant research and practice.

Spinal Cord Injury

In the United States an estimated 11,000 people each year acquire a spinal cord injury. Currently 247,000 people are living with SCI in the United States (Institutes of Medicine, 2005), 40,000 in Canada (International Collaboration on Repair Discoveries, 2009), and 40,000 in the United Kingdom with approximately 1,000 new cases each year in the United Kingdom (Spinal Injuries Association, 2009). Global statistics are difficult to find as a result of significant variations in data collection between countries. Individuals with SCI have lost motor and/or sensory function below their site of injury, leading to a lack of voluntary muscular control and limited mobility. While researchers initially focused on increasing life expectancy and functional ability for individuals with SCI, more recently they have focused on improving quality of life for those with SCI (Hicks et al., 2005). Studies by numerous investigators have clearly established that exercise has a positive impact on both the physiological and the psychological well-being of individuals with SCI. Despite the clear evidence that exercise is critical to health, functional ability, quality of life, and alleviating depression, the majority of the SCI population remains relatively sedentary (Hicks et al., 2005; Martin Ginis et al., 2003). In the following discussion I will present research that has focused on SCI from the perspective of sport, exercise, and the relatively new training technique termed *body weight supported treadmill training* (BWSTT). Additionally, I will discuss how my work with several colleagues and the work of Smith and Sparkes (2005, 2008; Smith, 2008; Sparkes & Smith, 2002) have embraced the cultural turn.

Sport studies

There are several researchers who have considered the sporting experiences of individuals with SCI. Wu and Williams (2001) identified the factors that led to sport participation after a spinal cord injury. They found that individuals who had been active prior to their injury identified sport clubs within the rehabilitation context to be important for reestablishing an exercise or sport routine. Individuals who were inactive prior to their injury identified education regarding exercise as an important impetus for participation. Wu and Williams's work is important in that rather than looking at inactive or sedentary individuals they identified active participants and then sought to determine what was most influential in their sport and exercise participation.

Sparkes and Smith (2002) offered a significant departure from previous research in sport psychology on disability, and specifically SCI. They interviewed four individuals who sustained SCI while participating in rugby. In their paper the authors proposed considering disability from an embodied perspective. Sparkes and Smith suggested that the consideration of the body has been conspicuously absent in the disability literature, and employed theoretical perspectives from disability studies and the sociology of disability that highlight the importance of the body in the experiences of disability. They contended that disability is experienced and understood within the lived body, and that the ways that men with SCI tell stories about themselves and their experiences with their disabilities are shaped and informed by the knowledges they gain in their body. The men interviewed by Sparks and Smith stated that prior to their injuries they had not considered the ways they had used their bodies and how their masculinity had been connected to their physical abilities. However, after injury they were acutely aware of their bodies and also questioned their masculinity. The men also experienced a loss of athletic identity. Central to the analysis of Sparkes and Smith (2002) was an interest in the narratives told by men with SCI. They were not only interested in what their participants had to say, but the ways in which their stories of injury and disability were told. Using this same narrative analysis Smith and Sparkes (2005) focused on 14 men from the same population as their previous study and found 3 distinct narratives in the ways that the men told their stories. The first was one of concrete hope, the second transcendent hope, and the third a despair narrative. Concrete hope was characterized by a belief that they would once again be healthy and able to walk. Those with transcendent hope found meaning in their injuries, and did not necessarily expect or hope to regain their ability to walk. They had found a sense of meaning through their injury. Finally, individuals with a despair narrative were not hopeful and saw little meaning in their current lives.

Rees, Smith, and Sparks (2003) found that emotional support, esteem support, informational support, and tangible support were important to men who had sustained a SCI while playing rugby. For individuals who have sustained a significant injury such as SCI, all of the types of support are critical. The sudden lack of ability to perform tasks of everyday living and having to reorganize one's life, physically and sometimes socially, can be challenging.

Sparkes and Smith (Smith, 2008; Smith & Sparkes, 2002, 2005, 2008) have published numerous studies on various aspects of the experiences of men who have acquired spinal cord injuries while playing rugby union. Their work highlights the possibilities of what the cultural turn can, and does, look like. "Culture provides people with a menu of narrative forms and contents from which the person selectively draws in an effort to line up lived experience with the kinds of stories available to organize and express it. Indeed, the story menu goes so far as to shape lived experience itself: we live in and through stories" (Smith, 2008, p. 24).

Sparkes and Smith have argued that the ways that individuals tell stories about themselves are inherently influenced by the social context in which they live, and advocated for the use of narrative analysis to interrogate these stories. Smith and Sparkes have repeatedly argued that it is the social context that delimits and influences the stories that are available to individuals with disabilities. Smith (2008) stated, "There is no real or true self that exists as some entity in our brain. Rather, the stories that we compose, in the social medium of language, function to create to [*sic*] the illusion of seamlessness in our self-perceptions and a sense of self-sameness" (p. 24). Smith further insisted that "narratives *do* matter. They are important resources to explore people's self-perspectives of disability, sport and physical activity" (p. 25).

Exercise studies

As discussed earlier, there is substantial evidence that exercise improves the psychological well-being of individuals with SCI, yet the majority of individuals with SCI remain sedentary. Martin et al. (2002) found that individuals with SCI identified several barriers that prevented them from exercising, including difficulties finding accessible and affordable exercise programs and facilities, pain, psychological variables (such as a lack of confidence), lack of time, and lack of information. Despite this, individuals with SCI were well aware of the benefits of an active lifestyle and identified improved physical functioning and an improved sense of well-being as outcomes of exercise participation.

Latimer et al. (2004) considered the mediating effect of exercise-related reductions in pain on increases in psychological well-being. They found that for individuals with SCI, exercise reduced pain, and that changes in pain mediated positive changes in psychological well-being. In a follow-up study Ditor et al. (2006) found that after the nine-month exercise intervention program there was a significant decrease in adherence to exercise, although the participants had access to continued engagement in the exercise program. They also found that the reductions in pain and increased psychological well-being that had occurred during the exercise program were not maintained when individuals did not continue the exercise program, highlighting the need for continued participation in order to maintain the psychological benefits of exercise.

Levins et al. (2004) looked at constraints and "enablers" to participation. They found that one barrier to participation was that individuals no longer saw themselves as capable of engaging in physical activity or sport. Loss of able identity was followed for some by a turning point where participants decided that they needed to change and engage in physical activity to increase their physical functioning and improve their mental well-being. The majority of participants in the study identified lack of access as a significant barrier. Some participants reported that the stigma of disability and the injustices they experienced in the able-bodied world discouraged them from participation; however, supportive others facilitated participation. While physical therapists were at times encouraging, some participants expressed that physical therapists underestimated the participants' abilities and dissuaded them from participation in physical activities.

Latimer et al. (2004) used the theory of planned behavior as a framework for understanding determinants of exercise for individuals with SCI and found only perceived behavior control to be significantly related to exercise intentions. They argued that while the theory of planned behavior had limited utility in explaining exercise behaviors among individuals with SCI, increasing a sense of control over the ability to exercise may result in increased participation for individuals with SCI, once again highlighting the need for exercise environments that individuals can easily access.

I, along with my colleagues Ray deLeon and Jesus Dominguez, conducted a 5-year study that measured changes in a variety of physiological measures, quality of life, and body satisfaction after participation in a 10-week exercise program (Semerjian, Montague, Dominguez, Davidian, & de Leon, 2005). In addition to using exercise equipment that was adapted for individuals with SCI, our participants also engaged in body weight supported treadmill training (BWSTT). In conjunction with questionnaires and physiological data that were collected to identify changes during the training period, I also conducted in-depth interviews with all 30 participants. Our work was initially conceived as a multimethod and multidisciplinary project. Ray de Leon is a neurophysiologist, and Jesus Dominguez is a physical therapist. I was initially invited to the project as an exercise psychologist, although I had every intention of bringing my cultural studies perspective to the research. Our hope was that through simultaneous collection of data related to physiological and psychological outcomes and interview data, we could present a more nuanced understanding of the experience of exercise for individuals with SCI. The ongoing analysis of the interviews was informed by my use of thematic analysis, as well as postmodern, queer, and feminist theories (Semerjian, 2006a, 2006b, 2007, 2008). This project is intended to embrace Ryba and Wright's (2005) suggestion that research "move toward interdisciplinarity, the bridging of the gap between research and practice and the incorporation of gender issues, social difference and power dynamics" (p. 196). Thus, in addition to demonstrating increased strength, endurance, and flexibility among individuals with SCI who participated in the exercise program, we also focused on psychological outcomes. We found that after 10 weeks participants exhibited significant improvements in quality of life and body satisfaction as measured by questionnaires.

In addition to the data relating to quality of life and body satisfaction, I have used thematic analysis to identify participants' motives to exercise, their experiences in their bodies during exercise, and the ways that race, class, and gender have shaped their exercise experiences, as well as their experiences post-injury (Semerjian, 2005, 2006a, 2006b, 2007, 2008). Incorporating a multimethod approach has been helpful in understanding the experiences of individuals with SCI more fully and providing a nuanced perspective on our data. For example, we measured changes in pain via a questionnaire, but found no significant differences pre- and post-exercise. The lack of change in pain perception originally surprised us and was inconsistent with previous research. However, an analysis of the interviews helped to make sense of this finding. Nearly all the participants reported that exercise had changed their experiences of pain; however, some reported that their pain sensations had increased, whereas others reported that their pain had decreased. All those who reported changes interpreted them positively, either as an indication of increased sensation, and therefore neurological recovery, or as a decrease in discomfort. Without the use of interviews in conjunction with the questionnaire data this finding would have gone unnoticed.

Implications of body weight supported treadmill training (BWSTT)

BWSTT has been used by several research groups in multiple countries, and increasingly there has been an interest in the psychological outcomes of this training. BWSTT allows individuals with mobility impairments to walk on a treadmill while being supported from above with a harness. Trainers assist the individual by guiding the hips and legs through the gait pattern. BWSTT allows individuals with SCI (as well as stroke and other mobility impairments) to walk, which can be a profound experience for someone who has been unable to stand independently since her or his injury. Effing, van Meeteren, van Asbeck, and Prevo (2006) tested 3 participants on their functional health status and quality of life after 12 weeks of BWSTT. The authors found that the three participants had varying results, with some physical improvements in all three participants, but improvements in quality of life for only one participant. Hannold, Young, Rittman, Bowden, and Behrman (2006) found that the physiological changes associated with BWSTT led to feelings of hope and motivation to continue exercise, and Martin Ginis and Latimer (2007) found that even a single bout of BWSTT led to positive mood states and decreases in pain related to improved mood states. Hicks et al. (2005) found that participation in a 12-month walking program resulted in increased life satisfaction and satisfaction with physical functioning, and that increases in subjective well-being were maintained when assessed 8 months after the conclusion of the training program. Hicks et al. indicated that BWSTT training can have an important impact on the psychological well-being of individuals with SCI.

In addition to using adapted exercise equipment, the participants in our study engaged in BWSTT (Semerjian et al., 2005). During the interviews our participants identified BWSTT as having a significant psychological impact. Seeing themselves walking was profound for a variety of reasons. Some had not seen themselves standing for nearly 30 years, and the ability to look someone in the eye, and not have to look up, was significant. For others BWSTT and the improvements that they attributed to this training led to hope that they would one day walk again. Although BWSTT has shown to lead to improvements in over ground walking in some studies, but not in others, we agree with Hicks and Martin Ginis (2008), who argued that there are psychological benefits to this type of training that go beyond the physiological measures. Again, the use of interviews allowed an articulation of the experience of walking for individuals with SCI that would have gone unheard otherwise. Walking was a profound experience for many of the participants in our study. As one participant put it: "I feel like I'm no longer broken. I feel more connected. I don't know even how to explain it because you can't. It's nothing you can describe to somebody who's normal or doesn't have a broken back or doesn't know that sensation of being paralyzed. And you never want to be there. . . . Yeah, before I felt broken, now I don't feel broken" (Semerjian, 2007 p. 8).

Qualitative research on the experience of exercise and rehabilitation captures the experiences of individuals with SCI in ways that are simply unavailable through quantitative methods. While the collection of such data is helpful in identifying trends, generalizations, and average responses, the embodied perspective on healing is not conveyed. Additionally, it is important to highlight that individuals with disabilities occupy bodies that are also gendered, raced, and marked by class, and the intersections of these experiences are critical to an understanding of the experience of disability.

Critical Analysis

Since the mid-1980s there has been a greater interest in athletes with disabilities and more recently the use of exercise as a modality for rehabilitation and increasing psychological well-being. Sport and exercise psychology researchers, however, have rarely engaged in an analysis of the cultural aspects that are relevant for individuals with disabilities in sport and exercise contexts and have relied primarily on positivistic and quantitative theoretical models and methodologies. A cultural turn in sport and exercise psychology utilizing cultural studies is warranted (Ryba & Wright, 2005), particularly in the study of individuals with disabilities in order to critically interrogate the category of disability as well as to understand experiences of disability as contextualized within other intersecting power relations. As articulated by Ryba and Wright (2005):

> Sport psychology as a cultural studies praxis moves away from looking at the athlete in isolation as a whole, singular unified individual in the way orthodox sport psychology tended to do. Instead the athlete is considered to be a subject of multiple discourses and various identifications, a member of numerous social and cultural groups, and a part of sport as an institution immersed in a particular sociocultural and historical context. (p. 204)

Thus the cultural turn requires that athletes and exercisers with disabilities be considered not solely on the basis of their disability identity, but with an acknowledgment of their multiple identities and their position as a result of the historical and social context they are located within. Theoretical paradigms that question the stability of identity categories, interrogate power relations, and make use of a variety of methodological tools including qualitative methods are required for work that espouses the cultural turn. In the following sections I will discuss how research addressing embodiment and the intersections of race, class, gender, and sexuality with disability can inform future investigations.

Embodiment

The majority of researchers considering disability in sport and exercise have failed to focus on experiences of embodiment as they relate to disability. Because disability by definition resides within the body, examining the experiences of embodiment seems critical. Hughes and Patterson (1997) have written, "Disability is experienced in, on and through the body. . . . Most importantly, the (impaired) body is not just experienced: It is also the very basis of experience" (p. 335). Thus, experiences of athletes with disabilities must be understood within the context of their bodies, and for athletes who participated in sport prior to their injuries, the changes in the embodied experience of sport must be acknowledged. Wu and Williams (2001) argued that individuals who had participated in sport and exercise prior to their injury were more likely to engage in these activities after their injury and began to participate sooner than those who had been inactive. However, in our research we found that individuals who had participated in sport prior to their injury often did not see wheelchair sport or, in the case of one participant, dance, as "real" or equivalent to what they had done previously (Semerjian, 2006). They implied that these sports were a cheap imitation of what they had done previously. Their bodies simply could not move in the same ways, and the ways they could move did not feel the same and therefore were not nearly as satisfying as they had hoped. Similarly, some of the men Sparkes and Smith (2002) interviewed reported a disinterest in wheelchair sports. These men stated that because they could not use their bodies in the same ways they had when they had previously played rugby, modified sports did not satisfy their need to move their bodies in powerful ways.

Qualitative methodologies are particularly helpful in considering embodiment. The works of Smith and colleagues in particular (Smith, 2008; Smith & Sparkes, 2002, 2008) highlight the narratives that individuals with SCI use to make sense of their lives, and often the stories told center on the body. The body is central to identity, and when individuals experience disability their sense of self changes profoundly, specifically because their self-presentation through the body has changed. As stated earlier, identities can be seen as multiple, and thus embodied identities are not understood simply based on ability but also intersect with the embodiment of race, class, gender, and sexuality.

Intersections of race, class, gender, and sexuality

Crenshaw (1995) considered the importance of intersections of power. She wrote, "My focus on the intersections of race and gender only highlights the need to account for multiple grounds of identity when considering how the social world is constructed" (p. 358). A consideration of the intersections of power lines of disability, race, class, and gender is also necessary. Disability is not the only aspect of individuals' identity, and their experiences occur within the context of their bodies that are marked not only by disability but also by race and gender. In the research that I have conducted with my colleagues we found that men of color were assumed by others, both strangers and friends, to have been involved in a gang- or drug-related shooting when they were in wheelchairs (Semerjian, 2006). As one participant stated, "If you're black or you're brown, that's the first thing that comes to their mind . . . he's in a gang, he got shot." This racialized component of disability is rarely discussed in sport psychology literature. In fact, in most studies authors fail to discuss the ethnicity of the participants at all, and race is rarely considered as an important component in the experience of disability. The cultural turn in sport psychology would require researchers to address the reasons for differences between groups in a sociocultural and historically contextualized manner, as well as problematizing the socially constructed categories that are used, such as disability, race, class, gender, and sexuality.

Another aspect of power in society is socioeconomic class. Individuals without the material resources to purchase what they need and desire are typically at a disadvantage in capitalist societies. This is exceptionally clear in the context of sport and exercise for individuals with disabilities. Wheelchairs, prosthetic devices, and hiring assistants to aid in activities of daily living are all expensive endeavors. Health insurance may cover some expenses, but not all individuals have private insurance and many rely on state-sponsored programs that may be difficult to negotiate and cover only their most basic health needs. Sport psychology researchers simply have not considered the implication of class and sport and exercise participation. Although access issues are often discussed as a barrier to participation, these issues are exacerbated when individuals do not have the material resources to purchase adapted vehicles that they can drive or ride in, pay for memberships to gyms that are accessible, and hire trainers who are familiar with their specific needs. To participate in wheelchair sport, specialized wheelchairs are often required and for individuals with amputations, specialized prosthetics may be necessary. This specialized equipment is not covered by insurance, and only those with significant wealth or sponsorship can afford to play. Thus, much of the research conducted on disability sport has likely included participants who occupy a particular social class. A significant portion of the population of individuals with disabilities is likely excluded from this research. In our research we found that participants appreciated the accessibility of the low-cost program (no-cost while they participated in the study). All the equipment that they used was adapted for individuals with SCI, and there were trainers with specialized knowledge to assist them (Semerjian et al., 2005). After completion of the study, they could continue to exercise at the university for a relatively small fee, and while some did, the difficulty of transportation or the cost of the program (even though it was low) may have limited their adherence to the exercise program. Without a consideration of the implications of class on sport and exercise experiences of individuals with disabilities, only a partial understanding of these settings and the individuals who participate in them is possible. Working with diverse populations is critical for future projects.

In the area of disability sport and exercise there have been few studies where gender has been considered (Semerjian, 2007; Smith & Sparkes, 2002, 2005; Sparkes & Smith, 2008). In our study, we found that disability had a significant impact on individuals' gender identity. Women did not feel that they could embody their femininity because of their lack of mobility. They discussed strategies they used to enhance their feminine image, such as crossing their legs in their wheelchairs and dressing in hyper-feminine ways. One woman stated, "I mean, they are going to see the chair period, but I just want something more petite, something more for a girl . . . smaller tires, you know, little, smaller frame." This equation of femininity with taking up less space mirrors the social imperative on women to be small, not particularly muscular, and to conform to hegemonic notions of femininity (Krane, 2001). The ability to conform to those notions may be compromised by disability (Potgieter & Khan, 2005). Sparkes and Smith (2002, 2008) have highlighted that men are similarly challenged to display hegemonic masculinity. The men they interviewed found that ability to display masculinity was at times "shattered and lost" (2002, p. 269). We found that one of the major motivators to exercise for the men in our study was to develop a more muscular body, which they related to masculinity. They expressed that their ability to be seen as masculine was compromised by their SCI, and the development of a muscular body would help them to attain a masculine image once again.

While limited discussions of gender exist in the study of athletes with disabilities, no researcher has considered the implications of sexuality and its intersections with disability. It is not clear what direction this research might take, and as discussed in chapter 7 there is a general lack of research on sexuality in sport and exercise psychology more broadly. While the population of gay, lesbian, bisexual, and transgender athletes and exercisers with disabilities may be small, the imperative to demonstrate a heteronormative image is an imperative in mainstream sport (King, 2008) and may have implications for individuals with disabilities as well.

Researchers in the field of disability studies have begun to undertake projects that grapple with these intersections. Snyder and Mitchell (2001) stated that "like feminized, raced and queer bodies, the disabled body became situated in definitive contrast to the articulation of what amounted to a hegemonic aesthetic premised on biology. Within this cultural belief system, the 'normal' body provided the baseline for determinations of desirability and human value" (p. 369).

One potential framework for such research has been proposed by McRuer (2006), who introduced "crip" theory, which much like queer theory, is intended to problematize and disrupt commonly understood notions about the able-body and the disabled-body. He argued that just as there is an imperative toward heteronormativity in Western cultures, there is an equally compelling imperative toward being able-bodied. "Like compulsory heterosexuality, then, compulsory able-bodiedness functions by covering over, with the appearance of choice, a system in which there actually is no choice" (p. 8). Theoretical perspectives such as postmodernism (Foucault, 1995; Grosz, 1994), cyborg theory (Haraway, 1991), crip theory (McRuer, 2006), and feminist disabilities studies (Thomas, 2001) can inform the shape that the cultural turn takes in future research with individuals with disabilities.

Conclusion and Future Directions

Every investigation of the barriers to exercise and sport participation of individuals with disabilities highlights accessibility as a central concern. Without access to sport and exercise spaces, adapted equipment, transportation, and the like, participation is simply not possible. It is clear from the research outlined in this chapter that sport and exercise participation has a positive impact on the psychological health and well-being of individuals with disabilities. The ability to be strong, powerful, and competent in one's body may be of particular significance to individuals who live in a society that views their bodies as less able (Asken, 1991). Sport and exercise psychology researchers and applied practitioners should be active agents in the promotion of exercise for individuals with disabilities.

The Paralympics is a powerful space for athletes with disabilities to display their strength, power, and skills. Currently the Paralympics follow the Olympics by two weeks, using the same venues used by able-bodied Olympic athletes. Ironically, however, the mainstream media does little to promote this event, particularly in comparison to the Olympics (DePauw & Gavron, 2005). Increased visibility of such events could certainly boost the public's awareness of the ability of athletes with disabilities to perform fantastic physical feats. That said, the promotion of a "supercrip" image that encourages the perception that if one exemplary individual with a disability can perform, then anyone with a disability should be able to engage in similar events is problematic. The promotion of a "supercrip" image can lead to blaming individuals with disabilities who are not able to perform phenomenal physical feats (Schell & Rodriguez, 2001). Berger (2008) has presented a more nuanced perspective on the "supercrip" narrative. Berger argued that athletes with disabilities see media images of other athletes with disabilities as an affirmation, and stated that there are readings beyond the "supercrip" narratives. Berger noted, "The blanket condemnation of the supercrip prevalent among disability activists and scholars misses the perspective of youths" (p. 658) who see other athletes with disabilities as role models and mentors. He suggested that there are multiple readings of exceptionally talented athletes with disabilities. Berger's study is another example of how the use of qualitative interviews and a cultural turn in sport psychology research focusing on disability could lead to valuable insight into the experiences of individuals with disabilities. Additionally, because able-bodied individuals' perceptions of individuals with disabilities can profoundly impact behavior toward those with disabilities, and lead to oppression and discrimination, an investigation into these perceptions is warranted.

While the Paralymics is an important event for elite athletes with disabilities and their supporters and fans, there have been calls to eliminate these separate games, and instead to integrate the participation of all athletes, those with disabilities and those who are able-bodied, into the Olympics (DePauw & Gavron, 2005). Increased media coverage of the Paralymics would increase visibility for athletes with disabilities, and not marginalize their participation. Additionally, athletes with disabilities may be able to compete with able-bodied athletes. Prior to the 2008 Beijing Olympics, Oscar Pistorius of South Africa succeeded in his petition to be allowed to compete for a spot on the South African track and field Olympic team (Joyner, 2008). While he did not qualify, his fight to be allowed to compete in the Olympics highlights the instability of the category of disability. As athletes who use wheelchairs and prosthetics continue to demonstrate that they are as capable, and at times, more capable, than athletes without disabilities, debates about their inclusion in mainstream sport will no doubt continue. Sport and exercise psychology researchers are well positioned to investigate the impact of media images of athletes with disability on perceptions of disability among both those who are able-bodied and those with disabilities. Additionally, qualitative research with athletes who use assistive technologies and their embodied experiences would be valuable contributions to the field. Frameworks such as cyborg theory, as used by Butryn (2003) to discuss track and field athletes' narratives regarding their cyborg identities, could be particularly useful.

Finally, future researchers in sport and exercise psychology should widen their focus from elite sports and include exercise and participation in sport for all. As discussed earlier, the ability to compete in sport at elite levels is an expensive endeavor, available only to those with the resources to purchase specialized equipment. It is clear, however, that exercise participation is profoundly beneficial to individuals with disabilities, just as it has significant positive effects on the mental well-being of able-bodied individuals. Advocating for spaces where individuals with disabilities are able to exercise with equipment adapted to their needs and with trainers who are able to provide appropriate assistance and advice is critical. Future researchers could address the impact of having accessible exercise settings, the psychological outcomes and determinants of exercise, and how to promote long-term exercise participation.

An understanding that individuals with disabilities are individual is also imperative. The diversity and the heterogeneity of the disabled community cannot be underestimated. Mastro, Burton, Rosendahl, and Sherrill (1996) found that there was a hierarchy of preference among elite athletes toward other athletes with disabilities. The less severe the disability was perceived to be, the more favorable the perception. These differential perceptions highlight the need for research within the disabled community and a better understanding of the nuances within the group rather than assuming that all athletes with disabilities are the same, or in this case, even view one another similarly. Researchers examining perceptions of others often rely on quantitative methodologies, which can be useful in identifying general trends. In addition to questionnaires, qualitative methodologies that allow for interrogation of how perceptions of individuals with disabilities are formed and vary would add a more nuanced understanding of such perceptions.

Just as disability advocates argue for inclusion and integration of individuals with disabilities into all sport and exercise settings, inclusion and integration needs to occur at the level of research. Athletes and exercisers with disabilities should no longer be considered a special population, but rather a part of the sport and exercise community at large. The special considerations of this population do need to be acknowledged, but by treating the disabled community as "other" and "different," researchers may further marginalize a group of athletes that has historically struggled to find spaces to play, exercise, and compete.

References

Arbour, K. P., & Martin Ginis, K. A. (2007). Does the environment matter? Exploring the role of the physical environment in predicting leisure-time wheeling among people with spinal cord injury. *Journal of Sport & Exercise Psychology, 29*, S144–S145.

Asken, M. J. (1991). The challenge of the physically challenged: Delivering sport psychology services to physically disabled athletes. *The Sport Psychologist, 5*, 370–381.

Berger, R. J. (2008). Disability and the dedicated wheelchair athlete: Beyond the "supercrip" critique. *Journal of Contemporary Ethnography, 37*, 647–678.

Breckenridge, C. A., & Vogler, C. (2001). The critical limits of embodiment: Disability's criticism. *Public Culture, 13*, 349–357.

Brewer, B. W., Van Raalte, J. L., & Linder, D. E. (1993). Athletic identity: Hercules' muscles or Achilles heel? *International Journal of Sport Psychology, 24*, 237–254.

Butryn, T. M. (2003). Posthuman podiums: Cyborg narratives of elite track and field athletes. *Sociology of Sport Journal, 20*, 17–39.

Cox, R. H., & Davis, R. W. (1992). Psychological skills of elite wheelchair athletes. *Palaestra, 8*, 16–21.

Crenshaw, K. (1991). Mapping the margins: Intersectionality, identity politics, and violence against women of color. *Stanford Law Review, 43*, 1241–1299.

Crocker, P. R. (1993). Sport and exercise psychology and research with individuals with physical disabilities: Using theory to advance knowledge. *Adapted Physical Activity Quarterly, 10*, 324–335.

DePauw, K. P., & Gavron, S. J. (2005). *Disability sport* (2nd ed.). Champaign, IL: Human Kinetics.

Ditor, D. S., Latimer, A. E., Martin Ginis, K. A., Arbour, K. P., McCartney, N., & Hicks, A. L. (2003). Maintenance of exercise participation in individuals with spinal cord injury: Effects on quality of life, stress and pain. *Spinal Cord, 41*, 446–450.

Edwards, S. D. (2008). Should Oscar Pistorius be excluded from the 2008 Olympic Games? *Sport, Ethics and Philosophy, 2*, 112–125.

Effing, T. W., van Meeteren, N. L. U., van Asbeck, F. W. A., & Prevo, A. J. H. (2006). Body weight-supported treadmill training in chronic incomplete spinal cord injury: A pilot study evaluating functional health status and quality of life. *Spinal Cord, 44*, 287–296.

Ferreira, J. P., & Fox, K. R. (2008). Physical self-perceptions and self-esteem in male basketball players with and without disability: A preliminary analysis using the physical self-perception profile. *European Journal of Adapted Physical Activity, 1*, 35–49.

Foucault, M. (1995). *Discipline and punish: The birth of the prison* (2nd ed.). New York: Vintage.

Greenwood, C. M., Dzewaltowski, D. A., & French, R. (1990). Self-efficacy and

psychological well-being of wheelchair tennis participants and wheelchair non-tennis participants. *Adapted Physical Activity Quarterly, 7*, 12–21.

Grosz, E. A. (1994). *Volatile bodies: Toward a corporeal feminism*. Bloomington: Indiana University Press.

Hannold, E. M., Young, M. E., Rittman, M. R., Bowden, M. G., & Behrman, A. L. (2006). Locomotor training: Experiencing the changing body. *Journal of Rehabilitation Research & Development, 43*, 905–915.

Hanrahan, S. J. (1998). Practical considerations for working with athletes with disabilities. *The Sport Psychologist, 12*, 346–357.

Hanrahan, S. J. (2005). Able athletes with disabilities: Issues and group work. In M. B. Andersen (Ed.), *Sport psychology in practice*. (pp. 223–247). Champaign, IL: Human Kinetics.

Hanrahan, S. J. (2007). Athletes with disabilities. In G. Tenenbaum & R. C. Eklund (Eds.), *Handbook of sport psychology* (3rd ed., pp. 845–858). Hoboken, NJ: Wiley.

Hanrahan, S. J., Grove, J. R., & Lockwood, R. J. (1990). Psychological skills training for the blind athlete: A pilot program. *Adapted Physical Activity Quarterly, 7*, 143–155.

Haraway, D. (1991). *Simians, cyborgs, and women: The reinvention of nature*. New York: Routledge.

Heimer, S., & Relac, M. (1998). The importance of recreational sport and sports programs during rehabilitation and post-rehabilitation of the physically disabled. *Kinesiology, 30*, 57–62.

Henschen, K. P., Horvat, M., & Roswal, G. (1992). Psychological profiles of the United States wheelchair basketball team. *International Journal of Sport Psychology, 23*, 128–137.

Hicks, A. L., Adams, M. M., Martin Ginis, K., Giangregorio, L., Latimer, A., Phillips, S. M., et al. (2005). Long-term body-weight-supported treadmill training and subsequent follow-up in persons with chronic SCI: Effects on functional walking ability and measures of subjective well-being. *Spinal Cord, 43*, 291–298.

Hicks, A. L., & Martin Ginis, K. A. (2008). Treadmill training after spinal cord injury: It's not just about the walking. *Journal of Rehabilitation Research and Development, 45*, 241–248.

Hughes, B. (2007). Being disabled: Towards a critical social ontology for disability studies. *Disability & Society, 22*, 673–684.

Hughes, B. & Patterson, K. (1997). The social model of disability and the disappearing body: Toward a sociology of impairment. *Disability and Society, 12*, 325–340.

Institutes of Medicine (2005). *Spinal cord injury*. Washington, DC: The National Academies Press.

International Collaboration on Repair Discoveries. (2009) *SCI facts and stats*. Retrieved February 15, 2009, from http://www.icord.org/sci.html.

Joyner, J. (2008). Oscar Pistorius, double amputee Olympic sprinter. *Outside the Beltway Sports*. Retrieved January 19, 2008, from http://sports.outsidethebeltway.com/2008/05/oscar-pistorius-double-amputee-olympic-sprinter/.

King, S. (2008). What's queer about (queer) sport sociology now? A review essay. *Sociology of Sport Journal, 25*, 419–442.

Kosma, M., Ellis, R., Cardinal, B. J., Bauer, J. J., & McCubbin, J. A. (2007). The mediating role of intention and stages of change in physical activity among adults with physical disabilities: An integrative framework. *Journal of Sport & Exercise Psychology, 29*, 21–38.

Krane, V. (2001). We can be athletic and feminine, but do we want to? Challenging hegemonic femininity in women's sport. *Quest, 53*, 115–133.

Latimer, A. E., Martin Ginis, K. A.,

Hicks, A. L. & McCarteny, N. (2004). An examination of the mechanisms of exercise-induced change in psychological well-being among people with spinal cord injury. *Journal of Rehabilitation Research & Development, 41*, 643–651.

Levins, S. M., Redenbach, D. M., & Dyck, I. (2004). Individual and societal influences on participation in physical activity following spinal cord injury: A qualitative study. *Physical Therapy, 84*, 496–509.

Longman, J. (2007) An amputee sprinter: Is he disabled or too-abled? *The New York Times*. Retrieved January 19, 2008, from http://www.nytimes.com/2007/05/15/sports/othersports/15runner.html.

Martin, J. J. (1996). Transitions out of competitive sport for athletes with disabilities. *Therapeutic Recreation Journal, 30*, 128–136.

Martin, J. J., Eklund, R. C., & Mushett, C. A. (1997). Factor structure of the athletic identity measurement scale with athletes with disabilities. *Adapted Physical Activity Quarterly, 14*, 74–82.

Martin, K. A., Latimer, A. E., Francoeur, C., Hanley, H., Watson, K., Hicks, A. L., & McCartney, N. (2002). Sustaining exercise motivation and participation among people with spinal cord injuries: Lessons learned from a 9-month study. *Palaestra, 18*, 38–40; 51.

Martin Ginis, K. A. M., Latimer, A. E., McKechnie, K., Ditor, D. S., McCartney, N., Hicks, A. L., et al. (2003). Using exercise to enhance subjective well-being among people with spinal cord injury: The mediating influences of stress and pain. *Rehabilitation Psychology, 48*, 157–164.

Martin Ginis, K. A., & Latimer, A. E. (2007). The effects of single bouts of body-weight supported treadmill training on the feeling states of people with spinal cord injury. *Spinal Cord, 45*(1), 112–115.

Mastro, J. V., Burton, A. W., Rosendahl, M., & Sherrill, C. (1996). Attitudes of elite athletes with impairments toward one another: A hierarchy of preference. *Adapted Physical Activity Quarterly, 13,* 197–210.

McRuer, R. (2006). *Crip theory: Cultural signs of queerness and disability.* New York: New York University Press.

Paulsen, P., French, R., & Sherrill, C. (1991). Comparison of mood states of college able-bodied and wheelchair basketball players. *Perceptual and Motor Skills, 72,* 396–398.

Potgieter, C. & Khan, G. (2005). Sexual self-esteem and body image of South African spinal cord injured adolescents. *Sexuality and Disability, 23,* 1–20.

Rees, T., Smith, B., & Sparks, A. C. (2003). The influence of social support on the lived experiences of spinal cord injured sportsmen. *Sport Psychologist, 17,* 135–156.

Roeder, L. K., & Aufsesser, P. M. (1986). Selected attentional and interpersonal characteristics of wheelchair athletes. *Palaestra, 2*(2), 28–32; 43–44.

Ryba, T. V., & Wright, H. K. (2005). From mental game to cultural praxis: A cultural studies model's implications for the future of sport psychology. *Quest, 57,* 192–212.

Schell, L. A., & Rodriguez, S. (2001). Subverting bodies/ambivalent representations: Media analysis of Paralympian, Hope Lewellen. *Sociology of Sport Journal, 18,* 127–135.

Semerjian, T. Z. (2005, October). *The influence of exercise on quality of life and body satisfaction among individuals with spinal cord injuries.* Paper presented at the meeting of the Association for the Advancement of Applied Sport Psychology, Vancouver, Canada.

Semerjian, T. Z. (2006a, May). *A qualitative investigation of the experience of exercise for individuals with spinal cord injury.* Paper presented at the meeting of the Ameri-

can College of Sports Medicine, Denver, CO.

Semerjian, T. Z. (2006b, November). *Intersectionalities of gender, race, class, and disability.* Paper presented at the meeting of the North American Society for the Sociology of Sport, Vancouver, Canada.

Semerjian, T. Z. (2007, November). *Traversing the borderlands in the body: Experiences after SCI.* Paper presented at the meeting of the North American Society for the Sociology of Sport, Pittsburgh, PA.

Semerjian, T. Z., Montague, S. M, Dominguez, J. F., Davidian, A. M., & de Leon, R. D. (2005). Enhancement of quality of life and body satisfaction through the use of adapted exercise devices for individuals with spinal cord injuries. *Topics in Spinal Cord Injury Rehabilitation, 11,* 95–108.

Shakespeare, T. (Ed.). (1998). *The disability reader: Social science perspectives.* London: Cassel.

Smith, B. (2008). Disabled bodies and stories, selves: An example of qualitative research and narrative inquiry. *European Journal of Adapted Physical Activity, 1,* 23–34.

Smith, B., & Sparkes, A. C. (2005). Men, sport, spinal cord injury, and narratives of hope. *Social Science and Medicine, 61,* 1095–1105.

Smith, B., & Sparkes, A. C. (2008). Changing bodies, changing narratives and the consequences of tellability: A case study of becoming disabled through sport. *Sociology of Health & Illness, 30,* 217–236.

Snyder, S. L., & Mitchell, D. T. (2001). Re-engaging the body: Disability studies and the resistance to embodiment. *Public Culture, 13,* 367–389.

Sparkes, A. C. (1998). Validity in qualitative inquiry and the problem of criteria: Implications for sport psychology. *Sport Psychologist, 12,* 363–386.

Sparkes, A. C., & Smith, B. (2002). Sport,

spinal cord injury, embodied masculinities, and the dilemmas of narrative identity. *Men & Masculinities, 4,* 258–285.

Sparkes, A. C., & Smith, B. (2008). Men, spinal cord injury, memories and the narrative performance of pain. *Disability & Society, 23*(7), 679–690.

Spinal Injuries Association. (2006, September 20). "*. . . because life needn't stop when you're paralyzed . . .*" Retrieved February 15, 2009, from http://www.mascip.co.uk/pdfs/Briefing%20Note%20Sep%202006%20FINAL2.pdf.

Swanson, S. R., Colwell, T., & Yushan Zhao. (2008). Motives for participation and importance of social support for athletes with physical disabilities. *Journal of Clinical Sport Psychology, 2,* 317–336.

Thomas, C. (2001). Feminism and disability: The theoretical and political significance of the personal and the experiential. In L. Barton (Ed.), *Disability, politics and the struggle for change* (pp. 48–58). London: David Fulton.

Tasiemski, T., Kennedy, P., Gardner, B. P., & Blaikley, R. A. (2004). Athletic identity and sports participation in people with spinal cord injury. *Adapted Physical Activity Quarterly, 21,* 364–378.

van Hilvoorde, I., & Landerweerd, L. (2008) Disability or extraordinary talent—Francesco Lentini (three legs) versus Oscar Pistorius (no legs). *Sport, Ethics and Philosophy, 2,* 97–111.

Warms, C. A., Belza, B. L., Whitney, J. D., Mitchell, P. H., & Steins, S. A. (2004). Lifestype physical activity for individuals with spinal cord injury: A pilot study. *American Journal of Health Promotion, 18,* 288–291.

Wetterhahn, K. A., Hanson, C., & Levy, C. E. (2002). Effect of participation in physical activity on body image of amputees. *American Journal of Physical Medicine & Rehabilitation, 81,* 194–201.

Wu, S. K., & Williams, T. (2001). Factors influencing sport participation among athletes with spinal cord injury. *Medicine & Science in Sports & Exercise, 33,* 177–182.

12

PROFESSIONAL CULTURE OF CAREER ASSISTANCE TO ATHLETES: A LOOK THROUGH CONTRASTING LENSES OF CAREER METAPHORS

Natalia Stambulova

CHAPTER SUMMARY

This chapter considers career assistance to athletes as a profes-sional culture with related concepts, theoretical frameworks, tra-ditional and emergent working issues, professional principles, val-ues, strategies, and tools. A multiple metaphor approach suggested in social (Morgan, 1986) and vocational psychology (Inkson, 2004, 2006) is used as a framework. More specifically, nine career meta-phors—*inheritance, cycle, journey, action, fit, relationship, role, resource,* and *story* (Inkson, 2004, 2006)—are applied to career develop-ment and transition research and practice in sport psychology. Three case examples are followed throughout the chapter and viewed through the lenses of the various career metaphors. Fi-nally, advantages, limitations, and future uses of the multiple meta-phor approach in summarizing career assistance to athletes as a professional culture are discussed.

As an author, I am aware that the material in this chapter has been shaped by my personal views of the career assistance profes-sional culture, and that this culture is examined not only through the lenses of nine career metaphors, but also through my own eyes (i.e., my professional, athletic, and lived experiences in Russia for many years and later acquaintance with Western approaches in career research and practice since my move to Sweden in 2001). In this chapter, career assistance is shown as a complex and multi-faceted culture, but because of my personal biases in its descrip-tion, some of its aspects may not have received proper coverage. Therefore, I invite my colleagues within the career assistance field around the world to complement and challenge this view.

Professional Culture of Career Assistance to Athletes

Metaphors may enable us to examine career phenomena through contrasting lenses, triangulate the different views, and hopefully arrive at a synthesis, which recognizes the validity of each view point and its integration with others.

—Kerr Inkson, 2004, p. 107

Career assistance is a relatively new trend in sport psychology consulting focused on helping athletes with various issues related to their careers in and outside of sport. Since the end of the 1980s, career assistance programs for retiring/retired athletes, active elite junior/senior athletes, and student-athletes have been established in different parts of the world. Examples include the "Olympic Athlete Career Centre" (Canada), "Career Assistance Program for Athletes" (USA), "Athlete Career and Education" (Australia and United Kingdom), and "Life Style Management Program" (United Kingdom). These services generally involve the assessment of athletes' needs, support for personal growth, guidance on balancing lifestyle, education and career, help with social psychological issues, and life development interventions that emphasize transferable skills to use both in and outside sport (see overviews in Gordon, Lavallee, & Grove, 2005; Hackfort & Huang, 2005; Wylleman, De Knop, Ewing, & Cumming, 2004). One specific area in career assistance relates to helping athletes cope with athletic transitions, for example, from junior to senior sports or from sport to the post-sport career, as well as with non-athletic transitions, such as from childhood to adolescence or from high school to college (Petitpas, Brewer, & Van Raalte, 2002; Stambulova, in press; Wylleman & Lavallee, 2004).

Career assistance is based on career development and transition theoretical frameworks, relevant sport psychology research, and a set of applied principles (e.g., a whole career approach, a whole person approach, individual approach, and others); it also contains a number of strategies/tools used by career consultants (see Alfermann & Stambulova, 2007, for overview; Stambulova, in press). Therefore, career assistance can be viewed as a professional culture with a system of related concepts; underlying theoretical frameworks and research; consultants' shared values, principles, and ethical norms; as well as the typical working issues and professional strategies/tools used in consultants' work with athlete-clients. The career assistance professional culture can be defined as a subgroup culture relevant to a professional group of career consultants (i.e., consultants specializing in helping athletes with career issues), who create and maintain this culture as well as transmit it to the next generation in the profession. More specifically, career assistance professional culture is about *what* career consultants deal with (working issues), as well as *how* and *why* they work and serve their clients (tools and strategies, values and principles, as well as underlying theories and research).

Sport psychology literature illuminates some aspects of the career assistance culture, such as classifying career development and transition theoretical frameworks (Alfermann & Stambulova, 2007), comparing career assistance programs (Gordon et al., 2005; Wylleman et al., 2004), and structuring career assistance working issues (Hackfort & Huang, 2005). But thus far there has been no attempt to create a holistic description of career assistance to athletes as a professional culture. In this chapter I am going to undertake such an attempt, using *career metaphors* as descriptive frameworks.

There are several examples in the literature where sets of metaphors were used as descriptive *frameworks* for complicated phenomena. In social psychology, Morgan (1986) used the multiple metaphor method to analyze *organizations*. He proposed that because organizations are complex and multifaceted, no single metaphor could adequately describe them. Therefore, to paint a complete picture, he considered them as *machines, organisms, cultures, brains*, and *political systems*. The same method was recently used in vocational psychology by Inkson (2004, 2006) to describe *careers* in nine metaphors: *inheritance, cycle, journey, action, fit, relationship, role, resource,* and *story*. As Inkson (2006) explained, "Careers can be any, or all, of these [nine metaphors]. Each of these metaphors has something to say about careers. Each is true up to a point, but only up to a point. Each represents a particular way of thinking about careers. Taken together, they may provide a wide understanding of careers" (Inkson, 2006, p. 15).

In this chapter, following an interdisciplinary approach emphasized in cultural research (Ryba & Wright, 2005), I am going to borrow the nine career metaphors from vocational psychology and use them as frameworks to describe the career assistance professional culture in sport psychology. Each of the nine career metaphors reflects particular facets in athletes' careers and correspondingly in career assistance (e.g., principles, strategies used, etc.), and altogether these metaphors might contribute to creating a holistic description of career assistance as a multifaceted culture. To begin with, I consider how the nine career metaphors can be applied to analyze career definitions.

Career Definitions and Metaphors

In vocational psychology, *career* is defined as "the evolving sequence of a person's work experiences over time" (Artur et al., 1989, p. 8). Based on this definition, each person has just one career lasting potentially a lifetime, involving continuity and change in objective and subjective work experiences and related experiences outside work (Inkson, 2006). Taking into account this broad career definition, an athletic career appears to be just one part or aspect of a life career.

Several definitions of an athletic career proposed in sport psychology emphasize its different aspects. Wylleman et al. (2004) defined athletic career as "a succession of stages and transitions that includes an athlete's initiation into and continued participation in organized competitive sport and that is terminated with the athlete's (in)voluntary but definitive discontinuation of participation in organized competitive sport" (p. 511). In this definition, the authors adopted a developmental perspective and viewed career as a *cycle*, with the career stages and transitions unfolding within the structure of organized competitive sport. Alfermann and Stambulova (2007) gave a metaphoric definition of an athletic career as "a miniature life span course, with stages analogous to childhood, adolescence, adulthood and older ages" (p. 713), which also referred to a career as *cycle*. These authors further defined athletic career as "a multi-year sport activity voluntarily chosen by the person and aimed at achieving his/her individual peak in athletic performance in one or several sport events" (p. 713). Their definition highlighted other facets of athletic career relevant to the *action* and *journey* metaphors: a choice, a long-term commitment, a striving for upward career movement, and a possibility of having a specialized or a generalized career. Combining these definitions yields a more holistic view of athletes' careers.

Career development in sport psychology has been defined as proceeding through career stages and transitions (Stambulova, Alfermann, Statler, & Côté, in press). A transition has been defined through the metaphor of a *turning point/phase* in the course of a career, with a set of demands an athlete has to cope with to continue in sport or adjust to the post career (Alfermann & Stambulova, 2007). Crises have been defined as transitions where athletes are unable to cope on their own and feel a need for psychological assistance (Stambulova, 2000). Metaphorically, crises are often described as being in *a blind alley, dead end*, or *dead circle*. The essence of crisis-metaphors relates to *being locked* and/or *having no exit* (Stambulova, 2003). Later in this chapter I illustrate how the nine career metaphors enrich our understanding of athletes' career/transition/crisis experiences using case examples from my consultancy practice. (See author note at end of chapter.)

Metaphors in Career Assistance to Athletes: Case Examples

Metaphors with their symbolic nature help us understand something unknown (or difficult to describe) through the similarity to something already known or described (Comb & Freedman, 1990), with an emphasis on the most personally relevant and important shades of meaning (Hanin & Stambulova, 2002). The two case examples below illustrate how metaphors help athletes relate their career experiences, and also how consultants might use metaphors to find an entry point, analyze the client's situation, and search for its solution.

Case A. This case refers to a 17-year-old female Russian swimmer. She turned to me for help with the situation she described as follows:

> I feel like one day I entered a very high building that was my sport and took an elevator to go to the top. My coach and parents were with me, and with their support I moved up quickly. I was successful in a series of junior competitions and became a candidate for the national team. Then my life situation changed: I met my love. This person has become very important to me and I wanted to spend as much time as possible with him. I also hoped that I could continue moving up in my athletic career, but my coach and parents didn't think that I could practice and prepare for competitions as good as before. They even said it was too early for me to have a boyfriend. . . . So, one day the elevator stopped, the door opened, and my coach and parents walked out. Then the door closed, and I was alone. I pushed the button to open the door, but it did not work. I started to push other buttons in the elevator to go up, or even down, but again it did not move. I found myself locked in the broken elevator. . . . You are my alarm button.

When working with this athlete, I used her metaphors to establish an entry point to my work:

> Let us imagine that the alarm button worked and I opened the elevator's door. Can you consider getting out on that floor and

analyzing what has happened? Then you may decide whether or not to continue your journey in the elevator; to go up or down, alone or with other people and also with whom; or even consider leaving the building.

In that first consulting session, the metaphors generated by the athlete-client helped me to establish a connection with her by speaking her language, and in the following sessions we continuously used the client's metaphors in searching for solution of her situation.

Case B. The present case refers to a Russian figure skating pair, in which the female-partner complained that the male-partner had become aggressive and even cruel to her during practices. Here is an excerpt from my dialogue with the male-partner:

> Skater: When she is making stupid mistakes, I just lose control over my emotions and behavior. Yes, at such times I am not in full control over what I am doing.

> Consultant: Do you drive a car?

> Skater: Yes, of course.

> Consultant: Do you always stop for the red light?

> Skater: Yes, of course.

> Consultant: Good. It means that in principle you have your own brakes and you can control yourself when you want to.

> Skater: But this is a completely different situation.

> Consultant: It is not that different. Let us apply the "driver" metaphor to your relationship with your skating partner. On the road, other drivers may also make stupid mistakes, but you always stop for the red light because you know that if you do not, it may cause an accident. The same is true in the situation with your partner. If you are not able to control yourself, your pair will fall apart and all the years of joint practices will be lost. Can you consider using the "red light" image as a stop signal for yourself? For example, you can say to yourself: "Red light! Stop!" and imagine that you are on the road and your skating partner is with you there. Think about yourself as the experienced "driver" of your pair.

In this case the metaphors such as *driver on the road, brakes, red light,* and *driver of the pair* appeared illustrative for the client and helpful in changing his attitude to his skating partner.

Later in this chapter, I follow these case examples to show how the nine career metaphors can be used as *career archetypes* helping career consultants view athletes' career situations/experiences from various and complementing perspectives. Such analysis will be incorporated into a narrative of the professional culture of career assistance to athletes, in which the nine career metaphors will serve as a descriptive framework.

Using Career Metaphors to Describe Professional Culture of Career Assistance to Athletes

1. Career as Inheritance

Inkson (2004) briefly explained the metaphor of career as inheritance as follows: "Each career, in some way and to a varying extent, is inherited from the 'families' of which we are part" (p. 100). Career inheritance in sport is multifaceted, with genetic (athletic talent), psychosocial (e.g., parental involvement), and sociological (e.g., social structure/sport system) components.

The talent development topic has a longer history in sport psychology than the career development topic. Talent development theoretical frameworks, such as Bloom's three stages in talent development model (1985) and Ericsson's 10 years rule to reach expert performance level (1996), can be seen as predecessors of athletic career descriptive models and related research. Recently, three ISSP Position Stands considered talent detection, talent development, and career development in sport (Côté, Lidor, & Hackfort, 2009; Lidor, Côté, & Hackfort, 2009; Stambulova et al., in press). The authors emphasized that the talent development process occurs within a career development context and contributes to the athlete's internal resources to cope with career transitions. However, it was also highlighted that the early disposition of an athletic talent and related early social recognition of young and often immature athletes can lead to their single-minded focus on sport and additional difficulties (e.g., overinflated expectations) in the transition to senior sport (see also Stambulova, 2009). Therefore, there is a niche for career consultants to help young talented athletes realize their potentials in sport while balancing their sport and other activities to facilitate their future transitions to senior sport and a post-sport career.

Through the inheritance metaphor, career consultants are encouraged to investigate athletes' family background. The role of parents in athletes' careers has been well documented in sport psychology research (Côté, 1999; Wuerth et al., 2004; Wylleman et al., 2000), focusing on optimal parental involvement (i.e., adequate support to athletes) in contrast to their under-involvement (lack of support) or over-involvement (parental pressure). The authors emphasized that many children "inherit" their parents' interest either in sport in general or in particular sport events and learn many athletic skills and attitudes from their parents. Besides, parents' educational, social, and financial statuses are not neutral for athletes' careers. For example, African children playing football in the street and well-equipped young golfers from North America inherit different resources from their families. Athletes from less privileged families (or social structures), as well as their parents, often consider sport as a way to move up the social ladder (Stambulova, 2009). In order to reach athletic success, these athletes have to find ways to overcome structural constraints imposed by their career development environments.

One interesting phenomenon related to career as inheritance is career *imprisonment* (Inkson, 2006), that is, the individual's feeling of being "locked in the structure." *Case A* can be interpreted as a mild case of imprisonment, where the athlete is faced with constraints of the Russian sport system reflected in the underlying views of her coach and parents: "If you are a candidate to the national team, then sport should be prioritized." Imprisonment in sport/training system may lead to serious negative consequences (e.g., severe injury, burnout, or an eating disorder), and career consultants should be able to recognize such situations in time to develop strategies helping athletes find a reasonable way out.

Such factors as social class, gender, or race may work as either resources or barriers in athletes' career developments and transitions. For example, the "genderquake" (Wolf, 1993) in sport during the 20th century is reflected in increased female participation at all levels in sport and emergence of many new sport events for female athletes. Male hegemony in sport has been challenged but not completely eliminated, as women in many countries still experience financial and social/cultural barriers to sport participation (Gill, 2007). Structural constraints may also influence athletes' access to career services. Therefore, the inheritance metaphor may serve as a trigger for the social justice principle in career services. D'Andrea and Daniels (2005) suggested the RESPECTFUL Sport Psychology model, which acknowledges clients' diversity in terms of their religious/spiritual identity, economic class identity, sexual identity, psychological maturity, ethnic/racial identity, chronological challenges, trauma and threats to well-being, family history, unique psychological characteristics, language, and location of residence. Taking all of these factors into account is a challenge for career consultants. Recently, a set of strategies to cope with this challenge was suggested by a cultural discourse of sport psychology (e.g., Ryba, 2009; Schinke & Hanrahan, 2009). The authors emphasized cultural reflexivity and related cultural/multicultural competencies and skills of sport psychology/career consultants, such as awareness of one's own cultural values and biases, understanding of the client's worldview, and development of culturally appropriate intervention strategies.

2. Career as Cycle

Career as a cycle has been an underlying metaphor for several descriptive models of an athletic career (Côté, 1999; Salmela, 1994; Stambulova, 1994; Wylleman & Lavallee, 2004). In these models, career is defined as a succession of stages, such as the initiation/sampling stage, development/specialization stage, perfection/mastery/investment stage, final/maintenance stage, and discontinuation stage of competitive sport involvement. When describing career development, the authors emphasized: (1) changes in athletes' perceptions of/attitude to sport and in the degree to which they identified themselves with the athlete role; (2) changes in athletes' social networks and support; (3) changes in time/energy investment across the stages; and (4) changes in the degree to which they sacrificed in other spheres of life to reach their sport goals (Alfermann & Stambulova, 2007). Additionally, descriptive models provide career consultants with prediction of normative transitions (i.e., turning phases between adjacent career stages), such as the beginning of sport specialization, the transition from development to mastery stage, the transitions from junior to senior and from amateur to professional sports, and the transition from athletic career to the life after.

Recently, athletes' transitions in non-sport contexts have been receiving increased attention from researchers and practitioners (Cecić Erpič, Wylleman, & Zupančič, 2004; Wylleman & Lavallee,

2004). Career consultants work on helping athletes balance their complementary careers: sports and studies, sport and work, or sport and family. Among the five classic stages of vocational career development (Savickas, 2002; Super, 1957) the first two — the exploration and establishment stages — often coincide with the athletic career, and then they are followed by the progress, maintenance, and work retirement stages in the athletes' life after sport.

To briefly conclude, the cycle metaphor contains triggers for the two basic principles of career assistance culture: a whole career approach that is helping athletes cope with transitions throughout the whole course of an athletic career, and a whole person approach that is helping athletes deal with not only athletic but also non-athletic transitions.

3. Career as Journey

Many athletes feel compelled to describe their careers as journeys. Here is a fragment from the career narrative of a Russian female volleyball player (**Case C**):

> Sport is like a train journey. Once you take it, you go forward and forward. The speed gets higher and higher, and the destination seems far away. But the time flies, and at some point you feel that you soon must leave the train. It is a sad point and you try to continue your journey, even if it is not as fast and lucky as before.

This athlete was a long-term player for a team in the highest volleyball league and perceived her career as a movement forward defined by the "rails" set up by her head coach. As she got older, the time she spent playing in official games decreased (her career movement slowed down) and she perceived it as signal to think about athletic retirement (pay attention to the overlap with the cycle metaphor). However, she was not quite ready to retire. Her goals were to continue in volleyball, while finishing up her university studies that had suffered due to the intensive traveling, practices, and games. Her solution was to "change the train," by transferring to a lower-level team that let her enjoy playing volleyball while getting more time for her studies.

The journey metaphor highlights the two key facets of careers: "movement between places, and time" (Inkson, 2006, p. 103). Therefore, this metaphor brings us to the idea of different career trajectories in sport. The following three alternative athletic career paths have been defined by the developmental model of sport participation (Côté et al., 2007): (1) early sport specialization and deliberate practice (i.e., high in structure/efforts and low in enjoyment) leading to top performance in one chosen sport; (2) early sampling and deliberate play (i.e., more flexible and diverse sport involvement) with transition to deliberate practice and top performance in one chosen sport following; and (3) early sampling and deliberate play followed by transition to recreational sport (see also Côté et al., 2009). The first two paths have an objectively defined destination that is top performance, whereas in the third an altogether different goal for the career journey is proposed: enjoying the athletic experience.

In career assistance, there are several career planning tools that help athletes map their career journeys and clarify their particular trajectories. For example, the five-step career planning strategy (Stambulova, in press) leads the athlete through analysis of his or her past experiences, current situation, and perceived future followed by bridging the past with the present and the present with the future. These bridging experiences are indeed a distinctive feature of this strategy, where the present situation (i.e., the current moment in the career journey) appears as a focal point integrating the past and the perceived future in the athlete's career development.

The journey metaphor is useful in career counseling because it is rich in producing related metaphors such as career turns, crossroads, blind alleys, traffic, traffic jams, as well as career maps and a compass. *Case B* illustrates how the traffic/driving metaphor helped resolve a difficult situation between partners in a figure skating pair. The case also raises an interesting question about the athlete's own role in the career journey that is of a passenger or a driver. The volleyball player in *Case C* perceived herself as a train passenger, and her solution was just to change the train and consequently her driver (a new coach). In *Case B*, the skater was encouraged to become "a driver of the pair," that is, to take responsibility for the more efficient work with his younger and less experienced skating partner.

One more career aspect that fits into the journey metaphor is athletes' international mobility or transfer to a different geographic location (e.g., from a small town to a large city). For career consultants, it creates a niche in helping athletes with their sociocultural adaptation when their career paths lead them out of their countries or places of origin (e.g., Schinke et al., 2007; Stambulova et al., 2009).

4. Career as Action

For many athletes, careers do not just happen to them. They build their careers by their own actions. The action metaphor sends a message that athletes may benefit from greater empowerment and expression of themselves in their careers.

By making career decisions (e.g., signing a professional contract, starting in a new team or sport club, choosing a new sport partner or coach), athletes involve themselves in normative or non-normative (i.e., idiosyncratic, less predictable) transitions and related coping processes. Career researchers (e.g., Savickas, 2002) consider career maturity (i.e., an ability to master the tasks at each of the career stages), and career adaptability (i.e., readiness for coping with current and anticipated career demands) among an individual's coping resources. One form of adaptability is career resilience, that is, "a reactive ability to stand up to hard knocks" (Inkson, 2006, p. 83). In sport psychology, athletes' career maturity and preparedness to transition out of sport were examined in a cross-cultural study of German, Lithuanian, and Russian athletes by Alfermann, Stambulova, and Zemaityte (2004). The authors emphasized the role of contextual factors (e.g., sport system, cultural tradition to plan for the future) in facilitating or interfering with the athletes' readiness to athletic retirement.

There are several professional tools/strategies used by career consultants to help athletes in their career decision making and planning. Petitpas, Champagne, Chartrard, Danish, and Murphy (1997) offered the athlete's guide for career planning aimed at helping the still active as well as retiring athletes to make a sequence of effective decisions related to professional education, career choice and planning. In this tool, career planning is presented as a three-phase process with self-exploration, career exploration, and career acquisition (phase 1), planning for transition (phase 2), and career action planning (phase 3). The authors provided detailed advice on how to proceed through the process in a way that at each phase the athletes develop all the necessary resources to proceed to the next phase.

According to my counseling experience, athletes find it especially difficult to make decisions while being in a crisis-transition and experiencing the corresponding crisis symptoms, such as a decrease in self-esteem, chronic emotional discomfort, increased sensitivity to mistakes/failures, and disorientation in decision making and behavior (Stambulova, 2003). As mentioned earlier, athletes usually perceive a crisis situation as being in a dead end, being locked, and having no exit. The "mobilization" counseling model (Stambulova, 2000; in press) outlined the three strategic alternatives in a crisis-transition: (1) "rejection," or getting away from the traumatic situation (e.g., dropping out from an activity or terminating a relationship); (2) "acceptance," or staying in the situation as it is but changing the client's reaction(s) and attitude(s) to the situation/activity or people involved; or (3) "fighting," or trying to radically change the situation for the better. To illustrate these alternatives, let us consider how they were used in helping the female swimmer in *Case A*. We discussed several scenarios related to the rejection strategy: to terminate in sport and to continue with her boyfriend; to continue in sport but to change the coach; or to continue in sport but to separate from her boyfriend. All these were not very attractive to the client. Next, we discussed the acceptance strategy: to accept the people around her as they were, for example, not to expect her coach to share her joy related to her love relationship. The athlete found this strategy to be a good starting point in normalizing her relationship with the coach. More specifically, she decided to stay with the same coach, focus more on his professional advice, and try to eventually prove to him her ability to combine sport and her relationship with her boyfriend. But in the case of her boyfriend, she selected the fighting strategy by choosing to involve him more in her athletic life (e.g., inviting him to visit her competitions and practices) and making him a resource rather than a barrier (remember that in the client's initial story, he was not in the sport "building" at all). Besides, she felt confident that her parents could support her decisions related to the coach and the boyfriend. In our discussions of different transition alternatives available to the athlete, her own metaphors, such as building and elevator, were continuously used. The approach proved to be useful to help the athlete make decisions that clarified her career path.

5. Career as Fit

In the counseling process given in the previous section, the swimmer from *Case A* was unwilling to reject any aspect in her life situation. Instead, she wanted to find a better fit between them. In *Case B*, the skater was helped in finding strategies to create a better fit in the interactions with his skating partner. The volleyball player from *Case C* chose to move to a lower-level team because she started to feel a lack of fit in her previous team and because she hoped to find a better fit in her new team and also between her sport and studies.

These three cases illustrate several career issues triggered by the fit metaphor, such as a fit between a person and his or her team; a fit between the different cycles in the athletes' life; a fit in relationships with or between people in the athlete's micro-environment. All these cases also fit into the historical, sociocultural, and sport system contexts in the 1990s Russia. Athletes' perceptions of their career situations were affected by their knowledge of these contexts. For example, the swimmer in *Case A* did not see any sense in changing her coach. She expected the new coach to think the same of her boyfriend, because Russian elite sport coaches typically prioritized the interests of the sport system over any personal interests and wanted athletes to focus exclusively on sport (see also the inheritance metaphor section). The volleyball player in *Case C* started her elite career during the Soviet times and felt secure in terms of her life after sport. Her university studies followed an individualized schedule designed to accommodate the demands of her sport. At the moment of our talk, she had been a student for about 10 years. When the 1990s brought on a historical shift and an economic crisis in Russia, she understood that in this new situation she had to take full responsibility for her life after sport. Therefore, finding a better fit between her sport and studies has acquired a new sense of urgency.

Introducing the fit metaphor Inkson (2006) stated: "you cannot put a square peg in a round hole," but "one problem is that neither the peg nor the hole stays the same shape for long" (p. 19). These images provide several connotations for career assistance to athletes. The first one is in the sport orientation area when helping athletes find the sport events suitable to their potentials and interests (i.e., putting a round peg into a round hole). The second one is in assisting athletes to adjust in the chosen sport (i.e., to make the peg fit into the hole). The third one is in stimulating athletes to be proactive in anticipating how sport in general and their sport events in particular will change in the near future and what resources need to be developed in advance to make a good fit with the forthcoming demands (i.e., adjusting the peg to the changing shape of the hole).

Using the fit metaphor, we can consider career transitions as changes in fit between the athlete, the task, and/or the environment (Hackfort & Huang, 2005). Career transition models used in sport psychology research and applied work (Schlossberg, 1981; Taylor & Ogilvie, 1994; Stambulova, 2003) emphasize the preconditions and demands, coping and related factors (e.g., resources and barriers), outcomes, and later consequences of a transition. A common pattern in these models is viewing the coping processes/strategies as central in a transition, with a fit between the transition's demands and the athlete's resources being a key factor in successful coping. Athletes have successful transitions when they are able to develop and effectively use all the necessary resources in the coping process. Crisis-transition is an alternative outcome with athletes' perceived need in psychological assistance. Lack of career assistance to athletes in crises may lead to negative consequences of not coping with the transition (e.g., premature dropout, neuroses, eating disorders, etc.). The three perspectives in assisting athletes to cope with career transitions have been defined: (1) preventive, (2) crisis-coping, and (3) negative-consequences-coping (Stambulova, 2003). Preventive interventions help athletes build awareness of the forthcoming transition demands and emphasize the timely development of necessary resources for effective coping (i.e., create a fit). Crisis-coping interventions help athletes analyze the crisis-situation and find the best available way to turn ineffective coping into more effective strategies (i.e., correct the lack of fit or help find a new fit). Interventions dealing with negative consequences of not coping with the crisis correct new issues or problems (often clinical ones) caused by the long-term lack of fit in the transition.

Some non-normative transitions like injuries pose a sudden lack of fit between an athlete's ability and demands of the sport that can be difficult to prepare for in advance. Injury researchers (Johnson et al., 2005; Pargman, 2007) have provided evidence that teaching athletes relaxation, goal setting, stress management, and other mental/ life skills may help prevent injuries, and also help athletes within the rehabilitation period to restore fit between them and demands of the sport.

All in all, the fit metaphor triggers a set of career transition frameworks and taps into several principles of career assistance culture, such as activity-specific approach (i.e., taking into account not only common, but type of sport-specific career demands), individual approach (i.e., focusing on the athlete's idiosyncratic resources and barriers), culturally specific approach (i.e., helping athletes adjust within a particular sport system, society, and culture), and transferable skills approach (i.e., teaching skills applicable both in and outside of sport).

6. Career as Relationships

The relationship metaphor highlights the athletes' social networks and relevant demands, as well as their social skills. In many senses, other people (coaches, managers, parents, peers, opponents, referees, etc.) make athletes' careers possible and meaningful. A body of knowledge exists in sport psychology about the dynamic social context of athletes' development and the roles of the people involved (see, e.g., Jowett & Lavallee, 2007). In the developmental model of transitions faced by athletes (see also the cycle metaphor section), Wylleman and Lavallee (2004) presented the most important social agents for athletes at different stages of their careers based on the analysis of literature on the athletic triangle (i.e., athlete-coach-parents), relationships within the athletic family, and peer and marital or lifetime-partner relationships of athletes. The authors suggested that during the initiation career stage, athletes perceive their parents, siblings, and peers as the most influential in their sport involvement. During the development career stage, peers, coaches, and parents form athletes' major social network. In the mastery stage, coach and partner (or own family) are listed among the main supporters. The latter is also considered the major supporter during the discontinuation career stage.

A more holistic perspective in considering the athletes' social network was recently presented by Henriksen and co-authors in the athletic talent development environment (ATDE) model that demonstrated the embeddedness of athletic careers within a series of overlapping social structures and cultures (Henriksen, Stambulova, & Roessler, under review). The focus in this study is shifted from studying athletes to investigating successful ATDEs (e.g., teams or clubs) that regularly produce elite senior athletes by effectively helping young talented athletes make a successful transition from junior to senior sport. The authors emphasized relationships between the different components of an ATDE (e.g., between young and senior athletes) and investigated how this environment and its specific organizational culture are influenced by higher-level social structures (e.g., federation, educational system, mass media, etc.) and cultures (national, youth, sport, and sport event specific cultures). They also stressed that the team/club organizational culture integrates other factors and plays a key role in providing continuity between generations in the environment and thus contributing to the environment's success in the talent development task. Such culture stimulates young athletes to build relationships and communicate effectively in order to use all the resources available in the environment.

Compared to young athletes, senior and especially professional athletes in the dynamic contemporary sports have to possess a greater set of social life skills, including self-regulation in social situations (as in *Case B*), self-promotion, impression management, reputation building, and contract-hunting skills. Such social skills become important coping resources for retired athletes building new careers. Therefore, practicing social life skills in both athletic and non-athletic contexts is accentuated in life development interventions within career assistance to athletes (e.g., Danish, Petitpas, & Hale, 1993; Lavallee, 2005).

When discussing athletes' social networks and diversity of relationships in sport, the consultant-client relationship cannot be overlooked. The core values attached to it include empathy, congruence, trust, and unconditional positive regard to the athlete-clients (Lavallee & Andersen, 2000; and others). One emerging relationship issue in elite and professional sports is communication and interactions between the different professionals helping athletes with various aspects of their careers (e.g., coaches, physiotherapists, managers), among which career consultants have to find their place.

7. Career as Role

When looking through the lens of the role metaphor, an athletic career appears as a role behavior. Starting in sport, athletes begin to master the role of an athlete and develop athletic identity, which is the degree to which the individuals identify themselves with the athlete role (Brewer et al., 1993). Over the course of their athletic careers, athletes change their roles within the sport system (see also the cycle metaphor section). They start as novices and proceed as young prospects. After the transition to senior sports, they become senior and/or elite amateur athletes. When some of the elite athletes sign professional contracts, they transit to the role of professional athletes. Sooner or later, all of the athletes transfer to the role of retired/ former athletes. Role transformations refer to the changes in career demands and coincide with normative career transitions. Athletic identity is strengthened throughout the initiation, development, and mastery stages (Stambulova, 2009), but it is expected to shrink as athletes approach athletic retirement. Multiple personal identities reflecting the different roles of an athlete (e.g., a family member, a friend, a student, an employee, and others) serve as resources in the transition to the post-career (Lavallee, Gordon, & Grove, 1997; Petitpas et al., 2002). In contrast, athletes' early social recognition facilitates their athletic identity foreclosure (single-minded focus on sport and athletic role) and one-sided development that later become risk factors for the identity crisis (self misinterpretation) during athletic retirement (e.g., Stambulova, 2009). Career assistance interventions are often related to working on identity issues with still active and retired athletes (e.g., Lavallee & Andersen, 2000; Lavallee et al., 1997; and others).

One way to understand roles is to use the concepts of "role set" and "role expectations" (Katz & Kahn, 1966). A role set is a set of other people who define parts of the role of the focal person. Each member of the role set has role expectations and communicates them directly or indirectly to the focal person. The expectations of the various members of the role set can be incompatible, leading to intra-role conflict. Two or more different roles held by the same person may get in the way of each other, leading to inter-role conflict. The sum of total expectations experienced in a particular role may be more than the focal person can handle, leading to role overload (Inkson, 2006). All such issues can cause significant stress in clients and thus become working issues for career consultants.

The role metaphor provides further insights into the three cases followed in this chapter. In *Case A*, the swimmer experienced an intra-role conflict in terms of her athletic role (i.e., coach and parents expected her to prioritize sport against her love relationship, and her boyfriend expected her to prioritize him). She also experienced inter-role conflict in which being a good girlfriend got in the way of being a good daughter and a good athlete. Her decisions described earlier (see the action metaphor section) led her to solving both conflicts through trying to make her boyfriend's expectations of her sport more compatible with the coach's and the parents' expectations. The skater in *Case B* was good at his athletic role (i.e., skating), but his role behavior as a skating partner was unacceptable to his female partner, who expected him to be supportive and patient. This intra-role conflict was solved by helping the male partner to change perception of his role in the pair and develop self-regulation skills to use in the critical situations during practices. The volleyball player in *Case C* experienced an inter-role conflict between her athletic and student roles, which was solved through moving to a lower-level team to get more time for studies.

There are other interesting aspects of athletes' careers triggered by the role metaphor. One of them relates to athletes' self-expressions in the psychological roles they play in their sport groups/teams (e.g., dictator, supporter, workaholic, clown, etc.) or for spectators and opponents in competitions in order to be visible and distinct from other athletes (e.g., superman, aggressive machine, sport hero, reckless gambler, etc.). Career consultants might help an athlete to creatively search for his or her individual image and style of performance that feel subjectively comfortable to the athlete and are complementary to his or her athletic success.

Mass media nowadays often creates sport heroes and even idols. Such a role attached to the athlete holds both pluses and minuses for the role holder. On the one hand, it is inspirational to be popular and a role model for many youngsters. On the other hand, the hero role implies a lack of privacy with a feeling of being constantly "on stage." Because the role set is huge for the hero-athletes, it is easy to anticipate role overload with related stress, which may lead to negative consequences, such as injury or drug use. Besides, people tend to idealize heroes and perceive them as having no weak points. Such perception may work as a barrier for athletes to seek psychological assistance when they need it. Based on my experience of communicating and working with socially recognized and popular athletes, I would like to emphasize a multilevel treatment approach that addresses not only the symptoms/role behaviors (e.g., anxiety, conflicts), but also determinants behind the role play (e.g., athletes' perceptions, attributions, personal meanings) in the difficult career situations.

And last but not least, the role metaphor stimulates us to consider what roles career consultants may play in their work with athlete-clients. Such roles as advisor, supporter, listener, believer, instructor, or coach showcase the various facets of consulting work. In all these roles, the consultant is expected to play professionally by following professional culture, especially the basic ethical norms (e.g., competence, confidentiality, avoiding dual relationships, and others).

8. Career as Resource

Athletic careers may be considered as resources for sport organizations or sport systems they belong to, and also as "career capital"

(Inkson, 2006) for athletes themselves. When athletes are considered as resources for their teams, clubs, or federations, several working issues for career consultants get illuminated. For example, elite athletes at the top of their careers experience a high level of organizational support but also of organizational pressures, such as planning for Olympic gold medals or stimulating them to take part in competitions when they are ill or not fully recovered after injury. In situations like these, athletes might feel imprisoned and require psychological assistance. When elite athletes retire, their typical complaint is about the indifference of sport organizations to their fate after sport, leading to feelings of being "used and forgotten" (Alfermann et al., 2004; Stambulova et al., 2007). Therefore, one more task for career consultants is helping former athletes renew their social networks and find supporters outside sport.

Viewing athletic career as a capital for athletes' life career, we can consider it as a developmental event characterized by the *duration* of sport participation, *sport event (s)* practiced, *achieved* sport titles/ results, perceived *benefits* and *costs* of the multiyear sport involvement, as well as by *career satisfaction* (i.e., one's self-esteem with regard to the athletic career) and *career successfulness* (i.e., social recognition of one's athletic career) (Stambulova, 1994). Successful careers are usually associated with athletic excellence and high social recognition, whereas satisfactory careers are associated with achieving individual peak in athletic performance corresponding to the individual resources and environment (Hanin & Stambulova, 2004).

Important indicators of earning good career capital in sport are occupational success and life satisfaction after termination of the athletic career. Elite sport is often used as a means for upward social mobility that opens up new opportunities in the post-athletic career. Non-elite athletes also get career capital from sport (e.g., they can chose careers in sport-related fields or use the skills acquired through sport, such as ability to focus, self-discipline, and others, in non-sport occupational careers). A body of knowledge has been collected about athletes' occupational development and life satisfaction after sport leading to the following conclusions: (1) former athletes are no less successful in life than non-athletes; (2) professional athletes are more at risk than amateurs for downward social mobility in the post-athletic career; and (3) educational level and sport involvement are better predictors for life satisfaction than sport alone (see Alfermann & Stambulova, 2007, for an overview).

Helping athletes turn their athletic careers into capital, investment, or resource for their life careers can be seen as an umbrella goal for career assistance to athletes, to which all the approaches discussed across this chapter (whole person, whole career, transferable skills, individual approaches, and others) make their contributions.

9. Career as Story

During my research and applied work, I have listened to a diversity of athletes' career stories. My study of normative career transitions of Russian athletes involved 552 essays on "My athletic career" written by student-athletes and 16 in-depth career interviews with elite athletes (Stambulova, 1994, 2009). In another study, I qualitatively examined the symptoms of athletes' crises via 126 crisis-narratives (Stambulova, 2003). From these written and oral stories, I have learned that athletic careers are dramatic and meaningful life experiences not only for elite but also for lower-level athletes, and that even retired athletes tend to do some retrospective sense making when reflecting about sport. Many athletes I talked to acknowledged that my interest in them was broader than just their athletic performance, and study participants with problems sometimes turned into clients. When telling crisis-stories, many athletes really dramatized their experiences. For example, the swimmer from *Case A* presented a very personal interpretation of her situation. My impression was that she dramatized the situation to show me how important it was for her to find the balance between different cycles of her life and have social support from/keep good relationships with all her significant others. But other people involved in her situation could tell different stories about the case.

The story metaphor triggers several strategies in the career assistance professional culture. First of all, it is the multilevel approach described earlier (see the role metaphor section) that stimulates the consultant to think and understand what is behind the athlete's story. Second, the story metaphor brings up an association with all the existential psychology consulting strategies dealing with key existential concepts such as death, freedom, isolation, and meaninglessness (Lavallee et al., 2000). Third, this metaphor leads us to an information-processing strategy based on account making in response to stress that can be used to describe transition experiences to someone who can respond with empathy (Grove, Lavallee, Gordon, & Harvey, 1998).

Considering career as a story, it is important to remember that much of our imagery of sport is derived from the stories that sport people and media tell. These stories communicated to and by people as a means to share and negotiate experiences and meanings of sport contribute to (re)shaping of sports culture.

Conclusion and Future Directions

My attempt to employ the multiple metaphor approach for summarizing the professional culture of career assistance to athletes was a challenging and enriching experience. The nine career metaphors borrowed from vocational psychology proved to be a useful descriptive framework for sport psychology and career assistance in sport. More specifically, the career metaphors have been beneficial in: (1) demonstrating different and complementary aspects in existing athletic career definitions; (2) summing up career development and transition theories and research in sport psychology; (3) analyzing the traditional and emerging career demands for contemporary athletes and clarifying the current and potential working issues for career consultants; (4) illuminating various internal and external factors that serve as resources or barriers in athletes' careers/transitions; (5) reviewing career assistance values and principles, as well as various professional tools and strategies; and (6) considering the consultants' roles in career assistance interventions and their professional challenges (e.g., cooperation with other sports professionals and more). Altogether, the nine career metaphors contributed to a holistic narrative of the career assistance professional culture, which revealed that athletes' careers and the corresponding professional culture are complex and multifaceted.

The nine career metaphors can be seen as universal career archetypes through which people from different cultures might share ideas about careers, including careers in sport. At the same time there can also be nuances in interpretation of career archetypical metaphors in different national cultures. For example, applying the cultural syndromes framework (see more in Stambulova & Alfermann, 2009; Stambulova et al., in press), it is possible to hypothesize that the fit metaphor might be interpreted differently in individualist versus collectivist cultures. In the former, athletes typically search for a fit in a form of consensus between their individual goals and team goals, and in the latter, they just subordinate individual goals to the team goals. The journey metaphor might be interpreted differently in process-oriented versus outcome-oriented cultures. In the former, athletes might tend to emphasize the process and direction of their career movement, while in the latter, a particular destination. Therefore, when an athlete and a consultant share a cultural background, the metaphors work as cultural narratives facilitating their mutual understanding. But when a consultant works with an athlete from another cultural background, the consultant's cultural awareness and reflexivity (e.g., Ryba, 2009) become a virtue, implying, among other things, negotiations of metaphors and their meanings.

Following the three cases throughout the chapter and analyzing each of them from different viewpoints suggested by career metaphors, a great deal can be learned about the athletes involved and their career situations. Therefore, the archetypical career metaphors can be incorporated into career assistance culture as practical frameworks or professional tools stimulating consultants to consider each athlete and his or her career situation from various perspectives. Some content overlap between these metaphors may facilitate integrating different facets of each case. The cycle metaphor showed the most connections with the other metaphors (e.g., journey, role, relationship) and might be established as a basic career archetype to which the other archetypical metaphors add facets or nuances. Using the archetypical career metaphors as professional tools, consultants might stimulate the athlete-clients to generate their idiosyncratic career metaphors, illuminating the most important personal meanings of their career experiences. It is interesting to note that the working issues presented in the Russian case examples followed throughout this chapter look universal in a sense that athletes from other countries might experience similar career situations. But, as it was briefly illustrated in the fit metaphor section, the perception and interpretation of career experiences by Russian athletes in *Cases A–C*, as well as solutions to their problems, were shaped by the Russian historical and social contexts of the 1990s. In all these cases, it is also possible to see an impact of the Russian collectivist vertical culture with its hierarchy, competitiveness, and group interests overweighting the individual interests (see also the inheritance metaphor section and Stambulova et al., 2009; Stambulova & Alfermann, 2009; Stambulova et al, in press).

More generally speaking, professional culture of career assistance to athletes is embedded in wider historical and sociocultural contexts that shape its content. For example, in individualist cultures (e.g., United States, Australia, some west European countries) career assistance emphasizes helping athletes with athletic retirement and adjustment to the post-career, whereas in collectivist cultures (e.g., Russia, China) more attention is paid to helping athletes with the "within career" transitions, such as from junior to senior sports (see more in Stambulova et al., in press). At the same time, career assistance professional culture is also influenced by globalization tendencies in sport, sciences, and more generalized fields. Therefore, career assistance culture might have both culturally specific and common features across different countries. Using the system's theory (Ganzen, 1982), career assistance professional culture can be defined as an open system with certain *elements* (e.g., values, principles, frameworks, tools, etc., that can be universal or culturally specific), *structures* (the one based on career metaphors is presented in the chapter), *functions* (professional identification, education, clients' protection), and *development* (in terms of both content of the culture and number of career consultants and career assistance programs). The content of career assistance culture consists of accumulated experiences and professional philosophies of career consultants that are grounded in sport psychology/applied sport psychology knowledge and knowledge transmitted from the adjacent areas (e.g., other sport sciences, clinical, vocational and counseling psychology). This professional culture is negotiated at the conferences, described in the professional literature, and communicated to applied sport psychology students in the related programs. What is presented in this chapter is no more than my personal view or narrative of the career assistance culture affected by my professional, cultural, and other backgrounds and experiences. Therefore, other consultants are urged to complement and/or to challenge this view.

Regarding the future directions for research, I would like to stress several potentially interesting issues. First, it will be useful to further investigate and describe the professional culture of career assistance to athletes using either the multiple metaphor approach or other frameworks, as well as in relation to the various sociocultural contexts. Second, career development and transition researchers in sport psychology may enrich the career assistance professional culture by providing career consultants with athletes' culturally specific perceptions of career demands, resources, barriers, career success, and the like (Stambulova & Alfermann, 2009; Stambulova et al., in press). Third, the case examples followed in this chapter demonstrated the importance of athletes' idiosyncratic metaphors when expressing their career experiences. Therefore, it would be interesting to apply the metaphor self-generation method (Hanin & Stambulova, 2002) to study athletes' idiosyncratic career metaphors within one culture and/or cross-culturally.

Acknowledgments

I am grateful to Dr. Tatiana Ryba, Dr. Robert Schinke, and the anonymous reviewer for constructive comments on the early draft of the chapter. I am also thankful to Dr. Maria Cypher for improving the overall readability of the chapter.

Author Note

My career consultancy experience includes two decades of working with athletes and coaches from various sports in Russia and since 2001, in Sweden. However, my applied work is secondary to my academic career insofar as I have never been a full-time consultant. All the case examples described in this chapter are real. I tried to present the athletes' stories as well as I remember them. To ensure the clients' anonymity, I do not use any names, exact locations, and time.

References

Alfermann, D., & Stambulova, N. (2007). Career transitions and career termination. In G. Tenenbaum & R. C. Eklund (Eds.), *Handbook of sport psychology* (3rd ed., pp. 712–736). New York: Wiley.

Alfermann, D., Stambulova, N., & Zemaityte, A. (2004). Reactions to sports career termination: A cross-national comparison of German, Lithuanian, and Russian athletes. *Psychology of Sport and Exercise, 5*, 61–75.

Arthur, M. B., Hall, D. T., & Lawrence, B. S. (Eds.). (1989). *Handbook of career theory*. Cambridge: Cambridge University Press.

Bloom, B. S. (1985). *Developing talent in young people*. New York: Ballantine.

Brewer, B. W., Van Raalte, J., & Linder, D. E. (1993). Athletic identity: Hercules' muscles or Achilles heel? *International Journal of Sport Psychology, 24*, 237–254.

Cecić Erpič, S., Wylleman, P., & Zupančič, M. (2004). The effect of athletic and non-athletic factors on the sport career termination. *Psychology of Sport and Exercise, 5*, 1, 45–60.

Combs, G., & Freedman, J. (1990). *Symbol, story, and ceremony. Using metaphor in individual and family therapy*. New York: Norton.

Côté, J. (1999). The influence of the family in the development of talent in sport. *The Sport Psychologist, 13*, 395–417.

Côté, J., Baker, J., & Abernethy, B. (2007). Practice and play in the development of sport expertise. In G. Tenenbaum & R. C. Eklund (Eds.), *Handbook of sport psychology* (3rd ed., pp. 184–202). New York: Wiley.

Côté, J., Lidor, R., & Hackfort, D. (2009). To sample or to specialize? Seven postulates about youth sport activities that lead to continued participation and elite performance. *International Journal of Sport & Exercise Psychology* (7)1, 7–170.

D'Andrea, M., & Daniels, J. (2005). RESPECTFUL sport psychology: A multidimensional-multicultural competency model. *ESPNews, 19*(1), 9.

Danish, S. J., Petitpas, A. J., & Hale, B. D. (1993). Life development intervention for athletes: Life skills through sports. *The Counseling Psychologist, 21,* 352–385.

Ericsson, K. A. (1996). *The road to excellence: The acquisition of expert performance in the arts and sciences, sports and games.* Mahwah, NJ: Erlbaum.

Ganzen, V. A. (1984). *Sistemnye opisaniya v psihologii* [System descriptions in psychology]. Leningrad: Leningrad State University Press.

Gill, D. (2007). Gender and cultural diversity. In G. Tenenbaum & R. C. Eklund (Eds.), *Handbook of sport psychology* (3rd ed., pp. 823–844). New York: Wiley.

Gordon, S., Lavallee, D., & Grove, J. R. (2005). Career assistance program interventions in sport. In D. Hackfort, J. Duda, & R. Lidor (Eds.), *Handbook of research in applied sport and exercise psychology: International perspectives* (pp. 233–244). Morgantown, WV: Fitness Information Technology.

Grove, J. R., Lavallee, D., Gordon, S., & Harvey, J. H. (1998). Account-making: A model for understanding and resolving distressful reactions to retirement from sport. *The Sport Psychologist, 12,* 52–67.

Hackfort, D., & Huang, Z. (2005). Considerations for research on career counseling and career transition. In D. Hackfort, J. Duda, & R. Lidor (Eds.), *Handbook of research in applied sport and exercise psychology: International perspectives* (pp. 245–255). Morgantown, WV: Fitness Information Technology.

Hanin, Y., & Stambulova, N. (2002). Metaphoric description of performance

states: An application of the IZOF model. *The Sport Psychologist, 16,* 396–415.

Hanin, Y., & Stambulova, N., (2004). Sport psychology, overview. In C. Spielberger (Ed.), *Encyclopedia of applied psychology* (Vol. 3, pp. 463–477). New York: Elsevier.

Henriksen, K., Stambulova, N., & Roessler, K. (under review). Holistic approach to athletic talent development environment: A successful sailing milieu. *Psychology of Sport and Exercise.*

Inkson, K. (2004). Images of career: Nine key metaphors. *Journal of Vocational Behavior, 65,* 96–111.

Inkson, K. (2006). *Understanding careers: The metaphors of working lives.* Thousand Oaks, CA: Sage.

Johnson, U., Ekengren, J., & Andersen, M. B. (2005). Injury prevention in Sweden. Helping soccer players at risk. *Journal of Sport and Exercise Psychology, 1,* 32–38.

Jowett, S., & Lavallee, D. (Eds.). (2007). *Social psychology in sport.* Champaign, IL: Human Kinetics.

Katz, D., & Kahn, R. L. (1966). *The social psychology of organizations.* New York: Wiley.

Lavallee, D. (2005). The effect of a life development intervention on sports career transition adjustment. *The Sport Psychologist, 19,* 193–202.

Lavallee, D., & Andersen, M. B. (2000). Leaving sport: Easing career transitions. In M. B. Andersen (Ed.), *Doing sport psychology* (pp. 223–236). Champaign, IL: Human Kinetics.

Lavallee, D., Gordon, S., & Grove, R. (1997). Retirement from sport and the loss of athletic identity. *Journal of Personal and Interpersonal Loss, 2,* 129–147.

Lavallee, D., Nesti, M., Borkoles, E., Cockerill, I., & Edge, A. (2000). Intervention strategies for athletes in transition. In D. Lavallee & P. Wylleman (Eds.), *Career transitions in sport: Interna-*

tional perspectives (pp. 111–130). Morgantown, WV: Fitness Information Technology.

Lidor, R., Côté, J., & Hackfort, D. (2009). To test or not to test? — The use of physical skill tests in talent detection and in early phases of sport development. *International Journal of Sport & Exercise Psychology*, 7(2), 131–146.

Morgan, G. (1986). *Images of organization*. Beverly Hills, CA: Sage.

Pargman, D. (Ed.) (2007). *Psychological bases of sport injuries* (3rd ed.). Morgantown, VW: Fitness Information Technology.

Petitpas, A. J., Brewer, B. W., & Van Raalte, J. L. (2002). Transitions of the student-athlete: Theoretical, empirical, and practical perspectives. In E. F. Etzel, A. P. Ferrante, & J. W. Pinkney (Eds.), *Counseling college student-athletes: Issues and interventions* (pp. 137–156). Morgantown, WV: Fitness Information Technology.

Petitpas, A., Champagne, D., Chartrand, J., Danish, S., & Murphy, S. (1997). *Athlete's guide to career planning: Keys to success from the playing field to professional life*. Champaign, IL: Human Kinetics.

Ryba, T. V. (2009). Understanding your role in cultural sport psychology. In S. Hanrahan & R. J. Schinke (Eds.), *Cultural sport psychology* (pp. 33–44). Champaign, IL: Human Kinetics.

Ryba, T. V., & Wright, H. K. (2005). From mental game to cultural praxis: A cultural studies model's implications for the future of sport psychology. *Quest*, 57, 192–212.

Salmela, J. H. (1994). Phases and transitions across sports career. In D. Hackfort (Ed.), *Psycho-social issues and interventions in elite sport* (pp. 11–28). Frankfurt: Lang.

Savickas, M. L. (2002). Career construction: A developmental theory of vocational behavior. In D. Brown & associates (Eds.), *Career choice and development*

(4th ed., pp. 149–205). San Francisco: Jossey-Bass.

Schlossberg, N. K. (1981). A model for analyzing human adaptation to transition. *The Counseling Psychologist*, 9(2), 2–18.

Schinke, R. J., & Hanrahan, S. (Eds.) (2009). *Cultural sport psychology*. Champaign, IL: Human Kinetics.

Schinke, R. J., Gauthier, A. P., Dubuc, N. G., & Crowder, T. (2007). Understanding athlete adaptation in the National Hockey League through an archival data source. *The Sport Psychologist*, 21, 277–287.

Stambulova, N. (1994). Developmental sports career investigations in Russia: A post-perestroika analysis. *The Sport Psychologist*, 8, 221–237.

Stambulova, N. (2000). Athlete's crises: A developmental perspective. *International Journal of Sport Psychology*, 31, 584–601.

Stambulova, N. (2003). Symptoms of a crisis-transition: A grounded theory study. In N. Hassmén (Ed.), *SIPF Yearbook 2003* (pp. 97–109). Örebro: Örebro University Press.

Stambulova, N. (2009). Talent development in sport: A career transitions perspective. In E. Tsung-Min Hung, R. Lidor & D. Hackfort (Eds.) *Psychology of Sport Excellence* (pp. 63–74). Morgantown, WV: Fitness Information Technology.

Stambulova, N. (in press). Methods and tools for career assistance. In D. Hackfort (Ed.), *New approaches for advancement in elite sports*. Morgantown, WV: Fitness Information Technology.

Stambulova, N., & Alfermann, D. (2009). Putting culture into context: Cultural and cross-cultural perspectives in career development and transition research and practice. *International Journal of Sport & Exercise Psychology*, 7, 292–308.

Stambulova, N., Alfermann, D., Statler, T., Côté, J. (in press). Career development and transitions of athletes: The

ISSP Position Stand. *International Journal of Sport & Exercise Psychology*.

Stambulova, N., Johnson, U., & Stambulov, A. (2009). Sport psychology consulting in Russia and Sweden. In R. J. Schinke & S. Hanrahan (Eds.), *Cultural sport psychology: From theory to practice* (pp. 125–140). Champaign, IL: Human Kinetics.

Stambulova, N., Stephan, Y., & Järphag, U. (2007). Athletic retirement: A cross-national comparison of elite French and Swedish athletes. *Psychology of Sport and Exercise, 8*, 101–118.

Super, D. E. (1957). *The psychology of careers*. New York: Harper & Row.

Taylor, J., & Ogilvie, B. C. (1994). A conceptual model of adaptation to retirement among athletes. *Journal of Applied Sport Psychology, 6*, 1–20.

Wolf, N. (1993). *Fire with fire: The new female power and how it will change the twenty first century*. New York: Random House.

Wuerth, S., Lee, M. J., & Alfermann, D. (2004). Parental involvement and athletes' career in youth sport. *Psychology of Sport and Exercise, 5*, 21–34.

Wylleman, P., & Lavallee, D. (2004). A developmental perspective on transitions faced by athletes. In M. Weiss (Ed.), *Developmental sport and exercise psychology: A lifespan perspective* (pp. 507–527). Morgantown, WV: Fitness Information Technology.

Wylleman, P., De Knop, P., Ewing, M., & Cumming, S. (2000). Transitions in youth sport: A developmental perspective on parental involvement. In D. Lavallee & P. Wylleman (Eds.), *Career transitions in sport: International perspectives* (pp. 143–160). Morgantown, WV: Fitness Information Technology.

Wylleman, P., Theeboom, M., & Lavallee, D. (2004). Successful athletic careers. In C. Spielberger (Ed.), *Encyclopedia of applied psychology* (Vol. 3, pp. 511–517). New York: Elsevier.

13

SEXUAL ABUSE IN SPORT: IMPLICATIONS FOR THE SPORT PSYCHOLOGY PROFESSION

Trisha Leahy

CHAPTER SUMMARY

International research documenting the occurrence of sexual and other forms of violence against young athletes (e.g., physical and psychological) in sport has led to a more critical analysis of the sporting environment, and its impact on young people. The International Olympic Committee (IOC) has recently issued a Consensus Statement on sexual harassment and abuse in sport specifically recognizing all the rights of athletes, including the right to enjoy a safe and supportive sport environment. UNICEF has now taken up the issue under its mandate, defined by the Convention on the Rights of the Child, of preventing violence against children (those under the age of 18). As well as a human rights framework, the scientific biopsychosocial paradigm is also being brought to bear in the development of preventative policy and practice.

My goal with this chapter, using current knowledge about the sexual abuse of athletes in sport and its impact, is to advocate for the sport psychology profession to actively participate in a multidisciplinary engagement with all support professionals working in sport, to maximize our potential as gatekeepers for athletes' safety in identifying, intervening, and acting to prevent the sexual abuse of athletes in sport systems.

I begin with an introduction to the role of sport as a social institution with social responsibilities and obligations to protect children's rights in sport. Following the Convention on the Rights of the Child, I include all young athletes under the age of 18 in the term *children*. I then propose that under the biopsychosocial framework upon which most elite sports systems are built, the sport psychologist has a key safeguarding role. I then provide an overview of some of the literature on sexual abuse of athletes and specify the implications for the sport psychology profession to be able to engage effectively with the current human rights and biopsychosocial discourse on the prevention of violence against gifted young athletes in our sporting systems.

Sexual Abuse in Sport

I was having so much trouble trying to deal with it, 'cause the [sport organization] kept saying, "This is so confidential. You can't talk to anyone about it." And I needed to get it out. But they kept saying, "It's confidential, if the media gets to this and blah, blah , blah. . . ."

It's [pause], it's just awful to that that happened and the people who could have stopped it, and not just for me. . . . I can't believe that they couldn't [pause], you know what I mean. They just [long pause], they saw that things were wrong, and they didn't do anything about it so [long pause], yeah [sighing, long pause], not only the fact that I fell out of a sport that should have protected me. . . . I lost so much. I lost my relationship with my family, I could have saved a few years of my life.

He was in such a powerful position that no one interfered, I think no one questioned what he was doing. But now when I speak to people, they do say he stepped over the line with us, but . . . they didn't say anything, they didn't want to interfere with him. Yeah, I'm a bit angry about that you know because, when people now say, you know we knew, you know he was stepping over the line, and I'm just like, "Well, why didn't you interfere?"

I spoke to the sport psychologist a couple of times but not once did [the sport psychologist] get it.

But it was crazy, like the [sport psychologist] just sat there and just [pause]. . . . I mean I was 17 [long pause] and [pause], I mean [long pause], I can't say that I had any thoughts of saying, "No" [to the perpetrator], which is hard to justify to someone who says you're old enough to say no . . . and like the [sport psychologist] couldn't understand that, uhm at 17, or 16, I couldn't say no. . . . At the time it was crazy for me to try to explain how I felt, uhm, and so I actually said, "I can't do it." . . . I just didn't go back.

The above firsthand narratives, reported with permission from athletes who were systematically sexually abused within the elite sports environment over a number of years by their coaches, provide bleak and compelling evidence of the systemic failure of the sports system to protect and safeguard young athletes sexually victimized while under its care. All of the athletes quoted above, regardless of gender, had been sexually abused from a young age over a period of years by coach-perpetrators who had been simultaneously abusing other members of the squad.

These poignant records are in direct contrast to our consensus vision of competitive sport as a positive, empowering environment for gifted young people. They point to inadequate training of sport psychology professionals to be able to respond appropriately to sexually abused athletes in distress. Research shows that these are not isolated incidents, but reflect systemic vulnerabilities within the sports system and the training of professional sports psychologists that need to be addressed if we are to be effective in safeguarding young athletes (Leahy, Pretty, & Tenenbaum, 2003, 2004). In the following sections, I present an overview from critical public health, human rights, and biopsychosocial frameworks of some of the relevant issues related to the safeguarding of young athletes in sport.

Role of Sport

Given the well-researched public health benefits of physically active and sporting lifestyles, sport development constitutes an important policy priority for many countries. International research documents the importance of sport and physical activity in the prevention and amelioration of several chronic diseases and conditions, such as cardiovascular disease, diabetes, cancer, hypertension, obesity, depression, and osteoporosis (Taylor et al, 2004; Warburton, Nicol, & Bredin, 2006). The enhancement of young people's academic, personal, and social development has also been documented (Castelli, Hillman, Buck, & Erwin, 2007; Donaldson & Ronan, 2006), as has the reduction of high-risk youth behaviors, such as substance abuse, teenage pregnancy, and gang membership (Nichols & Crow, 2004; Smith & Waddington, 2004). On a community level, sport has been associated with the promotion of social inclusion, tolerance and community spirit, and national identity (Blauwet, 2005; Posner, 1999; Ross & Jameson, 2007).

The United Nations has recently recognized sport as an important tool to build community spirit and bridges across ethnic and community divides (United Nations, 2002). Sport then, is not simply seen as a national enterprise but potentially stretches beyond borders with multinational influence. Not surprisingly, therefore, organized competitive sport constitutes an important social institution in many countries with multiple public health, and community development goals.

The documentation of sexual abuse of athletes within sport systems has, however, challenged the commonly accepted view of sport as an unproblematic facilitator of public health policy initiatives. A more balanced view of sports systems has begun to emerge with challenges to the assumption of sports systems as free from social problems, coming primarily from sport sociology critiques (e.g., Brackenridge, 2001; Fisher, Roper, & Butryn, 2009; Kirby, Greaves, & Hankivsky, 2000). These critiques point to the sociocultural context of competitive sport as a unique subculture with its own norms based very much on power and hierarchical relations (McKay, Messner, & Sabo, 2000). It is only relatively recently that researchers have begun to document the links between these power structures and the creation of an environment that facilitates, rather than challenges, the abuse of power that is the defining feature of sexual abuse (Brackenridge, 1997; Herman, 1997; Leahy et al., 2004).

Human Rights and Sport

For many years, sport escaped critical investigation as a possible site for violence against children, as it was dominated by a characteristic set of beliefs about sport as a site of fair play grounded in an apolitical meritocracy and outside the sphere of legal scrutiny (Brackenridge, 1994). The organized sports sector has, therefore, largely avoided any substantive reflection on the human rights implications stemming from young athletes' involvement in this sector of community life, despite the fact that since the democratization and expansion of the sport system from the 1970s onwards, numerous rights-related issues have progressively emerged in the public domain (David, 2005). Consequently, sport has lagged behind other sectors of the community in establishing regulatory safeguarding policies and practice for young athletes (Leahy, Pretty, & Tenenbaum, 2002).

Organized competitive sport is a permitted social institution obliged by the requirements of the UN Convention on the Rights of the Child. The Convention has been ratified by all but two nations across the world (the United States and Somalia) and provides a legal and policy framework to guarantee the protection of children's rights. While no provision of the Convention on the Rights of the Child explicitly mentions sport, 37 of the 42 substantive provisions apply directly to sport (David, 2005). These include the provision that children have the right to play and to recreation (Article 31), and the right to have their talents and mental and physical abilities be developed to their fullest potential (Article 29). Specifically related to the topic of this article, the Convention on the Rights of the Child explicitly recognizes in Articles 19 and 34 the right of children to be protected from sexual abuse. Article 19 directs that states must take "all appropriate legislative, administrative, social, and educational measures to protect the child from all forms of physical or mental violence, injury or abuse, neglect or negligent treatment, maltreatment or exploitation, including sexual abuse while in the care of parent(s), legal guardian(s) or any other person who has the care of the child" (UNICEF, 2005, p. 5).

In addition, protective measures should include "effective procedures for the establishment of social programmes to provide necessary support for the child and for those who have the care of the child as well as other forms of prevention, and for identification, reporting, referral, investigation, treatment and follow up of instances of child maltreatment" (UNICEF, 2005, p. 5).

The obligations under the Convention on the Rights of the Child apply to the state, parents, and *any other person who has care of the child* (Article 19). Within organized competitive sport, therefore, not only state sports organizations, but all personnel involved are obliged to ensure that sport is violence-free and that effective systems are in place to support and rehabilitate victims of any form of violence against children in sport (UNICEF, 2005).

Sport requires thoughtful stewardship if it is to fulfill its social responsibility and its obligations to protect children's rights. No individual within the institution of sport can be considered exempt from this responsibility, including coaches, athletes, parents, volunteers, administrators, and scientific, medical, and welfare support staff. However, the sports industry, like other organizations, represents a very complex social system in which structural and relational characteristics are inherently value laden. To be a successful professional coach, a coach needs to produce winning teams; to be a successful professional sport, a sport needs to attract fans, provide entertainment value, and at the same time provide value for money for sponsors. To attract and retain young gifted athletes, sports at all levels need to provide developmentally appropriate and safe training environments. It is well recognized that when power is unequally distributed among groups or individuals, ethical and moral conflicts will inevitably emerge (Newman & Fuqua, 2006). In such a climate of competing interests, how can the sport psychology profession contribute to efforts to ensure that socially responsible or ethical directions are consistently taken and that the rights of young athletes are not being violated?

In the following section, I propose that a biopsychosocial framework of elite sports development provides a platform for support personnel including sport psychologists to act in the role of gatekeeper in promoting a best-practice sports environment that facilitates the development of athletic giftedness within a safe, ethical delivery system.

The Biopsychosocial Framework

Within behavioral medicine and the social sciences, the term *biopsychosocial* is used to refer to the interaction between biological, psychological, and social factors, which are integrally linked in the overall development of any individual. The biopsychosocial framework is commonly applied within the elite sport sector, whose objective is to develop gifted athletes to world-level performance standards. Internationally, servicing infrastructures that facilitate elite sport development generally operate within a biopsychosocial, integrated support system targeting all aspects of each athlete's medical and physiological, psychological, social support, and welfare needs (Leahy, 2008a).

A multidisciplinary approach is a core feature of the biopsychosocial paradigm, which assumes that athletes rarely, if ever, exhibit unidimensional problems. Solutions therefore, are invariably the result of multidisciplinary, integrated, science- and evidence-based interventions. Additionally, office- or laboratory-based servicing is increasingly not the norm in elite sport scientific support service delivery. Scientific support staff members, including sport psychologists, are highly mobile, traveling to local and overseas training and competition venues with the athletes.

Within the biopsychosocial model therefore, sport psychologists are key frontline members of the athletes' entourage, which is tasked with providing a scientific training methodology to support coaching, training, and performance. In general, there is now a sound scientific base and well-established practice guidelines to monitor individual health and performance parameters. However, systemic health and performance parameters, from the social end of the biopsychosocial spectrum, have been less visible in our performance-related research and applied interventions. Sport sociology contributions in this area, particularly those from the cultural studies field, appear to have been largely ignored by the sport psychology profession.

Systemic parameters are an important component of the biopsychosocial framework, requiring our attention if we are to effectively use it as our operating model of high-performance service delivery. For example, similar to other institutionalized cultural forms, sport is affected by and in turn affects existing structures of power and inequality in society (Hall, 1996; Leahy, 2001a). Feminist and critical cultural studies colleagues remind us that central to an understanding of the impact of systemic parameters is the critical analysis of the construction of power and the impact of powered social structures on individual athletes' health and performance (Brackenridge, 2001; Leahy, 2001a; Ryba, 2009).

The sport psychologist as part of the biopsychosocial, multidisciplinary support system is in a key position to monitor the maintenance of a psychologically, physically, and sexually safe sports system in which athletes can achieve their potential. Sport psychologists, because of their close involvement with the team, are often the first point of contact for athletes in distress and therefore need to be aware of the potential for these forms of harm and the relevant social policy and procedures for reporting and referring. Using a sports injury analogy, sport psychologists, as members of the multidisciplinary scientific support team, can effectively use their positions within the athlete's entourage to contribute to the prevention of "systemic injuries" and to advocate for appropriate child and youth protection policies within the sports system. The increasing recognition that social institutions, including sport, should provide systemic harm reduction strategies has stimulated policy initiatives in a number of countries such as the United Kingdom (Child Protection in Sport Unit, 2006) and Australia (Australian Sports Commission, 2007) focusing on safeguarding athletes (Brackenridge, Bishopp, Mousalli, & Tapp, 2008). Sport psychologists should be at the forefront of such policy initiative developments, from the design planning phase, to the implementation phase, to the evaluation phase. However, sport psychology training programs that primarily teach mental-skills as performance enhancement techniques at the expense of training in related systemic policy, advocacy, and ethical systems will not equip entrants to the profession with the necessary competencies to enable effective engagement with a biopsychosocial discourse and praxis (Leahy, 2001a; Ryba, 2009).

Before sport psychologists, as members of the biopsychosocial support team, can step up to the role of gatekeeper, effectively acting to protect the rights of young people in sport, we must first insist on our own rights to be educated and provided with clear guidelines and core competencies embedded in a support system that empowers us to act on behalf of young athletes at risk. Sport psychology training programs that lead to a critical analysis of the multiple intersections of power and powerlessness in society (e.g., across gender, race, socioeconomic status, ethnicity, sexuality, and [dis]ability) and in sport as a microcosm of that society are needed. Sport psychologists must be equipped to be able to effectively help athletes through practice and research that is relevant to and grounded in athletes' lived experiences in the sports system.

Violence against children, in all its forms, physical, psychological, or sexual, is a social problem and the sports sector, similar to other sectors of the community, cannot totally secure itself. What we can perhaps achieve is to increase deterrence and decrease risk by empowering all adults in the system, starting with ourselves as sport psychologists, with the specific knowledge and resources required to understand and to act to empower and protect athletes. To this end, in the following section, I present an overview of relevant aspects of current knowledge on the sexual abuse of athletes.

Understanding Sexual Abuse in Sport

During the past few years, the occurrence of sexual abuse in sport has been systematically documented by researchers in a number of countries in Europe, Australia, Canada, and the United States (e.g., Brackenridge et al., 2008; Fasting, Brackenridge, Miller, & Sabo, 2008; Kirby, Demers, & Parent, 2008; Leahy et al., 2002, 2008; Vanden Auweele et al., 2008). Research in the area began with both prevalence studies (Kirby et al., 2000; Leahy et al., 2002) and qualitative investigations of the experiences of sexually abused athletes (e.g., Brackenridge, 1997; Cense & Brackenridge, 2001, Leahy et al., 2003; Toftegaard-Nielsen, 2001). Prevalence rates suggested by research reports across different countries vary according to the definitions and methodologies used, with rates of between 2% (Tomlinson & Yorganci, 1997) and 22% (Kirby et al., 2000), depending on the broadness or narrowness of the definition.

In one study using an Australian sample, the researchers provided indications of prevalence using a more precise legally based definition of sexual abuse (Leahy et al., 2002). In that study, sexual abuse was considered to be any sexual activity between an adult and a child (under 18 years old, following the Convention of the Rights of the Child), regardless of whether there is deception or the child understands the sexual nature of the activity. This included sexual contact accomplished by force or the threat of force regardless of the age of the victim or perpetrator. Sexual abuse also included noncontact (e.g., exhibitionism, involving a child in sexually explicit conversation, engaging a child in pornographic photography), contact (sexual touching, masturbation), and penetrative (oral, vaginal, anal penetration) acts. Results indicated that of 370 elite (national representatives) and club (regional representatives) male and female athletes surveyed, 31% of female athletes and 21% of male athletes reported having experienced sexual abuse before the age of 18. Of these, 41% of the sexually abused female athletes and 29% of the sexually abused male athletes indicated that the abuse was perpetrated by sports personnel. The sport-related abuse was largely perpetrated by those in positions of authority or trust with the athletes. These included primarily coaches and, less frequently, support staff and other athletes. The vast majority (more than 96%) of perpetrators were men.

Long-term Impact

Prevalence studies suggest that sexual abuse and its psychological sequelae is an area of significant practice application for sports psychologists working with athletes. Yet, empirical evidence about the psychological sequelae associated with sexual abuse in athlete populations and implications for specific interventions is an area of research that has been conspicuously absent in the sport psychology literature (Leahy et al., 2008). In the clinical psychology and psychiatric research literature, researchers and clinicians have for some time now been applying a trauma framework to understand the impact of sexual abuse. Central to this still-evolving theoretical framework are the concepts of posttraumatic stress and dissociation as key responses to traumatizing events. Core posttraumatic symptoms of reexperiencing, avoidance, and hyperarousal have been frequently identified in sexual abuse populations (e.g., Carlson et al., 1998; Johnson et al., 2001). Symptoms related to reexperiencing and hyperarousal can include intrusive thoughts, physiological arousal, reactivity to trauma cues, and hypervigilance (American Psychiatric Association: *DSM-IV-TR*, 2000). Avoidant symptoms can include avoidance of thoughts, feelings, places, or people associated with the trauma (*DSM-IV-TR*, 2000).

Dissociation is understood as "a disruption in the usually integrated functions of consciousness" (*DSM-IV-TR*, 2000, p. 477). Dissociative symptomatology (e.g., amnesia, derealization, depersonalization) involves a splitting between the "observing self" and the "experiencing self." During a traumatic experience, dissociation provides protective detachment from overwhelming affect and pain, but it can result in severe disruption within the usually integrated functions of consciousness, memory, identity, or perception of the environment (van der Kolk et al., 1996.).

Clinical and research evidence indicates that those manifesting core posttraumatic symptoms generally also appear to develop a complex set of other interrelated, or secondary, symptoms (Carlson, 1997). These can include, for example, depression, impairment of self-esteem, and a disruption of important developmental processes leading to affect and impulse dysregulation and deformations of relatedness and identity (Briere, 1997; Courtois, 1999; Herman, 1997).

In one published report to date, the researchers specifically investigated from a trauma framework the long-term impact of sexual abuse on athletes (Leahy et al., 2008). Taking into account the multiple contexts of childhood physical and psychological abuse and adult trauma exposure in a group of 90 (45 men and 45 women) athletes, the study results suggested that childhood sexual, physical, and psychological abuse were strongly correlated. Of the three forms of abuse reported in the study, the primary unique correlate of long-term traumatic symptomatology was psychological abuse. This is not surprising, as individual forms of abuse are unlikely to be experienced unidimensionally (e.g., Higgins & McCabe, 2000a, b). Both sexual and physical abuse may be understood as inherently psychological forms of abuse (Hart, Binggeli, & Brassard, 1998). It may be, therefore, that it is the embedded psychological abuse of sexually abusive experiences wherein lies the harm (Hart et al., 1996; Jellen, McCarroll, & Thayer, 2001; Sanders & Becker-Lausen, 1995).

Within the environment of competitive sport, the psychological abuse variable may have particular salience, as researchers have documented apparently normalized coaching and instructional practices and team initiation rituals that constitute psychologically abusive practices (Brackenridge, Rivers, Gough, & Llewellyn, 2006; Kirby & Wintrup, 2002; Leahy, 2001). It may also specifically relate to the particular strategies that appear to be used by sexual abuse perpetrators within the athlete's environment, as described below.

Perpetrator Methodology

Leahy et al. (2004) published qualitative data describing the relationship between specific perpetrator methodologies and long-term traumatic outcomes in a sample of 20 athletes. The group was purposefully selected to balance male and female participants with similar sexual abuse experiences, half of whom scored within the clinical range of traumatic symptomatology clinical assessments. Two general dimensions of perpetrator methodology were revealed from a thematic content analysis. These strategies were designed to engender feelings of complete powerlessness in the sexually abused athlete and, conversely, to present the perpetrator as omnipotent. What seemed to characterize the perpetrator's methodology, and this was particularly obvious in cases where the abuse was prolonged and repeated, was the need to impose his or her version of reality on the athlete and to isolate the athlete within that reality. The perpetrator successfully maintained that reality by controlling the psychological environment, silencing and isolating the athlete from potential sources of support. In addition to controlling the athlete's outer life, her or his inner life was controlled through direct emotional manipulation and psychological abuse.

From the psychological literature we know that the repeated imposition of a powerful perpetrator's worldview, and the lack (due to isolating and silencing strategies) of alternative reference points, can result in the victim being entrapped within the perpetrator's viewpoint (Herman, 1997), as described by a male athlete who was sexually abused by his coach:

> It was just like a different arena, and I was so young, and training with people that were so well known, that were already there, you know which is a big thing, so, uhm . . . like I was so overawed by this whole situation, as well as this big team, and

going places I'd never been and stuff . . . and I hadn't been there that long, and you know maybe, this, this is the way it goes.

The athletes' reports described an unpredictable and volatile emotional reward-punishment cycle pervading the sports environment. This cyclical repetition of fear and reprieve, punishment and reward, in the closed context of a competitive sports team can result in a feeling of extreme dependence on the perceived omnipotent perpetrator (Herman, 1997). As one female athlete sexually abused by her coach said,

> If we had anything to say we'd say it to him, whether it's regarding sport or life, whatever. . . . I used to think that the most important thing was that I was training and listening to him, 'cause to us at that time, his word was like gospel.

From the psychology literature we understand this state as a traumatized attachment to the perpetrator. Under these conditions, disclosure simply does not happen and commonly expected indicators of distress may not be apparent. Silencing is an integral, not separate, part of the experience achieved through aspects of the perpetrator's methodology that keep the athlete in the state of traumatized confusion, fear, and entrapment, as illustrated in the statements below by three athletes sexually abused by their coaches:

> It was more emotional, everything he did . . . he'd put me down, he'd really put me down as an athlete and then build me up with his affection and then it got really confusing and I didn't know the difference, if he was a coach or somebody who was just playing with my emotions. *(Female athlete)*

> I remember going to the motel room and being terribly scared . . . that internal fear, just so scared . . . and the intense fear of telling. *(Male athlete)*

> So what do you do when you trusted this person, and you've got all this at your feet like your sport and a whole bunch of new friends, so what are you going to do? . . . It's just your word against his . . . and you don't know, maybe it happens to everybody. Maybe this is the way it goes. *(Male athlete)*

The Bystander Effect

In a further examination of athletes' experiences of sexual abuse, Leahy et al. (2003) described a pervasive bystander effect, which appeared to compound long-term psychological harm for sexually abused athletes. The bystander effect (Latané & Darley, 1968) refers to the situation where the victim perceived that others, who knew about (or suspected) the sexual abuse, did not do anything about it.

The athletes' experiences of the bystander effect, quoted at the beginning of this chapter, make clear the distress-amplifying impact of abandoning the sexually abused athlete to isolation and silence (Leahy et al., 2003). They illustrate how the system exactly replicated the dynamics of silencing and isolating strategies used by the perpetrator. They also point to the apparent lack of systemically sanctioned accountability in relation to the power of the coach-perpetrator that allowed the abuse to continue for many years unchallenged by other adults in the system. These included coaching and other support staff or volunteers who were not as senior in the competitive sport hierarchy as the perpetrator. This was especially notable among in elite sport context:

> We were such an elite squad, we were so much better than all the other squads that we were training with and we very much kept to ourselves, no one ever interfered with us because we were so elite and no one ever questioned what we were doing.

Non-intervention by other adults in a young person's environment is likely to be interpreted as meaning that those adults are also powerless in relation to the perpetrator. For children, disclosure may be preempted if the child believes or is aware that other adults know about the abuse (Palmer, Brown, Rae-Grant, & Loughlin, 1999). If observing adults take no action, the child may assume that the behavior is socially acceptable, or in the case of older children, as mentioned above, that perpetrator's message that she or he is omnipotent is really true and that therefore the child really is trapped.

Implications for Sport Psychology Practice

There is a clear need for more research on sexual and other forms of violence against children in sport to substantiate the scientific database and improve on the methodological limitations of the research to date. For, example, data are needed to support preventative policy and practice for athletes with disabilities, athletes with differing sexual orientations, and athletes from differing racial and ethnic backgrounds. Nevertheless, indicative implications for the sport psychology profession relate to training and supervision programs, and the children's rights advocacy role of sport psychologists as system-privileged service providers in the biopsychosocial sports system.

Research and clinical evidence indicates that athlete survivors of sexual abuse, whether perpetrated within sport or outside of sport, form a significant percentage of the athlete population with which sport psychologists will come into contact. Therefore, sport psychology training programs need to include comprehensive training in the assessment and treatment of sexual and other forms of abuse and in traumagenic symptomatology in order for professionals to be able to respond therapeutically to athletes in distress. The importance of maintaining a psychologically safe and consistent therapeutic environment when working with athletes who have experienced sexual abuse cannot be overstated. Therapy is a trust-based relationship that requires not only authentic engagement but also vigilance in maintaining a healing dynamic within the therapeutic environment (Leahy et al., 2003). Maintaining this quality requires close attention to relational dynamics with vulnerable athletes. The risk of even minor countertransferential errors being experienced as harmful replications of perpetrator dynamics is high. Sport psychologists working with such athletes should ensure that they have access to ongoing supervision to maintain the quality of the therapeutic environment.

Effective abuse-related therapy must address the sociocultural context of the survivor's distress (Briere, 1992). Particularly evident from research reports across a number of countries is the manner in which certain aspects of the culture of competitive sport provide an environment that facilitates, rather than inhibits, perpetrator methodology in the sport environment (Brackenridge, 1997, Kirby et al., 2000; Leahy et al., 2004; Toftegaard-Nielsen, 2001). In the cases mentioned in this chapter, the coach-perpetrator's ability to create a version of reality positioning himself or herself as the omnipotent central figure in the athlete's life, and the power of the coach to control a reality exclusively defined by his or her abusive agenda went unchallenged, in some cases, for many years. As poignantly reported by a male athlete abused by the coach who abused many members of the squad over many years:

> He was very well known . . . and people would say [after the perpetrator had been caught], "Oh, and all those teams that he coaches, and he gave such a lot of time to junior sport." And

[pause], and people say, "Oh, was any of it, was any of it genuine or was it all abuse?" . . . And I don't know what the answer is.

It has long been argued by feminist and cultural studies researchers, and more recently within the human rights field, that a transformation in the culture and institutional practices in sport, specifically related to equity and power sharing, is necessary to minimize the risk of athlete abuse (e.g., Brackenridge, 2001; David, 2005; Hall, 1996; Hargreaves, 1994; Leahy 2001a).

Sport psychologists working with athletes who are survivors of sexual abuse also need to take into consideration the documentation of psychologically abusive coaching strategies, which have apparently become normalized within the sociocultural context of some organized competitive sport systems (Brackenridge, 2001, Leahy, 2001; Leahy et al., 2004). There is an urgent need to eliminate any psychologically abusive behavior in sport. Psychological abuse has been uniquely implicated in long-term traumatic outcomes (Leahy et al., 2008). It also effectively masks sexual offender behaviors, which rely on psychological abuse and emotional manipulation as primary strategies (Leahy et al., 2004, Toftegaard-Nielsen, 2001).

To overcome the bystander effect, comprehensive and ongoing sexual abuse awareness education is imperative for all those involved in organized sport, including athletes, parents, and all associated support personnel. Particularly, it is the responsibility of adults in the system to ensure children's safety. This responsibility should not be relegated to the children themselves. Silencing is an integral, not separate, part of the sexual abuse experience. Nondisclosure is the norm. Nevertheless, as specified by the Convention on the Rights of the Child, children's voices should be incorporated in the development of policy and practice that concern their welfare.

Every person in the athletes' entourage has a right to be informed and specifically empowered to act to safeguard athletes' welfare through clear ethical and procedural guidelines. However, most ethical guidelines tend to be prescriptive in nature rather than facilitative of ethical decision-making strategies in the sometimes very complex and intense relational situations that can characterize sport relationships. Understanding ethical relationships; how relationships become exploitative; the meaning of harm in relational terms; and the process through which relational errors of judgment can occur all need to be explicit targets of educational programs for frontline support personnel in elite sports systems. The sport psychologist is in a key position to be at the vanguard of ethical competency training for support personnel, as among all the support professions ethics training is particularly emphasized in psychology training programs.

While codes of ethics and policy guidelines are fundamentally necessary, they are, alone, insufficient to safeguard athletes from abuse. A more fundamental intervention might be one that addresses the way power is constructed within the sociocultural milieu of competitive sport. The development of an ethical, psychologically safe, power-sharing coaching system may offer considerable challenge to existing systems and practices. This is particularly true at the elite level, where coaching careers are sometimes directly predicated on athletes' performance results (Brackenridge, 1997). Autocratic leadership styles, unaccountable power, and hierarchical organizational structures further compound the risk of exploitation of athletes at all levels and the inability of others to act in support of victimized athletes. Engagement of the sport psychology profession is essential to inform in the critical, but ultimately facilitative systemic evaluation necessary to ensure the sport system is safe for individual children.

Conclusion

Those of us working in the competitive sports sector all recognize and understand the influential role of sport in the physical, psychological, and social development of individuals and communities. We acknowledge its importance to public health and as a vehicle to bridge ethnic and communal divides (United Nations, 2002). However, if we are to achieve these aims, we need to engage in a more thoughtful stewardship of sport and help to confront broader social issues, including violence against children, which also occur in sport (Chan, 2006). The sport psychology profession, similar to the psychology profession in general, must become a more socially engaged discipline. To paraphrase past American Psychological Association President Philip Zimbardo (2004), the sport psychology profession should use its areas of expertise and knowledge to offer a more positive contribution to and to promote athletes' welfare.

At the highest level of elite sport the International Olympic Committee (IOC) has made it clear that it is the right of all athletes to enjoy a safe and supportive sport environment, and that it is in such conditions that athletes are more likely to flourish and optimize their sporting performance (IOC, Medical Commission, 2007). The sport psychologist is in a key position to monitor the maintenance of a safe sporting environment for athletes and to be an advocate for athletes' well-being, so that they can optimize their athletic giftedness in safety. The sport psychology profession must engage more fully with the multidisciplinary research, practice, and advocacy efforts to address systemic risks in sporting systems and to "develop a culture of dignity, respect, and safety in sport" (IOC Medical Commission, 2007).

References

American Psychiatric Association. (2000). *Diagnostic and statistical manual of mental disorders* (4th ed.). Text revision. Washington, DC: American Psychiatric Association.

Australian Sports Commission (2007). *Ethics in sport: Child protection in sport* (n.d.) Retrieved January 20, 2007, from http://www.ausport.gov.au/ethics/child protect.asp.

Blauwet, C. (2005). Promoting the health and human rights of individuals with a disability through the Paralympic movement. Retrieved March 17, 2009, from *International Paralympic Committee* website, http://www.paralympic.org/...Development/Development_tools/Health_as_a_Human_Right_Final_long_Version.pdf.

Brackenridge, C. (1994). Fair play or fair game? Child sexual abuse in sport organizations. *International Review for the Sociology of Sport, 29*, 287–299.

Brackenridge, C. (1997). "He owned me basically . . .": Women's experience of sexual abuse in sport. *International Review for the Sociology of Sport, 32*, 115–130.

Brackenridge, C. H. (2001). *Spoilsports: Understanding and preventing sexual exploitation in sport*. London: Routledge.

Brackenridge, C. H., Bishopp, D., Moussalli, S., & Tapp, J. (2008). The characteristics of sexual abuse in sport: A multidimensional scaling analysis of events described in media reports. *International Journal of Sport and Exercise Psychology, 4*, 385–406.

Brackenridge, C. H., Rivers, I., Gough, B., & Llewellyn, K. (2006). Driving down participation: Homophobic bullying as a deterrent to doing sport. In C. Atkinson (Ed.), *Sport and gender identities: Masculinities, femininities and sexualities* (pp. 120–136). London: Routledge.

Briere, J. (1992). *Child abuse trauma: Theory and treatment of the lasting effects*. Newbury Park, CA: Sage.

Briere, J. (1997). *Psychological assessment of adult posttraumatic states*. Washington, DC: American Psychological Association.

Carlson, E. B. (1997). *Trauma assessments: A clinician's guide*. New York: Guilford.

Carlson, E. B., Armstrong, J., Lowenstein, R., & Roth, D. (1998). Relationships between traumatic experiences and symptoms of posttraumatic stress, dissociation and amnesia. In J. D. Bremner & C. R. Marmar (Eds.), *Trauma, memory and dissociation* (pp. 205–228). Washington, DC: American Psychiatric Press.

Castelli, D. M., Hillman, C. H., Buck, S. M., & Erwin, H. E. (2007). Physical fitness and academic achievement in third- and fifth-grade students. *Journal of Sport and Exercise Psychology, 29*, 239–252.

Cense, M., & Brackenridge, C. H. (2001). Temporal and developmental risk factors for sexual harassment and abuse in sport. *European Physical Education Review, 1*, 61–79.

Chan, K. M. (2006). FIMS Leadership: Prof Kai-Ming Chan — Hong Kong. In K.M. Chan & W. R. Frontera (Eds.),

Sports medicine (pp. 26–31). Hong Kong: FIMS.

Child Protection in Sport Unit. (2006). *Strategy for safeguarding young people in sport, 2006–2012*. Leicester: Sport England/Child Protection in Sport Unit.

Courtois, C. (1999). *Recollections of sexual abuse: Treatment principles and guidelines*. New York: Norton.

David, P. (2005) *Human rights in youth sport: A critical review of children's rights in competitive sports*. London: Routledge Taylor & Francis Group.

Donaldson, S. J., & Ronan, K. R. (2006). The effects of sports participation on young adolescents' emotional well-being. *Adolescence, 41*, 369–389.

Fasting, K., Brackenridge, C. H., Miller, K. E., & Sabo, D. (2008). Participation in college sports and protection from sexual victimization. *International Journal of Sport and Exercise Psychology, 4*, 427–441.

Fisher, L. A., Roper, E. A., & Butryn, T. M. (2009). Engaging cultural studies and traditional sport psychology. In R. S. Shinke & S. J. Hanrahan (Eds.), *Cultural sport psychology* (pp. 23–34). Champaign, IL: Human Kinetics.

Hall, M. A. (1996). *Feminism and sporting bodies: Essays on theory and practice*. Champaign, IL: Human Kinetics.

Hargreaves, J. (1994). *Sporting females: Critical issues in the history and sociology of women's sports*. London: Routledge.

Hart, S., Binggeli, N. J., & Brassard, M. R. (1998). Evidence for the effects of psychological abuse. *Journal of Emotional Abuse, 1*, 27–58.

Hart, S., Brassard, M., & Karlson, H. (1996). Psychological abuse. In J. Briere, L. Berliner, J. Bulkley, C., Jenny, & T. Reid (Eds.), *The APSAC handbook on child abuse* (pp. 72–89). Newbury Park, CA: Sage.

Herman, J. L. (1997). *Trauma and recovery. From domestic abuse to political terror* (2nd ed.). New York: Basic.

Higgins, D., J., & McCabe, M. P. (2000a). Multi-type abuse and the long-term adjustment of adults. *Child Abuse Review, 9*, 6–18.

Higgins, D., J., & McCabe, M. P. (2000b). Relationships between different types of abuse during childhood and adjustment in adulthood. *Child Abuse, 5*, 261–272.

IOC Medical Commission, (2007). *Consensus statement on sexual harassment and abuse in sport*. Retrieved August 17, 2008, from http://multimedia.olympic .org/pdf/en_report_1125.pdf.

Jellen, L. K., McCarroll, J. E., & Thayer, L. E. (2001). Child psychological abuse: A 2-year study of US Army cases. *Child Abuse and Neglect, 25*, 623–639.

Johnson, D. M., Pike, J. L., & Chard, K. M. (2001). Factors predicting PTSD, depression, and dissociative severity in female treatment-seeking childhood sexual abuse survivors. *Child Abuse and Neglect, 25*(1), 179–198.

Kirby, S., Greaves, L., & Hankivsky, O. (2000). *The dome of silence: Sexual harassment and abuse in sport*. Halifax, NS: Fernwood.

Kirby S. L., Demers, G., & Parent, S. (2008). Vulnerability/prevention: Considering the needs of disabled and gay athletes in the context of sexual harassment and abuse. *International Journal of Sport and Exercise Psychology, 4*, 407–426.

Kirby, S., & Wintrup, G. (2002). Running the gauntlet: An examination of initiation/hazing and sexual abuse in sport. *The Journal of Sexual Aggression, 8*, 49–68.

Latané, B. & Darley, J. M. (1968). Group inhibition of bystander intervention in emergencies. *Journal of Personality and Social Psychology, 10*, 215–221.

Leahy, T. (2001a). Reflections of a feminist sport psychologist. In G. Tenenbaum (Ed.), *The practice of sport psychology* (pp. 37–47). Morgantown, WV: Fitness Information Technology.

Leahy, T. (2001b). Preventing the sexual abuse of young people in Australian sport. *The Sport Educator, 13*, 28–31.

Leahy, T. (2008a). A biopsychosocial approach to sports excellence at the Hong Kong Sports Institute. *Journal of Youth Studies, 11*, 50–58.

Leahy, T. (2008b). Editor's note: Understanding and preventing sexual harassment and abuse in sport: Implications for the sport psychology profession. *International Journal of Sport and Exercise Psychology, 4*, 351–353.

Leahy, T., Pretty, G., & Tenenbaum, G. (2002). Prevalence of sexual abuse in organised competitive sport in Australia. *Journal of Sexual Aggression, 8*, 16–35.

Leahy, T., Pretty, G., & Tenenbaum, G. (2003). Childhood sexual abuse narratives in clinically and non-clinically distressed adult survivors. *Professional Psychology: Research and Practice, 34*, 657–665.

Leahy, T., Pretty, G., & Tenenbaum, G. (2004). Perpetrator methodology as a predictor of traumatic symptomatology in adult survivors of childhood sexual abuse. *Journal of Interpersonal Violence, 19*, 521–540.

Leahy, T., Pretty, G., & Tenenbaum, G. (2008). A contextualised investigation of traumatic correlates of childhood sexual abuse in Australian athletes. *International Journal of Sport and Exercise Psychology, 4*, 366–384.

McKay, J., Messner, M. A., & Sabo, D. (2000). *Masculinities, gender relations and sport*. Newbury Park, CA: Sage

Newman, J. L., & Fuqua, D. R. (2006). What does it profit an organization if it gains the whole world and loses its own soul. *Consulting Psychology Journal: Practice and Research, 58*, 13–22.

Nichols, G., & Crow, I. (2004). Measuring the impact of crime reduction interventions involving sports activities for young people, *The Howard Journal, 43*, 267–283.

Palmer, S. E., Brown, R. A. Rae-Grant, N. I., & Loughlin, M. J. (1999). Responding to children's disclosure of familial abuse: What survivors tell us. *Child Welfare, 78*, 259–283.

Posner, J. K. (1999). After-school activities and the development of low-income urban children: A longitudinal study. *Developmental Psychology, 35*, 868–879.

Ross, C. M., & Jameson, L., M. (2007). Research update: Using recreation to curb extremism. *Parks & Recreation, 42*, 26–29.

Ryba, T. V. (2009). Understanding your role in cultural sport psychology. In R. S. Shinke & S. J. Hanrahan (Eds.), *Cultural sport psychology* (pp. 35–44). Champaign, IL: Human Kinetics.

Sanders, B., & Becker-Lausen, E. (1995). The measurement of psychological abuse: Early data on the child abuse and trauma scale. *Child Abuse and Neglect, 19*, 315–323.

Smith, A., & Waddington, I. (2004). Using "sport in the community" schemes to tackle crime and drug use among young people: Some policy issues and problems. *European Physical Education Review, 10*, 279–298.

Taylor, R. S., Brown, A., Ebrahim, S., Jolliffe, J., Noorani, H., Rees, K., Skidmore, B., Stone, J. A., Thompson, D. R., & Oldridge, N. (2004). Exercise-based rehabilitation for patients with coronary heart disease: Systematic review and meta-analysis of randomized controlled trials. *The American Journal of Medicine, 116*, 682–692.

Toftgaard-Nielson, J. (2001). The forbidden zone: Intimacy, sexual relations and misconduct in the relationship between coaches and athletes. *International Review for the Sociology of Sport, 36*, 165–183.

Tomilson, A., & Yorganci, I. (1997). Male coach/female athlete relations: Gender and power relations in competitive sport. *Journal of Sport and Social Issues, 2*, 134–155

UNICEF. (2005). *UN human rights standards and mechanisms to combat violence against children*. Florence: UNICEF Innocenti Research Centre.

United Nations. (2002). *Right to play belongs to everyone: Secretary-General tells Olympic Aid forum*. Press Release SG/SM/8119, February 11, 2002. Retrieved August 17, 2008, from http://www.un.org/News/Press/docs/2002/sgsm8119.doc.htm.

van der Kolk, B. A., Pelcovitz, D., Roth, S., Mandel, F., McFarlane, A. C., & Herman, J. L. (1996). Dissociation, somatization, and affect: The complexity of adaptation to trauma. *American Journal of Psychiatry, 153*, 83–93.

Vanden Auweele, Y., Opdenacker, J., Vertommen, T., Boen, F., Van Niekerk, L., De Martelar, K., & De Cuyper, B. (2008). Unwanted sexual experiences in sport: Perceptions and reported prevalence among Flemish female student athletes. *International Journal of Sport and Exercise Psychology, 4*, 354–365.

Warburton, D. E. R., Nicol, C. W., & Bredin, S. S. D. (2006). Health benefits of physical activity: The evidence. *Canadian Medical Association Journal, 176*, 801–809.

Zimbardo, P. G. (2004). Does psychology make a significant difference in our lives? *American Psychologist, 59*, 339–351.

14

NARRATIVE COACHING:
A COMMUNITY PSYCHOLOGICAL PERSPECTIVE

Reinhard Stelter

CHAPTER SUMMARY

This chapter presents a new understanding of coaching defined as the coach's participation in and facilitation of the developmental and learning process of coachees (i.e., individuals or groups being coached[1]). New social trends and societal changes are put forward as the central reason for introducing a new perspective on coaching—an approach significantly different from traditional sports coaching. A theoretical framework of this coaching approach is presented by balancing between an individual, experiential, embodied perspective on the one hand and a social, cultural, community-oriented perspective on the other. Meaning making is highlighted as the central concept in this approach and as the pivotal point for the coaching dialogue. Concrete suggestions of how to focus on experiential and social dimensions are given as ideas for the concrete coaching intervention. A case is presented to give a concrete example of this narrative, community psychological-oriented intervention, a process that helps people to develop a sense of personal or cultural identity and an understanding of their doing as being in correspondence with their values and intentions. The overarching focus of narrative coaching as presented in this chapter is on shaping modified, uplifting, and/or alternative stories about experiences and activities athletes or exercisers are able to share in their concrete community of practice. These joint actions might be a way to build up local cultures in different sport and exercise settings.

Narrative Coaching

In this chapter I present a new approach to coaching, which breaks with the common understanding of the term in the field of sport psychology. The main reason for this development lies in the social and cultural changes that our society has undergone over the past 20 to 40 years (Giddens, 1991; Beck, 1992), changes that are also noticeable in the sport and movement culture. Social scientists see people's needs and aspirations as twofold: (1) to achieve self-understanding and develop an "acceptable" identity, one that provides satisfaction and lets us realize our potential and resources in all aspects of life; (2) to learn more from each other's differences than we do at present. These two goals are the main reasons for the growing interest in coaching in all domains of our society, but traditional sport psychological interventions do not take these social implications and their possible impact on athletes and exercisers sufficiently into account, and thereby neglect some of the basic psychological needs that characterize sport participants (see, e.g., Schinke et al., 2007; Stelter, 1998).

In sport psychology, coaching is generally understood as a psychological and educational discipline that is applied to sport, an interactional strategy in the realm of *teaching* or *instruction* where the coach also pays attention to the psychological aspects inherent in sport and performance. The focus is very much on winning and performance enhancement, whereas other aspects of sport and exercise, and their developmental value and significance as lifelong leisure activities, are not significantly included in the sport coaching literature (see, e.g., Martens, 1997; Vealey, 2005).

The intention with this chapter is to: (1) build a bridge between the growing literature in coaching psychology (Cavanagh, Grant, & Kemp, 2005; Palmer & Whybrow, 2007; Stober & Grant, 2006) and the coaching tradition in sport psychology; (2) introduce a narrative, cultural, and communal psychological dimension to coaching; and (3) couple theory and practice by presenting a case study that will form the basis for further reflections on the applicability of this approach.

How to Define Coaching?

In contrast to sport psychological literature, coaching will be defined here as the coach's participation in the development and learning process of the coachee—the person or group to be coached—(Stelter, 2007). Coaching is a form of conversation that is always related to a specific context and situation in which the coachee(s) experience something significant and challenging—challenging in the sense that they seek to reflect upon events and understand the circumstances and changes in themselves, their lives, sport, and so on (Stober & Parry, 2005). Coaching, as a discipline of learning and

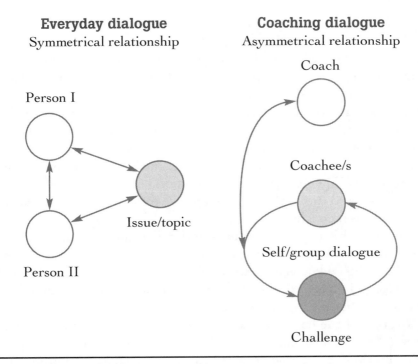

Everyday dialogue
Symmetrical relationship

Person I

Issue/topic

Person II

Coaching dialogue
Asymmetrical relationship

Coach

Coachee/s

Self/group dialogue

Challenge

Figure 1. Differences between an everyday dialog and a coaching dialog (Stelter, 2002).

development, is a process based on the coachees' interests and preparedness to have their current view of reality *unravelled*. In coaching, the coachees' "internal dialogue" is stimulated by an emphasis on selected situations, contexts, and challenges; in such a process the coach acts as a *facilitator* of the dialogue. The figure above illustrates the difference between a "normal," everyday dialogue and the dialogue between coach and coachee.

In an *everyday dialogue* all participants relate to the topic at hand in a similar way. They wish to contribute to the issue or topic by sharing their views and opinions with the other participant(s). In that sense we can speak about a *symmetrical relationship* among all participants. In their idiosyncratic way, the participants have some knowledge of the topic and they share this knowledge equally. They may agree or disagree, they may fight for a specific standpoint, or they may come to some common conclusion. For example, this form of dialogue takes place when players share their experiences and attitudes about their last game.

In a *coaching dialogue*, the coachee(s) are recognized as the experts with regard to the challenges they face. The *conditio sine qua non* of a fruitful coaching dialogue is when it is the coachees who choose the topic and articulate their interest in further reflecting on it, perhaps with the aim of gaining a deeper understanding of the situation or to work toward a solution to a specific problem or challenge. The built-in *asymmetry* of the dialogue arises from the situation; it is the coachee who defines the topic, and it is the coachee who is considered the expert with an understanding and knowledge of the circumstances. The coachee may sometimes also be able to offer new perspectives to the challenge at hand. There can never be an argument between coachee and coach. The coach is "only" a participant who—with his or her questions and reflections—can invite the coachee(s) to further reflect on the issue. But in the end it is the coachee who will determine the level and quality of new insights and knowledge inherent to the challenge that has been the point of departure of the coaching dialogue.

In spite of the coachees' central position in their developmental process, new understanding and shaping of new realities takes place in a process of *co-creation* between coach and coachees. Both parties create a dialogical and social space where their ways of making meanings meet, and where they are able to co-create meaning for the benefit of the coachees' development. Bruner (1990) stressed meaning making as a fundamental process that constitutes *culture*—a perspective that he believed should hold a central position in psychology. In the dialogical space between coach and coachee(s), their speech, reflections, and actions evolve during the process of negotiating meanings. This negotiation can take place verbally during communication and/or arise from the activity itself, namely, by mutual engagement in a community of practice.

Anchoring Coaching in Experience and Social Discourse: A Theoretical Framework

In this section I present a theoretical framework for a new form of coaching intervention, where I try to balance between an individual, experiential, embodied perspective on the one hand and a social, cultural, community-oriented perspective on the other. By doing so, I combine theoretical roots from phenomenology with social constructionism. Phenomenology casts a light on immediate embodied experiences upon which individuals can focus with regard to a specific situation in which they are involved. Social constructionism, on the other hand, deals with discourses between people, the social implications of relationships, and the relational and cultural construction of reality. Although these two theoretical approaches differ in many ways, they share some connections, which allow them to be used in an integrated model for coaching. These connecting concepts revolve around (1) the construction of reality and (2) the concept of meaning, which I discuss in the following two sections. The integration of these two aspects is the central basis for the understanding of my theoretical framework where phenomenology and social constructionism meet and can fuse in an integrated coaching model, a model that I finally synthesize by taking a narrative, community psychological approach.

The Construction of Reality

In both phenomenology and social construction, reality is not something definite and final. Reality is either constructed in the present moment of experiencing and will change from one situation to another (phenomenology), or is socially constructed in relationship with others (social constructionism).

Phenomenology has developed as a genuine "science of experience," with its main focus on how individuals create their own world. Husserl (1985), the founder of phenomenology, spoke about a "descriptive psychology," where the point of departure for psychological investigation is phenomena as *perceived by the subject*. Ihde (1977) wrote:

> Phenomenology begins with a kind of empirical observation directed at the whole field of possible experiential phenomena. Initially, it attempts to see things in a particularly open way that is analogous to Copernicus' *new* vision of the universe. Ideally, this stance tries to create an *opening* of a particular type towards things; it wishes to capture the original sense of wonder which Aristotle claimed was the originating motive for philosophy. Thus, its first methodological moves seek to circumvent certain kinds of predefinition. (p. 31)

Phenomenologists have developed an empirical method for that open approach to phenomena called *epoché*, meaning suspension of judgment. In epoché, the individual attempts to grasp the pure subjectiveness of the world — the individual's world in itself. In that sense we can speak about an *individual, experiential construction of reality*. There are a number of strategies that allow an individual's perceived experience to be explored in depth (see Stelter, 2007, 2008). To counter the accusation of subjectivism, phenomenologists draw a sharp line between them and rational and empiricist traditions in philosophy and psychology, as represented through the method of introspection, a process of "looking within" one's own mind, that is, thoughts, emotions, and sensations are explored through a method of reflective self-observation.

How do *social constructionists* regard the term *reality?* In social constructionism, the focus is on relationships and how social relations develop and form the individual and the social context itself. This relational perspective also sees the evolvement of emotions and thoughts as *socially* constructed and not formed internally by the individual. Reality is constructed exclusively though social discourse and interaction with others — in a workplace, family, or sports team — and thereby evolves in the *relationships* that people are part of (Gergen, 1994). What appears as "reality" is, indeed, a social construction. From a sociological perspective, Berger and Luckmann (1966) set the stage by saying, "The sociology of knowledge understands human reality as socially constructed" (p. 211).

As a consequence of this epistemological assumption, it becomes "possible" — as a strategy of intervention — to deconstruct and reconstruct a specific social reality (e.g., in a sports team, a group of exercisers, or an organization) by influencing the way people talk to each other. Gergen (1994) put it like this: "The degree to which a given account of the world or self is sustained across time is not dependent on the objective validity of the account but on the vicissitudes of social process" (p. 51).

It is here intervention strategies such as Appreciative Inquiry (AI) (Cooperrider & Sekerka, 2003) are seen as valuable. The goal of AI is to bring about organizational change, not through problem solving by means of finding the causes of the problem but rather by enabling the members of the organization to articulate and activate their positive core values and focus on situations where they once shared success. This new way of dealing with challenges — approaching them from another perspective — is the starting point of seeing social reality in a team or organization in a different, encouraging and positive way. Van der Haar and Hosking (2004) wrote in their evaluation of AI:

Reality making is achieved in and through co-ordinations of, for example, written and spoken words, non-verbal actions, voice tone, and artifacts of human activities (interior design, house magazines, technology . . .). But how are these construction processes to be theorized? We cannot speak of "inter-personal" processes — if these are taken to mean what happens between already theorized and independently existing human actors (with personality, attitudes, etc.). This is because we wish to treat relational processes as the medium within which social realities — including what it is to be human and what it is to be "this particular human" — are located. So, instead we speak of coordinations, inter-actions, or text-con/text relations. More narrowly, when acts (texts) are brought into relation they construct relational processes. This means that constructing: (i) becomes understood as co-constructing, rather than an individual affair; and (ii) social construction becomes talk of relational processes and realities rather than meanings, so to speak, "inside someone's head." (p. 1021)

The AI process is jointly constructed by the participants, who through interaction are able to co-create a new social reality for themselves. By choosing *positive* topics as the starting point for their dialogue, by discovering and imagining possibilities, the participants have a chance of creating a reality that furthers their development, both personally and as a group or team. AI can easily be integrated into the coaching process, because it is often much more helpful not to focus on the problems of the situation but on possibilities and strengths of the participants involved.

The Concept of Meaning

The underlying assumption of traditional objective theories of perception and understanding is that there is a reality *out there* in the world; we perceive the world while creating a *picture* of it. This approach lets us understand the world through concepts that focus on internal representations of external reality. This traditional view can be replaced by a definition of reality as something that is constructed through the individual's interplay with a concrete environment.

From the *phenomenological perspective*, Husserl (1950) spoke about *constitution*, which he regarded as a function prior-to-meaning and as part of transcendental intersubjectivity, which offers the individual a set of prefabricated meanings embedded in culture through the medium of language. In our world, we become conscious of meanings, which we receive through a cultural originator as part of a transcendental intersubjectivity. Meaning is formed through the experiences and (implicit) knowledge that an individual acquires in various social contexts. This process is constitutional: the individual develops *meaning* by being in action in a specific sociocultural context. Hence the "outer" world becomes real, namely *meaningful* — through an individual's reflection and interpretation of a situation. From a phenomenological point of view, "meaning is formed in the interaction of experiencing and something that functions as a symbol" (Gendlin, 1997, p. 8). This symbolization often takes a verbal form, but can be expressed by other means, such as painting, drama, dance, or writing. In sport we use words like *flow, lightness in movement,* and *excitement* to describe our experiences and thoughts about an activity in which we are involved (Berger, Pargman, & Weinberg, 2002; Stelter, 2000). By highlighting and giving space to experiential meaning, the coach can establish a *contextual ground* for individuals as embodied and settled in the cultural context of concrete situation.

In *social constructionism* meaning is negotiated between the participants in the specific social setting. Gergen (1994) wrote: "There is an alternative way of approaching the problem of social meaning: removing the individual as the starting point opens a range of promising possibilities. Rather than commence with individual subjectivity and work deductively towards an account of human understanding through language, we may begin our analysis at the level of the *human relationship* as it generates both language and understanding" (p. 263).

Ideally, all participants realize that their position and opinion is only one of many possibilities, only one worldview. Hence, open-mindedness and curiosity about whether others see the world in different ways or how they regard a specific task is extremely helpful in the negotiation process or social discourse. The views of other persons should inspire an individual's personal or professional growth. This would enable all members of a social group or organization to grow and mature in their perception of the world and ideally come to a form of agreement or acknowledgment of differences.

In a community of practice such as a sports team, where all participants take part in the process of meaning making, we observe that social negotiation often unfolds through personal accounts and narratives. Narratives tie in with the concrete context and to actions and events that the person either is or has been part of and that are often related to other people (friends or opponents, colleagues, team members, etc.). A narrative is formed with a specific "plot" that gives the narrative coherence in terms of action and meaning and provides a basic orientation in the form of a guiding clue in the story (Polkinghorne, 1988). Encouraging and uplifting narratives strengthen cooperation in the community of practice. For example, an uplifting narrative in a sports team could be shaped around the good experiences of playing together and enjoying each other's company despite the defeat in the last game. On the other hand, narratives myths can be created about certain members of the group or team, and external relations or events. For example, a myth can emerge when a mistake of one player in one specific situation is unfolded as the reason for having lost the whole game. In this way narratives can create a form of reality that comes into existence through the social discourse of the involved parties.[2]

Integrating Meaning Making in Two Streams of Coaching

In the previous section I presented the concept of meaning as central for the two lines of thought I am going to integrate in my applied approach to coaching. The importance of meaning making is also central for one grand old man of American psychology, Jerome Bruner (1990): "Given that psychology is so immersed in culture, it must be organised around those meaning making and meaning-using processes that connect man to culture" (p. 12). In this process of meaning making the two streams, one from phenomenology and the other from social constructionism, will be integrated. These two streams of meaning making will be presented in the following two sections.

Individual Experiences and Meaning Making

In the first stream, the focus of coaching intervention is on *individual experience and personal meaning making*. Together with the coach, coachees strive to understand their subjective reality or a subjective experience of the culture they live in. Their focus is on the implicit and embodied dimensions of their doing. As the starting point of the conversation, the coachees study detailed descriptions of certain activities and explore their felt sense (Gendlin, 1997; Stelter, 2000) at the time in order to reach a deeper understanding of their thoughts, feelings, and behaviors. Gendlin (1997) as one of the leading practitioner-researchers in this field defined the felt sense as a form of inner aura or physical feeling about a specific situation, event, or person. But this felt sense is often pre-reflective, namely, preconscious and not verbalized. The coach's sensitive questioning helps the coachees get in touch with these implicit, embodied, and pre-reflective dimensions of their doing. I will discuss strategies of sensitive questioning in a later section of this chapter. For now, I will simply say that this form of experience-based inquiry remains a challenge, because it is difficult to find words for experiences that are basically personal and embodied. Stevens (2000) mentioned that it depends on "how articulate, how skilled and expressive" (p. 115) people are to speak about their experiences. Another challenge for Stevens is "that the words used relate to a diffuse network of semantic assemblies both for the speaker and the listener" (p. 115), which means both speaker and listener have to create their universe of meaning together.

From a narrative perspective, White (2007) spoke about revisiting the absent but implicit, thereby describing the importance of personal meaning making. His idea was to relate forgotten experiences and episodes and join them with a storyline that is more uplifting than the training story the coach might have presented in the beginning of the session. By revisiting the absent but implicit reality, for example, by remembering the importance of a teacher in one's first school years, the coachee has a chance to retell and enrich her story on the basis of her cultural background and life history. This might allow her to modify story plots and couple events in a new way, thus leading to the creation of a more uplifting storyline and a positive, encouraging reality.

Co-creation of Meaning: Developing Alternative Stories

In the second dimension of meaning making — which is integrated with the first in the actual coaching conversation — the focus is on the *socially* co-constructed reality. This constructive process takes place in the dialogue between coach and coachee, but more significantly in dialogues in a group of coachees. The dialogues are initiated by the coach through a form of intervention called outsider witnessing — a method that is explicitly highlighted in the case discussed below. Social constructionists suggest that reality is shaped in a process of co-action and social and linguistic discourse. This form of discourse is comprised of collections of statements and other verbal activities which, in a given context, form the basis for developing meaningful linguistic systems. In these discourses, knowledge, understanding, and concepts are shaped in such a way that they find acceptance in the social context and verify the very same context. One of the central aspects of the discourse between coach and coachee or among different coachees is the co-creation of values and meaning: Which values do we find central and meaningful? Why do we do the things we do? Could we do things differently so that our activities would be more fun, more efficient, or more beneficial to our performance? The coach's questions or the contribution of others — if we are in a group context — can enrich the current reality of every participant in the dialogue, thereby making space for new meanings and the unfolding of new and alternative narratives. It is through relating to each other in words and actions that we create meaning and our ever-changing social reality. Gergen (1994) spoke about the communal origins of meaning. In a team context in sports this would mean that all participants co-construct the culture that they are part of at the same time. In this communal process, co-creating narratives and storytelling play a central role. Bruner (2006) highlighted the significance of storytelling as follows: "*The* principal way in which our minds, our 'realities,' get shaped to the patterns of daily cultural life is through the stories we tell, listen to, and read — true or fictional. We 'become' active participants in our culture mainly through the narratives we share in order to 'make sense' of what is happening around us, what has happened, and what *may* happen" (p. 14).

Narratives have the function to structure events and to tie events together in a timeline. That's how stories appear coherent and how life makes sense to us; stories are the source of meaning making. Narratives establish temporal coherence and shape how events, actions, other persons, and ourselves can be experienced and perceived as sensible and meaningful. The plot of every story is the basis for the development of an inner structure and drama (see also Sarbin, 1986, one of the early psychologists with a narrative orientation). By telling stories and listening to them, our lives become meaningful. Carr (1986) put it like this: "Lives are told in being lived and lived in being told" (p. 61).

Integrating the Experiential and Relational in Narrative

Narrative psychology can be understood as a further development of the social constructionist perspective — a new approach that integrates the experiential and subjective with the relational and discursive dimension and an objective I also strive for in the present contribution. Crossley (2003) wrote: "I felt there was a need for a different kind of psychology—one which retained the ability of appreciating the linguistic and discursive structuring of 'self' and 'experience,' but one which also maintained a sense of the essentially personal, coherent and 'real' nature of individual subjectivity" (p. 289).

Crossley (2003) built on Carr's ideas: "The whole point of Carr's argument is that the necessity of achieving a sense of structure and order in the course of our everyday activities stems not from an intentional act, but from our practical (obviously embodied and affective) orientation within the world. . . . The whole process of narration and the implicit orientation towards narrative structure operates to transform a person's physical, emotional and social world" (pp. 296–297).

Researchers who share this position of integrating the embodied-experiential with the relational-discursive concept are Shotter and Lannammann (2002), Stam (1990), and Sampson (1996). They all see the possibility of linking phenomenological with social constructionist thinking by establishing a narrative position. They are far from taking a naturalistic standpoint by, for example, regarding personality as anchored in more or less stable traits. Instead, they strive toward a culturally oriented psychology, where experiences and emotions are the basis for forming narratives shaping the personal and communal values of self and others. As Bruner (1990) stated "[Values] become incorporated in one's self identity and, at the same time, they locate one in a culture" (p. 29). Telling stories to one another and developing and sharing narratives and accounts, either in a coach-coachee relationship or in a group setting, is fundamental for the process of social meaning making; the grounding of an individual in a cultural context is always based on specific values and meanings. The central position of meanings and values is illustrated in the figure below.

In a traditional sport psychological intervention, one of the main objectives of mental training is goal setting with a focus on specific results. The purpose and meaning of one's sport involvement are not in focus. This narrow concentration on goals might work in an elite sport setting. However, for the development of the whole person, it is important to also focus on purpose and meanings in sport involvement. In exercise and all forms of sport practice, an exclusive focus

Meaning & Values
central in the concept of intentionality

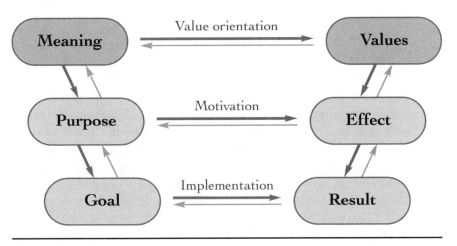

Figure 2. Meanings and values are central to the concept of intentionality.

on physical goals (losing weight, feeling more fit, getting in better shape) would be insufficient to keep sport participants engaged in their activity. Here, a stronger focus on personal and social meanings is essential for lifelong motivation to engage in sport and physical activity, which is especially highlighted by Berger et al. (2002).[3] These personal and social meanings are often embedded in narratives and personal accounts that are formed by the individual or in a group of participants. The teacher, instructor, or coach has a special responsibility to invite the participants to verbalize personal experiences and stories drawn from their sport involvement.

Coaching and Meaning Making: Application to Practice

In the previous section I presented theoretical evidence for my applied work. In the this section I will discuss some general ideas for a coaching practice based on the two streams of meaning making described above. These two streams lead to two basic strategies for coaching, strategies that are not separated in vivo, but are integrated in the flow of the coaching dialogue. The separation exists only for analytical reasons. The organization of my presentation follows that used in the previous section. In an applied perspective, coaching and meaning making represent different approaches to learning. Here I expand my definition of coaching to include learning — a central concept of applied coaching, where the coach is a participant and facilitator of the coachees' learning processes.

Coaching, Individual Meaning Making, and Aesthetic Learning

In this first strategy for coaching, the focus is on the experiential dimension of coaching, in which *aesthetic learning* is the central path for the coachees' developmental process. In the following I will present a number of procedures, which combine to form the constituents of the *aesthetic* or *sensual* focus of the coaching process. These procedures likewise enable the coachee(s) to describe experiential, embodied aspects of situations and events, which have become topics during the coaching process.

The present moment

The first premise of coaching for individual meaning making is the orientation toward the present moment, the here-and-now of the situation. To facilitate the sense of being in the moment, it is important to "*clear the space*" by, for example, taking a deep breath and mentally settling oneself in the moment. The experience enacted in the present moment gives rise to both Erlebnis (immanent lived experience) and Erfahrung (experiential apprehension of self and situation). This concept is also highlighted by Stern (2004), who stressed the present moment as the starting point for any developmental process in psychotherapy and everyday life.

Bracketing/epoché

The coach strives towards a nonjudgmental stance and as far as possible, to help the coachees bracket all presuppositions. This nonjudgmental position helps generate new sensibilities of the situation, new in the sense that coachees become aware of the implicit and experiential dimensions of their doings. Coachees are encouraged to stay on the "pure" level of experience, free of evaluation or judgment. In phenomenology, the term *epoché* is used to describe this state. Edmund Husserl (1985), the founder of phenomenology, saw epoché or the method of phenomenological reduction as the "basic method to a pure psychology" (p. 201). In epoché, the individual attempts to grasp the pure subjectiveness of the world — the individual's world in itself. Similar attempts can be seen in mindfulness — defined as the embodied and intentional effort of "paying attention in a particular way, on purpose, in the present moment, and non-judgmentally" (Kabat-Zinn, 1994, p. 4).

Descriptive questioning

The coach tries to phrase questions in a way that the coachee is able to respond to by presenting "pure" descriptions. The focus is on aesthetic dimensions of thoughts and feeling, on a concretely based descriptive exploration of the coachee's worldview. It is important to accept description without any focus on explanation. The coachee is encouraged to use language that refers directly to bodily experiences and metaphorical and visual language that is rich in imagery. The focus is on the "what" and "how" and not on the "why." If the coachee makes an abstract statement, such as "I am confused," the coach could ask, "How does that feel?" Such questions encourage the coachee to return to a creative and embodied description of personal experiences. Through descriptive questioning the coachee is guided to stay in the sensuous mode and does not start to move away from experiencing the concrete situation by moving on to further reflections.

Horizontalization

This method is inspired by Spinelli (in press), who suggested horizontalization "to avoid placing any unsubstantiated hierarchies of significance or importance upon the [coachee]'s statements of experience, and instead to treat each as having initially equal value." With this perspective in mind, the coach keeps the coachee in the descriptive-explorative, experiential position, where everything said appears novel to both (see also Ihde, 1977).

Connecting experiences to thoughts, emotions, and actions

The dialogue around the experiential descriptions generated by asking questions about feelings or sense of specific situations is expanded by also asking about thoughts, emotions, and actions. The idea is to balance these four dimensions: bodily experiences generate specific emotions and thoughts; they can also refer to actions in the past or lead to actions in the future. Graphically, this process of connecting experiences to thoughts, emotions, and actions is presented in the figure below.

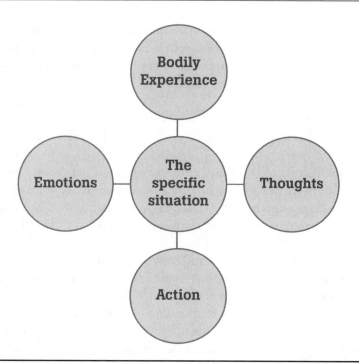

Figure 3. Balancing questions about bodily experience, emotions, thoughts and actions related to a specific situation.

Coaching, Social Meaning Making, and Relational, Cultural Learning

In this second strategy for coaching, the focus is on the cultural dimension of coaching. We take a closer look at how the coach can facilitate the process of social meaning making, a process that goes beyond the individual, experiential perspective. Social meaning making always involves several people, the minimum being the dyad of coach and coachee or a group or team led by a coach. Social meaning is developed by interacting with others in a form of negotiation that generates a social reality experienced as meaningful by the involved parties (Bruner, 1990). As this reality is constructed in socially coordinated processes, it will differ, depending upon the context (e.g., a sports team, in the family, or in the company of friends). Pearce and Cronen (1980) described this social interrelatedness with the term *coordinated management of meaning* (CMM). We co-create a life or team practice with the people we know. As described earlier, a central strategy in this process of meaning making is the narrative approach.

With inspiration from White (1990, 2007), a leading narrative therapist and counselor from Australia, I will outline ideas that are central for relational and cultural learning, both in the dyad of coach and coachee and in teams or groups of cooperating sport participants/ athletes. The idea is to (1) achieve a better understanding of the group culture in which coachees are participating, (2) enhance co-operation, and (3) enrich the coachees' understanding of their own doing through sharing with each other the diversity of being involved in practice .

Coach and coachee(s) are co-creators and co-authors of a positive, inspiring story about situations and events they have been or are a part of. An appreciation of the uplifting aspects of situations and events is the starting point of a narrative that is formed between coach and coachee or between all participants of a group coaching dialogue. Their practice will be strengthened by discourses that encourage good practice, collaboration, and commitment. In teams or groups of sport participants, everyone can contribute to improving the working culture, team spirit, and cohesion — concepts that describe the common practice and discourse toward which the team or groups are working.

In times of adversity or personal struggle, a single participant or any member of a team or group can be a co-author of alternative and uplifting stories about herself or himself, someone else, or the team/ group. These stories can be created by finding positive exceptions to the present situation. Some events can be viewed from different perspectives and thus be seen in an inspiring light. There is always something outside the difficult and problematic story — a stepping stone from where the new story can take its start.

Reality is not a fact, and that is why it always allows for several stories. Variations in stories can be enriching for individuals, a team, or a group of athletes/participants being coached. Stories can reveal a wealth and variety of opinions and understandings of the common practice. Different viewpoints can enrich the stories, the plot may be developed, and the stories may acquire an uplifting storyline. In teams of athletes, the members' sense of one another will grow, and in time the individual stories will become a part of the team's common narration about itself.

In team sports, teams develop faster and better if a problem is regarded as a *challenge*, rather than singling out individuals in the team and treating them as the *problem*. It is a common misconception to believe that problems in a team can be solved by making someone a scapegoat or by labeling individuals and describing their personal characteristics as "unfortunate" or "strange." Labeling a situation as a problem indicates that a practice or collaboration has become "unbalanced," and this can be illustrated by a conflict that has reached a deadlock. A new dialogic and affirmative strategy to resolve conflicts is — as mentioned earlier — appreciative inquiry, where the goal is to find positive elements in a situation. For example, this is done by creating concrete ideas about what is possible and then letting the participants express their hopes and wishes for an optimal solution of the conflict (Cooperrider & Sekerka, 2003). The idea is to move the spotlight away from the problem and toward the development of a new reality, grounded in the participants' visions and desire to collaborate and find a common practice.

Case of a Coaching Intervention

In this section I will present a case in which I have been involved as a sport psychological consultant. The case is an ideal-typical example[4] of a new way of understanding coaching dialogues, where the sociocultural dimension receives special attention and where I especially use an *experiential focus* in the beginning of the session and continue by introducing *outsider witnessing* to generate a new understanding and *storyline* for the participants involved in the session.

In my function as a professor of sport psychology with further education in applied psychology I was contacted by the chairwoman of a table tennis club who was worried about the negative influence of sport competition on the self-esteem and identity development of four of her adolescent players. In a long telephone conversation she described them — three boys and one girl, all between 13 and 14 years of age — as follows: "Three of the children are very talented, and one has the potential to be a good player but is very insecure. They all play well in training and in training contests. But when they compete with players whom they regard as more competent and self-confident, they become very nervous and often lose. I know that a lot is happening in their everyday lives; they are in a period where peers and social recognition are very important. They are developing their identities and seek social acceptance and acknowledgment. They do not like having their personalities challenged, and I'm afraid that they will give up playing because of the pressure they often feel in competition. Both our coach and I find it very difficult to reach the children on a personal level. I hope that your expertise both as a researcher and practitioner might be a good starting point to achieve closer contact with them and hopefully develop skills to handle competition and help them to grow as individuals."

I was impressed by the level of reflection of this chairwoman; maybe my prejudice about the nature of club chairpersons increased my surprise. I spontaneously expressed my highest appreciation of her way of tackling the situation. Furthermore I acknowledged her analysis: children in this age group are generally very insecure about themselves and about their social position in a group of peers. In addition, the four were in a very critical age period where a lot of adolescents drop out of sport, often because they lose motivation or feel treated badly by coaches who seem to focus only on success and achievement and do not have an eye for the social needs of their athletes. I asked her how she would like me to handle the situation."Oh, I don't know precisely," she responded. "I just think it would be great if they could go to a psychologist. Later on I will share your work with the coach in charge. The biggest problem for me is that we do not have very much money in our budget to pay you."

"I have a solution for that," was my spontaneous but sincere answer. "Send them all together; I would like to speak with them all at once. I believe that they can learn from listening to each other and by sharing something from their lives, some personal thoughts and feelings. These dialogues might help them grow together and gain qualities they will be able to use later, both in their training and in competition." "That sounds like a brilliant idea," she said. "I can drive them all to your office some day in the afternoon after they have finished school. I hope we can make an appointment right away. Perhaps I can speak with you after you have talked to them — also with regard to possible consequences for our future training."

We made an appointment and formulated a plan. I felt that something valuable would come out of it. Furthermore, I was convinced that the chairwoman and the young athletes' club coach cooperated in a sensible and reliable manner. The club coach was informed about her initiative, and I felt safe and confident about any conclusions they might draw for their work with the intended young athletes. I finished by informing her about my professional confidentiality, which would prevent me from talking about what the athletes shared with me.

The Intervention

In the following I will describe incidents from the first session with the four young athletes. My ambition for the session was that the kids learn to listen to each other, relate to each other's stories, be receptive to new aspects of their accounts, and form a more uplifting story.

After having picked up the children from school, the chairwoman entered my office with the girl and three boys in tow. The kids seemed a bit shy. I offered them chairs and expressed my appreciation of their courage in coming. The chairwoman left, saying that she would have a look around and come back in an hour. The children and I introduced ourselves and I described my ideas for our conversation, which was to be based on mutual trust and open-mindedness toward whatever anyone wished to contribute.

I turned toward the girl — let's call her Susie — asking what had brought her here. She talked about situations from training and how she enjoyed playing table tennis. My asking about her *experience* helped the athlete get truly in touch with her personal values and feelings about her sport. "But," she said,

> when it comes to competition, everything seems to be different, especially when my opponent is a good player. I lose my courage, my sense for the game. I start to think about what will happen if I lose, what the others will think. And then sometimes I lose touch with the situation and forget myself. My thoughts start to dominate: What will I tell the others, if I lose? If my thoughts take over, I'm lost — that's for sure. I do not enjoy the game anymore and most often I lose it.

The three boys had listened very attentively. Then I asked Peter: "How does that resonate with something in your own life? What came into your mind while you listened?" Peter took a deep breath. "I know exactly what Susie is talking about!" And he started to tell his story and how he could feel the difference between training and competition. After Peter's account I asked Tom and Philip to talk to each other (as outsider witnesses to the stories told by Susie and Peter), looking at neither me nor the other two. I asked the boys to speak about what impact the stories of Susie and Peter had on them, how these stories touched their own feelings and thoughts. While Susie and Peter listened, Tom and Philip talked about how their own stories were very similar to what they had heard. They were really amazed at Susie's and Peter's accounts. Tom said: "I had no idea that we all felt the same; knowing that will really help me. I won't feel so alone with my anxiety and tension in competition. Now I recognize that I have the others' backing and they are very familiar with my feelings."

After Tom and Philip's conversation, I asked the other two to comment on what they had heard and how they felt about it. They had both enjoyed listening and felt relieved. I tried to conclude the conversation by asking them how they would use this new knowledge in their future training and competitions. They all agreed to be more proactive by sharing their feelings and talking with their coach about how they could better handle their anxiety.

I was more than touched by the stories of these four kids and by their courage and willingness to share their innermost feelings. Their sharing was the starting point for a new story — co-created by the four of them — a story with a new plot: sharing feelings of tension and anxiety helps us to overcome them. It is part of our life and of many young people's lives: we are all on our way to finding ourselves. In our future training and when working together we will be able to create something different for ourselves, something that will help us enjoy our sport even more, in a new way of cooperating.

How Can a Coach Take Part in the Process of Developing Enriched or Alternative Stories?

Storytelling is a form of art. Curiosity, trust, and interest in each other's lives and worldviews are important prerequisites for the unfolding of a reflective space for all participants and for an atmosphere of development and growth. In the following I will present a number of key strategies and give some examples either by returning to the presented case or by sketching some examples from other sport situations. These key strategies may help to strengthen storytelling and can result in an uplifting, progressive storyline.

Focus on Positive Exceptions

Although we tend to focus on things that do not work, cause trouble, or create conflict, there are always elements in situations that can be defined as positive. For example, if two athletes come to you, the coach, complaining that they cannot work together because they are always fighting, your question to them could be: "Can you remember a situation where you actually worked together in a good and constructive way?"

Focus on Elements of Success

This strategy is similar to the one described above. Here the focus is on elements of success. So even if you have lost the game, or the exercise has been hard and exhausting, there might be elements of success in the game. For example, by asking the players about specific successes the team coach would be able to hear stories about some brilliant combinations and the fun of playing together. In an exercise setting the participants might tell stories of how they felt satisfied by doing the training together with a friend and by having mastered many small challenges of the different exercises through supporting each other.

Connect Stories with an Experiential and Embodied Implicit

Events and situations hide implicit dimensions that need to be unfolded. These hidden elements are somehow absent, but if we learn to identify and describe them, we might find a key to enriching our stories and eventually our lives. By talking about a specific current situation the participant might remember an uplifting moment from the past that can be connected to the current situation and by that enrich the story about a current event or situation. For example, by asking the boys about how they experienced listening to Susie's story, I tried to help them to unfold a new and somehow alternative story about the value of experiencing things in a similar way. From a story of feeling isolated we developed a story of cooperation and mutual support.

Enrich Stories by Relating Them to Values and Questions of Identity

The art of storytelling is to make stories richer, to develop a detailed plot that is clear and explicit. It is useful to ask questions about values that are based on concrete and embodied experiences and that evoke events, as well as questions dealing with identity and personal and social meaning. Let's look back at the case again. By asking them questions about personal values and meaning, I tried to help the kids to focus on the specific value of talking together about what happens with them in specific situations, for example, in competition. A renewed reflection on critical moments of their performance can help them to reshape their personal and social identity. By relating to their own values and identity issues, we were able to provide a keystone for enriching the story.

Link Events to Each Other

Stories always unfold by linking events. Stories unfold in a new way if we link certain events in a way not done earlier. And suddenly the storytellers are caught by surprise, because their actions suddenly can be seen and understood in a new and different light. In the presented case I supported the kids to link their own experience to the experience of others and by that helped them to see their experience of isolation in a totally different light.

Build Bridges between Stories and Imagined Future Actions

On the basis of stories that are further developed or on the basis of "alternative" or "new" stories, the participants become better equipped to take action on matters they have reflected and talked about. Furthermore, the values and meanings of participants/ coachees that emerged from their storytelling grow vivid and provide motivation. The focus turns to purposes and goals anchored in values based on personal and social meaning making. The imagined future in our case was about sharing a common future, where they can talk about difficulties in specific performance situations and thereby develop as a team.

Outsider Witnessing

Michael White developed a strategy to help us share our stories and experience the impact of other persons' stories. White (2007, p. 165) spoke about *definitional ceremonies* that provide "a context for rich story development." Through *outsider witnessing* we acknowledge the lives of others instead of merely judging or evaluating them, as is so typical in our culture. By listening to the stories of others, these witnesses are invited to focus on how stories resonate with events and experience in their own lives. Having someone witness the steps a person is taking in his or her life and having these acknowledged can make a real difference. It can enable people to feel connected to others, reduce their isolation and sense of worry, and strengthen the "alternative stories" being developed in the coaching session. By asking the three boys about how Susie's introductory story resonated with their own experience, the kids developed an understanding about challenging episodes in competition that helped them all to move on.

Conclusion and Future Directions

The provided case exemplified that sharing experiences and stories can create something new — a new culture of cooperation. The key to understanding this approach is to listen to others and not to judge them, to share with them how other stories are connected to one's own, how they might be different, how I might be touched by what I have heard, and how we can develop as communities by sustaining each other through our stories.

The narrative coaching approach presented in this chapter can be used in many areas of sport and exercise. We can develop our sport psychological consultation by including personal, social, and cultural differences to enrich our cooperation, by being open-minded to what others can give to me and what I can give to others.

A new future area for this narrative coaching approach could be in supporting people who have difficulty remaining involved in exercise. All participants must be regarded as experts in their own life. We instructors, teachers, and consultants should not act as experts, but as coaches who listen to the participants, who take them seriously, and who guide them toward self-development. The first step could be to introduce an exercise program with a strong focus on social interaction — for example, by introducing a variety of different games. In games and in shared activities in a community of practice, culture can unfold. It's not enough to put people with low motivation on a treadmill and let them exercise for 20 minutes. It is important for participants to have opportunities to share experiences, challenges, and successes. A coaching intervention that helps participants acquire an understanding of health and well-being, and to develop values and opinions about sport and exercise, might be a way forward. They must become experts in their own lives. We have to help them to build social capital through sport and exercise — like in the case of the four kids who took their first steps toward greater cooperation. The French sociologist Pierre Bourdieu (1985) defined social capital as "the aggregate of the actual or potential resources which are linked to possession of a durable network of more or less institutionalized relationships of mutual acquaintance or recognition" (p. 248). These durable networks are the basis for communal living, which is the central premise for human development and well-being, no matter whether we intend to help athletes to perform better or exercisers to enjoy their physical activities and stay motivated and involved in them. The overarching focus of narrative coaching as presented in this chapter is on shaping uplifting stories about experiences and activities athletes or exercises are able to share in their concrete community of practice. These joint actions might be a way to build up local cultures in different sport and exercise settings.

References

Beck, U. (1992). *Risk society: Towards a new modernity*. London: Sage.

Berger, P., & Luckmann, T. (1966). *The social construction of reality*. New York: Doubleday/Anchor.

Berger, B. G., Pargman, D., & Weinberg, R. S. (2002). *Foundations of exercise psychology*. Morgantown, WV: Fitness Information Technology.

Bourdieu, P. (1985). The forms of capital. In J. G. Richardson (Ed.), *Handbook of theory and research for the sociology of education* (pp. 241–258). New York: Greenwood.

Bruner, J. (1990). *Acts of meaning*. Cambridge: MA: Harvard University Press.

Bruner, J. (2006). Culture, mind, and narrative. In J. Bruner, C. Fleischer Feldmann, M. Hermansen, & J. Molin (Eds.), *Narrative, learning and culture* (pp. 13–24). Copenhagen: Copenhagen Business School.

Carr, D. (1986). *Time, narrative and history*. Bloomington: Indiana University Press.

Cavanagh, M., Grant, A. M., & Kemp, T. (Eds.) (2005). *Evidence-based coaching*, Vol. 1: *Theory, research and practice from the behavioural sciences*. Bowen Hills: Australian Academic Press.

Cooperrider, D. L, & Sekerka, L. E. (2003). Elevation of inquiry into appreciable world — toward a theory of positive organizational change. In K. Comeron, J. Dutton, & R. Quimm (Eds.), *Positive organizational scholarship*. San Francisco: Berrett-Kohler.

Crossley, M. L. (2003). Formulating narrative psychology: The limitations of contemporary social constructionism. *Narrative Inquiry, 13*, 287–300.

Foucault, M. (1972). *The archaeology of knowledge and the discourse on language*. New York: Pantheon.

Gendlin, E. T. (1997). *Experiencing and the creation of meaning*. Evanston: Northwestern University Press (original from 1962).

Gergen, K. J. (1994). *Realities and relationships—soundings in social construction*. Cambridge, MA: Harvard University Press.

Giddens, A. (1991). *Modernity and self-identity—self and society in late modern age*. Oxford: Polity.

Husserl, E. (1950). Konstitution der Intersubjektivität. In E. Husserl (Ed.), *Gesammelte Werke*. Bd. 1: *Cartesianische Meditationen und Pariser Vorträge* (pp. 121–163). Den Haag: Martinus Nijhoff.

Husserl, E. (1985). Encyclopaedia Britannica. In E. Husserl (Ed.), *Die phänomenologische Methode I* (pp. 196–206). Stuttgart: Reclam.

Ihde, D. (1977). *Experimental phenomenology: An introduction*. New York: Putnam's Sons.

Kabat-Zinn, J. (1994). *Wherever you go, there you are: Mindfulness meditation in everyday life*. New York: Hyperion.

Martens, R. (1997). *Successful coaching* (2nd ed.). Champaign, IL: Human Kinetics.

Merleau-Ponty, M. (1962). *Phenomenology of perception*. London: Routledge & Kegan Paul.

Nitsch, J. R. (1986). Zur handlungstheoretischen Grundlegung der Sportpsychologie. In H. Gabler, J. R. Nitsch, & R. Singer (Eds.), *Einführung in die Sportpsychologie*, Teil 1: *Grundthemen* (pp. 188–270). Schorndorf: Hofmann.

Palmer, S., & Whybrow, A. (2007). *Handbook of coaching psychology*. London: Routledge.

Pearce, W. B., & Cronen, V. (1980). *Communication, action and meaning*. New York: Praeger.

Polkinghorne, D. P. (1988). *Narrative knowing and the human sciences*. Albany: State University of New York Press.

Sabrin, T. R. (Ed.) (1986). *Narrative psychology: The storied nature of human conduct*. New York: Praeger.

Sampson, E. E. (1996). Establishing embodiment in psychology. *Theory Psychology, 6*, 601–624.

Schinke, R. J., Hanrahan, S. J., Peltier, D.; Michel. G., Danielson, R., Pickard, P., Pheasant, C., Enosse, L.& Peltier, M. (2007). The pre-competition and competition practices of Canadian aboriginal elite athletes. *Journal of Clinical Sport Psychology, 1*, 147–165.

Shotter, J., & Lannammann, J. W. (2002). The situation of social constructionism: Its "imprisonment" within the ritual of theory-criticism-and-debate. *Theory & Psychology, 12*, 577–609.

Spinelli, E. (in press). Existential coaching. In E. Cox, T. Bachkirova, & D. Clutterbuck (Eds.), *Sage handbook of coaching and mentoring*. London: Sage.

Stam, H. J. (1990). Rebuilding the ship at the sea: The historical and theoretical problems of constructionist epistemologies in psychology. *Canadian Psychology, 31*, 239–253.

Stelter, R. (1998). The body, self and identity. Personal and social constructions of the self through sport and movement (review article). *European Yearbook of Sport Psychology, 2*, 1–32.

Stelter, R. (2000). The transformation of body experience into language. *Journal of Phenomenological Psychology, 31*, 63–77.

Stelter, R. (Ed.) (2002). *Coaching — læring-og udvikling* [Coaching — learning and development]. Københaven: Psykologisk Forlag.

Stelter, R. (2007). Coaching: A process of personal and social meaning making. *International Coaching Psychology Review, 2*, 191–201.

Stelter, R. (2008). Exploring body-anchored and experience-based learning in a community of practice. In T. S. S. Schilhab, M. Juelskjær, & T. Moser (Eds.), *The learning body* (pp. 111–129). Copenhagen: Danish University School of Education Press.

Stern, D. N. (2004). *The present moment in psychotherapy and everyday life*. New York: Norton.

Stevens, R. (2000). Phenomenological approaches to the study of conscious awareness. In M. Velmans (Ed.), *Investigating phenomenal consciousness* (pp. 99–120). Amsterdam: John Benjamins.

Stober, D. R., & Grant, A. M. (Eds.). (2006). *Evidence based coaching handbook*. Hoboken, NJ: Wiley.

Stober, D. R., & Parry, C. (2005). Current challenges and future directions in coaching research. In M. Cavanagh, A. M. Grant, & T. Kemp (Eds.), *Evidence-based coaching, Vol. 1: Theory, research and practice from the behavioural sciences* (pp. 13–20). Bowen Hills: Australian Academic Press.

Van der Haar, D., & Hosking, D. M. (2004. Evaluating appreciative inquiry: A relational constructionist perspective. *Human Relations, 57*, 1017–1036.

Vealey, R. S. (2005). *Coaching on the edge*. Morgantown, WV: Fitness Information Technology.

White, M. (1990). *Reflections on narrative practice—essays and interviews*. Adelaide: Dulwich Centre Publications.

White, M. (2007). *Maps of narrative practice*. New York: Norton.

Notes

1. The term *coachee* is a parallel term to *interviewee* and is gaining traction in the coaching psychology literature. See: Palmer and Whybrow (2007) and http://www.societyforcoachingpsychology.net/page_1207144809625.html.

2. But we also have to be aware of power structures and boundaries, as well as opportunities that may influence our ability to participate freely in dialogues (Foucault, 1972). There are organizations and social contexts where it is impossible to negotiate because of the dominance of powerful stakeholders; for example, some coaches and trainers do not tolerate positions other than their own. Furthermore, it can be very dangerous, for example, for a coach or trainer to suggest standard solutions for specific situations, because then only his or her view of the situation seems to count.

3. Berger et al. (2002) have a whole chapter on "Personal meaning in physical activity" in their handbook *Foundations of Exercise Psychology*.

4. "Ideal-typical" means that there are several modifications possible. For example, sports coaches/trainer/teacher can use elements of my approach in small doses in their training or teaching.

15

PSYCHOLOGY OF EXTREME SPORTS

Holly Thorpe

CHAPTER SUMMARY

In this chapter I examine the current state of research on the psychology of extreme sports and offer some suggestions for advancing our understanding in this exciting new field of research and practice. More specifically, this chapter consists of three main parts. The first provides a critical overview of the existing psychological research on extreme sports. Despite offering some interesting psychological insights into the experiences of extreme sports participants, many studies reinforce stereotypes of extreme sports as dangerous activities enjoyed mostly by daredevil, risk-taking, and adrenaline-seeking youths; gloss over complicated cultural dynamics and complex political histories; and present participants as a homogenous group with similar personality types, motives, and experiences. In the second part, I argue that, to understand the behavior of extreme sports participants, sport psychologists need to contextualize their behavior within the larger social, cultural, and political structures in which they were produced. I then offer ethnography as a potentially fruitful research strategy for investigating the dynamic interplay of individual and social factors in extreme sports. In the third part, I describe my ongoing ethnographic research into the sociopsychological experiences of snowboarders and, to further illustrate the potential of this approach, offer a selection of insights from my research on the group dynamics and cultural hierarchies inherent in contemporary snowboarding culture. Lastly, I offer a brief conclusion and consider future directions for research on the psychology of extreme sports.

The Psychology of Extreme Sports

In the 1990s, some U.S. corporations grouped a number of formerly marginal, youth-dominated activities, such as skateboarding, BMX (bicycle motocross) riding, and BASE (building, antenna, span, Earth) jumping, under a new label: "extreme" sports. Participants in these sports *allegedly* sought risks, thrills, and new skills and subscribed to an "outsider identity relative to the organized sports establishment" (Kusz, 2007, p. 359). Over the past decade extreme sports have grown rapidly in many Western, and even some Eastern (e.g., China, Japan, South Korea), countries (see Booth & Thorpe, 2007; Thorpe, 2008). In 2003, for example, 5 of the top 10 most popular sports in the United States were extreme sports, with inline skating ranked first, skateboarding second, snowboarding fourth, and wakeboarding ninth (Survey Says, 2005). As extreme sports become increasingly popularized and incorporated into the mainstream, and adopt many of the trappings of traditional modern sports — corporate sponsorship, large prize monies, rationalized systems of rules, hierarchical and individualistic star systems, win-at-all-costs values, and the creation of heroes and heroines — they are also garnering more attention from sports psychologists (e.g., Boyd & Kim, 2007; Celsi, 1992; Diehm & Armatas, 2004; Feher, Meyers, & Skelly, 1998; Griffith, Hart, Goodling, Kessler, & Whitmire, 2006; Self, Henry, Findley, Reilly, 2007). In much of the existing psychological literature, however, researchers tend to pay scant regard to the distinctive sociocultural and historical contexts of extreme sports. My key argument here is that in-depth knowledge of so-called extreme sports cultures and their development, and the values of cultural members, is an essential prerequisite for those hoping to understand and explain the behaviors of athletes and practitioners in extreme sports (see Thorpe, 2009).

Overview of Research

The mania for risk in extreme pursuits — captured by the "If it can't kill you, it ain't extreme" annual tow-in surfing event — suggests that devotees accept higher levels of danger than participants in established sports (Booth & Thorpe, 2007). Statistical evidence seems to provide confirmation. In climbing and air sports, around 800 participants will die for every 100 million days of participation, compared with 70 for water sports, 30 for horse riding, 16 for rugby, and 5 for boxing (Watson, 1996). Such statistics, combined with the tendency of the mass media to sensationalize the risky and spectacular elements of extreme sports, have prompted the public and journalists to ask: "What drives some to embrace extreme risks, while the rest of us scurry for the safety of the sidelines?" (Handwerk, 2004, ¶ 4). In their attempts to answer such questions, sport psychologists have typically focused on individual motives and dispositions.

Extreme sports are a relatively new phenomenon, yet psychologists have been attempting to explain the experiences of participants in high-risk sports since the late 1960s (e.g., Huberman, 1968; Hymbaugh & Garrett, 1974). Recent studies have focused on various psychological dimensions (e.g., mood, quality of experience, risk perception, disinhibition, goal orientation, flow, self-efficacy, motivation) of an array of so-called extreme sports, including adventure racing (Schneider, Butryn, Furst, & Masuccin, 2007), BASE jumping (Griffith et al., 2006), high-altitude rock climbing (Fave, Bassi, & Massimini, 2003), skateboarding (Boyd & Kim, 2007), skydiving (Celsi, Rose, & Leigh, 1993; Lyng, 1990), snowboarding (Anna, Jan, & Aleksander, 2007), and surfing (Diehm & Armatas, 2004). However, the dominant approach has been to establish a relationship between participation in extreme sports and personality traits (e.g., Goma, 1991; Robinson, 1985). Some have compared personality traits of experimental and control groups as assessed by Zuckerman's Sensation Seeking Scale (SSS) (Breivik, 1996, 1999; Campbell, Tyrrell, & Zingaro, 1993; Cronin, 1991; Diehm & Armatas, 2004; Slanger & Rudestam, 1997). Others have drawn upon Frank Farley's (1986, 1993) series of continuums to measure the degree to which individuals demonstrate various levels of positive and/or negative, and physical and/or cognitive, thrill seeking characteristics (Self et al., 2007). Comparing extreme sports and nonparticipant groups, a number of researchers have revealed extreme sports participants as having a preference for novel, high-risk activities and for high levels of arousal, and thus having Type T and/or Sensation Seeking personalities (see Diehm & Armatas, 2004; Straub, 1982; Wagner & Houlihan, 1994).

In focusing, almost exclusively, on individual dispositions (e.g., Type T, Sensation Seeking), as well as individual behaviors, thoughts, and feelings, sport psychologists have typically drawn upon quantitative methods (e.g., questionnaires, surveys) to gather data, develop and test theories and concepts, and help make statements about human behavior in high-risk and extreme sports more generally. In so doing, however, many of the studies cited above reinforce stereotypes of extreme sports as dangerous activities enjoyed mostly by daredevil, risk-taking, and adrenaline-seeking youths; gloss over complicated cultural dynamics, complex political histories, and national and regional differences; and present participants as a homogenous group with similar personality types, motives, and experiences. To date, few researchers of the psychology of extreme sports have embraced qualitative methods; notable exceptions include Brymer and Oades (2009), Celsi et al. (1993), and Sparkes and Partington (2003).

Too many psychological studies of extreme sports are based on the problematic assumption that extreme sports are indeed more risky than traditional sports. Many activities labeled extreme are actually very safe. Sport journalist Rick Arnett (2006) might cast bungee jumping as "suicide on-a-string," but statistics indicate it is no more dangerous than riding a roller coaster (cited in Booth & Thorpe, 2007, p. 183). Certainly, there is an element of risk involved in all activities labeled extreme, but in most cases risk is a subjective calculation that individuals make in the context of their ability. Moreover, there is no evidence that disciples of extreme have abandoned concerns for safety. On the contrary, many deny accusations that they are risk takers and insist that they are as conscious of safety as participants in established sports. In his oft-cited study of high-risk competitors, including skydivers, racing car drivers, fencers, and aerobatic pilots, Bruce Ogilvie (1974) concluded that they are success oriented and rarely reckless risk takers; their risk taking is calculated, he said (also see Celsi et al., 1993). Similarly, Joe Tomlinson (2004) dismissed notions of extreme disciples as "lunatics seeking a buzz": they all "perform within their limits" (p. 6).

Thus, while advertisers, marketers, and corporate media tout the high-risk nature of extreme sports to serve commercial interests, on closer inspection, high risk per se does not stand out as a characteristic of extreme pursuits. But, if risk is not a defining feature of these sports, what classifies them as extreme? While some versions of so-called extreme sports are not overly dangerous for the majority of participants (e.g., surfing in two-foot waves; snowboarding on a slope of gradual gradient within ski resort boundaries), the term appears to have relevance in at least three distinct ways. First, the countercultural roots and irreverent lifestyle associated with many of these activities have contributed to the general public's perception of these sports and subsequent "extreme" labeling (see, e.g., Appleton, 2005; Booth & Thorpe, 2007; Heino, 2000). Second, in the late 1990s, television and corporate sponsors recognized the huge potential in extreme sporting activities to tap into the young male market, and thus went to great lengths to portray participants as extreme in their perilous approach to their activities and their personas. Third, while the majority of participants engage in these activities in a fairly conservative manner, some variants of these sports (e.g., big mountain snowboarding) are performed in high-risk environments (e.g., gale force winds, subzero temperatures, 60 degree slopes, ice, rocks, slides, avalanches, cliffs, and crevasses), and thus are undeniably extreme (see Booth & Thorpe, 2007). Simply put, while authors of previous studies have offered some important psychological insights into the experiences of extreme sports participants, they have overemphasized risk, overlooked the various styles and techniques within these sports, and ignored the broader contextual and cultural meanings of "extreme."

The lack of attention to context, however, is not unique to psychological research on extreme sports. As Gill (2002) argued in relation to sport more broadly, it seems highly doubtful that we can "fully understand the individual without considering the larger world — the social context" (p. 356). Similarly, Horn (2002) proclaimed that individual behavior cannot be completely understood without an accompanying analysis of "the cultures in which the individual subscribes, the value systems inherent within those cultures, and the degree to which the individual subscribes to or endorses those cultural values" (p. 281). Indeed, scholars from various backgrounds (e.g., identity development, indigenous psychology, feminist psychology, and cultural psychology) also question what Wilkinson (2001) referred to as the "contextual sterility" (p. 20) of traditional psychology. Miles (1996), for example, proclaimed that "psychology's narrow person-centered approach has cut it off from the realities of the inseparable context in which behavior occurs" (p. 143). Phinney (2000) also commented that, in its search for universal principles of human behavior, Western psychology has traditionally "ignored or treated as epiphenomena" cultural and historical considerations (p. 27). While understanding of the cultural context is particularly important for those attempting to explain and/or enhance the experiences of extreme sports athletes and practitioners, it has remained peripheral in studies where researchers continue to focus primarily on individual dispositions.

In contrast to psychological explanations, critical sports sociologists interested in extreme sports have tended to privilege broader social, cultural, economic, and political processes (e.g., commercialization, mediatization, institutionalization) and power relations (e.g., gender, class) within particular historical conjunctures. Drawing largely upon qualitative methods such as ethnography, interviews, and discursive analysis of various media sources (e.g., magazines, websites, videos) and an array of theoretical perspectives (e.g., phenomenology, symbolic interactionism, Pierre Bourdieu's theory of embodiment, Foucauldian theorizing) and concepts (e.g., hegemonic masculinity), researchers adopting such sociological approaches have shed light on various dimensions of a plethora of extreme sports cultures, including adventure racing (Kay & Laberge, 2002), inline skating (Rinehart, 2003), rock climbing (Robinson, 2008), skateboarding (Beal, 1995), sky-diving (Laurendeau, 2006), surfing (Ford & Brown, 2006), snowboarding (Anderson, 1999; Heino, 2000; Humphreys, 1997), and windsurfing (Wheaton & Tomlinson, 1998). Recently, however, some scholars have argued that the emotional, sensual, and aesthetic aspects of individuals' lived experiences are missing from many of the studies cited above (see Evers, 2006; Thorpe & Rinehart, in press).

When studying extreme sports, psychologists have tended to focus on the individual, while sociologists have typically examined processes and dynamics within the broader cultural context. There are, however, notable exceptions. In their attempts to better understand the lived experiences of extreme sports participants, some scholars employ social-psychological approaches that consider both the individual and the broader social, cultural, political, and historical context. In particular, Stephen Lyng (1990) adopted an interesting social-psychological perspective to offer a contextualized explanation of voluntary risk taking. He developed the concept of "edgework" to help illustrate the connections between various aspects of risk-taking behavior and structural characteristics of modern American society at both the individual and structural levels. He offered the concept of edgework in response to the "seemingly irreconcilable nature of studies that focus on the psychological or interactional dimensions of a phenomenon and of those that examine the influence of macro-level social structural factors" (Lyng, 1990, p. 856; also see Laurendeau, 2006; Lyng, 2005). Despite some psychologists adopting alternative methodological and theoretical perspectives and placing real importance on the power of cultural, social, and historical context to elucidate the psychological enterprise and, more specifically, the experiences of extreme sports participants, such approaches tend to remain on the margins of a field dedicated primarily to the development of universal concepts and theories of human behavior.

Understanding Extreme Sports: A Social-psychological Approach

Many contemporary sport psychologists know that both individual characteristics *and* the social situation affect behavior. This premise is, of course, reflected in the basic tenet of social psychology as set forth in Kurt Lewin's (1935) formula $B = f(P, E)$, where behavior is a function of the person and the environment. While sport psychologists are increasingly adopting social-psychological approaches that examine factors in the immediate social environment (e.g., motivational climate, and parental, peer, and coach behavior) that may influence athletes' psychological responses and behaviors, fewer adopt a sociocultural perspective where focus is placed squarely on the "broader social, economic, political and cultural forces that affect people's behavior in sport and physical activity contexts" (Horn, 2002, p. 281; see also Brustad & Ritter-Taylor, 1997; Schinke & Hanrahan, 2009). Moreover, sport psychologists have conspicuously neglected the *dynamic* context in which individuals live and construct their sporting behaviors (Gill, 2000). This is particularly problematic for those seeking to understand, explain, and enhance the experiences of individuals in extreme sports cultures. Rather than being "immutably fixed phenomena, frozen statically at a particular point in history" (Osgerby, 1998, cited in Thorpe, 2006, p. 209), extreme sports cultures are in a constant state of change and flux. Indeed, styles and techniques seem to "mutate rapidly as devotees add twists to established activities, or combine existing sports in ways that sometimes spawn bizarre variations" (Booth & Thorpe, 2007, p. 186).

Extreme sports athletes and practitioners are actively making sense of their social worlds and constructing different meanings in particular social, cultural, political, historical, local, national, and geographical contexts. Thus, rather than looking at the extreme athlete in isolation as a whole, singular, unified individual in the way that orthodox sport psychology has tended to do, we need approaches that can recognize that each individual is a subject "immersed in a particular socio-cultural and historical context" (Ryba & Wright, 2005, p. 204). But, *what* precisely does "taking the broader context more seriously" mean for sport psychologists, and particularly those studying extreme sports? *How* do we develop a multilevel understanding of extreme sports cultures and their development, and the values and experiences of cultural members?

Seeking to provide rich, multilevel understandings of the various contextual factors influencing the experiences of extreme sports athletes requires a unique methodological approach. Here I suggest that drawing upon multiple qualitative methods has the potential to greatly facilitate such a task. More specifically, I believe ethnography offers an important methodological tool for gaining in-depth understandings of the unique cultural contexts within which extreme sports participants live, practice, and perform, as well as the behaviors, values, and experiences of cultural members (see Brustad, 2008; Krane & Baird, 2005; McGannon & Johnson, 2009). In other words, ethnography can help sport psychologists "elucidate the linkages between the macrological and the micrological, between the enduring and structured aspects of social life and the particulars of the everyday" (Herbert, 2000, p. 554) in extreme sports cultures.

Ethnography broadly refers to a unique approach to data collection that involves "the researcher participating—overtly or covertly—in people's daily lives for an extended period, watching what happens, listening to what is said, and/or asking questions through informal and formal interviews, collecting documents and artifacts" (Hammersley & Atkinson, 2007, p. 3). More specifically, ethnography encompasses a variety of different approaches and subtypes (e.g., micro-, macro-, virtual-, auto-, critical-, global-ethnography). Depending on the topic under investigation, the philosophical underpinnings and commitments of the ethnographer (e.g., anthropology, sociology, cultural studies, social geography, social psychology), and resources (e.g., time, finances, cultural access) available to the researcher, ethnography may be practiced at an array of levels—ranging from long-term, depth immersion studies to more fleeting forms of "ethnographic visiting" (Sugden & Tomlinson, 2002)—and adopt different levels of proximity (or distance) in relation to respondents (e.g., insider research), as well as utilize different methodological tools, processes of analysis, and presentation styles. Unfortunately, a detailed discussion of the diversity in perspective and practice of ethnography is beyond the scope of this chapter, and has been done well elsewhere (see, e.g., Hammersley & Atkinson, 2007; Silk, 2005). However, to illustrate how such an approach might be applied, in the following part I offer a brief discussion of the multiple ethnographic methods (e.g., participant-observation, interviews, analysis of cultural sources such as websites, magazines, films) I employed to produce knowledge about snowboarding culture and the sociopsychological experiences of snowboarders. This is, of course, just one of many possible applications of ethnography.

Understanding Snowboarding: An Ethnographic Approach

Contemporary research on sport cultures draws upon a variety of interpretations and uses of ethnography (Silk, 2005). The approach adopted here, however, is unique in a number of ways. First, I employed a theoretically informed approach to ethnography. Rather than waiting until the conclusion of the data-gathering phase before generating concepts or theories from emergent themes, I refined and developed my ethnographic interpretations throughout the research process by engaging the empirical insights in dialogue with key concepts common to many social theoretical approaches (e.g., structure, agency, power, gender, the body and embodiment, culture) (see Thorpe, 2007b, 2008). In so doing, the theoretical concepts helped set out questions and direct me to particular sources, and they also enabled me to organize evidence and shape explanations of snowboarding culture. Throughout this research, however, I continually sought "negative instances or contradictory cases" (Mason, 2002, p. 124) from *all* the sources in order to avoid including only those elements of the snowboarding culture that would substantiate my analyses.

Like many ethnographic studies of sport cultures, this project drew upon multiple sources, including personal observations and experiences, magazines, websites, newspapers, interviews and personal communications, videos, Internet chat rooms, promotional material, television programs, press releases, public documents, reports from snowboarding's administrative bodies, and promotional material from sporting organizations and associated industries. More specifically, the analysis drew upon 80 interviews with 40 snowboarders, 13 instances of fieldwork in 6 countries (the United States, Canada, France, Italy, New Zealand, and Switzerland), and access to 51 websites, 23 videos, and more than 100 magazines from 17 different publishers. "Even the humblest material artifact is," as T. S. Eliot has explained, "an emissary of the culture out of which it comes" (cited in Vamplew, 1998, p. 268). Indeed, cultural sources, such as magazines, films, and websites, play a decisive role in the lives of extreme sports practitioners, by confirming, spreading, and consolidating cultural perceptions. Analysis of such documents facilitated my understanding of snowboarding's cultural complexities at the micro- (e.g., intra-individual emotions and cognitive processes as described in interviews with professional snowboarders), meso- (e.g., interactions between editors and readers; narratives describing the group dynamics at international snowboarding events), and macro- (e.g., discourse analysis of advertisements and photos) levels.

The approach adopted in this study was atypical, however, in that rather than focusing upon a particular site, I adopted a multisited, "global ethnographic" approach with the aim to examine the values, practices, and interactions unique to local snowboarding cultures, as well as regional, national, and global flows of people, objects, value systems, information, and images within and across these places (Burawoy et al., 2000). Attempting to further expand my multilevel contextual understanding of snowboarding culture, I conducted numerous "ethnographic visits" in an array of snowboarding communities in New Zealand, North America (Canada, the United States), and Europe (France, Switzerland, Italy) during the 2004, 2005, 2006, 2007, and 2008 winter seasons. The prolonged nature of this project allowed me to observe cultural change, as well as providing time for reflection on the data gathered and my conceptual interpretations.

During the ethnographic visits, observations were made in natural settings both on and off the snow (including lift lines, chair lifts, resort lodges, snowboard competitions, prize giving events, video premiers, bars, cafes, local hangouts, and snowboard shops). During this fieldwork, I observed, listened, engaged in analysis, and made mental notes, switching from snowboarder to researcher depending on the requirements of the situation.[1] In conjunction with my ethnographic visits, I also conducted semi-structured interviews with 20 female and 20 male snowboarders. Participants ranged from 18 to 56 years of age, and included novice snowboarders, weekend warriors, committed/core boarders, professional snowboarders, an Olympic snowboarder and Olympic judge, snowboarding journalists, photographers, film-makers, magazine editors, snowboard company owners, snowboard shop employees and owners, snowboard instructors and coaches, and event organizers and judges.[2]

Of course, research is a process that occurs through the medium of a person — "the researcher is always and inevitably present in the research" (Stanley & Wise, 1993, cited in Wheaton, 2002, p. 246). In contrast to the "detached" position too often adopted by traditional psychologists located within positivist paradigms, ethnography demands greater researcher reflexivity before, during, and after fieldwork (Davies, 1999; McGannon & Johnson, 2009; Van Maanen, 1995). Researchers conducting ethnography must regularly reflect upon how their gender, sexuality, age, race, ethnicity, nationality, and previous lived experiences might be influencing their approach to the topic (e.g., research questions posed, methods employed, writing style adopted), as well as their dynamics with the subject and their ability to gain access to the sporting culture under investigation. Prior to commencing this project I had already held many roles in the snowboarding culture (i.e., novice, weekend-warrior, core boarder, semi-professional athlete, snowboard instructor, event organizer, terrain-park employee, and journalist). My physical abilities and previous knowledge about snowboarding gave me access to the culture and a head start in recognizing the significant issues and sensitizing themes and concepts, and in discerning relevant sources. However, this "insider knowledge" also carries potential pitfalls (see Hodkinson, 2005; Wheaton, 2002). Perhaps one of the hardest tasks in this research was negotiating the path that allowed me to understand and acknowledge the participants' worldviews and their subjectivities, while also gaining the "critical distance" necessary to contextualize those views and actions (Wheaton, 2002). As my research progressed, and I spent more time writing and less time on the mountain, I acquired greater analytical distance from snowboarding culture, which greatly facilitated the important task of "demystifying the familiar" (Wheaton, 2002, p. 262). Throughout this study, however, I self-consciously reflected on my constantly shifting positions as a female researcher and an (increasingly less) active snowboarder, and how these roles influenced the empirical development of my study.

A particularly salient lesson learned from my ethnographic experiences is that, when conducting fieldwork in extreme sports cultures, such as snowboarding, the researcher should be prepared for an array of potentially high-risk situations. During fieldwork in extreme sports cultures, researchers may find themselves directly or indirectly involved in unforeseeably dangerous or threatening situations (e.g., witnessing — and/or being coerced to participate in — excessive drinking; offers from cultural participants to partake in practices that may put the researcher in physical danger, e.g., hiking out-of-bounds of a ski resort despite avalanche warnings) in which instantaneous decisions must be made based on the dynamics and complexities of the particular social, cultural, and/or physical environment. In such situations, researchers need to act in a manner that will best protect the rights of their participants (i.e., anonymity), but they must also take into consideration their own physical and sociopsychological safety. While the former is discussed extensively in the plethora of literature regarding research ethics and ethnography (see, e.g., Hammersley & Atkinson, 2007; Silk, 2005), concerns about the dangers ethnographers may face in the field have garnered less attention (see Ferrell & Hamm, 1998; Giulianotti, 1995; Lee-Treweek & Linkogle, 2000). Such concerns, however, are particularly pertinent for those engaging in fieldwork in extreme sports cultures.

In summary, while previous cultural experience is beneficial to knowledge acquisition, researchers and practitioners new to a particular sporting culture are able to develop an intimate *understanding* of the values and beliefs of participants by reflexively employing an array of ethnographic approaches (Sands, 2002, 2008; Silk, 2005). As Krane and Baird (2005) proclaimed, adopting various ethnographic tools and methods, including cultural sources (e.g., magazines, websites, and videos), participant-observations and interviews can "help enrich our understanding of sport cultures and concomitant behaviors and mental states of athletes" (p. 102). Indeed, such an approach lent insights into the complexities of snowboarding culture and the behaviors, values, and emotions of individual participants.

Unfortunately, it is beyond the scope (and purpose) of this chapter to offer a detailed description of the data analysis process that led to such insights. It should be noted, however, that as well as drawing upon an array of theoretical concepts to help guide my interpretations, combining the empirical evidence with secondary sources (especially scholarly research relating to the kindred activities of surfing, skateboarding, and windsurfing) also greatly facilitated my data analysis and enhanced my understanding of the social, cultural, political, and historical contexts within which snowboarders participate. Thus, researchers and practitioners could consider delving into the secondary sources (e.g., autobiographies of athletes, pioneers, or other key persons; cultural histories; existing sociocultural-historical research on the sporting culture under investigation) to further inform their *understandings* of the broader context within which a particular sporting behavior or event occurred or is taking place.

A Partial Snowboarding Ethnography: Some Sociopsychological Insights

To illustrate the potential of the ethnographic approach being advocated here, within the remainder of this chapter I offer a selection of insights from my ongoing project on the sociopsychological experiences of snowboarders. Traditional sport psychologists reading this chapter, however, should be forewarned. In contrast to the tidy findings offered by researchers working within the positivistic paradigm, the multilayered ethnographic approach adopted here reveals a more multifaceted, uneven, and somewhat fragmentary picture of the extreme sports experience. Another well-recognized virtue of ethnography is that it offers a "thick description" of lived experiences (Geertz, 1973), which, of course, requires considerable space. The findings from my ethnographic research cannot be reduced to a few key themes, and certainly cannot be summarized in the final few pages of this chapter. Thus, the following discussion offers just one exemplar from my research; below I present an array of (unapologetically) messy insights into the unique group dynamics and cultural hierarchies in contemporary snowboarding culture.

Emerging in the late 1970s and early 1980s, the first snowboarders tended to be young, white, middle-class males. Since the mid-1990s, however, snowboarding has attracted an influx of participants from around the world, and from different social classes and age groups. Snowboarding experienced a 385% increase in participation between 1988 and 2003 ("Select Snow," 2004, ¶ 3), and more than 18.5 million individuals currently snowboard worldwide ("Fastest Growing," 2005). But the influx of new participants during the late 1990s and early 2000s fueled struggles within the snowboarding culture between insiders and newcomers, and various subgroups. Andy Blumberg (2002), editor of *Transworld Snowboarding*, explained that "once united, we seem today divided" (p. 16). Indeed, various subgroups exist within the contemporary snowboarding culture, including professionals and competitive athletes (e.g., half-pipe, big-air, alpine racers, slope-style, boarder-cross), highly committed "core" boarders, recreational boarders, and weekend warriors, novices, and poseurs. While the most obvious division is between insiders and newcomers, tensions continue to run high between core boarders and marginal participants.

Core participants include males and females whose commitment to the activity is such that it organizes their whole lives (Wheaton &

Tomlinson, 1998). According to snowboarding journalist Jennifer Sherowski (2005):

> Not everyone who rides a snowboard is a snowboarder, but for those who do bear this illustrious title, it's an undeniable way of life. High school ends, and the road starts calling — off to mountain towns and the assimilation into weird, transient tribes full of people who work night jobs cleaning toilets or handing you your coffee in the early mornings, all just so they can shove a fistful of tips in their pocket and ride, their real motives betrayed by goggle tans or chins scuffed by Gore-Tex. (p. 160)

Snowboard instructor, ski lift operator, journalist, photographer, competition judge, and coach are other jobs held by passionate snowboarders committed to the lifestyle rather than the economic rewards.

Various identities, and preferred styles of participation (e.g., free-riding, free-styling, and alpine), exist within this core group. Free-riders prefer to hike, ride a snowmobile, or pay for a helicopter ride, to access remote back-country terrain, where they might drop off rocks or cliffs, ride down chutes, and snowboard in powder and among trees. Others, including free-style boarders, prefer to ride the more accessible, yet typically more crowded, ski-resort slopes. Free-style riding, which includes snowboarding on artificially constructed features such as half-pipes and terrain parks, is currently the most popular form of participation. This style rests upon creative and technical maneuvers (e.g., spins, grabs, inverts), many of which have their roots in skateboarding. Alpine, another style of participation, privileges speed and carving over jumping or jibbing, but is the least popular style among core snowboarders, who tend to dismiss participants as "skiers on boards" (field notes, 2007). The alpine racer tends to receive very little cultural respect (and thus, minimal media attention and industry support) in the current generation where freestyle is the most prized form of participation. For sport psychologists working with snowboarders and other extreme sports participants, it is important to recognize that different styles of participation often require different equipment, skills, and knowledge, and carry different sets of risks and reward systems. Understanding the unique cultural values, styles, motives, and goals of different groups of boarders will not only facilitate sport psychologists' ability to develop rapport with their clients, it will also inform decision making regarding the most effective techniques to use for enhancing performance.

In contrast to core boarders, less committed snowboarders — including male and female novices, poseurs, or weekend warriors — have lower cultural status within the community. Rather than demonstrating commitment via participation, poseurs display what Beal and Weidman (2003) have called a "prefabricated version" of a boarding identity by consciously displaying name-brand clothing and equipment (p. 340). With core participants often dedicating many years to snowboarding, it is inevitable that struggles occur when outsiders and newcomers endanger such cultural investments. Core participants tend to employ an array of overt and covert practices and strategies (e.g., distinctive clothing and language) to maintain and reinforce the cultural boundaries and clearly distinguish themselves from outsiders, newcomers, and marginal boarders. But, as the following comments illustrate, the aggressive attitude often adopted by young male (and increasingly female) core snowboarders frustrates some boarders, particularly older participants and novices, who *do not experience snowboarding in the same way*:

> I hate it when the young guys think they're too cool for school. Like too cool to wear a helmet. Too cool to apologize to an older man or woman whose skis they just ran over, too cool not to spit on people from chairs, too cool to ride an older board that's not a brand name, too cool . . . geez, I could go on. Snowboarding rocks, but the punky, rebellious, "I don't give a damn" attitude has been around since day one, and I hate it. (Kelsey, personal correspondence, September 2004)

Clearly, not all snowboarders align with specific groups or subscribe to the latest fashions. Relatively older participants, who presumably have more identities beyond snowboarding, tend to express such attitudes more frequently. A marginal participant explains, "I'm one of those geeks who wears old geeky stuff, and just wants to have fun. I don't think image matters if you are comfortable with who you are" (Dan, personal correspondence, May 2004). It seems that even those unconcerned about the latest snowboarding fashions and their marginal position in the snowboarding culture are aware that clothing styles influence their cultural positioning (e.g., "I'm one of those geeks").

Knowledge of social hierarchies and latest fashions, symbols, and styles, and their value within different subgroups within the culture, is particularly important for sport psychologists attempting to work with extreme sports athletes. As I discovered on numerous occasions throughout my research, core snowboarders—like many extreme sports participants—are efficient at reading the body and all its symbols.[3] Of course, the researcher or psychologist cannot control the interpretations that others draw from their performances, but *subtle* attempts can be made to manage impressions so as to facilitate rapport and cultural access (e.g., sport specific clothing or argot). Such efforts can go a long way when working in extreme sports cultures where many participants are cautious of outsiders—and particularly suspicious of authority figures (e.g., coaches, sport psychologists, administrators, event organizers)—infiltrating their culture for research, education, commercial, or other professional purposes.

While core boarders constitute a dominant force in the contemporary snowboarding culture, various other identities exist. Examples of such marginalized groups include older, gay, disabled, or non-white snowboarders. For example, on a blog titled "Stuff white people like: #31 snowboarding," Adisa recalled taking a snowboarding lesson with a group of black friends where "the white instructor . . . frustrated by how slowly we were picking up the basics . . . said (I kid you not): 'Come on guys! You people are natural athletes. This should be easy!' We laughed about it then, as we do now" ("Stuff White," 2008, ¶ 3). While cultural demographics continue to change, the majority of snowboarders, like many extreme sports participants, are white (89%), middle-upper-class, and heterosexual (Thorpe, 2007a). In 2002, however, American snowboard racer Ryan Miller became the first professional snowboarder to declare his homosexual status. According to Miller, the initial response from teammates and the industry was "colder than a Canadian winter": "invitations to social events dried up, the camaraderie ended," and he was "basically shunned" by both his peers and snowboarding companies "not eager to be associated with an openly gay snowboarder" (cited in "Snowboarder Ryan," n.d., ¶ 10). Despite experiencing marginalization from some of his peers, Miller is "out and proud" and clearly distinguishes himself from others on the mountain by displaying stickers from a variety of gay organizations (e.g., Outboard, a gay and lesbian snowboarding group) on his snowboard. Some "others" also find pleasure in disrupting stereotypes of snowboarders as young, white, heterosexual males. Marcia, a 58-year-old Canadian snowboarder, for example, has been boarding for more than 12 years and enjoys "surprising people when I take off my helmet and show my long silver hair" (personal correspondence, 2004).[4] The key point here is that sport psychologists need to carefully consider the potentially racist, homophobic, sexist, and ageist aspects of extreme sports cultures that often circulate at the broader social levels, yet (implicitly and explicitly) affect the everyday interactions and lived experiences of *all* cultural participants.

Adopting an ethnographic approach, this exemplar has revealed a highly fragmented snowboarding culture. Snowboarders do not constitute a homogenous group; participants approach the activity with different motives, goals, and values, depending on an array of variables, including style of participation (e.g., free-ride or backcountry, freestyle, half-pipe, alpine), level of commitment, skill level, age, sexuality, race, gender, nationality, and so forth. Not only do individuals' motives, goals, and styles of participation change during their lifetime, but also the dynamics between these groups are constantly in flux. Yet, much of the existing research on the psychology of extreme sports overlooks the diversity of extreme sports participants and glosses over messy cultural complexities. In previous studies, most research participants have been young, white, heterosexual males. This is particularly problematic, however, when findings from these studies are used to support and/or produce grand narratives explaining the behavior of *all* extreme sports participants. While the diversity of participants and the dynamic complexity of extreme sports behaviors make precise prediction nearly impossible, contextual and ethnographic methodological approaches can help us better understand individual and social processes and their relationships with behavior.

Ethnography helps amplify the "polyphony of voices" of cultural participants, and shed light on the variegated experiences of extreme sports athletes (Wheaton, 2002). However, I do not wish to make exaggerated claims for the value of ethnography, as against other methodological, theoretical, and applied approaches. While the conduct of ethnography may seem "deceptively simple," it can be "humiliating, belittling, at times dull, boring and downright exhausting" (Silk, 2005, p. 75). Furthermore, ethnography alone is not directly an effective means for enhancing the interactions between sport psychologists and extreme sports athletes; its value is typically "restricted to facilitating the production of knowledge" (Hammersley & Atkinson, 2003, p. 236). Yet, the value of such knowledge must not be underestimated. Armed with in-depth understandings about

the dynamic and multilayered experiences of participants, sport psychologists can make better-informed choices to enhance the experiences of all extreme sports participants. While it is beyond the scope
of this chapter to consider the full practical implications of these
suggestions, it is important to recognize the psychology of extreme
sports as both (social) science *and* art. In other words, working effectively with extreme sports participants requires: (1) an in-depth
understanding of the multiple and fractured identities within the culture (e.g., high-performance athletes, highly committed yet noncompetitive participants, recreational participants, younger athletes), as well as complex intersections of class, race, gender and/or
sexuality; and (2) the ability to draw upon this knowledge to develop
creative strategies that cater to the unique needs of extreme sports
athletes within particular cultural, social, and historical contexts.

Conclusion and Future Directions

As extreme sports athletes increasingly compete in global events
such as the X-Games and Olympics, and sign six-figure contracts
with corporate sponsors such as Nike, Mountain Dew, Coca-Cola,
Visa, and Boost Mobile, they are also garnering more attention from
sports psychologists. Yet, much of the existing psychological research
focuses, almost exclusively, on individual dispositions, behavior,
thoughts, moods, and emotions. To date, most sport psychologists
researching high-risk and extreme sports have drawn predominantly
upon quantitative methods (e.g., questionnaires, surveys) to gather
data, develop and test theories and concepts, and help make statements about human risk-taking behavior more generally. But, in so
doing, many researchers have overlooked complicated cultural dynamics and complex histories; presented participants as a homogenous group with similar personality types, motives, and experiences;
and reinforced stereotypes of extreme sports as dangerous activities
enjoyed mostly by daredevil, risk-taking, and adrenaline-seeking
youths.

In this chapter, however, I have argued that to better comprehend
the complexities of individuals' behavior in extreme sports cultures
we must consider the dynamic social, cultural, and historical contexts within which participants practice, perform, and live. Since the
late 1990s, extreme sports have attracted an array of participants
from different social classes and age groups who approach the activities with distinct motives, values, and goals. Moreover, the motiva-

tions, expectations, and aspirations of extreme sports athletes and practitioners are not static, but continue to change throughout their lifespan; they are also specific to the particular historical conjuncture within which they participate. It is also important to acknowledge that all extreme sports have their own distinctive histories, environments, geographies, identities, and development patterns. Thus, in-depth knowledge of the particular sporting cultures and their development and of the values of cultural members is an essential prerequisite for those seeking to understand, explain, and enhance the behaviors of athletes in extreme sports. Advocating broader sociocultural contextual psychological analyses of individuals' sporting behavior, I offered a multimethodological ethnographic approach to help us move research on the psychology of extreme sports forward in this direction.

In sum, while it is difficult to predict the future of extreme sports, it seems inevitable that they will continue to grow and change for many years to come. To understand the experiences of participants within these dynamic sports cultures, psychologists must consider the broader cultural, social, and historical contexts. Ethnography offers a useful and nuanced tool for those of us pursuing this exciting and important endeavor into the 21st century.

References

Anderson, K. (1999). Snowboarding: The construction of gender in an emerging sport. *Journal of Sport and Social Issues, 23*, 55–79.

Anna, T., Jan, B., & Aleksander, T. (2007). Goals in sports career and motivation as the measure of professionalism in snowboarding. *Medicina Sportiva, 11*, 27–31.

Appleton, J. (2005, August 30). What's so extreme about extreme sports? Retrieved August 16, 2008, from http://www.spiked-online.com.

Atkinson, P., Coffey, A., Delamont, S., Lofland, J., & Lofland, L. (Eds.) (2001). *Handbook of ethnography*. London: Sage.

Beal, B. (1995). Disqualifying the official: An exploration of social resistance through the subculture of skateboarding.

Sociology of Sport Journal, 12, 252–267.

Beal, B., & Weidman, L. (2003). Authenticity in the skateboarding world. In R. E. Rinehart & S. Sydnor (Eds.), *To the extreme: Alternative sports, inside and out* (pp. 337–352). New York: New York State University Press.

Blumberg, A. (2002, January). Launch. *Transworld Snowboarding*, p. 16.

Booth, D., & Thorpe, H. (2007). The meaning of extreme. In D. Booth & H. Thorpe (Eds.), *Berkshire encyclopedia of extreme sports* (pp. 181–197). Great Barrington, MA: Berkshire.

Boyd, M., & Kim, M. (2007). Goal orientation and sensation seeking in relation to optimal mood states among skateboarders. *Journal of Sport Behavior, 30*, 21–35.

Breivik, G. (1996). Personality, sensation

seeking and risk-taking among Everest climbers. *International Journal of Sport Psychology, 27*, 308–320.

Breivik, G. (1999). Personality, sensation seeking and risk-taking among top level climbers, parachute jumpers and white water kayakers. In G. Breivik (Ed.), *Personality, sensation seeking and arousal in high risk sports* (pp. 8–26). Oslo: The Norwegian University of Sport and Physical Education.

Brustad, R. (2008). Qualitative research approaches. In T. Horn (Ed.), *Advances in sport psychology* (3rd ed., pp. 32–43). Champaign, IL: Human Kinetics.

Brustad, R. J., & Ritter-Taylor, M. (1997). Applying social psychological perspectives to the sport psychology consulting process. *The Sport Psychologist, 11*, 107–119.

Brymer, E., & Oades, L. G. (2009). Extreme sports: A positive transformation in courage and humility. *Journal of Humanistic Psychology, 49*, 114–126.

Burawoy, M., Blum, J., George, S., Gille, Z., Gowan, T., Haney, L., et al. (2000). *Global ethnography: Forces, connections and imaginations in a postmodern world*. Berkeley: University of California Press.

Campbell, J., Tyrrell, D., & Zingaro, M. (1993). Sensation seeking among whitewater canoe and kayak paddlers. *Personality and Individual Differences, 14*, 489–491.

Celsi, R. (1992). Transcendent benefits of high-risk sports. *Advances in Consumer Research, 19*, 636–641.

Celsi, R., Rose, R., & Leigh, T. (1993). An exploration of high-risk leisure consumption through skydiving. *Journal of Consumer Research, 20*, 1–23.

Cronin, C. (1991). Sensation seeking among mountain climbers. *Personality and Individual Differences, 12*, 653–654.

Davies, C. (1999). *Reflexive ethnography: A guide to researching ourselves and others*. London: Routledge.

Diehm, R., & Armatas, C. (2004). Surf-

ing: An avenue for socially acceptable risk-taking, satisfying needs for sensation seeking and experience seeking. *Personality and Individual Differences, 36*, 663–677.

Evers, C. (2006). How to surf. *Journal of Sport and Social Issues, 30*, 229–243.

Farley, F. (1986). The big T in personality: Thrill-seeking often produces the best achievers but it can also create the worst criminals. *Psychology Today, 20*, 44–48.

Farley, F. (1993). The type T personality. In L. Lipsitt & L. Mitmick (Eds.), *Self-regulatory behavior and risk-taking* (pp. 371–382). New York: Ablex.

Fastest growing sports (n.d.). Retrieved March 14, 2005, from http://www.extrememediagroup.com/xchannel/xcha_main.html#4.

Fave, A. D., Bassi, M., & Massimini, F. (2003). Quality of experience and risk perception in high-altitude rock climbing. *Journal of Applied Sport Psychology, 15*, 82–98.

Feher, P., Meyers, M., & Skelly, W. (1998). Psychological profile of rock climbers: State and trait attributes. *Journal of Sport Behavior, 21*, 167–180.

Ferrell, J., & Hamm, M. (Eds.) (1998). *Ethnography at the edge: Crime, deviance, and field research* (pp. 221–251). Boston: Northeastern University Press.

Ford, N., & Brown, D. (2006). *Surfing and social theory*. London: Routledge.

Geertz, C. (1973). Thick interpretation: Toward an interpretive theory of culture. In *The interpretation of culture: A selection of essays* (pp. 3–33). New York: Basic.

Gill, D. (2000). Psychology and the study of sport. In J. Coakley & E. Dunning (Eds.), *Handbook of sports studies* (pp. 228–240). London: Sage.

Gill, D. (2002). Gender and sport behavior. In T. Horn (Ed.), *Advances in sport psychology* (2nd ed., pp. 355–376). Champaign, IL: Human Kinetics.

Giulianotti, R. (1995). Participant observation and research into football hooliganism: Reflections on the problems of entrée and everyday risks. *Sociology of Sport, 12*, 1–20.

Goma, J. (1991). Personality profile of subjects engaged in high physical risk sports. *Personality and Individual Differences, 12*, 1087–1093.

Griffith, J., Hart, C., Goodling, M., Kessler, J., & Whitmire, A. (2006). Responses to the sports inventory for pain among BASE jumpers. *Journal of Sport Behavior, 29*, 242–254.

Hammersley, M., & Atkinson, P. (2007). *Ethnography: Principles in practice* (3rd ed.). London and New York: Routledge.

Handwerk, B. (2004, July 9). Fear factor: Success and risk in extreme sports. *National Geographic News*. Retrieved October 15, 2008, from http://news.nationalgeographic.com/news/pf/9078104.html.

Heino, R. (2000). What is so punk about snowboarding? *Journal of Sport and Social Issues, 24*, 176–191.

Herbert, S. (2000). For ethnography. *Progress in Human Geography, 24*, 550–568.

Hodkinson, P. (2005). "Insider research" in the study of youth cultures. *Journal of Youth Studies, 8*, 131–149.

Horn, T. (2002). Socio-environmental issues, socio-cultural issues, and sport behavior. In T. Horn (Ed.), *Advances in sport psychology* (2nd ed., pp. 281–283). Champaign, IL: Human Kinetics.

Huberman, J. (1968). *A psychological study of participants in high risk sports*. Unpublished doctoral dissertation, University of British Columbia.

Humphreys, D. (1997). Shredheads go mainstream? Snowboarding an alternative youth. *International Review for the Sociology of Sport, 32*, 147–160.

Hymbaugh, K., & Garrett, J. (1974). Sensation seeking among skydivers. *Perceptual and Motor Skills, 38*, 118.

Kay, J., & Laberge, S. (2002). The "new" corporate habitus in adventure racing.

International Review of the Sociology of Sport, 37, 17–36.

Krane, V., & Baird, S. (2005). Using ethnography in applied sport psychology. *Journal of Applied Sport Psychology, 17*, 87–107.

Kusz, K. (2007). Whiteness and extreme sports. In D. Booth & H. Thorpe (Eds.), *Berkshire encyclopedia of extreme sports* (pp. 357–361). Great Barrington, MA: Berkshire.

Laurendeau, J. (2006). 'He didn't go in doing a skydive': Sustaining the "illusion" of control in an edgework activity. *Sociological Perspectives, 49*, 583–605.

Lee-Treweek, G. & Linkogle, S. (Eds.) (2000). *Danger in the field: Risk and ethics in social research*. London and New York: Routledge.

Lewin, K. (1935). *A dynamic theory of personality*. New York: McGraw-Hill.

Lyng, S. (1990). Edgework: A social psychological analysis of voluntary risk taking. *American Journal of Sociology, 95*, 851–886.

Lyng, S. (Ed.). (2005). *Edgework: The sociology of risk-taking*. London and New York: Routledge.

Mason, J. (2002). *Qualitative researching, 2nd ed*. London: Sage.

McGannon, K., & Johnson, C. (2009). Strategies for reflective cultural sport psychology research. In R. J. Schinke & S. J. Hanrahan (Eds.), *Cultural sport psychology* (pp. 57–89). Champaign, IL: Human Kinetics.

Miles, S. (1996). The cultural capital of consumption: Understanding "postmodern" identities in a cultural context. *Culture and Psychology, 2*, 139–158.

Ogilvie, B. (1974). Stimulus addiction: The sweet psychic jolt of danger, *Psychology Today, 8*, 88–94.

Phinney, J. (2000). Identity formation across cultures: The interaction of personal, societal, and historical change. *Human Development, 43*, 27–31.

Rinehart, R. (2003). Dropping into sight:

Commodification and co-optation of in-line skating. In R. E. Rinehart & S. Sydnor (Eds.), *To the extreme: Alternative sports, inside and out* (pp. 27–53). New York: State University Press.

Robinson, D. W. (1985). Stress seeking: Selected behavioral characteristics of elite rock climbers. *Journal of Sport Psychology, 7,* 400–404.

Robinson, V. (2008). *Everyday masculinities and extreme sports: Male identity and rock climbing.* Oxford and New York: Berg.

Ryba, T. V., & Wright, H. K. (2005). From mental game to cultural praxis: A cultural studies model's implications for the future of sport psychology. *Quest, 57,* 192–212.

Sands, R. (2002). *Sport ethnography.* Champaign, IL: Human Kinetics.

Sands, R. (2008). Ethical ethnography: Epistemology and the ethics of good intentions. In. K. Young & M. Atkinson (Eds.), *Tribal play: Subcultural journeys through sport.* Bingley, UK: Emerald.

Schinke, R. J., & Hanrahan, S. J. (Eds.) (2009). *Cultural sport psychology.* Champaign, IL: Human Kinetics.

Schneider, T., Butryn, T., Furst, D., & Masucci, A. (2007). A qualitative examination of risk among elite adventure racers. *Journal of Sport Behavior, 30,* 330–357.

Select snow brands to show at ASR. (2004, December 2). *Transworld Business, Surf, Skate, Snow.* Retrieved November 14, 2006, from http://www.twsbiz.com.

Self, D., & Findley, C. (2007). Psychology of risk-taking. In D. Booth & H. Thorpe (Eds.), *Berkshire encyclopedia of extreme sports* (pp. 246–253). Great Barrington, MA: Berkshire.

Self, D., Henry, E., Findley, C., & Reilly, E. (2007). Thrill seeking: The type T personality and extreme sports. *International Journal of Sport Management and Marketing, 2,* 175–190.

Sherowski, J. (2005, January). What it means to be a snowboarder. *Transworld Snowboarding,* pp. 160–169.

Shoham, A., Rose, G., & Kahle, L. (2000). Practitioners of risky sports: A quantitative examination. *Journal of Business Research, 47,* 237–251.

Silk, M. (2005). Sporting ethnography: Philosophy, methodology and reflection. In D. Andrews, D. Mason, & M. Silk (Eds.), *Qualitative methods in sports studies* (pp. 65–105). Oxford: Berg.

Simons, H., & Usher, R. (Eds.) (2000). *Situated ethics in education research.* London and New York: Routledge.

Slanger, E., & Rudestam, K. E. (1997). Motivation and disinhibition in high risk sports: Sensation seeking and self-efficacy. *Journal of Research in Personality, 31,* 355–374.

Snowboarder Ryan Miller: Out on the slopes. (n.d.). *The Outskirts.* Retrieved October 12, 2008, from http://thehostess.wordpress.com/2008/09/05/snowboarder-ryan-miller-out-on-the-slopes/.

Sparkes, A., & Partington, S. (2003). Narrative practice and its potential contribution to sport psychology: The example of flow. *The Sport Psychologist, 17,* 292–317.

Straub. W. (1982). Sensation seeking among high and low-risk male athletes. *Journal of Sport Psychology, 4,* 246–253.

Stuff white people like: #31 snowboarding. (2008). Retrieved October 12, 2008, from http://stuffwhitepeoplelike.com/2008/01/27/31-snowboarding/?cp=16.

Sugden, J., & Tomlinson, A. (2002). Theory and method for a critical sociology of sport. In J. Sugden & A. Tomlinson (Eds.), *Power games: A critical sociology of sport* (pp. 3–21). London: Routledge.

Survey says: X-Games/action sports connect with today's youth. (n.d.). *ESPN event media.* Retrieved June 12, 2006, from http://espneventmedia.com/pr.php?p=945&e=554.

Thorpe, H. (2006). Beyond "decorative sociology": Contextualizing female surf, skate and snow boarding. *Sociology of Sport Journal, 23,* 205–228.

Thorpe, H. (2007a). Snowboarding. In

D. Booth & H. Thorpe (Eds.), *Berkshire encyclopedia of extreme sports* (pp. 286–294). Great Barrington, MA: Berkshire.

Thorpe, H. (2007b). Boarders, babes and bad-asses: Theories of a female physical youth culture. Unpublished PhD dissertation, University of Waikato.

Thorpe, H. (2008). Extreme sports in China. In F. Hong, D. Mackay, & K. Christensen (Eds.), *China gold: China's quest for global power and Olympic glory* (pp. 84–86). Great Barrington, MA: Berkshire.

Thorpe, H. (2009). Understanding alternative sport experiences: A contextual approach for sport psychology. *International Journal of Sport and Exercise Psychology*, special issue: Decolonizing methodologies: Approaches to sport and exercise psychology from the margins.

Thorpe, H., & Rinehart, R. (in press). Alternative sports and affect: Non-representational theory examined. *Sport in Society*.

Tomlinson, J. (2004). *Extreme sports: In search of the ultimate thrill*. London: Carlton.

Vamplew, W. (1998). Facts and artefacts: Sports historians and sports museums. *Journal of Sport History*, 25, 268–282.

Van Maanen, J. (Ed.) (1995). *Representation in ethnography*. London: Sage.

Wagner, A., & Houlihan, D. (1994). Sensation-seeking and trait anxiety in hanggliding pilots and golfers. *Personality and Individual Differences*, 16, 975–977.

Watson, T. (1996). Injuries in sport, Retrieved June 10, 2005, from http://www.ul.ie/~childsp/Elements/Issue3/watson.html.

Wheaton, B. (2002). Babes on the beach, women in the surf: Researching gender, power and difference in the windsurfing culture. In J. Sugden & A. Tomlinson (Eds.), *Power games: A critical sociology of sport* (pp. 240–266). London and New York: Routledge.

Wheaton, B., & Tomlinson, A. (1998). The changing gender order in sport? The case of windsurfing subcultures. *Journal of Sport and Social Issues*, 22, 251–272.

Wilkinson, S. (2001). Theoretical perspectives on women and gender. In R. Unger (Ed), *Handbook of the psychology of women and gender* (pp. 17–28). New York: John Wiley and Sons.

Willig, C. (2008). A phenomenological investigation of the experience of taking part in "extreme sports." *Journal of Health Psychology*, 13, 690–702.

Notes

1. In so doing, I engaged in "situated ethics," that is, I made ethical decisions regarding the overt and covert nature of my research based on the dynamics and complexities of the particular social, cultural, and/or physical environment (cf. Simons & Usher, 2000). While all participants have the right to know when their behavior is being observed for research purposes, in some situations it was not feasible (or, indeed, safe) to declare my researcher identity or ask for informed consent from *all* participants (e.g., observations from the chairlift of unidentifiable snowboarders interacting in the terrain park below; or at a Big Air event with thousands of young, intoxicated spectators).

2. The snowball method of sampling proved effective with many participants helping me gain access to other key informants by offering names and contact details (e.g., email addresses, phone numbers). All interviewees received both an information sheet that outlined the project and their ethical rights and a consent form. During the interviews, I asked participants to reflect on their beliefs about various aspects of their snowboarding experiences and encouraged them to express their attitudes, ideas, and perceptions. Interviews ranged from 30 minutes to 4 hours in length, depending on the willingness of participants. The majority of participants welcomed further communi-

cation, and thus most interviews were followed up with further email discussions or in-person communications; in some cases, participants with extensive cultural knowledge became key informants and were contacted on a regular basis throughout my research.

3. The following dialogue, which occurred after a presentation to a group of top-level New Zealand snowboarding coaches and instructors, illuminates how knowledge of the cultural intricacies of the extreme sports culture can enhance one's perceived cultural credibility among clients: *Attendee:* "Hey, thanks for a really great presentation. I think lots of us will try to use some of those ideas in our classes. I also think it really helped that you have street-cred". *Author:* "Thanks. . . . Do you mind if I ask what you mean by street-cred?" *Attendee:* "You know, you are one of us, you are a snowboarder. We can tell just by looking at your shoes and the shirt you are wearing. If you had come in here wearing a business suit, we probably would have been like, 'who is this idiot' and walked out" (field notes, 2007). Of course, overuse and inappropriate use of cultural symbols can be a clear giveaway of an outsider status and thus could potentially have the opposite effect.

4. While marginal participants may have limited access to gain respect and status within the snowboarding culture, many find the support they need to enjoy their snowboarding experience by forming social groups (e.g., Black Avalanche), creating websites (e.g., www.grayson trays.com, www. Outboard.com), and establishing specialized instructional programs and organizations.

REFLECTION ON THE CULTURE TURN METHODOLOGIES: A POSITIVIST PERSPECTIVE—DON'T SAY *NO* UNTIL YOU LEARN IT

Gershon Tenenbaum

To be honest, I was introduced to cultural methodologies in the form of feminist and postmodernist philosophies and methodologies some time ago. Then, in my capacity as the editor of the *International Journal of Sport and Exercise Psychology*, Tatiana and Robert introduced me to the *culture turn* concept of research in sport and exercise psychology by suggesting a co-edited special issue on emerging culturally reflexive methods in our field. I asked them to send me a short outline and a list of potential contributions. I was impressed by their enthusiasm, and also with the range of topics they suggested. The special issue has been published (*IJSEP*, 2009, Issue 3) and here I find myself joining them in editing a book on the culture turn. I was trained as a positivist methodologist (do not hold this against me, please!); more specifically, I was trained to develop introspective measures in the social-behavioral sciences intended to be culture-free! The *Rasch Model* was aimed at introducing a method that results in measures similar to a yardstick, one that contains an *origin* (i.e., a *zero-point*) and *equal units of measurement* spread along a *linear continuum*. Think for a moment, if indeed we could produce a latent-trait method in psychology that could measure objectively people of all origins, genders, language, and cultures; beliefs and attitudes could then be compared and analyzed just as we can compare height and weight of people of different genders, cultures, locations, and the like. Those trained at the University of Chicago (some 20 to 25 years ago) in this school of thought were convinced that such an approach would lead to a better scientific inquiry in the social sciences. The underlying assumption was that psychological entities, like physical entities, could be measured objectively with a given standard error of measurement (SEM). The smaller the SEM, the more accountable and trustful the measure would be.

At that time, I cannot recall any of us arguing that the *meaning of language* may differ from place to place, from culture to culture, and from men to women. Thus, is it possible that all these attempts to quantify depositions, traits, and states were flawed in essence? Well, one should admit that the probability that so many of us were, and are, wrong for such a long time is slim. After all, as scientists we search for the truth, and searching for truth necessitates the appropriate methodology. The strength of a methodology is only as strong as its weakest underlying theoretical assumption. Thus, can social behaviors be considered an entity, which is governed by some deterministic rules? If no, then a descriptive sequence of events, which happen to occur spontaneously in a given time under given circumstances, is sufficient for comprehension of the events. If yes, then how can we best capture the laws governing human behaviors? Coming from a positivistic philosophy and being open to the so-called culture turn, I believe that generally behaviors and attitudes are governed by some "general laws," while other behaviors and attitudes may be attributed to the uniqueness of the culture, gender, climate, geographical location, altitude, exposure to others, and factors that affect social behaviors. The question remains as to how we uncover these laws. What tools should we use to better capture the deterministic and the probabilistic rules of social behaviors? The intent of sharing with you my reflections is to challenge researchers from various standpoints to look beyond their own perspective and stimulate debate through their work, which will result in better research methods and designs in the social sciences.

While reading the book chapters, I realized that the authors use a different language than the one I use when asking questions about social issues. It is not only the methodology, which is of a different nature, but it is also a plea for social and scientific justice to issues, which were believed to be governed by political and religious institutions. I do understand the frustration of those who engage in the culture turn, but at the same time, it is hard for me to make the turn without questioning the underlying assumptions of the various cultural turn methodologies, which vary in scientific rigor. Are these alternative trajectories solely geared toward making better science of social issues, or are these methodologies part of a movement with a political-social agenda where rigorous scientific assumptions are placed on equal footing with other social and political considerations? My intention is to briefly *share* my opinions with the readers on some emerging issues presented in the book, while sending a message at the outset: do not say no to either the underlying arguments or the methodologies, until you make yourself acquainted with them.

Assumptions about the Origins of Positivism

Some of the chapters rely on the assumption that positivists' pro-Popperian methodology of making science is historically rooted in some kind of social-political-religious conspiracy aimed at exhibiting power of respective institutions. Some claim that scientific methods and tools were aimed at justifying the interests and policies of the formal institution. To do so, also the statistical methods of observing and analyzing data were developed to satisfy the "power intentions" of policy makers, who happen to belong, of course, to the upper class. To bring justice to this view, one may assume that political interests indeed govern research preference; this is the case also with U.S. National Institute of Health (NIH) and the National Science Foundation (NSF) grants today. Isn't it more reasonable to assume that the first British statisticians were driven more by developing statistical tools, which better fit the data and phenomena under investigation, than by "power and dominance" needs? Had the statistical methods not developed, would psychological variables not normally distribute in the population? Of course, the arguments about political and institutional power are valid today as they were in the 19th and 20th centuries, but the making of science and the development of scientific tools were independent of these needs, unless one comes and presents hard evidence of a conspiracy theory. This of course is not aimed at disputing the new trend of using qualitative and mixed methods in social and behavioral sciences. Despite the fact that the methods in the life and natural sciences are rigorous, we have uncovered that such methods are sometimes insufficient in capturing the underlying mechanisms of human and social behaviors. For example, the thoughts and feelings of athletes during competition or exercisers during practice cannot be fully captured using a Likert-type scale. Consequently, new methods have been developed that complement the traditional ones, some of which are presented in this book. However, if used in isolation, those employing new qualitative-ethnographic-personal methods will fall into the same trap, limiting the understanding of human and social phenomenon.

A final note here as it relates to the main assumptions of statistical procedures. Because the researcher can rarely measure an entire

population, the use of statistics for parameter estimation is the researcher's intention. It is simply to know about the many from the
few. This is not a political aim. The culture turn researcher's interest
is not necessarily in generalizing findings to the population, but
rather describing the uniqueness of certain social behaviors, which
happen to occur under certain conditions. Their uniqueness is the
core of interest. There are burgeoning methods where what is found
in the research is equivalent to what is achieved through the research. Examples include but are not limited to participatory action
research and decolonizing methodologies. Further, there are instances when methods are indigenous to a culture, such as where a
North American Aboriginal community develops talking circles in
place of focus groups, group-coauthored narratives in place of singular ones, and indigenous versions of thematic analysis that replaced hierarchical versions (the analysis was circular and cyclical).
The intent sometimes with these emergent methods is not to describe,
but to gain access to understanding where previously conventional
practices might have delimited researchers to different parameters in
their lines of questioning and analyses. Even in such new methods,
the intention is to move well beyond description (from understanding can come the shift toward predictive research, albeit with more
salient questions and nuances strategies that tweak the conventional
methods meaningfully). Once aims of scientific inquiry differ, methods differ and adjust accordingly. Blaming a methodology for the
lack of recognition of another methodology is the wrong way to go
from my vantage.

The Physical versus the Social

The physical is objective and the social is subjective, thus the em-
bracement of only the physical science is wrong and brings us
nowhere. I argue that human beings are biological entities who live
in a world filled with deterministic laws not yet fully explored. Humans and animals interact via communication channels, enabling
them to survive/adapt to the environment. Thus, some of the methods we use to explore adaptability of humans and societies should be
physical in nature, but not all, and the two methods must complement each other because neural networks do not account for all of
human and social variability. On the other hand, observing humans
and societies is not always sufficient in capturing the underlying
mechanisms and variability of humans and society in time and space.

Instead of declaring which method is better, the criterion for judging scientific quality must be dependent on the adequate method applied to answer specific questions, and not which method is "theoretically" and "practically" better than the other! The claim that social research follows naturalistic scientific rigor for recognition purposes, as well as for enabling "prediction and control," is not sufficient reason to disregard them as sound methods. When one wishes to understand how imagery affects exercise endurance, one must conduct a sound empirical study considering all the rigorous requirements of a sound science. Such requirements secure the internal and external validity of science bound validity guidelines. However, when one wishes to understand how disputes in a family get resolved, it may well be that a psychologist must observe disputes in the family and describe the various ways these disputes are resolved, and also speak to the meanings and language used within the unit to convey thoughts at the micro level. After all there can be nuances within the setting that also shed light on the problem/phenomenon, and some of these nuances may be a challenge to capture through a monocultural/conventional method.

Both methods are legitimate and acceptable; they *must fit* the questions a researcher is asking in relation to the given context within. When sufficient evidence accumulates, there is nothing wrong with predicting and hypothesizing about such cases when they occur again and again and form a trend or a pattern. A hypothesis is not an entity by itself, but rather an entity that reflects knowledge accumulation, which is an essential product of scientific inquiry, exposure to life events, and encounters with the environment (personal experiences).

Objectivity and Subjectivity

The authors of the book assume that people posses a specific agenda when planning, conducting, and interpreting research. How *valid* is such an assumption? People come to the world with genes, which are expressed when interacting with the immediate environment. The person (gene)-environment interaction results in knowledge accumulation in the form of neural schema (i.e., mental representation) enabling humans to *logically* make *preassumptions* about the world they live in and wish to better understand. They observe and interact with the environment, and develop attitudes and assumptions, which of course vary in nature and in essence. Thus, the question of *objectivity* remains the *core* issue here: can research methods be objective despite the inherent variations among people in so many dimensions? The Popperian rigorous approach to making science is an honest attempt to reach this goal, which many argue is unachievable. In contrast, some of the methods described in this book are meant to describe a phenomenon and reconsider it. Others are meant to emancipate people through research. Still others are meant to describe social processes through a cultural lens that is relevant and safe within the intended culture. When one assumes that subjectivity in social science is irrelevant, each testimony, each opinion, each observation counts, and the sum of these is the true social reality. Each one of us is allowed to interpret it subjectively. Interesting, and intriguing at the same time!

The Researcher and the Researched

Empiricism separates the researcher from the researched when it wishes to reach objective outcomes. When one wishes to study social phenomena as they occur he or she is *not* obliged to follow rigorous and predetermined rules. It may well be that we must develop some kind of a taxonomy of questions/aims, and then design a best-fitting method for judging a sound and "not so sound" research. Such an effort may result in some disagreements and conflicts, but may allow better judgment of research and science quality.

"Theory's" Place in Making Science

Some authors claim that a theory of truth cashiers the hope for universal criteria for judging research studies. Indeed? In a sound Popperian research design, both *true* and *error variances* account for human variability. Interventions and manipulations are *objective* tools applied to test and observe how and why humans vary each from the other. It is only through rigorous research method that the researcher can understand the *reasons* for humans to vary. Theory is as sound as its weakest link and arguments. No one has claimed to have a theory, which explains neither the physical nor the social universe. A theory is just an accumulation of presently known facts and rules observed in nature, and it exists for further exploration and change. And yet such observations might also reflect bias perhaps, be it singular or group bias. Those who conduct research without admitting they have a theory cannot claim they explore nature without any knowledge and bias. This claim is counter-productive to whatever they do and has no base.

Traditional Methods and Progress
in the Sport and Exercise Psychology Domain

One who compares the quality of research today with the research published in the 1960s–1990s will realize immediately the emergence of new disciplines, new approaches, new outlooks, and new methods and tools, which make our progress quite impressive. We continue to move forward and explore the domain employing both qualitative and qualitative methods, which expose us to both objective and subjective methods of inquires. Questioning methodologies is a scientific process, which contributes to sharpening our views about social phenomena, and is welcomed in the sport and exercise sciences.

The Scope of Studied Issues:
The Emergence of New Methodologies

Positivists tend to dichotomize research methodologies into experimental methods and correlational methods. Experimental methods consist of providing manipulation/intervention/treatment to a group and comparing its outcomes (and process) to a control group of subjects who were given attention, placebo, or nothing at all. Randomization of subjects to groups is a must. Correlational methods consist of providing measurement tools, which require their being valid and reliable, to a large representative sample and correlating the relationships between variables among them. Both methods range from simplistic to complex, depending on theory and availability of samplings. Internal and external validity of the research design must be followed to secure that effects/correlations are due to *true variance* among people rather than to *error variance* attributed to internal and external sources of error. The methods rely on stating hypotheses derived from a sound theoretical and/or conceptual framework. The concept of significance for securing generality is paramount to these methods, otherwise one cannot say anything about effects and correlations beyond the studied sample. Case studies are respected as long as they follow similar methodological rules, compromising significance and consequently generalizability (to some extent). The effects and correlations in the social sciences, where measures consist usually of introspection, are limited in scope because introspective measures do not allow inner reflection to come out. Much of the internal world of the phenomenon under investigation is ignored, and thus the truth is of limited value, and in some cases misleading. Indeed, the so-called error-variance stemming from internal and external sources and the limited scope of the studied subject matter resulted in extensive criticism and the rise of alternative methods of inquiry in the social sciences. One of them, ethnography, has a long-lasting tradition, although many alternative methods that better capture the individual-autonomous entity within a culture have been developed and shed more light on social behavior. The culture turn consists of powerful methods that aim at shedding more light on urgent issues, while avoiding as much as possible the *restrictions of response* posed by the mainstream methods. For example, Vikki Krane, Jennifer Waldron, Kerrie Kauer, and Tamar Semerjian used a *critical pedagogy* and *teaching queerly* approach in research, teaching, and consulting to elicit reflection about LGBT participants in sport activities. Trisha Leahy used athletes' *self-reflections* to highlight the phenomenon of sexual and other forms of violence against young athletes. Tamar Semerjian advocates the use of *cultural studies* considering race, class, gender, and sexuality with the experiences of individuals with disabilities. Janice Forsyth and Michael Heine examine theoretical and applied perspectives on *indigenous research* and *decolonizing methodologies*. Brett Smith and Andrew Sparkes highlight the use of *narrative inquiry* in studying sport, and Holly Thorpe conceptualizes extreme sport behaviors within a larger contextual social culture using *ethnography*. Her chapter illustrates elegantly how one can learn more from ethnography about behaviors, which otherwise would never be explored via traditional methods. She reviews the important findings about extreme-sport athletes, but also shows how these findings are restricted and limited in scope by using a single method of inquiry. Reinhard Stelter introduces a theoretical framework, *narrative coaching*, which balances between individual experiences and social, cultural, and community-oriented perspectives to know more about the phenomenon of coaching. Natalia Stambulova introduces a *multiple metaphor approach* to study and provide services to athletes in career transitions. Kerry McGannon and Rebecca Busanich present a *feminist post-structuralist perspective* on women's embodied physical activity. This approach allows them to encourage change and promote physical activity, which was to some extent ignored by findings using traditional methods of inquiry. Anthony Kontos outlines the *sociocultural perspective* that shaped the development of sport psychology, showing the limitation of approaches omitting this important perspective. Ted Butryn introduces *interrogating whiteness* to study issues in sport and exercise psychology, and Leslee

Fisher and Allison Anders explore ethical issues via careful analysis of particular political, moral, and ethical preferences in *cultural studies* examining power and social justice issues. Robert Schinke's chapter focuses on how project team reconceptualizes research through integrated involvement from Canadian Aboriginal community members. The researchers initially employed a mainstream post-positivist methodology and through close collaboration with Wikwemikong researchers modified their approach to reflect a version of PAR that forefronts matters of cultural and regional considerations. Diane Gill and Cindra Kamphoff cover representation, and particularly representation of cultural diversity in sport psychology. According to their view, integration of sport psychology as an academic and professional discipline is needed for social justice. Physical activity must be an activity open for all, with no more left-outs. Moving beyond inclusion to social justice requires action and advocacy. A wider scope of the discipline is offered. Tatiana Ryba and Handel Wright's articulation of sport psychology as cultural praxis suggests a discursive trajectory of sport and exercise psychology that is attuned to pressing issues of a globalized society. The proposed heuristic aims at broadening the epistemological spectrum of theory and practice in the field to address issues of transnational identities, representation, competing notions and sites of belonging, and contested cultures. Sport psychology as cultural praxis is located within the cultural turn and in this sense serves as a discursive backdrop of the book.

Thus, what do I see here? First, I must confess, epistemological, analytical, and moral/ethical concerns of a positivist research paradigm have not given appropriate emphasis to language, culture, gender, race, and other environmental issues because of lack of interest in and sensitivity to these issues. Second, national and international bodies financing research were governed by people who lack awareness (not necessarily political and interest-driven) of such issues. I strongly believe that progress in science emerges from the awareness of scientists and powerful others with respect to the limitations of any research methods and the scope of issues societies are engaged in within a time frame, geographical location, and political agenda. The culture turn as presented to me in this book is a sound mix of methods and issues I would have never considered seriously before. I urge all my colleagues to consider these emerging methods based upon their respective merits, and realize how much more we can learn from adopting them to our scientific life.

AFTERWORD:
RENEWING CULTURAL SPORT STUDIES

C. L. Cole

The Cultural Turn in Sport Psychology reimagines the discipline informed by the insights of cultural, feminist, post-colonial, critical race, disability, and queer studies and research. Importantly, these rich critical traditions — still too often neglected by sport psychologists and sociologists — enable the contributors here to position themselves and their projects in relation (but not simply in reaction) to the common-sense assumptions that guide many mainstream sport and exercise psychologists. More specifically, the collection expresses interdisciplinary ways of thinking about problems, power, knowledge, identities, and struggle. It joins with and contributes to much broader discussions about innovative directions in cultural studies and research. In so doing, it reflects new alliances made possible by academic structural and curricular changes.

Traditional social science fields, including sport and exercise psychology, establish and regulate their authority through presumptions about science, objectivity, methodology, innocence, and disciplinarity. Despite decades of substantial post-structuralist critiques regarding language, subjects, power, and interpretation that undermine such foundational beliefs and values, many social scientists still ignore or dismiss the critiques, continuing to engage in normative social science. Indeed, social scientists' motivations to adhere to — even insist upon — sanitized models of social science make sense: the stakes are high and there are negative consequences for not doing so. By denying any fundamental alteration of their relationship to scholarship, traditional social scientists preserve their field's imagined value, distinctiveness, and academic status.

The essays collected here — and written specifically for this volume — reject conventional investments, refuse the governing lines that regulate pure spaces, and undermine the boundary work required to produce disciplinary distinctiveness. The essays affirm — based on reformulations and reconceptualizations of power, particularly ways of thinking about how power operates in truths, spaces, bodies, and psyches—that there is no way back to social science or positivism *as usual*. They rethink respectability through academic responsibility, value through the lens of social justice and critiques of normalization, and the future through praxis and resistance. Especially in light of these revisions, the authors see the future of their field—its efficacy, ethics, and value—bound to reimagined social science ideals.

Working at the interface of power, knowledge, and embodiment, Donna Haraway (1991) answered the sort of questions about the future of social science that arise from social constructionist views of knowledge. In "Situated Knowledges: The Science Question in Feminism and the Privilege of Partial Perspective," Haraway seized the moment—not to dismiss or retreat from objectivity—but to reorient and sharpen its conceptualization. Anticipating a popular response to such criticisms, Haraway recognized and rejected the temptation to relativism. Indeed, a view from *everywhere* is as problematic as a view from *nowhere*. In this context, she redefined the problem:

> I think my problem and "our" problem is how to have *simultaneously* an account of radical historical contingency for all knowledge claims and knowing subjects, a critical practice for recognizing our own "semiotic technologies" for making meanings, *and* a no-nonsense commitment to faithful accounts of the "real" world, one that can be partially shared and friendly to earthwide projects of finite freedom, adequate material abundance, modest meaning in suffering, and limited happiness. (p. 187)

Haraway frames her definition of objectivity through *contextualization* and *specification*, rather than distance from worldly experience. The "view of infinite vision is," as Haraway puts it, "an illusion, a god-trick" (p. 189). Thus, she insists "metaphorically on the particularity and embodiment of all vision . . . and not giving in to the tempting myths of vision as a route to disembodiment and second birthing." She uses this affirmation and refusal to promote a "usable, but not an innocent doctrine of objectivity" (p. 189). As she neatly summarizes,

> The moral is simple: only partial perspective promises objective vision. This is an objective vision that initiates, rather than closes off, the problem of responsibility for the generativity of all visual practices. Partial perspective can be held accountable

for both its promising and destructive monsters . . . Feminist
objectivity is about limited location and situated knowledge,
not about transcendence and splitting of subject and object. In
this way we might become answerable for what we learn how
to see. (p. 190)

Like Haraway, the authors in this volume offer multiple paths to situated knowledge as they deal with the complex issues related to working with the subaltern. They problematize the researcher's representation of self and the researcher's representation of the subaltern. For Smith and Sparkes, this means rethinking the researcher as storyteller while recognizing the relational nature of storytelling. Although Smith and Sparkes make no definitive authorial claims, they attend to the researcher/researched relationship and the ethical task of dialogue. They draw attention to the points of contact between telling marginalized stories, creating space for counter-narratives, and the need for researchers to re-evaluate writing practices. And they use their personal shifting forms of embodiment to highlight the stakes in contextualization and specification.

Butryn considers how whiteness studies can be used to produce a white, anti-racist identity, an identity aligned with "progressive radical politics and larger battles for social justice. . ." He uses autobiographical reflections and the recognition of a situated, relational self to show how traditional social science narratives work to produce an illusory stable and coherent, white identity. Finally, Forsyth and Heine provide a model for situated knowledge by bringing together indigenous research, decolonizing methodology, and community-based participatory research. They take seriously the imperative to ground research about indigenous populations in indigenous political struggles and the problems that they identify as useful.

Notably, the relationship between knowledge production, normalizing practices, and the reproduction of moral hierarchies is a key feature of *The Cultural Turn*. Again Butryn's essay usefully shows how white normativity is advanced through the racial invisibility typically embraced by social scientists. Forsyth and Heine highlight the long history of pathologizing visions directed at indigenous communities in which they seek to intervene. Krane, Waldron, Kauer, and Semerjian underscore the need to address heteronormativity, homonegativity, and transphobia in sporting and research practices. And, they draw attention to the ways in which heteronormative assumptions—about gender, sexuality, bodies, kinship, and belonging—are regularly smuggled into research by researchers in ways that prescribe, moralize, and reify what is considered normal.

Given the focus on normativity, Cathy Cohen's (2004) "Deviance as Resistance: A New Research Agenda for the Study of Black Politics" demonstrates new possibilities for reimagining cultural psychology. What begins as an effort to develop a more queer informed black studies that simultaneously complicates the scope and intersections of queer studies ultimately turns into an urgent call to privilege *deviance* in research. Although Cohen's efforts are directed at deviance within black communities, it is easy to imagine how her project could be used by activist-oriented scholars—critical race, postcolonial, disability, and queer scholars—who engage other marginalized groups. Deviance, by Cohen's view, remains undertheorized and its analytic possibilities remain overlooked. As she problematizes deviance, she draws attention to people's willingness to repeatedly engage in acts that further their marginalization. For Cohen, these visible choices (she is not using choice in its liberal sense) despite negative consequences create counternormative spaces and affective critiques of the dominant order that hold definitional and political possibilities. In Cohen's words,

> Ironically, through these attempts to find autonomy, these individuals with relatively little access to dominant power, not only counter or challenge the presiding normative order with regard to family, sex, and desire, but also create new or counternormative frameworks by which to judge behavior. (p. 30)

To be clear, Cohen's project is not a return to what has been characterized as early cultural studies' tendency to celebrate everyday resistances; it is not a recovery or empowerment model; nor is it about giving those on the margin an unproblematized "voice." Instead, Cohen, who is careful not to confuse transgressive with transformative behavior, suggests serious and sustained analytic attention on the agency—however limited—of the marginal. For "critics of respectability," investigations into the counternormative spaces produced by "deviants" offers insights into the possibilities of oppositional politics and new ways of thinking, acting, and judging. In sum, she identifies the key challenges for scholars who seek to intervene in normalization practices in terms of differentiating and detailing the relationship between deviance, defiance, and resistance.

By way of conclusion, I want applaud the editors, who, in their introduction, offer a contextual strategy for understanding their project. Without question, the volume itself is an expression of various intellectual and political struggles going on behind the scenes for some time. Relatedly, *The Cultural Turn* is an expression of a concerted effort to build scholarly and political alliances in order to work in larger fields of thought. Typically, interdisciplinarity is imagined as exploiting the mutual productiveness of disciplines. Yet, far too often, cultural studies scholars have seen psychology as normative and counterproductive. Thus, for those invested in cultural psychology, such interdisciplinary work additionally requires making sure that critical insights and issues associated with the psychological are not simply diluted, subsumed, or neglected by cultural studies.

As this volume makes clear, the psychological is inextricably bound to the future of cultural studies and activist scholarship. In a context defined by neo-liberalism, neo-conservativism, and economic crisis: in an historical moment in which consumerism and empowerment are conflated and universities increasingly corporatized, the insights made possible through cultural psychology should matter deeply. Pleasure, desire, pain, anger, trauma, affectivity, motivation, experience, and resistance necessarily reverberate across the contemporary complex terrain of power. Sport and exercise psychology's commitment to applied work makes it a privileged site for situated research and intervention into normalization practices and processes.

Finally, *The Cultural Turn* cannot be reduced to a call for new directions for a discipline. Instead, it is a deliberate intervention into reconceptualizing the field and its mission. Although we cannot predict the final framing or questions that will guide the field, we can say that the cultural turn entails the ongoing and difficult work of reimagining its canon, revising its curriculum, rethinking strategic collaborations, and redirecting research. *The Cultural Turn* proposes a more responsible, accountable, and reflexive psychology: a situated scholarship that is at its best when it intervenes in normalizing functions. Such engagements are inspired by advocacy and hope, and what Cohen would call an ethics of deviance. In the first and final instances, such a project requires remaking subjects, forging alliances, and demanding accountability.

References

Brown, W. (2005). *Edgework: Critical essays on knowledge and politics*. Princeton and Oxford: Princeton University Press.

Cohen, C. (2004). Deviance as resistance: A new research agenda for the study of Black politics. *Du Bois Review, 1*, 27–45.

Haraway, D. (1991). *Simians, cyborgs, and women: The reinvention of nature*. New York: Routledge.

Rowe, A.C. (2008). *Power lines: On the subject of feminist alliances*. Durham: Duke University Press.

INDEX

ABOUT THE EDITORS

Tatiana V. Ryba holds a Ph.D. in sport studies with a double emphasis on sport psychology and cultural studies from the University of Tennessee. She is currently a senior lecturer in the European Master's Program in Sport and Exercise Psychology at the University of Jyväkylä Finland. Dr. Ryba undertakes research in the intersecting areas of cultural studies, sport psychology, identity, cultural history, and qualitative research. Her research has appeared in the *International Journal of Sport and Exercise Psychology*; *Journal of Applied Sport Psychology*; *Review of Education, Pedagogy and Cultural Studies*; *Quest* and the collections such as *Contemporary Sport Psychology*; *Contemporary Youth Culture*; and *Cultural Sport Psychology*. She also has taught extensively on questions of sociocultural diversity and research methodology in sport psychology. Dr. Ryba's latest projects include the special issue "Decolonizing Methodologies: Approaches to Sport and Exercise Psychology from the Margins" (2009), guest edited with Dr. Schinke for the *International Journal of Sport and Exercise Psychology*. In addition to her research and teaching contributions, Dr. Ryba is a member of the editorial board of the *Qualitative Research in Sport and Exercise*, and serves as Chair of the International Relations Committee, Association for Applied Sport Psychology. For her innovative work in the field, Dr. Ryba has received the Developing Scholar Award from the International Society of Sport Psychology in 2009.

Robert J. Schinke is an associate tenured professor at Laurentian University and holds a doctorate in education and a post-doctoral year in positive psychology. His research interests span cultural sport psychology, resilience, and adaptation and his methodological preferences span the qualitative methodologies, employing mainstream and culturally sensitive approaches dependent on population. A former Canadian Equestrian Team member and Pan American

Games medalist, Schinke has been funded by the Social Sciences and Humanities Research Council of Canada, the Canadian Foundation for Innovation, and the Canadian Institute for Health Research. His work, the most recent for which he has just been awarded the 2008 Canadian Sport Science Research Award for Community Research, has been published in the *International Journal of Sport and Exercise Psychology*, *The Sport Psychologist*, the *Journal of Sport and Social Issues*, *Quest*, and the *Journal of Physical Activity and Health*, among other publishing outlets. He has published two applied sport psychology books, each released in multiple languages, and has three edited compilations. Schinke is the editor of *Athletic Insight* and he has guest co-edited an installment of the *International Journal of Sport and Exercise Psychology* devoted to the intersection of culture and sport and exercise psychology. Schinke is also the chair of his university's research ethics board as well as the chair of Ethics and Qualifications for the Canadian Sport Psychology Association. He and his wife, Erin, have a new son named Harrison.

Gershon Tenenbaum, Ph.D., Benjamin S. Bloom Professor of Educational Psychology, a graduate of Tel-Aviv University and the University of Chicago, is a professor of sport and exercise psychology at Florida State University. He is a former director of the Ribstein Center for Research and Sport Medicine at the Wingate Institute in Israel, and coordinator of the graduate program in sport psychology at the University of Southern Queensland in Australia. From 1997 to 2001 he was the president of the International Society of Sport Psychology, and from 1996 to 2008 the editor of the *International Journal of Sport and Exercise Psychology*. He has published extensively in psychology and sport psychology in the areas of expertise and decision-making, psychometrics, and coping with physical effort experiences. Gershon has received a number of distinguished awards for his academic and scientific achievements, and is a member and fellow of several scientific and professional forums and societies.

ABOUT THE CONTRIBUTORS

Allison Daniel Anders is an assistant professor in the Department of Educational Psychology and Counseling at the University of Tennessee. Allison holds a Ph.D. in education from the University of North Carolina at Chapel Hill. She is an active member of the American Educational Research Association and the American Educational Studies Association.

Allison situates her research in education in social and political theory, social justice and human rights, cultural studies, narrative theory and postcritical ethnography, community-based participatory research, and feminist epistemologies, pedagogies, and methodologies.

Her current research involves the collection of educational narratives from incarcerated youth and the collection of resettlement narratives from refugee families and children.

Rebecca Busanich received her B.S. from the University of Michigan (athletic training) and her M.S. from the University of Oregon (sports medicine), and is currently pursuing her Ph.D. at the University of Iowa (psychology of sport and physical activity). She is currently a research assistant and teaches courses (i.e., Psychological Aspects of Sport and Physical Activity, Health in Everyday Life, Stress and Coping) in the Department of Health and Sport Studies, at the University of Iowa. Her specific research interests are in reconceptualizing female athletes' health and body experiences, specifically the concept of disordered eating, using feminist psychological approaches (i.e., social constructionism, critical feminism, post-structuralism).

Ted M. Butryn is an associate professor in the Department of Kinesiology at San Jose State University. Ted holds a Ph.D. in cultural studies and sport studies from the University of Tennessee and an M.A. in human performance (emphasis in sport psychology) from San Jose State University. Ted's primary research interests involve the intersection between cultural studies and sport, the application of cyborg theory to sport and the body, psychological and sociological aspects of pro wrestling and MMA, and issues related to whiteness in sport and exercise. He has published in *The Sport Psychologist*, the *Sociology of Sport Journal*, the *Journal of Sport & Social Issues*, and the *Journal of Sport Behavior*.

C. L. Cole is a professor of media and cinema studies and gender and women's studies at the University of Illinois at Urbana-Champaign. She has been the editor of the *Journal of Sport & Social Issues* since 2000, and currently is at work on several projects related to the media, sport, and national culture.

Leslee A. Fisher is an associate professor in the Department of Exercise, Sport & Leisure Studies at the University of Tennessee. Leslee holds a Ph.D. in sport psychology from the University of California at Berkeley and an M.S. in counselor education from the University of Virginia. She is currently serving as secretary/treasurer of the Association for Applied Sport Psychology (AASP). Leslee's primary research interests focus on the social psychological experiences of female athletes including the intersectional identities of gender/race/class/sexual/moral orientation, body issues, and the ways in which a cultural sport psychology can be used to enhance research and applied work within sport and exercise psychology.

Janice Forsyth is an assistant professor at the University of Alberta, where she holds a joint appointment with the Faculty of Physical Education and Recreation and the Faculty of Native Studies. Her research focuses on the way in which power relations, expressed as race, ethnicity, gender, and socio-economic status, have shaped, and continue to shape, the developing structure of Aboriginal sport in Canada. She has applied this analysis to representations of Aboriginal people in Olympic Games, sports and games at Canadian residential schools, the sporting experiences of Tom Longboat Award recipients, and Aboriginal women and sport.

Diane Gill is a professor in the Department of Kinesiology at the University of North Carolina at Greensboro. Her research emphasizes social psychology and physical activity. Her scholarly publications include the text *Psychological Dynamics of Sport and Exercise*, several book chapters, and over 100 journal articles. Current projects emphasize gender and cultural diversity and the relationship between physical activity and quality of life.

Michael Heine is an assistant professor in the School of Kinesiology at the University of Western Ontario. He holds a Ph.D. from the

University of Alberta, and has been involved in research relating to Arctic and sub-Arctic Aboriginal culture and history for the past 25 years.

Cindra S. Kamphoff is an assistant professor in the Department of Human Performance at the Minnesota State University, Mankato. She received her Ph.D. from the University of North Carolina at Greensboro. Her research has focused on gender and cultural diversity, including projects on women's issues in coaching, the diversity content in AASP conference programs, and cultural competence. She received the 2006 NASPE *Sport and Exercise Psychology Academy Dissertation Award*. She is an active member of AAHPERD and AASP, and has presented over 30 papers at national and international conferences.

Kerrie Kauer is an assistant professor of sport sociology in the Department of Kinesiology at California State University, Long Beach. Her primary areas of research interests include queer and feminist approaches to heteronormative sport environments, the body and body image, and social justice initiatives, particularly around girls and women in sport and physical activity. Kerrie completed her Ph.D. in sport studies with an emphasis in cultural studies and a cognate in women's studies in 2005 from the University of Tennessee, Knoxville.

Anthony P. Kontos is an associate professor at Humboldt State University, where he teaches courses in sport and exercise psychology, motor development/learning, research methods, and sport concussion; works as a sport and exercise psychology consultant; and is the director of the Behavioral Performance Lab and North Coast Sport Concussion program. Dr. Kontos received his Ph.D. in kinesiology/sport psychology from Michigan State University where he also received master's degrees in counseling and exercise science. He completed his B.A. in psychology at Adrian College. His research includes sport concussion, psychology of injury, risk taking, and multicultural sport and exercise psychology. Dr. Kontos has published over 30 articles/chapters and delivered over 55 professional presentations, and is a member of APA Division 47 and AASP.

Vikki Krane is a professor with the School of Human Movement, Sport, and Leisure Studies at Bowling Green State University and the former director of the Women's Studies Program. She has been the editor of *The Sport Psychologist* and the *Women in Sport and Physical Activity Journal* as well as president of the Association for Applied Sport Psychology. Dr. Krane currently is on the editorial boards of the *Journal of Applied Sport Psychology, The Sport Psychologist*, and *Qualitative Research in Sport & Exercise*. She is a fellow of the Academy of Kinesiology and Physical Education. She earned her doctorate at the University of North Carolina at Greensboro after receiving her master's degree from the University of Arizona and her bachelor's degree from Denison University.

Trisha Leahy is the chief executive of the Hong Kong Sports Institute. She has also previously worked as senior psychologist at the Australian Institute of Sport and was the unit head of the Sport Psychology Unit at the Hong Kong Sports Institute. She was an invited member of the International Olympic (IOC) Medical Commission's special working group on the prevention of abuse and harassment in sport. She is also an invited member of a UNICEF expert panel advising on research and policy strategies in child protection issues in sport. Dr. Leahy is the "Applied Issues in Sport" Section Editor of the *International Journal of Sport and Exercise Psychology*.

Kerry McGannon received her Ph.D. (health and exercise psychology) from the University of Alberta after receiving a B.A. (psychology) and an M.A. (sport and exercise psychology) from the University of Victoria. She is an assistant professor in the Department of Health and Sport Studies at the University of Iowa. Her research provides a "bridge" between traditional epidemiological approaches and cultural studies approaches, to understand physical activity participation. Her specific interest is in the social construction of the self and critical interpretations of physical activity and fitness using social theory and qualitative methodologies (e.g., narrative, discourse analysis). The journals in which her work is published, such as *Quest, Sociology of Sport Journal*, and *Journal of Sport and Exercise Psychology*, underscore the interdisciplinary nature of her research.

Duke Peltier is a member of the Wikwemikong Unceded Indian Reserve Band and Council. A former NCAA Division One ice hockey player, Duke has coached elite junior ice hockey for several years in Northern Ontario, Canada. As Director of Recreation in Wikwemikong, Duke oversees the sport programming for youth provided by Wikwemikong. In addition to his professional capacities, Duke has also collaborated on two successive SSHRC funded research projects with Robert Schinke and his colleagues from Laurentian University. The articles resulting from such work have been published in *The Sport Psychologist*, the *International Journal of Sport and Exercise Psychology*, *Quest*, *The Journal of Sport and Social Issues*, the *Journal of Physical Activity and Health*, and the *International Journal of Sport Psychology*. Duke has also co-authored several academic book chapters.

Tamar Z. Semerjian is an associate professor of sport psychology in the Department of Kinesiology at San Jose State University. She received her bachelor's degrees in psychology and human biodynamics at the University of California, Berkeley, and her master's and doctorate degrees in sport psychology at The University of Iowa. Her research focuses on marginalized populations and their sport and exercise experiences, incorporating theoretical perspectives from both social psychology of sport and cultural studies. She has published work based on her research with older adults, individuals with spinal cord injuries, and transgender athletes.

Brett Smith is honored to be in the School of Sport, Exercise, and Health Services at Loughborough University. His theoretical and empirical research interests concern the psycho-social dimensions of disability and health; the development of qualitative research methods and methodologies; and narrative inquiry. He has published extensively on each of these topics across a range of disciplines in international peer reviewed journals. Brett is founding co-editor of the journal *Qualitative Research in Sport & Exercise*.

Andrew Sparkes is a professor of social theory in the School of Health & Sport Sciences at the University of Exeter, UK. His research interests are grounded in methodological diversity and inspired by a continuing fascination with the ways that people experience different forms of embodiment over time in a variety of contexts. Recent work has focused on performing bodies and identity formation; interrupted body projects and the narrative reconstruction of self; sporting auto/biographies and body-self relationships; and the lives and careers of marginalized individuals and groups. He is currently editor of the annual British Sociological Association *Auto/Biography Yearbook*.

Natalia Stambulova is a professor in sport and exercise psychology in the School of Social and Health Sciences at Halmstad University,

Sweden. Her professional experiences in sport psychology refer to her work for about three decades as a teacher, researcher, and consultant in the USSR/Russia and since 2001 in Sweden. Her athletic background is in figure skating on the level of the USSR national team. She received her first Ph.D., in developmental psychology, at the Leningrad State University and the second one, in sport psychology, at the St. Petersburg State University of Physical Culture. Her research and publications relate mainly to athletic career with an emphasis on career transitions and crises. In applied work her specialization is helping athletes in crises, consulting athletes and coaches on various athletic/life career issues, and performance enhancement. She is a recipient of the Distinguished International Scholar Award of the Association of Applied Sport Psychology.

Reinhard Stelter holds a Ph.D. in psychology from the University of Copenhagen and is a professor of sport and coaching psychology at the University of Copenhagen and head of the Coaching Psychology Unit at the Department of Exercise and Sport Sciences. He has received further training in psychotherapy, coaching psychology, counseling, and applied sport psychology. He is an accredited member and honorary vice-president of the Society for Coaching Psychology, and from 1999 to 2007 a member of the managing council of FEPSAC, the European Federation of Sport Psychology. He has done research in the areas of sport and identity, body and learning, and is currently working with coaching psychology in a narrative and community psychological perspective.

Holly Thorpe is a lecturer in the Department of Sport and Leisure Studies at the University of Waikato, Hamilton, New Zealand. Holly teaches undergraduate and graduate courses in social-psychology of sport, leisure, and exercise. Her research interests include social theory, physical youth culture, gender, and extreme sports, particularly board-sports (e.g., surf, skate, and snow boarding). Her work has appeared in a number of journals including *Sport in Society*, *Journal of Sport and Social Issues*, and *Sociology of Sport Journal*. She is also co-editor (with Professor Douglas Booth) of the *Berkshire Encyclopedia of Extreme Sports* (2007) and is currently working on a book based on her doctoral research titled *Snowboarding Bodies in Theory and Practice* to be published by Palgrave Macmillan.

Patricia Vertinsky is a Distinguished University Scholar and professor of human kinetics at the University of British Columbia in Vancouver, Canada. She is a social and cultural historian working across the fields of women's history, sport history and sociology, popular culture, and the history of health and medicine. Her expertise lies in the study of normalizing disciplinary regimes in kinesiology and sport science and the social, political, and scientific context in which they have been conceived and promoted. Dr. Vertinsky was the first Canadian woman to become a Fellow of the Academy of Kinesiology and Physical Education, past-president of the North American Society of Sport History, vice-president of the International Society for Physical Education and Sport History, and Fellow of the European Committee for Sport History. She was recently awarded an honorary doctorate by the University of Copenhagen.

Mary Jo Wabano is the director of the Youth Center at Wikwemikong Unceded Indian Reserve. She and her staff provide sport and activity services to youth in collaboration with the Recreation Program at Wikwemikong. Presently Mary Jo has partnered with faculty members from Laurentian University and is serving as a community contact person. The nature of her present collaboration involves PAR and the ongoing provision of youth leadership training through an adventure leadership excursion, in which traditional teachings are provided as part of the experience. Mary Jo has contributed to peer-reviewed publications authored in the *Journal of Physical Activity and Health* and the *Journal of Sport and Social Issues*. She lives in Wikwemikong with her husband Mike, their two children and their grandchildren.

Mike Wabano served as the interim director for Sport and Recreation Services several years ago. He assisted Robert Schinke with an earlier externally funded project in which the cultural practices of elite Canadian Aboriginal athletes were considered. Mike has served as a community coach in Wikwemikong and he also continues to support the research partnership among Wikwemikong and Laurentian University.

Jennifer J. Waldron is an associate professor in the School of Health, Physical Education, and Leisure Services at the University of Northern Iowa. She received her Ph.D. in kinesiology from

Michigan State University. Dr. Waldron is interested in the relationship of sport and physical activity to self-esteem and body image, and potential health-compromising behaviors of participants engaged in sport and physical activity. She is actively involved in AASP and AAHPERD.

Handel Kashope Wright is Canada Research Chair of Comparative Cultural Studies, David Lam Chair of Multicultural Education, and director of the Center for Culture, Identity, and Education at the University of British Columbia, Canada. His research interests include cultural studies of education, cultural studies of sport, continental and diasporic African cultural studies, critical multiculturalism and anti-racism, critical pedagogy and (post)reconceptualization curriculum theorizing. His publications have appeared in *Quest*, *Cultural Studies*, and the *International Journal of Cultural Studies* and include the book *A Prescience of African Cultural Studies* (Peter Lang).